Knowing Feeling

Knowing Feeling

Affect, Script, and Psychotherapy

Edited by
Donald L. Nathanson

W. W. NORTON & COMPANY
NEW YORK • LONDON

Some chapters or portions thereof have appeared in other publications and are reprinted here with permission, specifically:

Chapters 1, 7, 8, and part of chapter 4 from *Psychiatric Annals*, 23:10, 1993.

Part of chapter 12 from *Archetypal Processes in Psychotherapy*, edited by N. Schwartz-Salant and M. Stein, Wilmette, IL: Chiron Publications, 1987.

Chapter 17 from the *Bulletin of the Tomkins Institute*, 1:1 (spring 1994), 1:2 (summer 1994), 1:3–4 (fall–winter, 1994), and 2:1 (spring 1995).

Copyright © 1996 by Donald L. Nathanson

Printed in the United States of America

First Edition

Manufacturing by Haddon Craftsmen, Inc.

For information about permission to reproduce selections from this book, write to
Permissions, W.W. Norton Company, Inc., 500 Fifth Avenue, New York, NY 10110

Library of Congress Cataloging-in-Publication Data

Knowing feeling : affect, script, and psychotherapy / edited by Donald L. Nathanson.
    p.   cm.
Includes bibliographical references and index.
ISBN 0-393-70214-6
1. Affect (Psychology) 2. Tomkins, Silvan S. (Silvan Solomon), 1911– . 3. Psychotherapy. I. Nathanson, Donald L.
BF531.K56   1996
152.4—dc20   95-49392 CIP

W.W. Norton & Company, Inc., 500 Fifth Avenue, New York, NY 10110
http://web.wwnorton.com
W.W. Norton & Company Ltd., 10 Coptic Street, London WC1A 1PU

1 2 3 4 5 6 7 8 9 0

To my beloved wife, Rosalind Helene Nathanson

Contents

Introduction

THE PAST FEW YEARS have witnessed rapid evolution in the clinical application of the affect theory introduced by Silvan Tomkins. The steady growth of the international network of study groups chartered by the Philadelphia-based Tomkins Institute has been accompanied by increasingly frequent public presentations by clinicians who have found these theories useful in their practice of psychotherapy. The present text is a group of essays by clinicians and researchers from a wide spectrum of disciplines, each of whom has found that using Tomkins's concepts as the theoretical base for clinical work has made it easier and more effective. It offers links to classical psychoanalysis and Jungian psychology, diagnostic evaluation, psychometrics, cognitive theory and cognitive behavioral therapy, image-oriented psychotherapy, psychopharmacology, couples therapy, sexual counseling, the theater, the evaluation and treatment of massive psychic trauma, and a new sociopolitical system for the management of juvenile offenders.

That so much attention has been paid to a theory, indeed to a rigorous, complex, and demanding theoretical system, is in itself remarkable, for all of us feel most comfortable with what we learned during our training and saw validated by articles in journals edited by peers who were similarly committed to that early training. Yet we have become uncomfortable as we survey our therapeutic failures, curious about research into brain mechanisms that disconfirm traditional theory but offer no clear model of the mind, and perturbed by the steady increase in anecdotal reports of therapeutic success involving techniques that seem foreign to our very nature. For many clinicians, the tried and true have become tired and false.

Take, for instance, the work that Jeanette Wright presents in her chapter on "Image-Oriented Psychotherapy." Trained as an art therapist and steeped in Freudian drive theory, Wright became fascinated by the faces drawn by her patients. With the permission of an artistically gifted woman who bore the diagnostic label of dissociative identity disorder, and whose concept of self seemed split into several distinct alternate personalities, Wright traveled from Iowa to show me a sheaf of her drawings. Not only could we see that these highly evocative pictures represented scenes characterized by intense affective experience, but we could with ease recognize each of the innate affects on the faces of the characters she depicted, even though the artist had no prior knowledge of affect theory. Wright has developed a novel therapeutic technique through which she encourages her clients to use drawings as a way of learning more about their affects, about the consistent and replicable systems through which they have learned to manage these affects, and about the historical sequences that produced these painful scripts, all while teaching new methods of affect modulation. In an era characterized by intense sociopolitical attention to the loss of natural resources and the scarcity of unspoiled territory, Wright's work reminds us that what we ignore as banal and ugly may be the doorway to the new and exciting. This is breakthrough work because it uses information that has always been available in the artistic productions of people in therapy and recognizes that the graphic depiction of facial affect display is all the more important in those whose affective experience has been so intense and painful as to foster dissociative defenses that interfere with awareness.

It was at the suggestion of a student that David Cook, now emeritus professor of counseling psychology at the University of Wisconsin in Stout, began to develop the Internalized Shame Scale (ISS). Previous shame scales had been based on lists of adjectives used by college students, perhaps the best studied cohort in the world of academic psychology. Cook went in the opposite direction, picking statements about shame experience culled from the work of such clinicians as Gershen Kaufman, whose 1980 book *Shame: The Power of Caring* was one of the first to introduce affect theory in the context of psychotherapy, and psychoanalyst Léon Wurmser, whose 1981 book *The Mask of Shame* was perhaps the most evocative ever written on what had until then been known as "the ignored emotion." Cook went on to revise and adjust his test in terms of the emerging work on affect theory and to determine the importance to clinical practice of this complex group of scripts. His chapter not only describes the science and logic behind the ISS, but is also a chronicle of his own journey from academic cognitive theory toward affect theory. In a later chapter, psychologist Shelley Milestone, also trained as a cognitive-behavioral therapist, offers a concise outline of her clearly stated and easily learned recommendations for the incorporation of affect theory into classical cognitive therapy.

Vernon C. Kelly, Jr., Training Director of the Tomkins Institute, has a career-long interest in the treatment of couples. Working with Tomkins in the months before the latter's death in 1991, Kelly produced an entirely novel definition of intimacy. In the intervening years, he has developed a new system of couples therapy based on these concepts. Briefly stated, it takes note of Tomkins's recognition that all humans are "wired" to enjoy the positive affects and dislike the negative affects. The basic "blueprint" of human psychological function requires that we try to increase positive affect, decrease negative affect, express all affect so these two goals may be accomplished, and develop scripts that foster these three goals. Kelly was the first to recognize that intimacy requires a private interpersonal relationship within which two people seek to mutualize positive affect so that it may be increased as a function of the relationship, to mutualize negative affect so that it may be downregulated, and to develop relationship-specific techniques for the expression of all affect so that it may be managed in the way best for the couple. Treatment, as he explains in this seminal chapter, requires far less attention to the content of quarrels and battles than to the affects that make these issues salient.

As a researcher and teacher for the Post Traumatic Stress Disorder unit of the Philadelphia Veterans Administration Hospital, Andrew M. Stone has found it useful to reevaluate our concepts of trauma in terms of innate affect mechanisms. His first contribution outlines a method of assessment that offers a bridge between the biological and the biographical factors operating in these devastating clinical conditions. My longtime colleague and collaborator, Dr. Stone was the first to suggest that we gather into one volume the growing collection of studies on the clinical applications of affect theory under the title *Knowing Feeling*.

Both Dr. Stone and Norfolk-based clinical psychologist Anthony Hite have become intrigued by the changes in the process of diagnosis made possible by an understanding of affect theory and script theory. Each offers a chapter that describes how to approach a new patient or to revise your way of dealing with a patient whose treatment has gotten stuck for lack of understanding of emotional issues — two contributions that differ dramatically in their focus and style.

A new theory should be capable of integration with the old so that the wisdom acquired by previous generations of clinicians is neither ignored nor lost in the excitement provided by novelty. It was Michael

Franz Basch, one of the best known and loved psychoanalytic writers, who first introduced Tomkins and his affect theory to the culture of psychodynamic psychotherapy and psychoanalysis. Here he reminds us that all of the defense mechanisms outlined by Freud are actually affect management scripts. Basch places affect at the center of all considerations of the mental mechanisms. Louis Stewart is a Jungian psychologist who points out that each of the archetypes defined by Jung may be viewed as a specific pattern of affect modulation. Moving easily between the concepts of Jung and those of Tomkins, Stewart asks us to think of myth, personality types, and psychic structure in terms of his own highly personal understanding of innate affect. And, just as it is important to build bridges between these classical systems for the understanding of human function and the new system offered by affect and script theory, our clinical work must be linked firmly to the research of psychologists who study infant and child behavior. Drs. Julie Faude, Wayne Jones, and Michele Robins have collaborated on a scholarly review of work that demonstrates both the innateness of affect and its importance in the establishment of a clinically relevant developmental theory.

Two of the authors are known for the intensity and duration of their work with Tomkins. Like most of us clinicians, I learned of affect theory through the work of Basch and, like so many others who saw in affect theory a way toward new clarity, wrote Tomkins asking for the privilege of a personal conversation. It was my great good fortune to work closely with him during the last decade of his life as I struggled to unlearn the theories of my training and adapt to both a system and a teacher at times clear and simple and at other times maddeningly obscure. Educated first as a research biologist, next as a physician and endocrinologist, and only much later in psychiatry, I kept trying to place the affect system in the body, hoping to establish it within the emerging fields of neuroendocrinology and psychopharmacology. In a series of papers and books, I have focused on the basic biological mechanisms involved in shame affect while trying to clarify the scripts through which it is incorporated into the range of experience from everyday life to severe psychopathology. This work is summarized as the opening chapter of *Knowing Feeling.* In a later chapter written with the invaluable assistance of psychopharmacologist and long-time colleague James Pfrommer, I suggest a way of understanding the interface between innate affect and the mechanisms of action postulated for some of the best known psychoactive drugs.

Exactly contemporaneous with my relationship with Tomkins was that of Donald Mosher, whose research into the emotionality associated with sexual behavior and experience had led him to affect theory. It was a peculiarity of Silvan Tomkins, possibly born of a professor's need to keep separate the research being done by his students, that neither of us knew anything about the other until Tomkins's death in 1991. Mosher's work on sexual scripts is the most sophisticated adaptation of script theory to date—often as complex as that of our mentor while at all times firmly linked to the world of psychotherapy. Here he summarizes what is to appear in his long-anticipated book on sexuality, offering what may be regarded as a glossary for the text of sexual scripts.

Using the emotionality of theatrical performance as their model, Miller James and David Read Johnson outline their novel and sophisticated treatment for posttraumatic stress disorder. Writing from the Veteran Administration's National Center for PTSD, they describe the "relationship lab" within which they use the teachings of leading drama theorists to enhance safer and more meaningful expression of emotion in this cohort. A contrasting view of the drama is presented by its originator, Bruce Shapiro, whose theory of iconicity has now been brought into conformance with our current understanding of human emotion. Shapiro sketches his revolutionary theory for the nature of dramatic performance, remarks on the significance of the theater for emotional health, and suggests the formation of an entirely new method of drama therapy that may be capable of producing deeper levels of change than those in use at this time.

Finally, just as Kelly insists that an understanding of intimacy must be informed by our affect-based theory of the person, the Australian political scientist and criminologist David B. Moore makes us realize that our understanding of society must be assisted by all valid theories of the personality. One of the leaders in the international movement to change the criminal justice system, Moore combines a willingness to read voluminously in any area of scholarship that might impinge on his topic with an unmatched ability to create working relationships among thinkers in disparate fields. When the town of Wagga Wagga, New South Wales, decided to implement the juvenile justice program suggested by John Braithwaite in his 1989 book *Crime, Shame and Reintegration*, Moore read the world literature on shame and became convinced that affect theory offered the best way of explaining the social phenomena being investigated by his group. His chapter offers a concise summary of modern criminology, describes the operation of the Wagga Wagga model of family group conferencing, and demonstrates how the conferencing system heals a community that has been wounded by crime. The same patterns of affect modulation that produce intimacy in private interpersonal relationships are necessary to create the sociality that forms the sense of community.

The day is long gone when any one therapist or one school of therapy can promise either explanation or cure for the woes of all. Neither affect theory nor script theory is a form of therapy, even though these concepts fit well into any system of treatment. All of us understand that a mood that persists despite sensible attention to its scripts may actually be due to abnormality of neurotransmitter function, just as the patient whose condition fails to improve no matter what medication is used may (for example) need attention to an interpersonal source of affect better handled in couple therapy. Therapeutic systems that depend on laboratory tests or the verbal productions of patients may be enlivened by attention to drawings. Psychodrama offers an opportunity to try out other ways of being—other patterns of affect modulation—just as hypnosis may allow access to parts of the personality held hostage by mental mechanisms earlier brought into use to manage affective overload. Cognitive therapy works better than psychodynamic insight or uncovering therapy in that fraction of the population for whom a highly structured therapeutic environment is needed to act as scaffold when the individual has little experience of affect modulation. Psychological tests may be used not just for diagnosis but to provoke skeins of associations that may be useful in therapy. A method of treatment based on preexisting sets of symbols, like Jungian psychology, may be used as a grid to anchor the individual who is otherwise skittish about depth psychology.

The history of our evolution as thinking beings changes greatly when one takes into account Tomkins's view of affect. A race of computers unable to assign salience, unable to determine which voice in the Babel of data required the most advanced form of attention, is unlikely to have been able to adjust to the ever-changing demands placed on it by the ability to move away from its roots and into new territory and new problems. We were not assigned the species name *homo sentiens*, the sentient or thinking human, but *homo sapiens*, the organism that lives according to innate abilities denoted by the Latin verb *sapere*, to savor or know, to be sensible or wise. This is a book about what makes us truly human, truly sapient. It is about knowing feeling in all of its aspects.

Good treatment is flexible, tailored to the needs of the individual or the cluster that has sought assistance, and capable of alteration on demand. It is our belief that the new attitudes toward human emotion described in these pages may alert the clinician to a wider variety of treatment options and illuminate ever-changing systems of therapy.

Acknowledgments

THERE IS SOMETHING about the urge to assemble a multi-author book that defies analysis. It starts with an editor's certainty that knowledge in some area of a field is distributed widely and deeply among a host of sober thinkers, none of whom is capable of representing the work of all. Next follows the task of convincing these individuals that they are less solitary than they had thought, and that their ideas might carry more weight if banded together with those of colleagues known only to the editor. Required is an implicit promise to allow each author the right to express these ideas with a certain purity unadulterated by the opinion of that editor, who is therefore placed in the position of a parent who loves equally all the children of this hastily assembled family. The production of each chapter is a chore taken on with some level of avidity dependent on the several realities that intersect to form the life of a busy professional.

The editor, then, receives these contributions not as a block of manuscripts, but one at a time over many months of anticipation; each chapter must be able to stand alone as a scholarly work but also fit into a gestalt that derives its unique power from assembly with the others. It is only as the sheer number of chapters increases to form a palpable mass that the editor can learn whether the originating concept was correct.

Yet much more is involved here than scholarly thought. A book must meet the standards of its publisher, which is also a group of people with several realities ranging from artistic to scholarly to commercial. Just as editor and author negotiate the expression of ideas that fit the needs of both, editor and publisher negotiate the method of assembly and the style of production. What started as a neat and simple idea, a somewhat theatrical inspiration for the edification of one's colleagues, achieves a rich complexity that must be completely invisible by the time a finished book arrives on the reader's desk.

My own ability to work on such a project is only one of the benefits accruing to me from a marvelously affirming marriage. By techniques as invisible to me as the work of editing should be to you as reader, Roz makes our shared space one in which writing and scholarship seem only natural and an outgrowth of what we do together. Vernon C. Kelly, Jr., has taken over more and more responsibility as Training Director of the Silvan S. Tomkins Institute, allowing me the freedom to concentrate less on administrative tasks that in his hands look easy and more on matters such as this. Our 20-year friendship has been a marriage of another sort, equally affirming and increasingly rewarding; it is a special pleasure to watch the development of his own creative ideas and to highlight them in this book. Troy Thompson, Chairman of the Department of Psychiatry and Human Behavior at Jefferson Medical College, has provided me with the opportunity to teach to my heart's content and therefore to interact with residents who challenge me to express ideas ever more clearly.

For more than a decade I have had the pleasure of working with John Ware, the highly literate literary agent who always forces me to pull my ideas into a form that will mean more to a publisher and thus guarantee their acceptance. His understanding that books represent commerce as well as art and scholarship and his ability to handle the realities and needs of a publisher have provided me with another form of freedom. This is the second book for which I have been privileged to work with Susan B. Munro of Norton Professional Books, by far the best editor I have ever met. Everybody's ideas seem a little bit clearer when they emerge after her attention to them and the resultant book somehow better designed and presented. There is a cabal of authors fortunate enough to have benefited from her skill, and we chuckle quietly about our luck.

Most of all, however, I wish to thank the 17 colleagues who diverted the stream of their own lives to fill the bowl of my needs and wishes. A decade ago I suggested that we were entering an era in which attention to affect would become the primary focus of our field. The validity of that prediction has been supported by a welter of books and articles about many aspects of human emotion and will perhaps be elucidated by this group effort to bring the affect theory of Silvan Tomkins into the foreground of our consciousness.

Contributors

Michael Franz Basch, M.D.*
The Cynthia Oudejans Harris, M.D., Professor of Psychiatry
Rush Medical College, Chicago

David R. Cook, Ed.D.
Professor Emeritus of Counseling
University of Wisconsin-Stout, Menomonie

Julie Abrams Faude, Ph.D.
Clinical Developmental Psychologist
Bryn Mawr College
Wayne, Pennsylvania

Anthony L. Hite, Ph.D.
Clinical Assistant Professor
Department of Psychiatry and Behavioral Science
Eastern Virginia Medical School, Norfolk

Miller James, B.F.A.
Supervisor, Creative Arts Therapies, VA Medical Center

National Center for PTSD
West Haven, Connecticut

David Read Johnson, Ph.D.
Associate Professor (Psychology), Dept of Psychiatry, Yale University School of Medicine
Director, Outpatient PTSD Services, National Center for PTSD
VA Medical Center
West Haven, Connecticut

C. Wayne Jones, Ph.D.
Director, Family Partnership Project, Philadelphia Child Guidance Clinic
Assistant Professor of Psychology in Psychiatry, University of Pennsylvania

Vernon C. Kelly, Jr., M.D.
Training Director, The Silvan S. Tomkins Institute

---

*Dr. Basch died on January 24, 1996, while this book was in production.

Clinical Associate, Department of
Psychiatry, University of Pennsylvania
Attending Psychiatrist, The Institute of Pennsylvania Hospital

Shelley F. Milestone, Ph.D.
Clinical Associate, Department of
Psychiatry, University of Pennsylvania
Adjunct Senior Staff, Center for
Cognitive Therapy, Philadelphia

David B. Moore
Director, Transformative Justice
Australia

Donald L. Mosher, Ph.D., ABBP
Professor of Psychology, University of Connecticut

Donald L. Nathanson, M.D.
Executive Director, The Silvan S.
Tomkins Institute
Clinical Professor of Psychiatry
and Human Behavior, Jefferson
Medical College
Senior Attending Psychiatrist, The
Institute of Pennsylvania Hospital

James M. Pfrommer, M.D.
Medical Director, Keystone Extended Care Unit, Chester,
Pennsylvania

Michelle Robins, Ph.D.
Clinical Developmental Psychologist, Philadelphia Child Guidance Clinic

Bruce G. Shapiro
Head of Performance, Acting Department, School of Drama,
Victorian College of the Arts,
University of Melbourne, Australia

Louis H. Stewart, Ph.D.
Clinical Professor in Medical Psychology, University of California San Francisco
Professor Emeritus in Clinical
Psychology, San Francisco State
University
Founding member, former president, and training analyst at the
C. G. Jung Institute of San
Francisco

Andrew M. Stone, M.D.
Clinical Assistant Professor of
Psychiatry, The University of
Pennsylvania
Director of Research and Training, PTSD Clinical Team, Philadelphia VA Medical Center

Jeanette Wright, ATR, M.S.
Associate Professor of Art Therapy, Drake University, Des
Moines

Knowing Feeling

1

About Emotion

Donald L. Nathanson

No matter how it is described or understood, all psychotherapy involves emotion. In this brief introductory chapter, our current theories of emotion are placed in the context of the 19th-century science from which they were derived and the links to a modern, affect-based theory for psychotherapy are suggested. A product of the same culture that spawned the revolution in information science, Tomkins disengaged affect and cognition into two separate but linked systems for the management of data. Throughout his work, Tomkins insisted that one of the most important attributes of living systems was that of duplication. On the macroscopic level, biological reproduction is the way we duplicate individuals to maintain a species; subserving this duplication of whole beings is a myriad of microscopic and submicroscopic processes working at the level of molecules like DNA that duplicate tiny fragments of themselves to produce the building blocks from which people are assembled.

Information, too, is the result of duplicative processes: What we see or hear or taste must trigger events that duplicate the original data in forms that can be handled by central processes. Light reflected from objects within the visual field is concentrated by a lens that reproduces these objects in miniature on the retina, where specialized cells transmit information that duplicates the form of the objects in several different areas of the brain. The rapid growth of modern neuroscience reflects the increasing sophistication of our understanding of the pathways for the duplication and transformation of information made possible by research tools capable of revealing ever more minute structures and processes. All of the duplicative processes that serve information transfer are here subsumed under the rubric of cognition.

Save for the occasional diehard creationist, few among us believe that the human sprung into existence fully formed as we know our species today. Life forms seem to have evolved from primitive toward complex, from simple and poorly organized to complex and highly integrated. Tomkins argued that an organism granted the ability to assemble information from such a wide range of electromagnetic sources as heat, sound, and light, as well as the presence or absence of a vast range of chemical substances, and compelled to process all of this information as equally important, might be at an evolutionary disadvantage when any one source of data was significantly more critical to life than the mass or welter of others. What, he asked, might be the most simple, the most universal factor involved in the transmission and duplication of information that might lead to the assignment of urgency and importance? What quality, what attribute of information–no matter what its nature or source–could the evolving organism use to assign salience where it might be most useful?

There is only one such arena within the whole realm of what we call information, one invariant realm of quality. No matter what happens, no matter when it happens, or to whom or why or where, it must happen at some rate of speed and at some intensity. Everything that happens does so over time. If we look at an event in terms of the system that will register or duplicate it, the event that produces *data* is the *stimulus* that triggers some bodily process. A stimulus occurs slowly or rapidly or constantly over time; it grows or decreases or remains steady in its intensity. In the language of affect theory, Tomkins states that there are only three qualities of stimulation: *stimulus increase*, *stimulus decrease*, or *stimulus level*. It was his great contribution to teach us that we have evolved to register these three qualities in special ways. We have evolved an affect system that responds to the qualities of stimulus increase, stimulus decrease, and stimulus level by making things happen all over the body in such a way that draws our attention to those specific qualities of the information suddenly made salient.

Is it surprising that our affects, our emotions, should at once be both mental occurrences and also bodily experiences? Should we reject out of hand a system of thought that refuses to acknowledge the traditional split between body and mind? How can we accept an explanation of emotion that draws us away from the brain and into so many realms of the body? Consider, for a moment, that complex life forms have evolved an autoimmune system to detect the difference between what is self and what is alien, and a hemopoietic system that makes and destroys blood elements–systems not linked to any particular organ or sharply distinct region but made of parts scattered all over the body. The difference between an organ and a system is one of order; despite the sophistication of their eventual evolution, organs are collections of cells that are clustered in space to enhance group action, while systems are more advanced organizations of cells and even organs to make a higher order of group action. The experience of affect is the result of data analysis that triggers something in the brain that in turn makes things happen all over the body. Save for pain, which calls attention to something that needs immediate correction, no other mechanism has evolved to produce the phenomenology of attention.

It is only when affect makes us pay attention to a stimulus that we may be said to be conscious of it; in the language of affect theory, consciousness itself occurs only when some mental content has been assembled with an affect to gain access to our highest cognitive functions. Whatever else is going on at the time will occur outside of consciousness and neither be noticed nor remembered unless it can be retrieved in some way that then makes it the trigger for affect. And just as one affect may bring something into consciousness, another may push the triggering event and its accompanying affect into a special compartment that makes it difficult to access or retrieve–this would represent the dynamic unconscious. Whereas generations of psychologists insisted that life was a matter of stimulus and response, and encouraged us to evaluate all situations in terms of "S-R pairs," we now know that no stimulus can evoke a psychological response unless it first triggers an affect. The entire concept of S-R pairs must be replaced by the language of stimulus-affect-response, or "S-A-R triplets." This opening chapter of *Knowing Feeling* presents some of the basic language and concepts of affect theory, and sets the stage for the clinical work to follow. –DLN

WE CLINICIANS MAKE the leap from theory to practice with such avidity, and so early in our careers, that often we are unaware of the degree to which our attitudes have been shaped by that early training. Nowhere is this more important than in our understanding of human emotion. Even though we know intuitively that people come to us for problems in living that are made urgent by the sort of emotionality called "symptoms," we tend to "cut through the emotional stuff" in order to get at what we perceive as the "real issues." To this end, we use a variety of therapeutic techniques that involve emotion in many ways.

Treatment based on psychoanalytic theory requires the therapist to be minimally interactive, gratifying as little as possible the patient's socially conditioned desire for normal conversation; the resultant "anxiety" impels the patient to reveal information not previously disclosed. Cognitive-behavioral therapy works on the principle that we are made uncomfortable by the thoughts and feelings triggered during an episode of emotion; by changing the pattern of these thoughts we are enabled to become more comfortable. Group therapy modeled on the 12-step program of Alcoholics Anonymous allows members the opportunity to learn new and less destructive ways of dealing with intense unpleasant emotion. Physicians prescribe medication to alter emotion that cannot be modulated by psychosocial means. In each of these therapeutic systems, emotion is viewed as an unpleasant, somewhat disorganizing experience.

It has been suggested that all therapeutic techniques might be viewed as either "glue" or "solvent" (R. R. Pottash, personal communication, September 1966). When our ability to function with competence in the adult world is limited by disorganizing emotionality, therapy works only when it reduces or modulates emotion and glues us back together. When our problems in living are not accompanied by intense emotion, treatment tends to loosen the sturdy structures that hold us together and thus produces enough emotion to motivate change. No matter how it is described or understood, all psychotherapy involves emotion.

Indeed, most of us tend to think of emotion with what infant researcher Daniel Stern (1985) calls a *pathomorphic distortion* — our view of the normal has been built from our attempts to comprehend and treat illness. Such a view is buttressed by lay thinking: When in the throes of an emotion we are likely to say that we are "disturbed," "upset," or that we "have a problem" with something. In our culture, emotion is discussed as something that interferes with rational, mature, neocortical thinking. It would appear that most of us, most of the time, would prefer a life without emotion.

Nonetheless, there does seem to be some need for emotional experience. Integral to the enormous societal expenditure of time and money on "entertainment" is the emotionality associated with the playing and viewing of sports and our immersion in the real and fictional exploits of others as seen on television, in films, and in literature. No matter what we think it is, we seem to crave emotion just as much as we try to avoid it.

THEORIES OF EMOTION

Many writers have provided lists of what are called "emotion labels," the several hundred names by which we know our adult emotions (DeRivera, 1977). The very word suggests motion, movement — heart racing during excitement and fear, voice rising in volume and fist clenching when we are angry, the agitation associated with anxiety. Some of emotionality is learned — an upper-class gentleman may raise one eyebrow or purse his lips slightly when angry in just the same situation that might move someone from another social grouping to raise his fist and take a truculent stance. Any expression of emotion can be faked. Some portion of emotion is undoubtedly biological: Hyperthyroid patients often complain of anxiety, while the persistent guilt, distress, and fear of classical depression respond best to tricyclic antidepressants. Infants cry, laugh, get excited, angry, and frightened just like adults. A competent modern theory must put all of this information into some usable matrix.

Instinct Theory

The easiest approach is to postulate that we are born with instincts, some kind of built-in circuitry for each emotion. In 1908, McDougall suggested that instincts are inherited or innate psychophysiological dispositions requiring perception of and attention to certain objects, followed by an emotion specific to that object and an impulse to act on that object in specific ways. In this system, I am said to react with fear to the charging elephant because my recognition of this stimulus releases a reaction for which I have been prepared by a built-in mechanism. This theory is dependent on an intact neocortex that allows perception and associative thinking; it cannot explain either the emotions of infants who are not yet capable of knowing about elephants nor the patient whose chronic sadness and lack of vitality can be traced to low blood thyroxine levels.

In 1884 and 1887, William James and Carl Lange (unaware of each other's nearly identical work) suggested independently that perception triggers visceral changes that are then appraised cognitively and labeled as emotions. In the James-Lange theory, I know I am frightened only because I feel my heart pounding and see myself running away from the lion. In this system of thought, everything we observe in the infant must be ignored, for only that which may be perceived and understood can trigger emotion.

Paulhan, in 1884, stated that "an affect is the expression of a more or less profound disturbance of the organism, due to the fact that a relatively considerable quantity of nervous energy is released without being able to be used in a systematic manner." This theory is a perfect example of late 19th-century rationalism, in which anything that interfered with useful work was considered as a disturbance. Discounted is the very idea that emotion may bring benefit to the organism. And nobody has been able to find "nervous energy," despite a century of excellent neurophysiological research.

Freud's (1915) understanding of emotion actually derives from that of Paulhan. The science of Freud's era demanded what are now known as "grand unifying theories." Einstein tried to present a unified field theory that linked all matter and energy in one equation; Sir William Osler (only seven years older than Freud) dominated Western medicine with his instruction to evaluate the patient so that each and every symptom might be explained as part of only one illness. Freud tried to explain all psychic function in terms of a life force he called *libido*—a basically sexual force capable of assuming many forms. Working in analytic therapy, Freud had studied men who were, by the mores and medicine of the times, forced to use *coitus interruptus* as a method of birth control and were dissuaded from masturbation by social pressure. Freud thought such men looked nervous.

Sexual arousal is normally accompanied by excitement and terminated by an orgasm that brings pleasurable calm; this Freud explained as the normal working of the sex drive. He suggested that when the drive was prevented from achieving its predetermined purpose, drive energy was sent along subsidiary paths to create anxiety. Furthermore, he extended this observation to define all emotion, pleasant or unpleasant, as a further derivative of misdirected drive energy. (A modern psychoanalyst, asking a colleague about the interests and pleasures typical of the patient being discussed, will ask "What are his derivatives?") Later, Freud added a second drive to account for anger and to plug the gaps left by this theoretical leap.

This system of drive-based emotionality suffers from the same defects mentioned in the theory of Paulhan: No science has ever found anything remotely like drive energy; nothing in the histology or electrophysiology of the brain suggests the presence of the little channels Freud's theory requires; the system demands a link to sexuality difficult to sustain in this era of modern biology; and his explanation ignores the fact that all the facial and bodily manifestations of emotion seen in the baby (whose libido energy is, by definition, not yet sexual) may be found in the adult. It certainly does not explain our constant observation that someone who drinks too much coffee can complain of anxiety in just the same terms as those used by a sexually frustrated lover. Although any theory of emotion must take into account its relation to sexual arousal, drive theory cannot explain enough to be maintained.

Perception of Value

Wundt, in 1897, pointed out that all emotion labels are dependent on a preexisting system of values. He described three dimensions of value-loaded, cognitively appraised feeling states: pleasantness/unpleasantness; excitement/calming; tension/relaxation. Any emotion could thus be graphed on each of these axes. A more recent version of this concept was proposed in 1941 by Angyal, who said that the quality of emotion is determined both by the perception of value and by proprioceptive feedback from bodily responses. Although it is clear that cognitive appraisal plays an important part in the adult experience of emotion, this system tends to ignore both the physiological basis of emotion and the type of emotion seen in the infant. Any modern textbook of psychology will provide a list of even more recent theories based on cognitive appraisal.

Transformation of Energy

It seems that wherever we find a theory for emotion that involves the idea of psychic energy, we also find emotion defined as a primitive, unwanted, or disturbing phenomenon. Sartre (1948) suggested that emotion occurs when a person discovers that he or she cannot act in the experienced world, thus transforming consciousness to the more primitive attitude of a magical world. To Sartre, then, emotion represents a basic response to failure, the energy of life turned from advanced, neocortical mechanisms toward the primitive. He seems to have known little about pleasure.

Pribram (1970) wrote that emotion arises when some stimulus situation disequilibrates the plan by which the neural system has organized behavior. He described two types of emotion, one of which operates to adjust the stimulus input to conform to our plans, another that adjusts our plans to conform to the stimulus input. Here, too, emotion only follows the breakdown of something better.

Jung (1923) was captivated by his concept of the unconscious world; his original and poetic theory for emotion was revised slightly by Hillman in 1961. In this system, emotion is instigated when the conscious and unconscious selves are united by a symbol, thus releasing psychic energy and transforming it into experienced emotion. Although few of us would argue about the existence of unconscious life, there is no evidence for an unconscious *self*, for the energy that might be released when these two hypothetical entities are fused, or for the mechanisms that might turn this energy into the broad range of known emotions.

One final adult-based theory is that of DeRivera (1977), who saw emotions as instructions that tell the organism how to move in relation to its stimulus situation—toward or away from self or other. If these instructions are written as clearly as DeRivera suggests, then something is quite wrong with the ways many of us interpret them. The actual experience of emotion differs so much from one culture to another that only by shifting emotion labels and constantly redefining each emotion can this system be made to work. It is based entirely on his arrangement of adult emotion labels, and denies both the biological and the infantile expressions of emotion.

Infant-based Theories

Charles Darwin evaluated everything he saw in terms of its utility to establish the concept of evolution. It was he who first noted that infants display all the facial and bodily signs of emotion seen in the adult, and that many of these signs may be seen in life forms that preceded us in the evolutionary sequence. From the responses to questionnaires he sent to correspondents all over the globe, Darwin established that a great portion of the expression of emotion is universal and independent of cultural training. He suggested that these expressions had evolved as a system of nonverbal communication, and that each emotion readied the organism to act in ways that conferred on it an increased ability to survive. Whenever the *display* of emotion was suppressed, the experience of that specific emotion was muted; to the extent that the expression was allowed full play, it seemed increased.

Darwin introduced the idea that we are born with a group of what would now be called "hardwired" mechanisms, each of which caused a specific facial expression, associated with which was a specific and reproducible emotional experience. His list included anger, fear, shame, amusement, grief, surprise, and delight; these were described as separate categories of emotion. Missing is any sense of human development, for Darwin could not have anticipated what was only later taught us by Freud—the vast number of psychic changes that take place during early childhood.

AFFECT THEORY

Published in 1872 as *The Expression of Emotion in Man and Animals*, Darwin's observations stood curiously ignored for nearly a century until the contemporary psychologist Silvan S. Tomkins (1962, 1963) expanded them into what is now known as *affect theory*. Observing the birth of his son, Tomkins recognized that the cry of the newborn does not occur because the organism has appraised the world as a vale of tears. Crying is a complex process involving tears, a great many facial muscles, and the voice; the mechanism for the cry must lie in some prewritten program that can be accessed without conscious control. And if the infant pushed some sort of button to produce this innate cry, there was no reason to suspect that the crying adult needed any other button. Signals for the innate cry travel over bulbofacial fibers, while simulated or intentional weeping involves corticofacial tracts (Nathanson, 1992).

Tomkins reasoned further that the very complexity of the innate cry implied another level of significance — it seemed unlikely to him that the organism would waste the information involved in so much auditory, muscular, and circulatory system activity. He suggested that the display itself became a source of data that tended to perpetuate its further display. Whatever triggered the cry therefore set in motion a mechanism that produced more crying; the mechanism acts as an amplifier of its stimulus conditions.

In an attempt to differentiate this new theoretical system from its predecessors, Tomkins used the term *affect* rather than emotion for the group of nine innate mechanisms he came to describe. (Affect is the root word for such terms as affection, disaffected, and affectionate, and had long been favored over *emotion* in the psychoanalytic literature.) In the infant, each of the nine innate affects is believed to be triggered not by experiences an adult would recognize as normal precipitants of emotion, but by alterations of such physiological parameters as the intensity and steadiness of whatever was then going on in the central nervous system. The affect responsible for crying is triggered by any stimulus that is both higher than optimal and of constant density (like persistent cold, or the gnawing sensation of hunger, or any mild and constant bodily discomfort); the steady quality of the sobbing affect itself is both an analogue of that steady-state stimulus and an amplifier of the discomfort. In the language of affect theory, an innate affect is therefore seen as an *analogic amplifier of its stimulus conditions*.

Seven of these innate mechanisms are given two-word names, the first indicating the mildest presentation of the affect, the second its most intense. For example, the affect *interest–excitement* is triggered by any optimal increase in information acquisition, as in the experience of novelty. Mild interest is demonstrated by the furrowed brow we associate with anybody who is "thinking hard" or "paying strict attention" to something; the fact takes on the appearance we think of as "track, look, or listen"; sometimes the tongue is thrust to the corner of the mouth. When this affect has been pushed to its higher range of activity, the infant will nearly leap from its position as it maximizes its attention to whatever has triggered the affect.

If interest–excitement is the analogic amplification of an *optimal* rise in stimulus density, then what happens when too much data is being handled? Tomkins suggests that the affect *fear-terror* is a programmed response to overmuch, a response pattern in which the face is blanched and cold, the eyes frozen in a stare, the pulse racing, and hair standing on end. Information that comes into the infant's system even more rapidly and then stops (as in the case of a hand clap or a pistol shot), triggers *surprise-startle*, the analogic amplifier of a sudden or abrupt stimulus. The affect itself is so brief that it cannot be said to have any positive or negative quality of its own; surprise merely readies us to evaluate whatever has co-opted our attention, no matter whether pleasant or unpleasant.

Intuitively, we understand that the relief of any preexisting stimulus produces a good feeling; Tomkins defines the affect *enjoyment–joy* as the calming analogic amplification of this stimulus decrease. A mild slope is associated with the smile of pleasure, while precipitous decrease produces laughter. Affects match their stimulus in many ways—the sudden rise and fall of surprise-startle resembles the profile of a thunder clap just as the constant-density stimulus of cold is matched by the *distress-anguish* it triggers. Should the triggering stimulus be both of constant density and even higher than that necessary to produce the sobbing affect of distress, the innate affect *anger-rage* results. Throughout life, the amplified analogues of high-density constant stimulation include such facial displays as a frown, clenched teeth, and the red face of anger.

Demos (1983) points out that the affect system converts quantitative information into a group of qualitative experiences. We have evolved to be an organism that is hardwired for two positive affects, a third so brief that it is neutral, and six that are decidedly negative.

What of the drives that assumed such importance to Freud? In general, Tomkins views the drives as mechanisms that sense a bodily need, indicate how and where it is to be satisfied, and initiate the process of consummation. The drive hunger detects such matters as lowered blood glucose, informs by making us hungry in the mouth, and then initiates sucking movements. But no drive is inherently linked to any affect. When hungry, we may be interested in food, afraid of it, humiliated by our hunger, distressed and therefore sobbing in our hunger, or angry at our hunger. Any affect can amplify any drive to make it urgent in its own particular way and therefore important to us.

Two additional mechanisms, *dissmell* and *disgust*, do relate to the drive hunger, even though they come to take on important roles in our later affective life. Initially triggered by food that smells or tastes bad, they provide a primitive mode of rejection. Even when hunger is at its height, dissmell can lead the organism to pull away from what had initially looked appetizing, while disgust impels us to spit out what had only a moment ago looked and smelled good. Later in development, they come to achieve the status of affects that involve not just food but also interpersonal distance. Tomkins gave them one-word names to indicate their derivation as auxiliaries to the drive hunger rather than the more purely physiological sources of the other seven affects.

Similarly, the affect *shame–humiliation* is considered to have evolved as an auxiliary to the affect system. Shame affect interrupts the interest or enjoyment amplifying whatever good scene had been going on only a moment ago by producing loss of tonus in the neck, downcast and averted gaze, and the blush. How it comes to be associated with such adult experiences as embarrassment and ridicule, or how fear-terror comes to be involved in anxiety, are matters yet to be presented. Table 1.1 lists all the innate affects, giving for each its triggering stimulus and facial display.

What Happens to Innate Affect as We Grow Older?

Every society on the planet requires that, in order to be considered adult, one must learn to mute the display of affect. So well have we adults learned this lesson that, past infancy, observers can detect little that really gives the sense of the true, innate mechanism. Yet to the infant, when an affect hits, it is the only game in town. It simply takes over the child's world. Tomkins believes that this sudden and powerful rearrangement of the infantile physiognomy is so remarkable an experience in the life of the infant that the data emanating from the face itself are responsible for the child's ability to identify the individual affects. This group of genetically based mechanisms causes so much to happen on the face that the associated facial feedback becomes the hallmark of our internal experience of affect.

Each affect program makes itself felt by taking over remote structures that have evolved for other purposes. (Surely hair did not evolve to

TABLE 1.1

The Innate Affects

Positive
1. Interest–excitement
   Eyebrows down, track, look, listen
2. Enjoyment–joy
   Smile, lips widened and out

Neutral
3. Surprise–startle
   Eyebrows up, eyes blink

Negative
4. Fear–terror
   Frozen stare, face pale, cold, sweaty, hair erect
5. Distress–anguish
   Cry, rhythmic sobbing, arched eyebrows, mouth down
6. Anger–rage
   Frown, clenched jaw, red face
7. Shame–humiliation
   Eyes down, head down and averted, blush
8. Dissmell
   Upper lip raised, head pulled back
9. Disgust
   Lower lip lowered and protruded, head forward and down

From Tomkins (1962).

stand up in fear, nor the circulatory system to thump harder in fear or excitement.) But the fibers responsible for facial expression are voluntary muscles. Sensing the arrangements of facial muscles associated with each of these programmed displays, the infant learns swiftly to imitate intentionally what was initially produced automatically by the innate mechanism. The skill of mimicry or *autosimulation* of affective expression and the accumulation of learned triggers to affect form significant parts of our emotional development.

It is these nine innate mechanisms that produce everything we call *motivation.* As Tomkins has pointed out, "affect makes good things better and bad things worse." At any moment, so much is going on in the human brain that nothing can be said to gain our *attention* unless it triggers an affect. Affect is responsible for *awareness,* for only that which gains affective amplification gets into the limited channel we call *consciousness.*

Basch (1976) offers an important connection between this complex physiological theory and the system of clinical observations with which we are more familiar. Affect, he has suggested, is best understood as a purely biological phenomenon that we appreciate as a *feeling* only when we become aware that it has been triggered. Growing from infancy toward adulthood, we accumulate experience of each affect, tending to group in memory those situations in which affect has been triggered. The older we are, the greater the store of previous affective experiences that come to mind when any one is triggered. Basch suggests that we use the term *emotion* to represent the assemblage of any affect with our associations to previous experience of that affect. I (1986) have summarized this formal definition by pointing out that affect is biology, while emotion is biography.

So it is that each member of this group of programmed physiological reactions (initially triggered by meaning-free alterations in specific physiological parameters) becomes linked with the history of a quite variable number and form of experienced triggers to achieve patterns of meaning and significance that will remain with us throughout life. Day by day, the growing child learns to group the experiences of each affect into categories of emotional experience. This is why no archaeological expedition, no psychoanalytic investigation of emotion can lead to an understanding of innate affect: Asked to study a piece of birthday cake, the biologist would make many accurate observations of the chemicals involved. But too much has been changed in the process of baking for that science to determine from cake the life cycle of cows, sugar cane, or wheat.

Of equal importance is the observation that relatively few of the possible affect–experience links achieve recognition in the form of an adult emotion label. Many situations trigger one or another innate affect, become thereby the momentary subject of our attention, and get solved without becoming known as a moment of emotion. Only a select group of often repeated and therefore significant triggers, affects, and responses earns such recognition.

Each of us grows up with the same palette of nine innate affects. We all start out with pretty much the same equipment. It is in our biographies that we differ so much, and therefore in the experience-affect combinations that come to represent what each of us knows as our emotions.

Affect in Our Shared World

There is yet another realm of affect to be considered. Even though this system of internal amplifiers has evolved to allow the organism such abilities as focused attention and intentional behavior, the very fact that each affect program is displayed on the face before it is processed by the organism ensures that it will also form an important part of our social interaction. When in the throes of positive affect (interest–excitement or enjoyment–joy), an infant is actually a beacon of pleasure for those around it; caregivers will gather happily around a smiling baby. And when some impediment triggers the painfully amplified analogue of impediment to positive affect that we call shame–humiliation, this pleasant interchange is interrupted.

Actually, it is only from the negative affect displayed by the preverbal infant that the caregiver first learns that the baby needs attention. Babies cry when any steady-state stimulus rises in density above an optimal level. That particular affect indicates only the presence of steady-state discomfort. It remains for the intelligence and experience of the adult caregiver to discern from among the host of possible sources the true nature of the need that has acted as a trigger to affect.

Some caregivers do no more than deduce the child's need and offer no more than a remedy. All of us have seen mothers who present the milk bottle as if they were plugging an electric cord into a socket, propping it on pillows so the infant can nurse unattended. Something different happens when the caregiver agrees to "tune in" to the infant's affect display by focusing on it to the exclusion of other stimuli. Just as our own affect, when initially triggered, so beautifully reproduces and amplifies the characteristics that make it a further trigger to affect, the displayed affect of another person can also be a trigger to our own affect. We speak, therefore, of the infant as a *broadcaster* of innate affect, and the caregiver as a *receiver* who experiences this affect by some process of *affective resonance*.

Basch (1976) points out that affective resonance is the beginning of empathy — what we share, initially, is one of the innate affects. But just as soon as we experience the affect, we form associations to it from our own biography; two people experiencing the same affect are not really experiencing the same emotion. Furthermore, I (1986) have suggested that the reason all of us do not walk around perpetually being taken over by the affects broadcast by others in our environment is that we build what I call an "empathic wall" that allows us to maintain our personal boundaries in society.

By tuning in to her child's affect display, the empathically competent mother does far more than tap into a major channel of data acquisition. The act of communing with the infant's affect display allows her to offer that infant some method of modulation, of improving or bettering the child's affective state. Mother's efforts at soothing these unmodulated displays of infantile affect teach the growing child what will, in later years, be known as the techniques of self-soothing. We believe that failures in this realm predispose one to use and abuse a host of substances, behaviors, and partners in an effort to quell roiling affective states. Furthermore, it is the child's dawning awareness that *affect is the link between need, its identification, and its later relief* that allows us to grow into adulthood trusting our emotions as an important source of information.

It is the affect system that mediates everything we call relatedness — our entire social and interactional world. The current attempt to turn all communication into affectless digital data that can be handled by computer may be viewed as a societal attempt to turn away from the disquieting information transmitted by the analogue devices of affect transmission. All of our attempts to understand and treat others must be based on a secure understanding of affect as part of both an intrapsychic and an interpersonal system.

Connection to Other Systems of Knowledge

In my review and extension of affect theory, I (1992) pointed out that each affect involves five separate moieties. For each, there are *sites of action* at which something happens that can be recognized as a feeling — the racing pulse of fear or excitement, the sudden intake of breath that accompanies surprise, the tuft of hair now standing stiffly erect that only a moment ago was limp and calm. The affect system has evolved to take over distant structures for use in this system of amplification.

In order for information to be transmitted from the basic affect programs to the periphery, there must be a group of *structural effectors* and *chemical mediators* capable of stimulating these sites of action. *Receptors* (like the tiny neurofibrils that surround each hair follicle) must be capable of returning data to the central assembly system. And all of these are grouped as the *organizers* of innate affect described by Tomkins.

I suggest further that we consider the human emotion system as if it were built something like the ubiquitous personal computer, with subsystems of hardware, firmware, and software (Table 1.2). The little machines that whir, buzz, and glow at us when given electricity are analogous to the body parts that serve the affect system — central nervous system (with its structural wiring and data handling capacity), skin and muscles of the face, chemicals that traverse the body to carry affect-related messages. Together, these are considered our hardware.

What we know of as "chips" in the computer actually contain instructions once written by extremely intelligent people, instructions that have been encrypted in such a way that they cannot be altered without destroying the chip. Neither "hard" nor "soft," they are considered firmware.

TABLE 1.2
Computer Model for the Human Emotional System

Hardware
- Central nervous system, including biochemical environment, neurotransmitters, structural "wiring," data handling capacity, information storage and retrieval.
- Striated muscles controlling face, posture, vocalization.
- Endocrine and exocrine systems.

Firmware
- Drives
- Affects

Software
- Learning
- Social conditioning
- Experience

From Nathanson (1992, p. 27).

Modern neurophysiological research reveals the presence of more and more built-in firmware packages like the drives and the affects. Emotion, however, depends on the system of amplifying affect mechanisms.

By software we describe sets of instructions that can be altered or varied; computer software allows a machine initially designed only to handle the numbers 1 and 0 to become a spreadsheet or a word processing device. In the human emotion system, it is the experience of life that operates as the controlling software. Each of us has grown up in a family, a neighborhood, an era; these structures influence our style of affect modulation simply because each requires a somewhat different attitude toward individual affects as such, and toward the display of affect. It should be immediately apparent that what is known traditionally as psychotherapy (psychoanalytic, cognitive-behavioral, or any other system) involves restructuring of our techniques and rules for affect modulation.

Equally apparent is the idea that any chemical capable of causing things to happen at a site of action normally associated with an affect display is therefore capable of triggering what can be experienced as an affect. Ingested chemicals like pseudoephedrine, a synthetic analogue of the adrenergic neurotransmitters, can produce enough effects that are similar to those produced by the affect *fear–terror* that we are often able to say that such medication (when taken for the discomfort of a stuffy nose) is a cause of anxiety. Much of modern psychopharmacology can be viewed as the study and relief of unpleasant affective states. These hardware malfunctions have been the subject of an enormous amount of research attention in recent years.

It is not much of a leap to consider bipolar affective illness as a disorder in which too much interest–excitement powers the manic phase; all depression involves some sort of lesion of the affect interest. While the history of our relation to the affect fear–terror can explain much of what we know as *anxiety,* sturdy research suggests the existence of many ways the biological circuitry for the innate affect may be distorted to produce specific illnesses. Family and population studies suggest genetic mechanisms for many such disorders. Yet, given the plasticity of the infant brain, it also seems likely that high-density, recurrent, unmodulated experiences of any affect might groove pathways for the production of affect mediators in amounts not seen in the normal adult. These, too, would be diagnosed and treated as hardware malfunctions effectively indistinguishable from those caused by heritable mechanisms.

If attention is always and only a product of the affect system, then what of the conditions known as disorders of attention? In bipolar affective illness, some aberration of normal affect mechanisms triggers an inappropriate amount of interest–excitement. Attention deficit disorder or attention deficit hyperactivity disorder (ADD or ADHD) may be viewed as malformations of the triggers for interest–excitement or any of the subsystems through which the brain processes the connection between the affect and whatever it amplifies. The relation between ADD/ADHD and the normal affect system is analogous to the relation between diabetes and the normal system for the metabolism of glucose. Medical science always learns about the normal through the study of disease.

Nothing is important unless it gains affective amplification; anything so amplified is important in direct proportion to the degree of amplification it achieves. Similarly, it will be clear that what an earlier generation thought of as "impulsive" behavior is not impelled by drive forces but overly amplified by affect. And there is a wide range of psychopathological conditions initiated by events that produce unmodulated affective amplification of terrible density—nothing can be called trauma unless it triggers affect.

The Example of Shame

In one short decade, shame has moved from the status of the least-studied emotional experience to one of the most discussed. Working within the archaeological tradition of the psychoanalyst, Wurmser (1981) demonstrated how any adult experience of embarrassment, humiliation, mortification, ridicule, or put-down could be related to a lifetime of similar discomfort.

Although in infancy the affect shame–humiliation is triggered by a meaning-free impediment to positive affect, the lifetime summation product of these experience-affect links falls into a limited number of groups. Using affect theory, I (1992) have determined eight categories of all the life situations in which the human organism might encounter this painful affect (Table 1.3). By the time we are adults, failure or inadequacy in any of these eight groups will trigger shame. The obvious and best known such triggers include loss in competition, sexual failure, the experience of betrayal, and the revelation of anything we would have preferred to have kept private or secret. Released next is the physiological mechanism itself, with the stigmata of blush, averted gaze, slump, and a sudden inability to think clearly described as a *cognitive shock* (Nathanson, 1987). So far, only innate affect is involved.

The third phase of the shame experience involves a rapid scan of all previous similar moments; it is this combination of affect and history that Basch (1976) describes as emotion. Now it becomes clear that there is much more involved in the concept of emotion than an assembly of affect and association. As soon as we recover from the cognitive shock of shame affect and the ensuing swirl of remembered incidents we must

TABLE 1.3
Categories of Shame Experience

- *Matters of personal size, strength, ability, skill*
  "I am weak, incompetent, stupid."

- *Dependence/Independence*
  Sense of helplessness

- *Competition*
  "I am a loser."

- *Sense of self*
  "I am unique only to the extent that I am defective."

- *Personal attractiveness*
  "I am ugly or deformed. The blush stains my features and makes me even more of a target of contempt."

- *Sexuality*
  "There is something wrong with me sexually."

- *Issues of seeing and being seen*
  The urge to escape from the eyes before which we have been exposed. The wish for a hole to open up and swallow me.

- *Wishes and fears about closeness*
  The sense of being shorn from all humanity. A feeling that one is unlovable. The wish to be left alone forever.

From Nathanson (1992, p. 317).

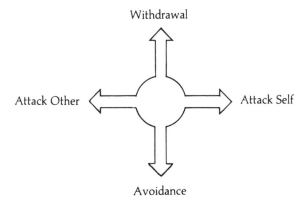

Figure 1.1. The compass of shame (from Nathanson, 1992, p. 312).

make some decision—what will we do with this new moment of self-knowledge made urgent by affective amplification? Shame comes to have terrible importance to our concept of self—either we accept what shame has now shown us and adjust our self-image, or we will be forced to defend against this experience by one of four highly scripted methods of behavior called the *compass of shame* (Figure 1.1).

The act of yielding to the push of the affect itself and turning away from the triggering stimulus utilizes the mechanism of *withdrawal*. At one end of its spectrum this may involve no more than the merest gesture of embarrassment (sometimes we put hand to lips as if to prevent ourselves from saying the very words that have just embarrassed us). At the other extreme, pathological withdrawal from all human interchange may be a hallmark of severe depression. Such an experience of shame leads to interference with our ability to be social; shame impedes interpersonal interaction. For those who fear most the sense of abandonment that can accompany unexpected shame, one time-tested strategy involves the intentional derogation of the self. The *attack self* pole of the compass of shame contains all the scripts and systems through which we demean ourselves in order to maintain association with others, ranging from simple deference to pathological masochism.

For those to whom any experience of shame is unbearable there exist myriad techniques for *avoidance*. Many street drugs, like cocaine and the amphetamines, provide a synthetic burst of the excitement that shame has impeded. Then, too, we can avoid shame by calling attention to anything that brings us pride. Most of what we have been taught to consider narcissistic can be understood and treated better as part of an avoidance script for the management of shame experience.

Finally, some people all of the time, and most people some of the time, experience shame as a moment of terrible inferiority that can be handled only by reducing the self-esteem of others. The *attack other* script library includes all the ways (from the normal interchange of banter and mild put-down to the outright abuse of the sadistic) that we adjust the balance of power between self and other in the language of shame. All manifestations of shame are controlled by the four script libraries described as the compass of shame.

It is too simple to say that shame involves a moment of exposure or a rift in the interpersonal bridge that we handle by "withdrawing in embarrassment." Shame is also the way we let people take advantage of us in order to avoid the feeling of isolation, as well as the way we escape "hurt feelings" by cruising for transient sexual conquests or drugs or the purchase of anything that makes us feel good about ourselves. Shame is also the sudden eruption of anger when we have been insulted. Our new definition of emotion must take into account the entire sequence of triggering stimulus, physiological affect, cognitive scan, decision phase, and reactive script.

Might there be for shame a cluster of syndromes powered by pathological alterations of biology much as we have described bipolar affective illness and ADD/ADHD in terms of interest–excitement? There is good evidence to suggest that the symptom complexes known as "social phobia" and "atypical depression" are afflictions involving the hardware for shame affect. Recently, I (1994) have presented a rationale for the understanding and treatment of "borderline illness" in terms of shame. All the symptoms exhibited by this otherwise puzzling group of patients may be understood better as variations on the themes mentioned above as poles on the compass of shame. The pathophysiology of shame-related disorders may be due to inborn errors of metabolism making an individual preternaturally susceptible to the affect of unpleasant impediment, or to poorly informed methods of nurturance that amplify shame experience and produce adaptive disorders of shame affect.

CONCLUSION

Affect theory offers a way of viewing emotion that removes it from its current position as the handmaiden of illness. By returning human emotion to its rightful place as the source of all that is colorful and interesting in life, this new system of knowledge suggests that the normal and the pathological lie as points along an easily understood continuum. All aspects of psychotherapy research and practice may be altered and improved by this new approach to the nature of human emotion.

REFERENCES

Angyal, A. (1941). *Foundations for a science of personality*. Cambridge, MA: Harvard University Press.

Basch, M. F. (1976). The concept of affect: A reexamination. *Journal of the American Psychoanalytic Association, 24*, 759-777.

Darwin, C. (1872). *The expression of the emotions in man and animals*. New York: St. Martin's Press.

Demos, E. V. (1983). A perspective from infant research on affect and self-esteem. In J. Mack & J. Ablon (Eds.), *The development and sustaining of self-esteem in childhood* (pp. 45-78). New York: International Universities Press.

DeRiviera, J. A. (1977). *Structural theory of the emotions*. New York: International Universities Press.

Freud, S. (1915). Instincts and their vicissitudes (J. Strachey, Trans.). In *The standard edition of the complete psychological works of Sigmund Freud, Vol. 12*, (pp. 159-204). New York: Norton.

Hillman, J. (1961). *Emotion*. Evanston, IL: Northwestern University Press.

James, W. (1968). What is an emotion? In M. Arnold (Ed.), *The nature of emotion*. Baltimore, MD: Penguin Press.

Jung, C. G. (1923). *Psychological types*. New York: Academic Press.

Lange, C. G. (1887). *Uber gemutsbewegunguen*. Leipsig, Germany.

McDougall, W. (1910). *An introduction to social psychology* (3rd ed.). Boston, MA: Luce.

Nathanson, D. L. (1986). The empathic wall and the ecology of affect. *Psychoanalytic Study of the Child, 41*, 171-187.

Nathanson, D. L. (1987). *The many faces of shame*. New York: Guilford.

Nathanson, D. L. (1992). *Shame and pride: Affect, sex and the birth of the self*. New York: Norton.

Nathanson, D. L. (1994). Shame, compassion and the "borderline" personality. *Psychiatric Clinics of North America, 17*, 785-810.

Paulhan, F. (1930). *The laws of feeling* (C. K. Ogden, Trans.). New York: Harcourt Brace.

Pribam, K. H. (1970). Feelings as monitors. In M. B. Arnold (Ed.), *Feelings and emotions*. New York: Academic Press.

Sartre, J. P. (1948). *The emotions: Outlines of a theory*. New York: Philosophical Library.

Stern, D. N. (1985). *The interpersonal world of the infant*. New York: Basic Books.

Tomkins, S. S. (1962). *Affect, imagery, consciousness, Vol. I: The positive affects*. New York: Springer.

Tomkins, S. S. (1963). *Affect, imagery, consciousness, Vol. II: The negative affects*. New York: Springer.

Wundt, W. (1907). *Outlines of psychology* (3rd ed.). New York: Strechert.

Wurmser, L. (1981). *The mask of shame*. Baltimore, MD: Johns Hopkins University Press.

2

Clinical Assessment
of Affect

Andrew M. Stone

What we know of people is neither the narrative by which they identify themselves nor the label by which they expect us to identify
them, but a complex gestalt of the feelings and memories evoked in
us and them during our interaction. Look at the face of the person
who has come to you for therapy–there you will read the roadmap
of their history and watch the display of their present. Patients have
always been telling us more than we have heard.

Clinical diagnosis involves both a process of assessment and a
placement of that assessment within some matrix built of what we
have learned from our work with others. If the psychotherapist is, as I
believe, a vendor of change, we are best able to understand another's potential for change when we know the meaning and significance of the moment-to-moment display of affect that characterizes them. Information is conveyed by what is hidden as well as what
is shown. Stone asks us to pay meticulous attention to the range over
which each of the nine innate affects is expressed, for the unexpressed affect may have been stifled, suppressed, or turned off in
response to historical sequences of cardinal importance. This chapter suggests ways that the therapist at any level of sophistication
may use the data of affective expression to inform the clinical process. –DLN

. . . the merely descriptive literature of the emotions is one
of the most tedious parts of psychology. . . . But as far as
"scientific psychology" of the emotions goes, I may have been
surfeited by too much reading of classical works on the subject, but I should as lief read verbal descriptions of the shapes
of rocks on a New Hampshire farm as toil through them
again. They give one nowhere a central point of view, or a
deductive or generative principle . . . Whereas the beauty of
all truly scientific work is to get to ever deeper levels.

— Willam James, 1890

THE ROLE OF AFFECT in conveying meaning has been seriously neglected
by many scholars. Part of the reason has been the lack of a clear framework in which to describe and account for the enormous and subtle
variations that in fact comprise the better part of human individuality.
As psychology and psychotherapy have evolved over the last hundred
years, their legitimacy has been drawn largely from correspondences
with the physical sciences. In pursuing the objective, the rational, the
deterministic keys to mental life, verbal cognitive material is most accessible and describable. As a place to start, it is fine. But to stop with the
purely verbal is to ignore much of what makes us who we are.

COGNITION : AFFECT = WORDS : MUSIC

Cognition is to affect as words are to music. Perhaps the correspondence
is not exact, but as far as interpreting the experience of another person is
concerned, we know for certain that going by cognitive content alone will
provide a very incomplete picture. Nonverbal, paralinguistic, kinesic/
proxemic, and other kinds of information must be interpreted as well to
give color and texture to our understanding (Shea, 1988).

When Meursault, the protagonist in Camus' *The Stranger*, tells us that
"Mother died today. Or perhaps it was yesterday," it is not the content
alone that disturbs us, but the way it is juxtaposed with his absence of
discernible affect. Applying the conventional expectations of our culture, an examining clinician might consider this combination of affect
and cognitive content to be "inappropriate." The words don't go with the
music, at least in the opinion of the observer.

How do we arrive at such determinations? What standards do we
apply? How can we assess affective display in a reproducible and clinically applicable way? What are we looking for? A succession of ques-

tions need to be answered. First, what affects are being displayed, and in what form and intensity? Second, how do these fit into their context?

What do we see? What do we hear? How do we know? We start with the face, the most important location of affect display. Izard, Dougherty, and Hembree (1983) have developed a scale to code facial affect response. The scale looks at nine different affects closely corresponding to the ones posited by Tomkins. Trained observers can produce reliable assessments of the presence of different facial affect displays. Recently, for example, the scale has been applied to a retrospective review of home movies of children who were later diagnosed as schizophrenic. Walker, Grimes, Davis, and Smith (1993) reviewed the films, identifying facial affect display and seeking differences in the frequency of the different emotional expressions. A significantly lower proportion of expressions of joy was found in the female pre-schizophrenic subjects compared with their non-diagnosed siblings. And both male and female pre-schizophrenic subjects showed more negative affect than same-sex comparison groups. These results are intriguing, and like most good research, raise many more new questions. But in this chapter, our concern is not so much with what they found as with how they found it. Using specified criteria for facial affect displays, they were able to distinguish reliably and reproducibly among different expressions of affect.

Doubtless we can all tell a smile from a frown. That seemingly intuitive discrimination will serve as the prototype for the necessarily less structured but no less rigorous identification of affect display that is an essential part of a clinical psychiatric evaluation.

DATA FROM ENCOUNTER

Observation

All real living is meeting.   —Martin Buber, 1958

What can we learn of the affective and emotional life of another person? How do we apply to the clinical setting what researchers and theorists have developed? As Tomkins (1962) suggests, and Demos (1983) confirms, the face is where we must begin. For research purposes, systems for the coding of affect display on the face use slow-motion or stop-action film or video; they separate the face into upper, middle, and lower facial zones; and they code for the onset, duration, and offset of specific expressive elements. For clinical use, the approach is necessarily somewhat more impressionistic and inexact. Still, there are enormous quantities of information to be gleaned.

The face in repose will (absent the effects of cosmetic surgery) reveal the lines and skin creases of habitual or characteristic predominant patterns of display. The skin and connective tissues are actually modified by the repeated contraction of the underlying musculature. The vertical line between the eyebrows associated with anger, the accentuated horizontal lines of the forehead in distress or anguish, even the "smile lines" at the eyes can each provide suggestions of frequently held positions of the face. While no single finding can itself be considered definitive, each adds a piece to our understanding of the affective range. In the young, these features will be subtle but still discernible. With the passage of years, frequently or intensely displayed affects are indeed etched more deeply into the face. When writers speak of "ravaged" features they refer not only to the effects of weather and nutrition, but also to the marks left by grief, pain, anger, and other emotional expressions. One evocative simile is that of a face that "looks like forty miles of bad road." The power of the phrase lies in the way it combines the description of a rough journey with the effects on the appearance of the traveler; the surface of the road and the surface of the visage are both implied in the trope. The efforts of physiognomists of old to determine character from facial features have relied in part on the observation of these resting patterns of redistributed collagen under the skin that result from the ceaseless movements of the muscles below.

In the course of conversation (or that special case of conversation which is called an interview), there will also be a flow of affective display on the face. Certain characteristic expressions may predominate. Some habitual patterns of presentation may operate totally out of the awareness of the person. Others may be consciously assumed: the "persona" in its original sense of a mask for a role. As with any other repeated behavior, we must assume that there has been at some point a sufficient environmental reinforcement for the organism to have found in this display some adaptational advantage.

A young woman from a turbulent family in a dangerous inner-city neighborhood was hospitalized on an inpatient psychiatric unit following a psychotic episode. As her recovery progressed, she participated more in the activities of the therapeutic milieu, including community meetings. She was slender but tall, generally moved quickly and purposefully, and usually held her face in a fixed expression with eyes narrowed, brows drawn down, and mouth in a tight straight line. Both staff and other patients found her presence somewhat intimidating. She was told of the effect that people around her were experiencing, and she was asked if she was aware of it. Her reply was succinct. "If you lived where I lived, you'd look like that too."

This woman's habitual display of anger served a purpose. It helped to create a safe zone, a distance around her into which others were reluctant to venture. It aided her passage through threatening streets. Like most defenses, it came at a certain price. In this instance the cost was an impairment of the possibility of closeness, warmth, spontaneous contact, and true intimacy. It was a price that she was willing to pay.

Beyond these fixed or habitual displays are the more fleeting and transient affective components of expression. There is no living visage that does not vary in its arrangement. Working from, within, and beyond the accustomed baseline or ground level of expression, every face has a repertoire and range of affect. This may be great and varied, or it may be limited and constricted. These very limits and distortions themselves become an important clinical finding in the course of our assessment of affect.

Neither can it be expected that the affective display on the face of an adult will consist solely of "pure" innate affects succeeding one another in distinct and separate phases. From the earliest social interaction, the negative and positive reinforcement of different components of expression will begin to modify an individual's own personal way of showing response. Especially in the case of the negative affects, such as anger or fear, learned modifications will superimpose and transform the initial basic response. Tomkins (1991) describes distorted or "backed-up" modes of displaying forbidden affects in which only a portion of the original response is permitted to surface (p. 430). Similarly, affects can be miniaturized, magnified, or otherwise transmuted through experience so that their expression is greatly modified. Observing, detecting, and interpreting these remnants and fragments become an ongoing exercise in pattern recognition for the interviewer.

The Affect Pattern Chart

One device for keeping in mind and visually presenting a profile of someone's affective expression during an interview is the Affect Pattern Chart that has been developed by Nathanson (1993) (see Figure 2.1). Listing each of the innate affects in turn, it invites the observer to record the extent and range of expression. By directing attention to each affect individually, the chart guides us to look not only at those affects that are predominant, but also to those which are conspicuous by their absence or suppression.

Figure 2.1. Affect Pattern Chart

Purpose of this chart is to show the range of expression of each innate affect. For each, list the degree to which it is seen overtly, the freedom of its expression, and/or its importance in the character structure of the individual.

Interest–Excitement _____

Enjoyment–Joy _____

Surprise–Startle _____

Fear–Terror _____

Distress–Anguish _____

Anger–Rage _____

Dissmell _____

Disguist _____

Shame–Humiliation _____

S–S usually followed by what affect?

E–J usually produced by what script?

For any affect registered at the higher end of the scale, is the trigger interpersonal, from internal preoccupation, or from biological aberration?

Where Dissmell and Disgust are prominent, is the affect triggered by self or other?

For S–H, sketch the compass and show prominent reaction pattern.

Is any affect described or experienced by the subject as coming more from outside the self than inside?

We may choose to describe the variations in expression, the coassemblies with other affects, the ones that are seen as a problem by the patient, and those that are so identified by the therapist. While not quantified or intended as a research instrument, the chart can serve the clinician as the scaffold for a quick sketch of someone's affective functioning at a point in time, and thus serve as a record for later comparison. Looking at affect as a first premise shapes the way we think of treatment, and training ourselves to observe it is an ongoing process as well. Using the affect pattern chart helps to establish the practice of attending to this layer of experience. As a quick, systematic overview of affective expression and functioning, it offers the therapist a checklist that supports the development of a thorough clinical inventory of a patient's behavior in this realm.

Affective Attunement in the Interview

Verbal description of visual observation, while essential, cannot convey all the information being generated during an encounter such as a psychiatric interview. Beyond the visual and auditory cues provided by the patient, another valuable source of data is the affective experience of the interviewer.

There is wide agreement among virtually all schools of thought in psychiatry that the reactions of the clinician provide pertinent information. The German objective-descriptive pioneers spoke of a *praecox-gefühl*, a feeling in the doctor that stems from an inability to match or comprehend the affective experience of the patient with dementia praecox, or what today would probably be seen as one of the schizophrenias. As Havens (1976) describes Jaspers' explanation of this, it is that very disjunction which indicates the presence of the illness. Here, the physician's response is considered as objective data and cited to support other diagnostic evidence.

The psychoanalytic investigation of the clinician's response has been extensive and revealing. In 1910, Sigmund Freud wrote:

> We have begun to consider the "counter-transference" which arises in the physician as a result of the patient's influence on his unconscious feelings, and have nearly come to the point of requiring the physician to recognize and overcome this counter-transference in himself. . . . every analyst's achievement is limited by what his own complexes and resistances permit, and consequently we require that he should begin his practice with a self-analysis and should extend and deepen this constantly while making his observations on his patients. (1910, p. 289)

Here the physician's response is no longer assumed to be merely a reflection of the patient's state. Rather, it is seen as depending on the personal "complexes and resistances" of the analyst, which determine how the therapist will react to the patient's emotional life.

Freud's injunction requiring the analyst to "recognize and overcome" these responses has provided material for a great deal of discussion and debate in the decades that have followed. In a sense, the pendulum has swung back and forth between recognizing and overcoming. While at one point the countertransference may have been viewed primarily as an error to be corrected, it has more and more been recognized as a necessary component of the human interaction involved in psychotherapy. The requirement for recognition of the affective response of the therapist has not diminished, and neither has that for the therapist to know himself or herself as fully as possible. It is only through such understanding that there is any chance of being able to tell which emotional material "belongs" to the patient, and is thus clinically pertinent to the problems at hand.

Early existential psychiatrists such as Minkowski made the contribution of acknowledging and valuing their own affects and emotional responses as part of the relationship that was being created. The interpersonal school, as introduced by Harry Stack Sullivan, began with an acute awareness of the patient's emotional and affective experience in the interview, and sought to consciously and deliberately modulate the patient's affective state, especially that of fear, by active intervention on the part of the therapist. All of which is to say that we have long been aware of the importance of observing affect in an interaction and of noting clearly the impact of that on the clinician. The effusive contagion of someone in a euphoric manic state, for example, is well-known.

In the course of my training, I had the opportunity to take night call at a state hospital that sometimes received direct admissions from the community in which it was located. Having been called at perhaps 3 or 4 in the morning, I made my way over to the unit where the patient was to have arrived. I was greeted by an unforgettable tableau in which a nurse and two aides were absolutely riveted on the engagingly hilarious performance of the patient, whose good humor, rapid speech, intermittent laughter, and expansive gestures combined with his broad smile to create a positive response in his audience. His high levels of enjoyment and excitement were readily transmitted to those around him. Given the time, place, and other possibilities, I was also grateful to receive some of this good feeling, which improved the experience without relieving the necessity of completing the admission evaluation.

Much more frequent in clinical practice, perhaps, is the encounter with any of the separate or combined negative affects. The angry patient can induce in the clinician an affective state that either provides valuable data if recognized or destroys the possibility of a successful meeting if ignored. Anxious or fearful patients can have a similar effect. Some of the people presenting with the disturbances of mood that are lumped together as "depression" may be displaying distress or sadness; the expressions and movements of others may be seen as predominantly shame-related. Nathanson (1992) has suggested that an underlying common thread in these patients may be an absence or deficit of the affect interest–excitement. The loss of this capacity is quite frequent in the states we refer to as depression, and its return in response to the proper treatment or the passage of sufficient time may be the single most important indication of recovery. The clinician's inward response to such people can be of a quite physical nature; a heaviness or hollow sensation in the chest, expressed by an outstretched hand clapped over the heart, is a not uncommon reaction after meeting with a person broadcasting this constellation of affects.

The clinician's awareness of her own capacity for affective attunement is an important variable in assigning weight and meaning to such sensations. The interviewer's own affective and emotional life has to be available to consciousness simply to aid in the process of sifting the data and identifying the sources of the affects that are found. Both daily vicissitudes and lifelong conflicts are fair game for this exercise and must be taken into account in assessing the affective experience of an interview that is at its root an interactive process.

Noticing and coding the affective characteristics of an individual at a given point in time lead us to consideration of longitudinal or diachronic affective patterns, viewed over the course of the individual's lifespan. Observation of the affective profile in the course of an interview begins to suggest areas of further inquiry, where problems regarding an individual affect or more general issues of affect identification, modulation, and expression can be explored in historical context.

HISTORICAL DATA

"Follow the Affect!"

Like the notorious injunction of "Deep Throat," Woodward and Bernstein's confidential source in the Watergate scandal, to "follow the money," one maxim for the therapist is to "follow the affect." For some, this has been taken to mean adopting a provocative style that elicits emotional responses from the patient. In another sense, however, it can be understood to guide the therapist to follow the already existing cues given by the patient, to note and pursue the variations in type and intensity of affective response as different material is touched on in the course of an interview.

A variety of interests is served by this commitment. First, the relative importance to the patient of different themes and material may be established. The rate, volume, and expressiveness of speech, as well as the passing facial display of affect, will help to indicate how and how much something matters. The juxtaposition of unexpected or "inappropriate" affect to content is another type of sign. Here a departure from the expected pattern becomes a signal for the interviewer. For example, a reduction or constriction of affective expression and display may be as significant as an increase or emphasis.

Thus, while the elements of anamnesis and chronology remain constant from one patient to the next, the actual course of conversation will vary. The variations in affect expression during the interview provide extremely valuable information that the interviewer will then combine with the content that has been presented in order to choose the direction of the next question. Affect provides us with a golden thread to trace the labyrinths of memory. (Though a monster may greet us at the center, the way back to freedom can be found.) If we consider memory to be a dynamic, ongoing, reiterative process in multiple brain locations, then taking a history is a journey through space as well as time. In the moment-to-moment branching of the possible pathways of interaction, the integration by the interviewer of the patient's affective data offers one of the best guides to discovering the structure of meaning and narrative as the patient has constructed it. Both the well-worn paths and those not taken are significant. The clinical experience and therapeutic goals of the interviewer still determine the choices that are made, but the information added by "following the affect" provides a more complete map with which to make those choices.

Family History of Individual Affects

We know that the innate affect of the infant is only the starting point for what becomes mature adult emotion. A lifetime of experiences in the family and society exerts a cumulative shaping influence on the patterns we see at the time of evaluation. While there are general cultural norms that may be found to apply, varying with socioeconomic, ethnic, regional, and other characteristics, the core of emotional education occurs in the family. Thus, it can be useful in the course of assessment to inquire as to the styles of displaying different affects that have become habitual within the patient's family of origin. Often, the patient will distinguish between the typical expressions used by each parent. The patient's own style may be closely patterned on one or the other parent, may be a reflection of the patient's role in the family system (e.g., peacemaker or parentified child), or may be a reaction against the affective atmospheres encountered while growing up.

It is rarely necessary to make exhaustive systematic inquiry into how
all nine innate affects were demonstrated by each member of the patient's
family of origin. Frequently, one or a few of the negative affects, by
their problematic nature for the patient, will recommend themselves for
this more detailed study. If the initial interview has not drawn attention
in this direction, material from later meetings may well suggest the help-
fulness of gaining additional understanding of the patient's experience
with a particular affect and emotion.

This focus on the affective experience of the patient within a particular
relationship and with respect to a particular emotion may seem at first
excessively simplistic or reductionist, but in practice is often a way of
arriving at greater clarity, as well as enhancing the patient's skills at
observation. Even for patients who have difficulty identifying their own
feelings, there has often been some form of understanding of the affects
and emotions of important others. Reinforcing the capacity for recognizing and classifying these displays in others becomes a therapeutic step-
ping-stone to the acquisition of the same skills in one's own emotional
life.

When the therapist asks, "What was your mother's anger like?" a
number of potential avenues of investigation appear. For one, the general collection of data about that individual is enhanced by the recall of
this affect-related material. For another, a crucial model for the patient's
own affective responses may be brought to light. Third, this line of
inquiry may begin to identify certain scenes that are in turn incorporated
into important scripts for the patient. The succession and juxtaposition
of affects, memories, and ideo-affective complexes form another level of
patterning to which the interviewer tries to remain alert. Often these
patterns can be found at the center of recurring problems in living cited
by the patient as reasons for entering treatment.

Affect Recognition, Expression, and Modulation Deficits as Problems in Living

Beyond noticing the individual affects as they become manifest during
the course of the interview, we look at the affective and emotional con-
textual matrix in which a person's life is embedded. As we will see in
chapter 10 on infant developmental research into affect, this is an irre-
ducibly interactive process. Thus, as we perform an assessment of an
individual's affective experience, we are reviewing both environmental
factors, such as family style, and personal patterns of response.

Difficulties may arise at any of several aspects of one's method for
processing affective and emotional information. The ability to distin-

guish among these can serve both the clinician and the patient in the work of repair.

The capacity of recognition or identification of affect can be impaired with respect to self, others, or both. The inability to interpret the affective communications of others has been seen as a crucial deficit in the social skills of individuals with schizophrenia. Morrison, Bellack, and Mueser (1988) have been able to show the differences between these patients and nonpatients in terms of their ability to recognize different affect displays in others. Seeing this as an important factor in a cycle of isolation and misunderstanding, they have developed training programs to improve these skills in schizophrenics and raise their level of social functioning.

The ability to recognize and identify different affect states in oneself can also vary considerably. Suggestions of difficulties in this area may arise in the elaboration of chief complaints as reported secondhand by the patient from the accounts of others who have noted such problems. For example, family members or co-workers may have noted an inability to express certain affects, or a lack of awareness of an affect until it has broken through in the form of a behavioral outburst.

Alexithymia, as described by Nemiah and Sifneos (1970), consists largely of an inability to recognize or describe one's own feeling states. Patients with this deficit are likely to present with somatic complaints that may eventually be understood as phenomenologically equivalent to experiences of negative affect without direct awareness.

Scripts That Are Problems

In the course of exploring the patient's presenting problem, one of the tasks is to clarify the affective phenomenology of any repeating patterns. The individual presenting what Sullivan (1953) called a problem in living can be asked to describe the circumstances of the problem's occurrence in terms of the prevailing affects and emotions that are experienced. Identifying the affective/emotional state that is perceived as the problem then leads to the related work of learning what states precede and follow. The information derived from this is a provisional script, a hypothesized succession of the customary manner in which the patient reaches the condition of a particular affective state, and what measures are taken to relieve or augment it. Further clarification is, in effect, a test of this hypothesis. The therapist inquires as to how the sequences of affect being described compare with those that the patient has been experiencing, perhaps in a particular recent experience.

Through this comparison, several aims are accomplished. A more ac-

curate impression of the patient's experience is constructed by the therapist. A language for describing affect is introduced to the patient. The
patient has the experience of being heard and understood, and is offered
the power to modify another's perception of what has taken place. A
different approach to the description of events provides the chance of
alternative interpretations of the meaning and significance of these
events, as well as the possibility of developing new approaches to response.

*A 38-year-old woman had requested evaluation for depression and
possible pharmacotherapy. She reported ongoing frustration with her
current job and lack of success in following the career she preferred.
What had been meant as a part-time stopgap had become a dead-end,
providing a livelihood but effectively preventing her from pursuing the
artistic work that she found most fulfilling.*

*In her second hour of treatment, she described her reaction to seeing a
classified advertisement for a job in the field in which she would have
liked to work. She reported an initial surge of interest, followed by a
memory of failure and rejection at a previous interview. Following this
recollection, she had set aside her plan and done nothing about the ads
for several days. When asked about the failed interview, she told of an
interviewer who seemed distant and became contemptuous and dismis-
sive. Although she could now see that the interviewer had been incorrect,
and that her own work had the merits she had claimed for it, this intellectual appreciation did not alter her feelings about the encounter.*

*It was a pattern she had been involved in before with teachers. In fact,
her professional training had consisted of three single years at different
schools, in considerable part because of her problems relating in class.
She felt that when she was being pressed for an answer, she would "shut
down," become confused, go blank, perhaps blush, and lose her train of
thought. Typically, she would then ask for clarification and quickly
reorient. She said that teachers often did not notice when she tried to
indicate that she could now continue, and would belabor the issues.
When they did not respond to her repeated nonverbal signals, she would
become angry, which they usually did notice. She said they would then
perceive her as hostile and standoffish, favoring other students who were
less talented but more easily reached.*

*The sequence of fear/anxiety followed by shame/embarrassment fol-
lowed by anger was proposed as a provisional script to describe the
maladaptive pattern she had developed. Framing it as a problem in communication and affective display permitted a less judgmental and thus
less shaming and self-deprecatory view of the hypothesized pattern.*

CONCLUSION

He [Dr. Levantes, the protagonist] compared the "human affects," as Spinoza called them, to a volcanic eruption. One must avoid the glowing lava, not try to swim in it. "There's only one question," he said. "Why did God or nature bestow on *Homo sapiens* such an abundance of emotions? What is their biological function? Neither Plato nor Spinoza nor Schopenhauer could really answer this."

—Issac Bashevis Singer, 1985

In the course of a clinical encounter, the therapist is presented with incredible amounts of information. This avalanche of data is screened and sifted. Probably more of it is ignored and discarded than is kept for conscious evaluation. Much of this occurs either outside the clinician's awareness or as the working of a set of practiced professional skills. The remaining information is organized further and processed according to the needs of the clinical situation and the theoretical frameworks available (and congenial) to the examiner.

The goal of this chapter has been to show that important clinical information about affect is available in every phase of an interview. This information is derived from observation of the patient, from recognition of the interviewer's own affective responses, and from historical material. Viewing personal history from the perspective of affect theory allows the therapist to recognize characteristic patterns and sequences of affective response. These scripts serve as platforms from which both successful and maladaptive strategies may arise. Many of the problems in living that bring people to seek the assistance of mental health professionals may be described in terms of the affect scripts that underlie them.

The clinician's task, then, is to integrate the information that has been derived from the interview. The assessment of the affect displayed in the course of conversation on various topics can shed much light on the meaning and relative importance of various areas of cognitive content. Historical and ongoing clinical evaluation of a patient's affect management skills and difficulties provides a crucial avenue toward understanding. History-taking, observation, and examination are the key elements in any medical evaluation or other form of healing relationship. No clinical evaluation in psychiatry, psychology, or other psychotherapy can be considered complete if it neglects the world of affect and emotion. The elements suggested here are offered as a starting point for knowing that world in each of the individuals who comes to us for treatment.

REFERENCES

Buber, M. (1958). *I and thou* (2nd ed.). (R. G. Smith, Trans.). New York: Scribners.

Camus, A. (1946). *The stranger*. New York: Knopf.

Demos, E. V. (1983). A perspective from infant research on affect and self-esteem. In J. Mack & S. Ablon (Eds.), *The development and sustaining of self-esteem in childhood*. (pp. 45-78) New York: International Universities Press.

Freud, S. (1910). The future prospects of psychoanalytic therapy. In *Collected Papers, Vol. 2*. (Joan Riviere, Trans.). New York: Basic Books. 1959.

Havens, L. (1976). *Approaches to the mind*. Boston: Little, Brown, & Co.

Izard, C. E., Dougherty, L. M., & Hembree, E. A. (1983). A system for identifying affect expressions by holistic judgements (AFFEX). Newark: University of Delaware, Instructional Resources Center.

James, W. (1890/1950). *Principles of psychology*, Vol. 2. New York: Dover Publications.

Morrison, R. L., Bellack, A. S., & Mueser, K. T. (1988). Deficits in facial-affect recognition deficit and schizophrenia. *Schizophrenia, 14*, 67-83.

Nathanson, D. L. (1992). *Shame and pride: Affect, sex, and the birth of the self*. New York: Norton.

Nathanson, D. L. (1993, October 1). *The affect pattern chart*. Paper presented at conference "Toward a New Psychotherapy," Philadelphia.

Nemiah, J. C., & Sifneos, P. E. (1970). Affect and fantasy in psychosomatic disorders. In O. W. Hill, (Ed.), *Modern trends in psychosomatic medicine*, Vol 2 (pp. 26-34). Stoneham, MA: Butterworth.

Shea, S. C. (1988). *Psychiatric interviewing: The art of understanding* (pp. 135-178). Philadelphia: Saunders.

Singer, I. B. (1985). The interview. In *The image and other stories*. New York: Farrar, Straus, Giroux.

Sullivan, H. S. (1953). *The interpersonal theory of psychiatry*. New York: Norton.

Tomkins, S. S. (1962). *Affect, imagery, consciousness, Vol. 1: The positive affects*. New York: Springer.

Tomkins, S. S. (1991). *Affect, imagery, consciousness, Vol. 3: The negative affects: Anger and fear*. New York: Springer.

Walker, E. F., Grimes, K. E., Davis, D. M., & Smith, A. J. (1993). Childhood precursors of schizophrenia: Facial expressions of emotion. *American Journal of Psychiatry, 150*, 1654-1660.

3

The Diagnostic Alliance

Anthony L. Hite

What do we see when we first talk with a new patient? As you know, people come to us psychotherapists only when their own techniques for affect modulation have failed and they have decided to investigate whether we have something better to offer. Always there is a first, or chief, complaint–a nearly poetic condensation of what may be a lifetime of dense affective experience. Dr. Hite explains that any interpretation of this greeting must be made within what he calls the "diagnostic alliance," a working relationship predicated on the ability of the therapist to read the subtle signs of affect that give special meaning to ordinary words.

He develops the concept of empathy as the result of joint work with "the two-handed hammer," the efforts of both participants to shape words into meaning that can foster therapeutic progress. Therapist reaction usually dismissed as transference or countertransference is evaluated for the possibility that it is a form of resonance with the affective experience of the patient and therefore a valuable source of information. At all times, Hite shows us that it is important to educate the patient by defining vaguely described experiences in terms of the specific affects involved; the two-handed hammer works best when both operators know what they are hitting.

An empathic relationship involves far more than affective resonance, for it requires the participants to know each other. How this knowledge is obtained, and the uses to which it may be put, form the core of this highly personal chapter. –DLN

> There are no "natural" perceptions apart from the organizing mind.
>
> — Alfred Margulies, 1989

SILVAN TOMKINS KNEW that we human beings *create* reality by our own lights; we are the architects of the worlds in which we live. We make them in response to the collision of sensory input with the innate affect system, what Nathanson (1988, 1992) has called the "firmware" of emotion. These neurobiologic preprogrammed computer chips are produced under the direction of the genetic code. Our worlds, Tomkins said, are structured in accordance with the scripts we develop to manage the affect, positive and negative, stimulated by that collision of sense data and the affect system.

Diagnosis is empathic living in those worlds with those scripts. You will not have a diagnosis worth the name without what Kohut (1971) called empathic immersion in the worlds created by your patients. Tomkins's explanations of the creative processes involved in such immersion, his explanations of affects and scripts, make our immersion and living in those worlds easier goals to achieve.

As clinicians, we are grateful to Dr. Nathanson (1992) for his "translation of Tomkins from the English." Tomkins provides the first comprehensive theory of human "being in the world" since Freud. Tomkins was more successful but, sadly, far less accessible than Freud. Nathanson provides us access to and, by adding much from his own resources, illumination of Tomkins's stunning contributions. Putting the two together will enable us to achieve a new level of diagnostic sophistication and effectiveness.

Using this blend of new information, one can avoid misdiagnosis, increase patients' treatment motivation and compliance, and move the process of therapeutic interaction toward higher levels of desired outcome. Traditional diagnostic processes and assessment protocols (emerging as they have from general medical models or the psychometric and statistical frameworks of academic psychology) as often as not *impede* rather than facilitate therapeutic success in our work as psychotherapists.

I doubt you will often hear physicians in *other* health-care settings say diagnosis doesn't have much to do with what they do in therapy. You hear it all the time among psychotherapists.

I will show you how using the Tomkins-Nathanson blend—affect theory, script theory, affective resonance (Tomkins, 1962, 1963), the "empathic wall" (Nathanson, 1986), and the compass of shame (Nathanson, 1992)—will enable you to see a different part of the spectrum of being human. The Tomkins-Nathanson contributions provide innovations as useful to us as infrared goggles are to commandos in the dark of night. They make *vivid* what has often been *invisible* to both patients and therapists in the context of their therapeutic interactions.

Now I want to replay an old clinical vignette on an imaginary split screen. On the left, yours truly, the rookie intern, listening with growing interest–excitement, enjoyment, and pride. Wilson, the veteran patient, is there sending urgent messages. Even though his *War and Peace*-sized chart had yet to be retrieved from the black hole of the medical records department, I was confident! I could locate this apparently alien planet in psychiatric space, within the framework of diagnostic categories. He was delusional, with both persecutory and grandiose elements; suspicious with a haughty and contemptuous air; paranoid schizophrenic!

Looking on the right screen, you see a different picture, however. Wilson was, in addition to being paranoid schizophrenic, a desperate, overwhelmed, and confused man whose struggle to fulfill his huge obligations and avoid menace and catastrophe left him exhausted and hopeless. I found myself drawn into Wilson's affectively charged struggle. Almost casually, I commented on the intense pressure under which he seemed to be crushed, desperate and hopeless. I could feel it! He *had* to succeed and he could *not*. I doubt I will ever forget the look on his face. In a world where no one could really be trusted, I had suddenly become an ally. Now I not only knew *about* Wilson, I knew *him*. And he knew I did. What I knew *about* his condition was different and, though ultimately important, far less useful than understanding his experience. From that point forward, on a monthly basis, I was the consultant for Wilson who began, with biological support (we restarted his Prolixin), to develop some alternatives to the nuclear scripts that had cast him into psychiatric hell.

On other occasions in later years, I remember my vertiginous shifts from excitement to horror in sessions where I figured out and shared with pride something *about a patient* only to discover his or her shame, disappointment, and justifiable anger at me for *knowing the patient* in a way for which he or she was not prepared. Let's shift back from the clinically specific to the conceptually general again before we examine other clinical vignettes.

I want to use the opportunities created by Tomkins and Nathanson to hammer out a conceptual framework for a user-friendly assessment paradigm I will call the *diagnostic alliance*. If it turns out to be persuasive, my argument might call for some radical revisions of the diagnostic procedures common in much of our everyday experience. But I will bet that much of what I want to formalize already occurs when you are proceeding effectively with your patients.

To really get a grasp on *this* diagnostic paradigm, however, we have to do two things: First of all, we have to distinguish it from our more familiar or traditional idea of diagnosis; secondly, we have to reintegrate the two. Both contain elements vital to valid diagnoses. In what I was saying regarding knowing *about* Wilson and *knowing* him, *understanding* him, you can *feel* the difference. I know it's a familiar feeling for practicing psychotherapists. The feeling lies behind their saying that traditional diagnostic "knowing about" means very little in their day-to-day psychotherapeutic work. I believe this attitude reflects a failure to understand how different kinds of knowing fit together in our work.

We must try to sharpen the distinction between *knowing about* and *understanding*. In traditional training in diagnosis, we are taught to gather information in an effort to determine whether and how observations fit first into a pattern and then into a category of patterns. And we try to gather enough information to classify the collection of observations exclusively. The observations should coalesce to represent *one* thing, not more than one. Tremendous advantages attend success here. If research and clinical experience have provided successful treatment strategies for one disorder/disease or another, knowing what category is the correct one can mean the difference between life and death.

The traditional definition of diagnosis, as taken from the Oxford English Dictionary, involves the determination of the nature of a disease condition, identification of a disease by a careful investigation of its symptoms and history, distinctive characterization in precise terms, and thorough perception. As the definition proceeds from top to bottom, the element of precision becomes explicit.

This description fits the process of finding out *about* things and processes better than it fits getting to know a person, however. Unfortunately, effective *treatment* depends as much if not more on knowing the person. At the same time, however, diagnostic acumen in the sense of knowing about is *also* critical. Well intentioned ignorance (in the sense of not knowing *about*) is very dangerous. A brief clinical example serves to underscore this point.

A young mental health professional called to refer me a patient after an exasperating, frightening, and disappointing series of clinical interviews with her. The therapy had been ongoing for months, and the clinician had a good empathic grasp of the subjective experience of her client, a 38-year-old married woman with two children. But the process had brought no relief and the patient was entertaining serious thoughts of suicide. The young clinician didn't know enough *about* her patient to make a complete diagnosis.

Making a diagnosis of bipolar II disorder (recurrent major depressive episodes with hypomanic episodes) shed considerable light on previously confusing clinical interaction. Exactly how knowing *about* and *understanding* ultimately fit together in this case is a matter to which we will turn shortly. Right now I just want to make sure, first, that we can feel the differences between the two kinds of knowing, and secondly, that we recognize both knowing about and understanding are central in the process of effective diagnosis.

There are very thorny problems for the diagnostician in his or her efforts to know the patient in both senses of the term I am describing here. Tomkins and Nathanson have laid the groundwork for understanding and solving these problems, however. Their revelations regarding the role of scripts in human development, the role of shame in interpersonal interactions, and the role of affective resonance and empathy in communication lead to workable solutions. First, however, a look at the problems. In the diagnostic phase of our work, we are trying to get information from the patient that includes his or her subjective experience as well as facts about him or her that can be observed independently. Of course, herein lies the rub. Diagnosis becomes an unparalleled opportunity for shame.

Nathanson (1987, 1992) points out, as have E. James Anthony (1981) and others, that therapy is an arena of shame. The diagnostic context is no less so. And the worst consequence of shame experienced during a diagnostic process aiming for a therapeutic intervention becomes chillingly clear. To feel "shorn from humanity," defective, isolated as unlovable, to crave for hidden solitude — all aspects of a shame experience — threaten the essential ingredient in all effective therapy: the empathic relationship. Hence, the essential diagnostic dilemma. The very most important information necessary for an accurate understanding, an empathic grasp of a particular person, may be most difficult to obtain at just the time when critical decisions are being made about treatment. And, as if this were not enough of a speed bump to slow our progress, consider another one.

While many of our observations of the patient's functioning *and* his or her subjective experiences can be described in relatively unambiguous ways, this happy circumstance does not always obtain. Through intro-

spection, and through observation of a relatively small number of patients met in our training, we diagnosticians learn to identify component
parts of diagnostic categories such as agitation, psychomotor retardation, apathy, anxiety, and the like. When exploring a particular patient's
affective experience, *our* particular scripts, including the conceptual
structure and imagery for such phenomena, may form Procrustean beds
into which we and/or the particular patient with whom we are working
at a given moment try to fit his or her experience. The goodness of fit
may be questionable. Worse, efforts to label these phenomena may obscure variations that might lead us to very different categories when
care is taken to ensure real consensus between the patient's and the
diagnostician's view of phenomena under study. When consensus resolves ambiguity, what starts out looking anxious might end up looking
fearfully sad and vice versa. Shame and defenses against it, for example,
may impel *either* patient *or* diagnostician to characterize phenomena in
erroneous ways.

To decrease the likelihood of this kind of collaboration and distortion, I employ the Principle of the Two-Handed Hammer. *Both* patient
and diagnostician try to shape the view of the patient's experience that
best represents it to *both* parties. The diagnostician eschews any attempt
to impose consensual reality constraints upon the patient's reality (or
even any attempt to see if the patient can impose such constraints unaided) until the patient is clear the diagnostician understands the patient's reality at an empathic level. We must do this even if the patient's
view of the world or his or her experience of it seems like a surrealist
canvas or a Fellini film. Patients frequently comment spontaneously on
the divergence between consensual reality, convention, and the like, on
the one hand, and *their* versions, on the other. How many times have
you heard the phrase, "*Intellectually*, I know, but *emotionally* . . . " or
"I know it sounds crazy, *but* . . . "? We make our reality under the aegis
of the affects. And we make the scripts with which we negotiate our
creation. Diagnosis is empathic living in that world with those scripts.

What actually occurs in dialogues designed to evoke such empathy
illustrates the Principle of the Two-Handed Hammer. The patient will
represent his or her experience in words, but not every patient is so
articulate or so fluent that he or she is satisfied with the first description.
I am, moreover, a little slow on the uptake. So the patient hammers out
the shape of his or her experience. Then I hammer at it with my words
until together we have a product we both know and recognize as the
patient's experience. Frequently, in these dialogues, one participant or
the other ignites a previously unknown luminous clarity with a previously
untried word or descriptive phrase. Remember, "scripts are sets of rules

for the management of scenes that are inevitable or desired or feared or despised but nonetheless will always assemble in predictable forms" (Nathanson, 1993). And scenes are defined as sequences of events linked by the affect triggered by them. These scripts or scenes are what we are trying to hammer out.

To some extent this intense focus on intersubjectivity should stimulate some curiosity in you about the role of *objectivity* in diagnosis. As Shedler, Mayman, and Manis (1993) have said, "In our enthusiasm for measures that appear 'objective' we must be careful that we do not lose the ability to study what is psychologically important" (p. 1129).

Shedler and his colleagues have stirred up quite a debate by highlighting the failure of objective diagnostic test instruments and checklists to distinguish illusory mental health, based on defenses, from the genuine article. The kind of knowing the patient that facilitates really effective treatment involves a set of data and a way of gathering them too fine for "objectivity" filters, and *our* wishes for objectivity in these contexts probably reflect *our* distress in the midst of uncertainty.

A story about referrals will serve to provide a clinical context within which to show how affect and script theory and Nathanson's (1986, 1992) discussions of affective resonance and empathy can solve the problems shame and ambiguity pose for us as diagnosticians. The story will also serve to illustrate the use of the two-handed hammer.

A divorce attorney with a lot of intuitive psychodiagnostic ability referred a young Army captain to me. "I think he's pretty depressed, Tony," the lawyer told me, "But I don't know if he needs drugs or therapy." Fortunately, by the time this patient was referred, I had abandoned the notion of depression as it comes to us through the tradition of psychoanalytic metapsychology. Nathanson (1994) has pointed out that when any of the six negative affects persists for a considerable period of time, both patients and mental health professionals will describe the clinical results in terms of depression. The important questions, of course, focus on the particular negative affect or combination of them that persist.

The young captain told me he had been in marriage counseling with his wife. As he relayed that message, he looked away and appeared disgusted. I asked immediately about what I thought I saw. He was startled, but he agreed that my description fit his experience better than "frustrated," the word he had been using. I asked if he wondered about coming to me in the wake of this unsatisfactory counseling. He was then able to talk about all the "help" that availed nothing and his cynicism and contempt for the helpers. He tried to apologize quickly for the implicit slight, but I pointed out his dilemma. Obviously sad and wanting desperately to halt the slide into chaos that marked his life these days, he had to rely on bunglers. His half smile revealed that "caught-with-my-hand-in-cookie-jar" embarrassment with which we are all familiar. It was my willingness to be a person he simultaneously needed, found contemptible, and distrusted that opened new possibilities.

The captain was able to talk in detail about his loss and reactions to it. Both he and I were surprised at what emerged. Initially, he had thought his wife crazy to leave him, and he was humiliated when she turned to another man. *But as we learned about his internal world, he realized that he saw his wife as a "cheap whore" and began to be terrified that his father's contemptuous warnings about fickle floozies were true after all. Worse! He had followed in his father's footsteps, the one thing that he* swore *to himself he would never do. Rage. Terror. A plaintive, confused and searching gaze marked his now-obvious bond with me. We had landed together in the territory of the nuclear script, and his dysphoria could now be plucked from the wastebasket term, depression, and the specific negative affects involved explored fully in the context of a group of scripts.*

In the captain's case, no pharmacologic intervention at the level of hardware seemed indicated; our discussions led to a satisfactory result. Detailed inquiry about every circumlocution, euphemism, vague statement, ambiguity, fidget, and restless shift allowed us entry into his affective life. The captain reported that three such sessions had taught him more about himself and why his marriage had gone sour than he had learned in months of counseling. His entire treatment with me lasted eight sessions. The search for the affect that lurked behind all the structures he had erected to hide, manage, or avoid it proved to be the critical factor in our success. When, early on, I explained this to the captain, he gave his best effort to cooperate in the search.

Do not for a moment think that his previous therapist was either incompetent or unconnected to his case. It makes a great deal of difference when you focus both the patient and yourself on the affect. This next case illustrates another facet of the problem — the need to identify the sources of each affect that has become problematic.

Ms. Stover, a married mother and college professor, had been in therapy for about a year. While she was feeling somewhat less "depressed" and confused about herself, I thought there was a lot being hidden. It was obvious that she liked me, and also that she was embarrassed about these feelings. When I understood why her discomfort about liking me now triggered my *anxiety, I was a lot more comfortable and tried to talk with her more about her embarrassment. Immediately, she reported a dream in which, as she put it, we were "intimate."*

An ambiguous message of that sort requires a speedy application of what I call the Principle of Particulars. I asked her if she remembered images from the dream. She became anxious and then angry with me. We turned first *to an examination of these reactions—all bearing upon shame. I told her that the details were obviously important because so much emotion in her was attached to my knowing them. We talked of the one-sided and unfair aspect of therapy in which I* didn't *have to reveal embarrassing thoughts and she did. I agreed it was unfair but I went on to say that I thought it would help us reach our goals in treatment.*

Ms. Stover said that we were having sexual intercourse in her dream. I asked her to describe the scene if she could. She looked puzzled, and I said, "Like positions, things like that. Who was on top, for example?" Though clearly startled by my shameless question, she responded, "I was." And she looked and sounded impish. I pointed out what I thought was the impishness, and she was aghast. But she could *sense her impishness in actually dreaming of having her way with me, as she put it. I asked about her distress in response to our discovering this in her. We were then rewarded with the first real breakthrough in a previously ho-hum treatment.*

Ms. Stover was able to speak about her worries about intense emotions of all kinds—anger, rage, hate, longing, lust—and her dread that any important person knowing of these things in her would be driven away in horror. The patient hid these feelings behind a persona of cheerful solicitude, rectitude, and warm compassion. If ever she were playful, she maintained a strong grip on it and worried about being "misunderstood." The feelings she worried about most were intense suicidal impulses. If she were to speak of them, I would hospitalize her instead of helping her understand the fears and confusion she felt about these impulses. Finally, I had a sense of actually knowing this particular person. She graduated therapy with honors. So much of our success as therapists depends on our ability to deal with our own affects—especially our own embarrassment!

The first five fundamental ingredients of the diagnostic alliance can now be distilled from the clinical vignettes presented thus far. First, the diagnostician:

- Starts with and maintains throughout the course of every interview an empathic focus on *immediate* affectively charged experiences.

Always on the lookout for all manner of sign and signal, muffled, camouflaged or blatant, one is searching for what has been made important in the moment by the affect it has triggered. That's what affect does. It plucks particular phenomena from the barrage of stimuli impinging on us all the time—from within and without—and makes one or another stimulus immediately important. Utterances occurring in the same moment as the postural, gestural, and facial correlates of aroused affect stimulate my inquiry, and my only responses are efforts to convey empathic understanding—how it feels for the patient to be thinking what the patient is thinking.

The second fundamental component of the diagnostic alliance disposes the diagnostician:

- To *explore in detail* what emerges in the field highlighted by the empathic focus.

You have heard "the devil is in the details," and Charles Darwin thought God could be found there as well. I believe the details reveal the scripts by which persons are guided in the particular pursuits and subjective experiences that define their individuality. For the purpose of diagnosis, *mental* health professionals cannot stop when we arrive in the neighborhood where the patient lives. We need to know much, much more about their house and their person. We require detail at the level of fingerprints. Many times we can't even find the neighborhood, the right category, without them.

This second fundamental—what I call the Principle of Particulars or Fingerprints—points us quickly to the third fundamental, a cautionary component of the diagnostic alliance. The diagnostician:

- Deals with shame affect in whichever of its myriad forms it becomes identifiable.

Shame is always the first on the agenda, at the top of the list. Many a student has inquired indignantly about my detailed inquiry into the intimate, if mundane, details of a stranger's days and/or nights. And believe me, I am nosy in very detailed ways. What about intrusive questions, embarrassing interrogations? My style of active inquiry threatens shame at any juncture. Of course it does. And I point that out in my introduction to the process. My patients and I have discussions about: undressing in school locker rooms; peeping Toms; TV reporters with unblinking cameras and relentless, *shameless* questions; getting caught with one's hand in the cookie jar; getting caught with some other vital part in a ridiculous light; being the *object* of pity, scorn, and derision. We also talk about doctors who look at, poke, prod, feel, and point out *parts* while we as *persons* cringe or wince or fume. Such discussions go a long way toward helping the person deal with the shame family of emotions, unavoidable in this context of being known.

At any point in the interview when eye contact is lost or shoulders slump or patients shift uncomfortably, I make note of it and we look together at the problem of *talking* with me about this, whatever *this* is. "I feel so *stupid* saying this, talking about this." "It's so *crazy* to think like this." "It's so *trivial*." "God, I'll bet you get tired of hearing this kind of shit." When any of these sentiments emerges — or the hundred other variants we all hear frequently — it becomes the focus of detailed inquiry regarding the patient's situation with me at the moment and at other times he or she can remember such sentiments. You might argue such excursions distract the patient and derail the unfolding story. *They make unfolding the story possible*. Without a mutual understanding between patient and therapist of the shame experience inherent in diagnosis, the "story" will be a pallid digest of the real data, a euphemism. I try my hardest to make sure empathy marks these excursions, and I'm prone to self-disclosure when my own experience might be reassuring and not burdensome.

The fourth fundamental component of the diagnostic alliance is necessitated by the approach to diagnostic interviews highlighted in the second and third principles. Exploring all those potentially shame-ridden details demands some didactic preparation. The diagnostician:

- Teaches the patient about emotions, feelings, tensions, and other later developments of affective life work — especially the shame family of emotions and their role in one's being known.

My didactic use of Nathanson's (1992) "compass of shame" is also very important in this context. The patient and I look together at his or her immediate responses to shame affect and try to locate them on the compass of shame. I point out that this affect family, and all that goes with it, can really impede our understanding and treatment if we don't get a handle on it. Every time we see it come, we stop, look, and listen for clues to the stimuli for shame responses in the particular material of the moment. Of course, for some patients, shame affect *is* the major issue; but for all patients it's a major factor. Attending to it serves the same therapeutic function as focusing *first* on what Freud called the resist-ances.

Avoiding shame affect or managing it so as to obscure underlying cognition closes off access to essential information about nuclear and other essential scripts. So, *first* shame and *then* what stimulates the shame affect responses. True for diagnosis; true for treatment. My em-phasis upon embarrassing detail is not *merely* disguised voyeurism.

The fifth fundamental component of the diagnostic alliance is the Principle of the Two-Handed Hammer.

- Two people collaborate to build an understanding of the patient's reality; one person (the diagnostician) does not categorize it in private.

And all this hammering is hard work! Both patient and therapist are active in a struggle for clarity. Active inquiry, moreover, is not the only source of sore muscles. Looking further at the demands on the therapist in the diagnostic alliance will give us a chance to expand on the role of empathy and the empathic wall. Maintaining an empathic focus and vigilant attention to fingerprint swirl level of detail in the diagnostic alliance sets up a periodic oscillation in the experience of the diagnosti-cian that is somewhat stressful. Basch has given us a colorful language for this oscillation:

> *Consternation*, or recognition of disorientation: I thought I under-stood what was going on, but this doesn't make sense. Now I can't seem to understand why this person is functioning the way he does. What makes him behave this way? Why is he saying what he is saying?
> *Reorientation*, or grasping the material from the patient's point of view: Oh, *that's* what it's all about! Now I think I know again what's going on. Let's check it out. (1988, p. 20)

These are descriptions of two phases of the therapeutic work Basch (1988) regards as definitive. Mostly, I live in constant consternation. (Dr. Basch is probably spending a lot more time in reorientation than I am.) The diagnostic phase *should* involve a lot of consternation, though, because fingerprints are harder to find than neighborhoods. The impor-tant point in this connection is this: The patient always reorients me and he or she really learns that what is in his or her head is in the long run far more important than what's in mine. We are focused together on finding out *how what's wrong works*, how it robs the patient of life. We are not "in therapy" yet. And I remind the patient of that fact every session until I'm ready to make recommendations about what to do about what's wrong. We are trying to find the scripts. Only then can treatment really be effective. But scripts are very idiosyncratic. They may be categorized just as more traditional signs and symptoms, but they must be explored in their particularity. We will return to this oscillation between consternation and reorientation after I show a bit more about how we get from one to the other, going either way.

So far, I have focused more on the content of knowing and less on the process. In the latter connection, the concepts of empathy, affective resonance, and, especially, the empathic wall, move into the foreground. Buie (1981)* suggests that there are four components of empathy: (1) *conceptual empathy* (emphasizing a cognitive understanding of the patient; (2) *self-help empathy* (referring to low-intensity memories, feelings, and associations experienced by the therapist); (3) *imaginative imitation empathy* (imagining and imitating in fantasy an ad hoc model of the patient's inner world); and (4) *resonant empathy*, which he describes as an affective contagion. Taken in order, Buie's components of empathy represent four mileposts on the road to a full, empathic understanding of another. Implicit in his discussion are some limits which deserve further attention, however. Nathanson's (1992) explication of Tomkins's view of innate affect and affective resonance and his own concept of the empathic wall (1986) go a long way toward diminishing the disruptive effects of unavoidable limits in therapeutic empathy.

Empathy obviously draws on commonalties in the experiences of both purveyor and pursuer of mental health. There must be at least enough overlap between patient and therapist for intelligent imagination to bridge experience gaps. Where there are *homogeneous* cultural backgrounds — those normative elements contributing to assumptions about what to seek and what to avoid in life — we have fewer problems with empathic communication. This notion is embedded in most discussions of empathy reflecting the first three components Buie outlines. (Of course, similarity breeds a false sense of security sometimes, as when the patient's experience only *sounds* familiar. Closer scrutiny, however, reveals important nuances and variations.) Buie's fourth component points in a direction Tomkins and Nathanson have mapped with great clarity. And the problem of diversity of backgrounds with its impact on

---

*I believe Buie would have placed resonant empathy *first* on the list had he grasped the preeminent role played by the affect system. Nathanson's discussions (1986, 1992, pp. 107–120) of affective resonance help realign the components of empathic experience in Buie's model.

the diagnostic process becomes more manageable in the context of these ideas.

Affective resonance is enormously adaptive. We can feel the innate affects broadcast by infants, who would have no other way to let caregivers know what is needed to ensure their ongoing viability and the comfort necessary for development. As Nathanson (1986) points out, however, a little broadcast affect goes a long way. It can be very disruptive and unwelcome. We learn therefore to muffle our *own* affect with various modulation strategies and disguises and *others'* affect with the empathic wall, a barrier between another's affect and our own. We learn to deaden our receptors to some degree and in that way preserve an acceptable range of affective attunement. That range will vary, of course, and, the variance will, with other temperamental traits and learning histories, give us folks with greater or lesser abilities to communicate on intimate emotional levels. Therapists, like good caregivers of infants and preverbal toddlers, need a greater range than most.

These observations make more understandable difficulties we all experience in our work. Take a lack of attunement (too thick a wall) and/or too few parcels of common ground and/or the patient having learned too well to muffle affect or transform it into what Tomkins called false affect, and it's a wonder we do as well as we do. Tomkins seemed more pessimistic about this than I am, however. That he was more researcher than clinician is, I think, only part of this story. I get the idea that he thought signs of innate affect were harder to read as people grew into older childhood and beyond, just as the contours of young mountains are more crisp and sharp than in the geologically older structures. Emotion grows from affect, through feeling, remember, and it is an integration of affect and cognition via the developmental scenes and, finally, scripts. As one becomes aware of affect, one starts to have feelings. Within increasing awareness of the circumstances with which feelings get connected, one develops emotions. Basch (1988) has traced this developmental line with great clarity in *Understanding Psychotherapy, The Science Behind the Art.*

Paul Ekman and others interested in and convinced of the cross-cultural universality of affective display in the face especially help account for my more optimistic view of the role of broadcast affect in diagnosis and treatment. Briefly put, enough affective cues—even though muffled and "noisy" in the sense of "signal" versus "noise" as in information theory—*can* be detected, especially in facial and gestural displays. Starting with rough approximations (reported to the patient with terms like "tension" or "restlessness" or "uneasiness"), the therapist many times more sharply attunes the patient to emotion. Obviously, patients will vary in their abilities to increase attunement. But I continue to be surprised by what a little pain-in-the-ass persistence produces in this regard. Urging patients to focus on cognitions occurring in the same time frame as detectable affective tension often produces useful data as well. For cognitive behavioral therapists, such an approach is a mainstay in their technical armamentarium.

Basch (1988) has described the *therapist's* experience of this dialogue very well in elaborating shifts from the processes associated with understanding the patient (what he calls "orientation") to consternation and on to reorientation. The therapist will from time to time get caught up in his or her own emotion because the patient's inputs will stimulate the therapist's affect system, triggering feelings and emotions. The patient's glum mood, for example, might stimulate fear and shame affects and their families of emotions in the therapist. The focus will likely center on the therapist's worries about competence. If these affects persist for a spell, the therapist may get angry. (This probably never happens to you, though, right?)

Basch uses his highly developed self-understanding in order to, as he puts it, "decenter." He steps back and uses the new information to get his bearings, to get the patient's experience back in the center of the therapist's focus. The value of knowing *oneself* in this process cannot be overestimated. The more I know about myself, the easier is the decentering process in the ongoing oscillation between consternation and reorientation.

In order to complete this discussion of the diagnostic alliance, to illustrate a bit further how it works, and to put in place the last fundamental principle on which it is built, you need to join me at the scene of a train wreck. She's the 38-year-old mother of two who was referred to me by a young colleague at the end of her therapeutic rope. The patient came to me prepackaged in that most forbidding diagnosis we all know and love: borderline personality disorder. Mary was mildly intoxicated but still able to communicate during our initial interview. Not an auspicious beginning, you say. Actually, it was a great beginning because her defenses were, well, fluid and porous. Data were abundant and her desperation easily accessible and understandable beneath a thin coating of rage. That's where we started. We moved quickly to her grief at the loss of the previous therapist and from there, as she got a little more sober, to my orientation to the diagnostic process. The fact that I had been able to convey a reasonably empathic understanding of her immediate experience — her feeling, while sitting with me, the emotions stirred in the wake of the referral to me — made the process I was proposing more interesting–exciting to her. In fact, because of her interest–excitement *and* her dread of loss and abandonment, bringing the first session to a close was a formidable challenge! The first principle of the diagnostic alliance was in place, however. I focused actively on whatever content her affects made salient.

When we resumed our dialogue two days hence, I began to put in place other fundamental components of the diagnostic alliance. After reestablishing the empathic focus and the degree of interaffectivity that had characterized that first session with me, I introduced her to the "framework of days." This device opens up the process to an identification of the patient's most important scripts and, ultimately, to his or her nuclear scripts. These, as we shall see, are the targets of choice for effective intervention.

I pointed out to Mary, as I do in various ways to all patients, that the act of trying to understand her difficulties so as to determine what we can do about them involves a somewhat different approach from those she may have experienced with the other doctors to whom she may have turned for help. I ask patients to tell me first what are the important things in their lives *each day* of each week. I want to know what they hope to do, whether alone or with others, each day or week or month, and what happens when they try to do these things. In this framework, one sees the way in which the *experience* of disorder, illness, and symptoms impedes in very concrete and detailed ways the patient's progress towards realizing ideals, goals, and objectives.

So I can say, as I did to Mary, "Not being able to stay focused, to keep stuff in your head, transforms you from a teammate building a business with husband Don into a constant drag and a disappointment to him and to yourself." That's different from knowing *about* Mary's impaired concentration and short-term memory functions. When we started, I told her it would take some time to understand what was wrong before we knew what we could do about it. Boy, did it. It took months. We found scenes and scripts involving her history of Bell's palsy, spinal stenosis, traumatic brain injury, attention deficit disorder, rapid bipolar changes sufficiently interesting to get the folks at NIMH involved (they decided her neuromuscular problems ruled her out of their research program, however), and a history of some sexual abuse. Oh, did I tell you she was adopted and found her biological family, or what was left of it, during our work? That was after we worked through the death of her adoptive mother two months after we started. It gets worse.

We sent Mary to a gifted neuropsychiatrist who tried everything. The medicines that worked she couldn't tolerate and the medicines she tolerated didn't work. She gained weight, lots of it, and felt even worse. But she thought I was wonderful. There is that empathy again. Using it, I stayed with her in her world of pain and humiliation and anguish and numbing fear. For a while, there seemed no end to it, just a question of acceptance. After a couple of suicidal gestures that might have ended it had she not called me in the midst of them, she decided to fight. She had disabilities and challenges, but she *herself* was a pistol. We both began to see her that way. And she decided to accept the fact that she got hit by a cosmic train.

At that point we got into therapy, into new behaviors and routines. She learned to collaborate with her husband, son, and daughter instead of running from or attacking them when shame overwhelmed her. She and I and her husband worked on strategies (counterscripts) to help everybody deal with her shifting moods and the frustrations born of her failure to be a better wife and mother than *either* of her mothers had been. Before the cosmic train crash, she'd been a gifted athlete. Now she was an athlete with disabilities and took some pride in the adjusted pursuits. I helped Mary and her father rewrite the history of their lives together within the context of her "affect disorder" and a new understanding of emotion — hers *and* his.

Her managed care company paid for every session for a year and half (in case anybody wondered about brief therapy and train wrecks). She went on after the year and a half, after a hug and a lot of tears. Pain management training. Cognitive rehabilitation training. She came by last Christmas with homemade cookies and a bottle of wine. She had lost a lot of weight and looked terrific. She cried. I cried. Haven't heard a word since. "You were the only one who knew me," she said.

Finally, we can state in summary form, the fundamental principles of the diagnostic alliance:

1. Start with and maintain throughout the interview the empathic focus on *immediate* affectively charged experiences — yours and the patient's.
2. Inquire in the context of the framework of days about what happens when the patient tries to do what seems to be important on a daily, weekly, monthly basis.
3. Use the two-handed hammer to shape a mutually clear reality of the patient's experience, one both can see.
4. Strive to develop as detailed a picture of the patient's experience of disorder as possible under the Principles of Particulars and Fingerprints.
5. Teach the patient about emotions, feelings, tensions and other later developments of the affect system. Teach, especially, about shame affect and the compass of shame.

6. Roll back the shadows of shame anywhere you detect them, since they will always make implementing principles 1 through 5 difficult or impossible.

Good luck!

REFERENCES

Anhony, E. J. (1981). Shame, guilt and the feminine self in psychoanalysis. In S. Tuttman, C. Kaye, & M. Zimmerman (Eds.), *Object and self: A developmental approach* (pp. 191–234). New York: International Universities Press.

Basch, M. F. (1988). *Understanding psychotherapy: The science behind the art.* New York: Basic Books.

Buie, D. H. (1981). Empathy: Its nature and limitations. *Journal of the American Psychoanalytic Association, 29,* 281–307.

Ekman, P. (Ed.). (1973). *Darwin and facial expression.* New York: Academic Press.

Kohut, H. (1971). The analysis of the self. New York: International Universities Press.

Margulies, A. (1989). *The empathic imagination.* New York: Norton.

Nathanson, D. L. (1986). The empathic wall and the ecology of affect. *Psychoanalytic Study of the Child, 41,* 171–87.

Nathanson, D. L. (1987). A timetable for shame. In D. L. Nathanson (Ed.), *The many faces of shame* (pp. 1–62). New York: Guilford.

Nathanson, D. L. (1988). Affect, affective resonance, and a new theory for hypnosis. *Psychopathology, 21,* 126–37.

Nathanson, D. L. (1992). *Shame and pride: Affect, sex and the birth of the self.* New York: Norton.

Nathanson, D.L. (1993, October). *Toward a new psychotherapy.* Paper presented at conference "Toward a New Psychotherapy," Philadelphia.

Nathanson, D. L. (1994). The case against depression. *Bulletin of the Tomkins Institute, 1,* 9–11.

Shedler, J., Mayman, M., & Manis, M. (1993). The illusion of mental health, *American Psychologist, 49,* 11, 1129.

Tomkins, S. S. (1962). *Affect, imagery, consciousness, Vol. 1: The positive affects.* New York: Springer.

Tomkins, S. S. (1963). *Affect, imagery, consciousness, Vol. 2: The negative affects.* New York: Springer.

Tomkins, S. S. (1992). *Affect, imagery, consciousness, Vol. 4: Cognition.* New York: Springer.

4

Affect and the Redefinition of Intimacy

Vernon C. Kelly, Jr.

Any extraterrestrial assigned the task of studying the individuals of our species would soon learn that we tend to assort into couples held together for unpredictable periods of time and for a wide range of apparent reasons. Each major psychological theory has attempted to explain the source of the binding energy that welds people into nuclei of variable stability. In a more prudish era, the need for a sexual partner seemed a logical reason, while the realities of child-rearing and mutual defense have led others to postulate economic rather than psychosexual forces for such assortment. In this chapter, Dr. Kelly establishes a new system through which we may both understand the nature of intimate relationships and assist in the repair of relationships that have developed impediments to intimacy.

His thesis, sketched roughly during several discussions with Silvan Tomkins and elaborated into a full-fledged system in the years since the latter's death in 1991, takes as a given that humans are born with both an affect system and a sexual system. Kelly presents a new way of assessing couples, of teaching them what is personal or internal to their psychological makeup and what is interactional, and of designing a method of treatment that fits each couple. It is the kind of work that, once stated, seems like something you always knew. I suspect that it will spark less controversy than imitation and become a new standard in our field.   –DLN

Each of the many thought-provoking definitions of intimacy found in the extensive academic and popular literature attempts to explain why intimate relationships succeed or fail. Although these definitions represent a variety of paradigms, three central themes can be deduced. First, and most prominent, is that intimacy is sought because it generates good or positive feelings and/or helps to remediate bad or negative feelings. Second, intimacy involves exposure and interchange of the inmost parts of those involved in the relationship. And finally, the ability to be intimate is a capacity forged in the emotional climate of childhood and adolescence. Each of these three facets of intimacy is dependent on *emotional* interactions between people. It is, therefore, critical to any definition of intimacy that it arise from a solid understanding of the origins and dynamics of affects, feelings, and emotions.

The affect theory of Silvan Tomkins (1962, 1963, 1991, 1992) is such a construct. It is utilized here to develop a new definition of intimacy that incorporates Tomkins's recognition that affect is the primary motivator of behavior. He has shown how nine innate affects link the biology and the psychology of our complexly evolved central nervous system (CNS). Affect theory provides a paradigm for understanding the basic characteristics of any specific moment of joy, excitement, distress, anger, startle, fear, shame, disgust, or dissmell. And it forms the underpinnings of the general theory of personality Tomkins has called script theory. This chapter extends affect and script theories by demonstrating (1) how affect directs the formation and maintenance of intimate relationships, (2) how affect determines in large part both what is inmost in each of us and how our inmost self is communicated to another, and (3) how the dynamics of the affect system influence the growth and development of one's capacity for intimacy. From this emerges a new definition of intimacy—one that allows us to understand how our innate biological endowment provides the basis for the development of intimate relationships. Arising from this new definition is an affect-theory-based model that clarifies how intimacy is nurtured, impeded, or destroyed, and a logical framework for the diagnosis and treatment of failures of intimacy in troubled couples.

A BRIEF REVIEW OF PRIOR DEFINITIONS

Although it is far beyond the range of this chapter to present an exhaustive list of prior definitions of intimacy, it is informative to review several before proceeding to a new one. When examined through the lens of affect theory, it is apparent that most definitions of intimacy are based on emotion. Many, in fact, contain direct references to one or more of the affects described by Tomkins even though their authors were oblivious to affect theory. Even those definitions that initially appear less directly concerned with emotion do not ignore it. Since such definitions come from paradigms in which emotion is either disregarded or poorly conceptualized, their basis in emotion is often difficult to discern. In this review, an effort will be made to reveal the emotional components of these definitions. First, however, it is interesting to consider two historically important paradigms.

The psychoanalytic literature seldom addresses the topic of intimacy directly. There is not one reference to intimacy in The *Standard Edition of the Complete Psychological Works of Sigmund Freud*. Kwawer (1982) states that "'Intimacy' is not addressed formally by object relations theory" (p. 53). Scharff and Scharff (1991), two widely published modern-day authors on object relations, offer no definition of intimacy in their recent book, *Object Relations Couple Therapy*. They describe projective identification as "the basis for intimacy" (p. 9), but leave readers to arrive at their own conclusions regarding the specifics of a definition of intimacy.

Two influential modern theorists of intimacy were Harry Stack Sullivan and Erik Erikson. Sullivan (1953a) described intimacy as follows:

> Intimacy is that type of situation involving two people which permits validation of all components of personal worth. Validation of personal worth requires a type of relationship which I call collaboration, by which I mean clearly formulated adjustments of one's behavior to the expressed needs of the other person in the pursuit of increasingly identical — that is, more and more nearly mutual — satisfactions, and in the maintenance of increasingly similar security operations. (p. 246)

Sullivan clearly implies that the "validation of personal worth" and "the pursuit of . . . identical . . . satisfactions" are interpersonal experiences with a positive emotional value. In his system, "security operations" are personality functions that ward off negative emotions, primarily anxiety. Sullivanian intimacy can therefore be understood as an interpersonal skill that increases positive emotions and decreases negative emotions. He postulated that the need for intimacy is a powerful motivator of human development and did not consider a person healthy unless capable of intimate relationships. As is true of many theorists in this area, his work represents a general overview of intimacy. It is not based on a precise theory of emotion and, therefore, it remains too general to allow an understanding of the dynamics of specific moments in interpersonal interactions. Such discrete instances of emotion, any of which may last only a few minutes or even seconds, can produce powerful, and at times persistent, positive or negative feelings between people. A truly comprehensive theory of intimacy must also explain how such feelings are triggered and the nature of their long-term effects.

Erik Erikson's theories are also too general to permit an understanding of specific moments in an interpersonal relationship. Nonetheless, his classic "eight ages of man" (1963) is an important overview of the life cycle of the individual. After struggling through the stage of *identity vs. role confusion*, the adolescent reaches the age of *intimacy vs. isolation*, about which Erikson (1968) says:

> Where a youth does not accomplish such intimate relationships with others — and, I would add, with his own inner resources — in late adolescence or early adulthood, he may settle for highly stereotyped interpersonal relations and come to retain a deep *sense of isolation*. If the times favor an impersonal kind of interpersonal pattern, a man can go far, very far, in life and yet harbor a severe character problem doubly painful because he will never feel really himself, although everyone says he is "somebody." (pp. 135–6)

This passage leaves no doubt that Erikson saw the failure to attain intimacy as a painful loss experienced at the core of a person, even though he does not specify the nature of the emotions involved. He, too, clearly believed that only one who achieves intimacy may be considered healthy.

Modern-day theorists also at least imply that there is an emotional component to intimacy. W. Robert Beavers (1985) approaches his work with families and couples from a paradigm that stresses the influence of the *family system* as a whole upon each member in that system. However, he states that: "The pursuit of emotional health and personal enjoyment by couples involves *intimacy* — the joy of being known and accepted by another who is loved" (p. 52). This is one of those definitions of intimacy that we sense intuitively as true. Of course we feel "joy" when our beloved knows and accepts us. But what is joy? Where does it come from, what makes it appear or disappear? Many descriptions of intimacy share with that of Beavers this sense of intuitive correctness because they use words or language that we all "understand" at an intuitive level. Within the context of affect theory, this kind of intuition is a result of the innate nature of affect. The innateness of affect confers upon all people the same group of core affective experiences. As a result, we each know what it is like to feel joy or excitement or fear or distress or anger. This allows us to know the experience of another at a core level. It is this type of knowing that forms the basis for empathy (Basch, 1983).

Another benefit of Tomkins's work is that it allows us a new understanding of a commonly used word like "joy," a concept previously as difficult to define as it is easy to talk about at great length. The affect *enjoyment-joy*, for which Nathanson (1992) has offered the cognate *contentment*, is an innate biological experience triggered by a decreasing gradient of stimulus density anywhere in the CNS. The cessation of any condition that produces a high level of neural firing will trigger enjoyment-joy in anyone at any age. Hence, if one is experiencing distress triggered by the steady-state uncertainty that one is loved by a desired other, and that other removes uncertainty by displaying love and an understanding of the distress, enjoyment-joy will be triggered as the distress dissipates. Likewise, if one is excited—a condition resulting from optimally increasing levels of neural firing—by the loved other and that excitement is satisfied by the other's display of love and understanding of the excitement, enjoyment-joy will also be triggered as the excitement dissipates. This is one means by which affect theory shows the causality behind Beavers's definition of intimacy as "the joy of being known and accepted by another who is loved."

In *The Art of Intimacy*, Malone and Malone (1987) write:

> The outstanding quality of the intimate experience is the sense of *being in touch* with our real selves. It allows us a fresh awareness of who, what, and how we are. It differs from introspection or meditation, which are ways of *looking* at ourselves. They are between us and ourselves, "alone" experiences, and, while valuable, do not energize, enhance, or create growth as intimacy does. In the intimate experience, our "seeing" happens in the presence of the other. It requires no looking or thinking but occurs directly; it is experiential. (p. 19)

Here the Malones direct attention to a very significant feature of intimacy—that, although dependent on the presence of another person, it is centered within the self of each individual. Affect theory suggests that this "experiential" happening is mediated by the affect interest-excitement. When triggered, interest-excitement, the response to novelty, captures consciousness and directs attention to the triggering stimulus. When they describe "a fresh awareness," the Malones are saying the intimate experience provides a novel way of looking at the self and the other. The novelty is provided by seeing the self through the eyes of another who has an abiding interest. Such novelty triggers interest–excitement in this new aspect of the self that is being seen. In essence, the intimate experience makes one more interested in both the self and the other. Affect theory expands the definitions of Beavers and the Malones and increases our awareness of the specific dynamic origins of the intimate experience. What definition emerges if one begins the exploration from within the affect theory paradigm?

TOWARD A NEW DEFINITION

Intimacy is defined in *Webster's Unabridged Dictionary, Second Edition*, as "the state or fact of being intimate; intimate association; familiarity." The word intimate is derived from the Latin word *intimus*, which is the superlative form of the word *intus* meaning "within." *Intimus*, therefore, refers to that which is the *most* within. This begins to explain why the Malones and many others refer to intimacy as an experience occurring within the self, and why interpersonal intimacy must be seen as an association between two people based on the dynamic interplay of the *inmost* parts of the self. From this idea as a point of embarkation, the central elements of affect theory will be woven into a redefinition of intimacy.

THE INMOST SELF

That which is inmost in a person has been scrutinized for centuries by theologians, philosophers, anatomists, biologists, psychologists, and psychiatrists. Tomkins considered all of these domains in developing affect theory. His theory is an answer to the question: What biological mechanism has evolved to ensure that conscious attention will be directed to that information which is most critical for survival? He recognized that information entering the CNS has only one of three possible effects on neural activity. Neural activity can increase, decrease, or remain steady. Tomkins saw that affect is triggered when a stimulus produces one of these three neurologic profiles, no matter whether that stimulus arises from outside or inside the body. Conscious attention is turned to the stimulus because the triggered affect is part of a system that amplifies the stimulus; attention is the result of the focus produced by affect.

When viewed this way, it becomes evident that the affect system, which responds immediately to stimulus changes, as opposed to the drive system, which responds only in a slow periodic fashion that is not as well attuned to environmental change, is more critical for immediate, first-line survival. A study of affect, therefore, permits better understanding of moment-by-moment interactions between people. Tomkins further postulated that without affect nothing is important, whereas with affect anything can be rendered important. Thus, consciousness is under the direction of the affect system, a system that can now be seen as a primary motivating force. This means that awareness of our inmost self only occurs when an affect is triggered, focusing attention on the inmost self. A working knowledge of the affect system becomes indispensable to any psychotherapist who is trying to help others increase their awareness of their inmost selves. To that end, a discussion of the inmost self follows. For the purpose of simplifying this discussion, the complexly interrelated components of the inmost self are divided into four parts: the physical body, memory, cognition, and personality (including one's sense of self).

The Physical Body

Generally speaking, our physical inmost self is comprised of a vast collection of biological operations, the majority of which remain hidden from awareness at all times. We do not feel our liver carrying out the enzymatic breakdown of chemicals, nor do we feel our bone marrow producing red and white corpuscles. Biological events that must register in consciousness in order to ensure survival arrive there through one of three mechanisms — *affects, drives,* or *pain*. A number of the theories for human motivation, most notably that of Freud, assign the primary role to the drives and a much lesser role to the affects. In fact, Freud's theory, simply stated, says that the negative affects arise only when something happens to a drive (repression, suppression, etc.) that transforms it into affect. He taught that one becomes anxious if not sexually satisfied and excited *only* when in the throes of sexual arousal.

Tomkins believed the affect, drive, and pain systems to be completely separate mechanisms. He saw the drives as providing information that was time and place specific. The hunger drive tells me I am hungry right now in my mouth; the sex drive tells me I am aroused right now in my genitals; and so on. In contrast to this, he saw the affect mechanism as providing information that was not specific to time and place. Thus, one can be distressed about the hunger experienced last night or that might be experienced later today, and one can be distressed about work, money, or anything else. Likewise, one can be excited about the sexual experience of last night or that one might engage in later today, and one can be excited about a good book, a movie, or anything else. To Tomkins, this difference between the characteristics of the drives and the affects is critical. The time and place specificity of a drive limits its sphere of influence. Tomkins believed the informational gain given the affects by their generality of time and place confers on them the central role in motivation.

Here are several examples that demonstrate the role of affect in relation to the drives: Everyone has had the experience of being too distressed to eat, too angry to eat, too afraid to eat, or so interested in something else that the hunger drive is ignored for extended periods of time. Conversely, people who are not experiencing hunger eat when distressed, angry, afraid, or made interested by the preparation of a favorite dish. An analogous situation occurs with the sex drive. Sexual arousal can be reduced by anything that provokes fear, shame, anger, disgust, dissmell, or distress. And in some, sexual arousal can be increased by fear, shame, anger, or disgust. Thus, the affects have the power to render the information of the drive system more important or less important.

Tomkins saw the pain system as separate from both the drives and the affects. He placed it midway between affect and drive in that it is sharply localizing (like drive) and powerfully motivating (like affect). Pain does not require amplification by affect to reach consciousness, but it can be overridden by affective amplification. For instance, I have long been susceptible to attacks of back pain from muscle damage sustained during my brief high school football career. A recent bout of back pain reminded me that I can be almost unaware of pain when working with a couple whose interest in therapy and growth contagiously triggers like interest in me. A short while later, with my attention to the pain no longer diverted by interest in my work, I was unable to sit still in my chair, fighting off discomfort that forced me to pace the floor in an attempt to find relief.

This abbreviated description of the affect, drive, and pain mechanisms indicates how awareness of the physical part of the inmost self is influenced by affect as the director of conscious awareness. Affect, a biological mechanism, assigns salience to the infinite amount of information bombarding the CNS at any given moment. This is necessary because people do not possess an infinite capacity to comprehend simultaneously all incoming data. Since there is only a limited capacity or "channel" for conscious awareness, the utility of affect in focusing attention is obvious. But it can cause problems as well. If you are interested in this book and you develop the pain of a toothache, or become hungry, or require relief from the pressure to urinate or defecate, your interest–excitement in the reading material will eventually be overpowered as the affect distress–anguish triggered by these stimuli directs your attention to them and makes you (consciously) aware of your need for relief. This process has a similar effect on interpersonal relatedness, because if you are interested in an intimate other and then begin to experience physical discomfort, you will become less and less responsive to that other as your attention is drawn more and more toward your physical needs. Affect and pain tune us to our physical inmost self, directing attention toward self and away from other. Many misunderstandings occur in relationships because this biological fact is neither clearly understood nor communicated.

Tomkins's theory allows clarification of such misunderstandings as one comes to recognize that affect is triggered by *normal* human biological operations. This eliminates the need to explain negative affects like anger, fear, or shame as resulting from some failed interaction of drive forces or some faulty cognition. These alternative explanations often carry judgmental implications. By replacing them with this biologically based paradigm of normal functioning, one eliminates the potential for shaming people in psychotherapeutic interactions by implying that they are weak and unable to resist domination by nasty drives and thoughts. That emotions are *only* activated by pathological processes is a severely limited and limiting concept. Affect theory replaces it with the idea that one's physical being generates affect — and thus emotion — because of a complexly evolved system, the function of which is nothing more or less than a way to increase chances for survival. The knowledge that all affects derive from physical events aids therapeutic endeavors aimed at helping people become more conversant with their feelings. Such a system makes it more likely that those feelings will be less shameful when communicated to a therapist or an intimate other.

Each affect is the biological precursor to a feeling. Basch (1983) has suggested that an affect becomes a feeling when one becomes aware of that affect. An emotion results from the coassembly of an affect with the memories of our life experience with that affect. Thus, Nathanson (1992) has suggested that affect is biology and emotion biography, and that affect forms the bridge between physiology and psychology. Finally, a mood is created when a feeling becomes involved in a feedback loop with its memories — often because those memories contain powerful or unresolved material. This prevents the usual dissipation of an affect not long after its original stimulus conditions have ceased. One may be left with anger, distress, joy, or any other affect that persists for hours or days, leading to the perception that one is in a good or bad mood.

Memory

Psychoanalytic investigation brought about a shift in awareness of the importance of childhood, of childhood trauma, and of the role of memory in creating and maintaining the inmost self. All modern theories of personality rely on the notion that some aspects of early interpersonal relationships are stored permanently in memory and play an ongoing, central role in determining how one interacts with others. Nevertheless, there remains widespread disagreement about how events are remembered, how memory is stored, and how it is retrieved.

One recent attempt to coordinate the many theories of memory into a theory of personality is that of Singer and Salovey (1993), as found in *The Remembered Self*. These authors conceptualize personality as based on "self-defining memories." Such memories, they suggest, are characteristically vivid, repetitive, linked to other memories, focused on enduring concerns or unresolved conflicts, and affectively intense. They say:

> We propose that each person has a unique collection of autobiographical memories and that these memories can be examined in an effort to define who a person is. Imagine that each individual carries inside his or her head a carousel of slides of life's most important personal memories. These slides have been carefully selected to represent the major emotionally evocative experiences that the person has ever had. The vividness of these memories and the intense affect they evoke ensure the memorability of the original event but also make recollection of that event particularly revealing to us of what matters most. Although memory is perpetually taking snapshots of each and every experience that we encounter, there always emerges a core of slides to which we return repeatedly. This dog-eared bunch of slightly obscured or distorted images comes to form the central concerns of our personality. (p. 12)

Another researcher in this area is Daniel Stern (1985), who works from the perspective of interpersonally based infant research. He, too, focuses on the role of memory as he delineates the sequential development of a sense of emergent self, core self, subjective self, and verbal self.

> The basic memorial unit is the episode, a small but coherent chunk of lived experiences. The exact dimensions of an episode cannot be specified here; they represent an ongoing problem in the field. There is agreement, however, that an episode is made of smaller elements or attributes. These attributes are sensations, perceptions, actions, thoughts, affects, and goals, which occur in some temporal, physical, and causal relationship so that they constitute a coherent episode of experience. Depending on how one defines epi-

sodes, there are no lived experiences that do not clump to form episodes, because there are rarely, if ever, perceptions or sensations without accompanying affects and cognitions and/or actions. There are never emotions without a perceptual context. There are never cognitions without some affect fluctuations, even if only of interest. . . . An episode appears to enter into memory as an indivisable (sic) unit. The different pieces, the attributes of experience that make up an episode, such as perceptions, affects, and actions, can be isolated from the entire episode of which they are attributes. But in general the episode stands as a whole. (p. 95)

For the current discussion, the point to be emphasized is that memory, a central element of the inmost self, is inevitably linked with affect. Tomkins's view of memory is that it functions as a vital part of the biological system for the purpose of preserving that which has been duplicated in consciousness. In other words, that humans are able to become aware of their environment is a survival mechanism which is made even more efficient because one is also capable of preserving and recalling this information. What once was, or happened, outside the self has now been duplicated within it. Tomkins also believed that only information of which one becomes conscious can be remembered, although not all of it will be. Earlier, we noted that only through amplification by affect can information enter the limited channel of consciousness. Thus, affect plays a significant — perhaps central — role in the formation and maintenance of the portion of our inmost self represented by memory.

Cognition

There are many modes of thinking and knowing, more than can be reviewed here. It is pertinent to our current consideration of the inmost world to concentrate on those thinking processes that one can know and control consciously. Awareness of this inner stream of consciousness or internal dialogue fluctuates markedly during waking hours. At times one can be very attuned to what one is thinking and be aware of being so attuned. At other times, especially when focused on things external to the self, one may be only intermittently aware of the internal dialogue. Most of the time this dialogue is not directed — it just happens. It does come under conscious control when one concentrates on a particular topic, works out a problem, or actively engages in such processes as fantasy and imagination. Is this part of our inmost self distinctly separate from our affect system? During logical, rational thinking, affect may seem absent, leading some to believe that normal cognition is affect-less, while affect-tinged cognition results only from pathological conflict. In such a system, a separation between affect and cognition may also appear warranted. Tomkins sees this as an artificial distinction. While he proposes that the affects are innate — present from birth — and that consciousness is limited and only accessed when an affect amplifies a stimulus and thereby draws attention to it, Tomkins (1992) clearly places affect and cognition in equal, interdependent relation when he says:

> Cognitions coassembled with affects become hot and urgent. Affects coassembled with cognitions become better informed and smarter. The major distinction between the two halves is that between *amplification* by the motivational system [the affect system — *author's note*] and *transformation* by the cognitive system. But the amplified information of the motivational system can be and must be transformed by the cognitive system, and the transformed information of the cognitive system can be and must be amplified by the motivational system. Amplification without transformation would be blind; transformation without amplification would be weak. The blind mechanisms must be given sight; the weak mechanisms must be given strength. All information is at once biased and informed. (p. 7)

It is important to remember that Tomkins was working from a Darwinian frame of reference wherein evolutionary change results from selection by survival. He saw the neocortical cognitive system as arising after the development of the affect system and as a distinct advantage for survival only if the two worked in conjunction. Nathanson (1992) is much more specific about this when he notes that:

> It was Basch who suggested to me that the much-vaunted neocortex, that part of the brain which is responsible for most of what people call "thinking" or "cognition," had evolved to enable the modulation of innate affect. "Look at it," he said. "It wraps around the rest of the brain like a cap." One at a time, little structures must have developed, each allowing a bit more opportunity to evaluate, understand, manage, control, and respond to innate affect, as well as the situations in which it had been triggered. Any increase in the potential for affective modulation might have conferred on the organism an increase in the potential for survival.

. . . The thinking of the new brain may have evolved to alter the thinking of the old. (p. 408)

Tomkins is clear that thinking and feeling are inextricably interwoven and cannot be separated. The internal dialogue, however, comes into awareness only under the direction of the affect system. On the one hand, if one notices what one is thinking, it is because one was directed there by an affect, as when the stream of thought triggers distress or fear or interest. On the other hand, thoughts tend to be centered on those issues that have already achieved affective amplification. If fearful of losing one's job, then thoughts about work will occupy the mind. If excited about an anticipated vacation, then the mind will wander off in fantasies about the vacation site. For these reasons, underlying affect should be suspected whenever one member of a couple struggles to share with the other what he *thinks*. Perhaps that person is ashamed of certain thoughts or fantasies, or afraid of provoking an angry response, or so angry that speech is impossible. In this context, an interesting therapeutic exercise for couples is to ask them to focus on their internal dialogue when around their loved one and notice what percentage of it they communicate. They are often amazed at how small a percentage it is. More importantly, it gives them and the therapist an idea of how open or closed they are and how difficult it is for them to expose the inmost self. In summary, our inmost thoughts and our attempts to communicate them are by their nature imbued with affect. The ability to know and control such thinking means that one can choose to share or withhold it from an intimate other — an aspect of personality that is often the critical element in disturbed intimate relationships.

Personality

Nathanson (1992) makes an interesting point when he says, "Generally speaking, I experience me as a self, but I experience your personality" (p. 162). Most would agree that the sense of self begins developing in the climate of an infant's relationship with the primary caregiver. From these early beginnings a personality emerges, experienced by each person as an individual self. For Tomkins and his proponents, the early child-caregiver climate is generated and mediated by affect — both the affect each brings to the relationship and the affect triggered in each by interaction with the other. In his script theory, Tomkins defines scenes as sequences of affect-driven interactions. From special collections of scenes are born scripts. Adults have a complex and unique set of scripts that shape their interpersonal interactions, scripts that form the basis of what others experience as one's personality. It is in the affective components of the earliest child-caregiver interaction that we see how innate affect provides the motivational source and the scripts for relationship formation.

Even though all the innate affects are visible on the infant's face quite early, parents of newborns will testify that distress–anguish is the most prominent early motivator of parent-child interaction. Triggered by anything that produces an above-optimal steady-state of stimulus density in the CNS, including hunger, pain, wetness, or cold, distress–anguish registers on the face of the infant as arched eyebrows and the down-turned corners of the mouth we know as "the omega of melancholy." If the stimulus condition persists, the baby will begin to cry with a rhythmic sobbing that is analogous to the steady-state uncomfortable condition triggering the affect. As the cry becomes louder, it produces a steady-state above-optimal auditory stimulus that by *affect contagion* triggers distress–anguish in anyone within hearing distance. Any affect, whether originating inside or outside the self, is a competent activator of that affect; the contagion occurs because affects are both analogs of and amplifiers of the stimulus triggering them. The parent, therefore, experiences distress–anguish at an intensity matching that of the child, and this produces strong motivation in the parent to limit this inherently punishing negative affect. So it is that the caregiver seeks to discover and remedy the source of the infant's distress.

The next step in this sequence is that while the baby is being fed, or changed, or rocked, there occurs a decreasing gradient of stimulus density as the cause of the unpleasant stimulus is removed or modulated. This triggers enjoyment–joy. The parent experiences like decrease in neural firing as the baby's cry diminishes and its facial expression is transformed to one of contentment. This shift in the baby's affective output triggers enjoyment–joy in the caregiver.

The overall sequence, which may be represented schematically as distress–anguish in infant → distress–anguish in caregiver → action → enjoyment–joy/contentment in infant → enjoyment–joy/contentment in caregiver, meets Tomkins's definition of a scene. A scene that is repeated with great frequency when one cares for a newborn, it sets the stage for a development that is a critical early precursor of future interpersonal relationships. As the infant begins to develop the ability to recognize that another person is present, it begins to associate the relief of distress and the ensuing enjoyment–joy with the presence of a person. Under normal conditions, this association becomes so powerful that eventually a baby will stop crying and smile at someone who comes near, even though the hunger, wetness, or cold persists. In other words, the act of recognizing another person itself becomes a powerful activator of enjoyment–joy when people can be relied upon to decrease the level of neural firing that would otherwise trigger distress.

In addition, because these scenes are *shared* by child and caregiver alike, and because enjoyment–joy is inherently rewarding, each seeks interaction with the other to produce more of the positive experience. This creates a state of reciprocal mutual amplification that makes the experience even more enjoyable and thus more memorable. Here is established the foundation for the process of sharing experiences of positive affect, interactions that later become so important in intimate adult relationships. I view these child-caregiver dynamics as the first interpersonal script — a script originating primarily from interaffective interactions in which other people are defined as the source of relief from unpleasant feelings. It is possible that this was the interactive sequence missing from the lives of Harlow's (1959) infant rhesus monkeys, the lack of which later caused them to be unwilling to relate to other monkeys. In this experiment, Harlow removed babies from their mothers to see if they would eventually prefer a wire surrogate mother with a bottle representing *food*, or a terrycloth surrogate representing *contact comfort* (love). Harlow successfully demonstrated the importance of contact comfort — except when feeding, the babies clung to the terrycloth surrogate. However, for the rest of their lives, these monkeys preferred their own company and would attack ferociously any monkey placed in their cage. Not only was it difficult to get them to mate, but those that did give birth paid little attention to their babies. If humans did not develop scripts that convey the sense that others are a potential source of relief from distress and, therefore, also a source of enjoyment–joy, one wonders whether we, like Harlow's monkeys, would eschew the company of others.

Human infant research continues to seek answers to such questions without the brutal measure of complete separation of babies from their mothers. In a section describing what he has labeled the subjective sense of self, Stern (1985) suggests that "Between the seventh and ninth month of life, infants gradually come upon the momentous realization that inner subjective experiences, the 'subject matter' of the mind, are potentially shareable with someone else" (p. 124). He goes on to say:

> Interaffectivity may be the first, most pervasive, and most immediately important form of sharing subjective experiences. Demos (1980, 1982), Thoman and Acebo (1983), and Tronick (1979), and others, as well as psychoanalysts, propose that early in life affects are both the primary *medium* and the primary *subject* of communi-

cation. This is in accord with our observations. And at nine to
twelve months, when the infant has begun to share actions and
intentions about objects and to exchange propositions in prelin-
guistic form, affective exchange is still the predominant mode and
substance of communications with mother. It is for this reason that
the sharing of affective states merits primary emphasis in our views
of infants of these ages. Most protolinguistic exchanges involving
intentions and objects are at the same time affective exchanges.
(pp. 132–3)

Research, therefore, supports Tomkins's theories concerning the central
involvement of affect in personality formation. That affect has a vital
role in the development of the interpersonal component of the inmost
self is also undeniable.

Each of the four components of the inmost self—the physical body,
memory, cognition, and the sense of self or personality—has been shown
to be deeply entwined with affect. One must infer that interaction
between the inmost selves of two people is also mediated by affect.
Although the affect dynamics of such interaction has already been suggested, it is necessary to present a more detailed description of interaffectivity before establishing a new definition of intimacy.

INTERAFFECTIVITY

The first principle of interaffectivity—affect contagion or affective resonance—was described in the previous section. It occurs when one mimics
another person's bodily display, facial expression, or tone of voice, thus
producing analogous affect in the self. Parents engage in affective resonance from the very first minute they see their baby. If the baby begins
to cry, they may make the same face as the baby in order to match the
baby's affect. Or they may intentionally override the distress triggered in
them by the baby's cry and make the smiling relaxed face of enjoyment-
joy as they coo in an effort to trigger in the baby this more pleasant
affect. Not long ago, I watched my nephew's wife carry out such a
maneuver with her six-week-old. Baby Lydia, when hungry, would often
become so intensely distressed within minutes that her cry shifted from
that of distress to the wail of anguish before her mother could begin to
feed her. So much was she taken over by these intense, anguished cries
that she was unable to nurse. Her mother would then hold her—instinctively placing her face within the short focal distance of a child of this
age—look directly at her, and begin to speak in a tone so steadily sooth-

ing that everyone within hearing range would begin to relax. Soon, Lydia too would relax and begin to nurse contentedly.

One of the most important events in the interpersonal life of an infant is the appearance of the ability to smile at will. The innate smile is an integral part of the enjoyment–joy mechanism, and it is triggered by any gradient of decreasing stimulus density. The social smile is made possible as the infant learns to perceive others more clearly, and it heralds the beginning of the second social script — a script made possible by affective resonance. The smile itself is explained by Tomkins (1962) as follows: " . . . the mother's face is one of the few objects in the environment with sufficient variation in appearance and disappearance to produce both excitement at its sudden appearance and the smile at the sudden reduction of this excitement when the face is recognized as a familiar one" (p. 372). The smile of a baby is so extraordinarily contagious that it is difficult to resist smiling back, and the enjoyment–joy experienced during this exchange is so inherently rewarding that one often feels compelled to continually retrigger the smiling response in the baby. The sequence of this social interaction is baby smiles → adult smiles → action by adult → baby smiles → adult smiles. This kind of play, based on affective resonance, further reinforces for the child that other people are a source of enjoyment–joy. Internalized with the first social script is the idea that enjoyment–joy appears when distress–anguish is relieved by people. In this second script, the infant learns that people are also a source of enjoyment–joy when they trigger interest–excitement followed by enjoyment–joy. These two scripts provide formidable motivation to seek intimate relationships in order to gain relief from negative affect and the pleasure of positive affect. In these ways and others, affect is the primary force behind the formation of the interpersonal inmost self. It is evident from such a description that intimacy is a developmental acquisition made possible by interaffectivity, especially affective resonance.

The end result of these sequences of interaffectivity between a child and its caregivers determines one's *capacity for intimacy*, which is based primarily on affective resonance. For example, if others in the child's environment show interest in that child, they will attempt to resonate with the child's interests. They will play ball, dolls, games of all sorts, and in general seek to teach the child interesting things and learn the child's interests so they can share those interests. From such experiences, scripts emerge that inform the child that it is inherently interesting to other people. Likewise, if others enjoy the child, that child will learn to experience the self as enjoyable and, because of the contagious nature of affect, enjoy enjoying the self and enjoy others enjoying it also. Adults who as children were raised in a climate of positive affect — exchanged interpersonally by affective resonance—usually have a well developed capacity for intimacy.

The consulting rooms of psychotherapists are filled with people who did not have such positive experiences. On the one hand, there are those who were raised in an emotional climate essentially devoid of positive affect. For example, if there is little interest shown in one as a child, then as an adult, that person may well find little interest in being with others or may not experience the self as interesting to others and, therefore, avoid them. Similarly, such a person may not think of himself as enjoyable to others. On the other hand, if the affective environment of one's childhood was primarily negative, then, depending on the negative affect of the caregivers, that person may perceive the self as distressing to others, or fear-inducing, or anger-inducing, disgusting, dissmelling, or shameful. The scripts developed are based on whatever negative affects were triggered in that person while resonating with the affects of the caregivers. Such a person's capacity for intimacy is severely limited because such scripts keep the inmost self unavailable, either by chasing others away with unpleasantness or closing off the inmost self for fear of exposure. Such scripts undermine relationships and produce the negative affect that brings these relationships into therapy or to divorce court.

One further psychological ability originates in the biological ability to resonate with the affect of others. *Empathy* occurs when, through affective resonance, the affect of another triggers the same affect in us. As Basch (1983) has noted, we then scan our inmost self to explain the affect triggered by the other and link it with the memory of our own life experiences involving that affect. Even though our biographies are different, we sense that we have been thrust into the other's shoes for a moment, and know what we would feel if we were in his or her experience. Empathy, therefore, is an affect-driven pathway connecting the inmost self of one to the inmost self of another.

FOUR GENERAL IMAGES OF HUMAN MOTIVATION

There is one further aspect of affect dynamics to introduce before proceeding to a new definition of intimacy. Tomkins (1962) says:

> In the case of the human being, the fact that he is innately endowed with positive and negative affects which are inherently rewarding and punishing and the fact that he is innately endowed with a mechanism which automatically registers all his conscious experience in memory, and the fact that he is innately endowed with

receptor, motor, and analyzer mechanisms organized as a feedback circuit, together make it all but inevitable that he will develop the following General Images: 1) Positive affect should be maximized; 2) Negative affect should be minimized; 3) Affect inhibition should be minimized; 4) Power to maximize positive affect, to minimize negative affect, to minimize affect inhibition should be maximized. (p. 328)

A general image is a partly learned and partly unlearned motivating "blueprint." This blueprint resides within the CNS and is ever-present in its motivating interaction with whatever else enters the CNS. In the passage above, Tomkins is saying that anything mediated by the CNS, including perception, memory, cognition, and behavior, is influenced by these four general motivating principles. Within affect theory, the blueprint is of equal importance at any age and during all interactions with self and others. From the preceding review of the inmost self, interaffectivity, and the four principles of motivation, a new definition of intimacy now emerges.

DEFINITION

Intimacy is an interaffective process through which the inmost parts of the self are communicated to the other by tangible displays of affect. These displays can take the form of verbal or nonverbal communication. They can involve touch, smell, hearing, facial expression, body language, sex, or cognition as when one shares with another some piece of information, a poem, a book, or a movie. The affect in an intimate relationship is triggered by stimuli generated in here-and-now interactions between the two people, the scripts formed in the childhood of both, and a complex interaction between these past and present phenomena.

Because affect is the central force driving intimate interactions, it follows that *the process of intimacy is directed by the same dynamic forces that direct the innate affects*. This means that in a healthy intimate relationship — regardless of the depth of the relationship — the two people are able to (1) maximize positive interpersonal affect, (2) minimize negative interpersonal affect, (3) minimize the inhibition of interpersonal affect, and (4) institute effective interpersonal processes (or scripts) that allow 1-3 above to be the primary affective modes within the relationship. In other words, the interaffective processes of a healthy couple are not in conflict with the central blueprint directing the affect system of each individual.

The depth of an intimate relationship is dependent upon the ability and the desire of each person to expose the inmost self to the other, as well as the ability and the desire to discern, interact with, and accept that which is exposed. In other words, if one imagines that there is a doorway to the inmost self, in order for intimacy to occur one must be willing and able to find the handle to one's door and open it, and the other has to be willing and able to look through the open doorway. The ability and desire to expose the inmost self are determined initially by the capacity for intimacy forged in the emotional climate of childhood. This capacity can and must evolve in the context of what is learned in one's adult relationships.

This paradigm for the process of intimacy can be applied to each of the definitions reviewed earlier, as well as most other definitions of intimacy. It asserts that the roots of social interaction grow from the universally shared experience of innate affect and that human biology predisposes people toward intimate relationships. The definition presented here includes in its scope the observation that in one's lifetime one can be involved with any number of people and at several levels of intimacy. The definition, therefore, has potential applicability for therapists working with any form of interpersonal relationship — parent and child, husband and wife, lover and lover, friend and friend, patient and therapist, or any other pair of humans who are seeking intimacy. It also allows the therapist to formulate and utilize a structured approach for treating disorders of intimacy.

DISORDERS OF INTIMACY

There are as many potential sources for a couple's failure of intimacy (be it short-lived or long-term) as there are statistically probable interactions between two people — but most dyads settle into regularly repeating patterns of such failures. In order to enhance the ability to diagnose and treat such couples, I have divided the various disorders of intimacy into two major categories based on the new definition of intimacy. These categories and their subdivisions are as follows:

1. Interaffective failures of intimacy:

    * failure to maximize positive interpersonal affect
    * failure to minimize negative interpersonal affect
    * failure to minimize the inhibition of interpersonal affect

2. Capacity for intimacy failures:

- lack of developmental acquisition
- biological interference

This classification is useful even though it must be acknowledged that there is significant overlap among the five problem areas. For instance, a couple involved in a chronically hostile relationship characterized by failure to minimize the negative affect anger–rage is unlikely to have achieved the goal of maximizing the positive affects interest–excitement and enjoyment–joy by engaging in sex. Someone who experienced infrequent resonance of interest–excitement in their family of origin, and thereby developed a limited capacity for intimacy, is also unlikely to be in a relationship that maximizes positive affect. Nor is someone with a depression well equipped to minimize negative interpersonal affect. In spite of this overlap, it appears valid to make a distinction between interaffective failures and capacity for intimacy failures.

The *interaffective failures* category includes difficulties with intimacy that arise primarily from here-and-now problems experienced by the couple as they attempt to deal with the interaffectivity arising from the vicissitudes of daily life. These problems can be addressed by the therapist in the here and now because their resolution usually does not require long-term intervention with deep exploration of the self. The category of *capacity for intimacy failures* is intended to include intimacy problems that derive more from that which is within each individual for biographical reasons. This category includes those whose interpersonal development was somehow compromised during childhood and/or adolescence. It also includes people with depressive, manic, or other affective disorders, as well as schizophrenia—in other words, it includes all disorders of human biology that can impede intimacy.

The division of the pathologies of intimacy provides a useful starting point for the therapist as it aids in formulating the diagnosis and prognosis of the couple's presenting problems. Additionally, it allows a more pragmatic focus for therapist and couple as they attempt to unravel what can initially appear to be a vastly complicated set of issues interfering with intimate interactions. What follows is a description of each of these categories from a clinical perspective.

INTERAFFECTIVE FAILURES OF INTIMACY

Failure to Maximize Positive Affect

Tomkins describes two positive affects: interest–excitement and enjoyment–joy. Interest–excitement is activated primarily by novelty; any novel stimulus entering the central nervous system at an optimal gradient of increasing neural activation triggers interest. Enjoyment–joy (or contentment) results whenever the level of neural activation begins to diminish, as when orgasm ends sexual arousal and excitement, or eating relieves hunger, or pain in any part of the body decreases. The two social scripts presented earlier describe the origins of the desire and ability of people to maximize positive affect, suggesting that these patterns evolve as a natural reaction to affective resonance. The theory was advanced that children whose interest–excitement is regularly stimulated by interactions with their caregivers are very likely to develop adult patterns of behavior (scripts) whereby they seek out others in order to engage in mutually interesting activities. It also follows that children who are isolated from the positive affect of others—as when the mother suffers from depression or the father is seldom present—are likely to develop scripts that lead to more solitary interests.

In adult life, the earliest stages of most love affairs are characterized by experiences of intense interest–excitement and enjoyment–joy. One's life suddenly includes a thrilling new person to talk to, to learn about, to have sex with, and with whom to expose things about your inmost self in ways you may have never shared before. New love presents a multiplicity of natural sources of interpersonal novelty, each of which activates interest–excitement. Interest–excitement, as predicted by the principle of affect contagion, resonates within the dyad. For instance, one is excited about a meeting with one's new lover both because of one's feelings for that person and *because that person's level of excitement about the meeting is also high.* The excitement in seeing the other brings relief from the negative affects involved in loneliness and from the moments when the two must be apart. This activates considerable enjoyment–joy, which also resonates with the dyad. Such intensity of positive affect makes falling in love great, and it encourages openness and the exposure of the inmost self to the other, because the presence of powerful good feelings makes most people willing and able to be vulnerable and open up the self to that cherished other. Since such intense openness is often new to both people, it provides a further significant contribution to the novelty of the experience and triggers even more interest–excitement. Maximizing positive affect is, therefore, natural and virtually effortless in the beginning stages of any new relationship.

Novelty diminishes, of course, as people get to know each other. The intensity of positive affect associated with novelty must decrease simply because the relationship is successful. The more time two people spend together, sharing aspects of the self with one another, the less novel they eventually become to one another, and the positive affect that once was present at high levels of intensity begins to diminish. Although the biography of each person is permanently altered by the experience of falling in love, the overwhelming mass of prior interpersonal experience — scripts from childhood — now begins to assert itself and influence the relationship. If the interpersonal patterns carried from childhood either do not include or defensively exclude methods for generating interest-excitement, then this can be the time in the life history of a couple when many of the sequelae of failures in maximizing positive affect are likely to surface. This is not to imply that all couples experiencing intimacy for the first time must get into serious difficulty, nor that previous experience provides the only source of difficulty. But all couples face this same loss of naturally occurring interest-excitement and enjoyment-joy, and must learn new interpersonal patterns for inducing positive affect. Some people are so distressed by this quite normal phase of an intimate relationship that they go outside the dyad and engage in affairs in search of greater novelty. It is also a time when many modern-day couples seek couples therapy or marriage counseling. This is an encouraging trend because it can interrupt the formation of destructive scripts for dealing with the discomfort that such loss of interest entails.

Many people mistake the powerful affects of the early relationship for "true love." They become very distressed, afraid, and even ashamed as the flamboyant sequence of interest-excitement and enjoyment-joy wane in concert with their deeper knowledge of each other. Some fear that it means they are capable of loving only briefly, and experience great shame at such inadequacy. Others take it to mean that the partner is insufficiently exciting. The shame engendered by such thoughts and feelings prohibits many people from exposing these inmost feelings to the other, who senses this decreased openness, which now triggers further feelings of rejection. Without therapy, many couples will then develop interpersonal patterns of distantiation as each hides the inmost self from the other in an effort to avoid these painful interactions.

The therapist encountering such couples hears presenting complaints like: "She/he takes me for granted," "The romance in our lives is gone," "We never do anything together anymore," and "Our sex life used to be great, now it's no fun at all." The general theme of such complaints is that interest-excitement and enjoyment-joy are gone from the relationship, and neither person knows how to rediscover these good feelings or overcome the impediments to them. Even when there are other factors involved — and there always are — therapy for such couples requires that something be done to help them rekindle positive affect. Without positive affect, relationships lack the resilience necessary to deal with even the most mundane causes of negative affect, and therapeutic endeavors require resilience if they are to succeed. The prognosis for change is grave if either member of the couple exhibits no tangible interest in engaging in therapy with the other, or if either has suffered significant rejection during the period of diminished interest. For this reason, most couples therapists develop a system of evaluation that includes seeing each partner individually at least once; this allows the partners to be more open about their true level of interest in or disgust for the other. The affect disgust, rarely discussed in marital and family counseling, is often involved in rejection. Since disgust signals the desire to spit out that which has been taken in, it is a powerful negative prognostic indicator for the continuation of the relationship and for couples therapy. The partner who feels most rejected is the one who will exhibit disgust for the other. Unless the therapist pays immediate and strict attention to whatever disgust or serious lack of interest has been uncovered, the therapy will be crippled.

Partners interested in engaging each other and the therapist in unraveling the mysteries of their lost ability to have a mutually interesting and enjoyable relationship have already begun to reestablish contact by calling the therapist and making an appointment – after all, for most people this is a novel experience. The therapist must help them develop insight into their inmost selves, a process through which they can learn to recognize the signs of painfully diminished levels of interest–excitement and enjoyment–joy. This requires us to help them become comfortable enough with self and other for them to communicate the negative affects arising from their decreased positive affect. It is important to teach people how to keep track of their affect on a minute-by-minute basis by increasing conscious awareness of each affect triggered by interactions during the session. Only by knowing what they feel in the here and now are people able to keep themselves and the other appraised of their inmost self, which is the necessary first step in the open disclosure of the inmost self. This is only possible if the therapist has created a therapeutic environment that conforms to the "safe place" described by Havens (1989). In such safety, and with the therapist's encouragement, people can practice exposing to the other these emotional experiences of the inmost self.

As therapy becomes successful, the spouses take charge of the work and begin to open up more of themselves to each other outside of the therapist's office. This process alone generates significant ongoing novelty for the couple because the inmost self of any person is a rich, complex arena in constant flux as various life events unfold, including the triggering of memories related to such events. The inmost self always contains a remarkable amount of new information. I am often amazed when my wife of over 25 years tells me startling things about her past that I have never heard before. One might think that after 25 years of living together each had gathered from the other a complete history; in reality this never happens. Memory is a vast, dynamic storehouse of information—dynamic in the sense that memories possess nuance that can change with every retelling of a story. Some couples boast that after just a few years of marriage they know "everything there is to know" about each other. More often than not, this is symptomatic of a failure of the ability to generate novelty and maximize interest-excitement by exposing major elements of the inmost self to one another.

The following case example illustrates a couple's failure to maximize positive affect.

Phil, the 31-year-old husband of a couple seen previously by me in couples therapy, called about a year after they left therapy. The earlier treatment terminated because most of their initial goals for therapy had been achieved, because their current economic status had become compromised by the expansion of his business, and because Cathy, at 29, was immersed in the care of their first child. Phil insisted on seeing me without Cathy present. In the first session he confessed tearfully that, after only four years of marriage, he had "fallen out of love" with Cathy. He had come to see me by himself because he could not possibly say such a devastating thing in front of her. He had not had an affair, but he was distressed that he was having regular sexual fantasies about other women, especially his new assistant. He didn't feel like spending any time with Cathy; when they were together, it seemed as if all they did was fight. He was afraid that their marriage was ending. He did not want it to end, particularly because of his infant daughter, but he was certain that he could not tolerate their incessant marital discord much longer, certainly not for a lifetime.

He told me that he had not shared many details of his feelings with Cathy, only that he wasn't happy. He came alone for a second session, during which he was unable to unearth anything more specific about his marital distress. He then agreed to ask Cathy to resume couples therapy. In the first conjoint session, Cathy expressed surprise that he was so unhappy. She knew things weren't perfect at home but had assumed that they were not feeling particularly close only because of the pressures of everyday life—a new baby, his expanding business, etc. She admitted to being more irritable than usual, which she attributed to the fatigue of child-rearing. She agreed with Phil that most attempts to discuss any topic of significance evoked almost instantaneous anger between them.

In the beginning of the session, they avoided looking at each other directly while either was speaking. Neither had any difficulty looking at me, and I could sense that the positive transference from our prior work remained intact. Although neither raised any major negative issue, even minor disagreements produced in each an obvious facial display of anger of an intensity greater than the issue appeared to merit. Each was aware that the anger was out of proportion to the topic being discussed, and that it seemed to reflect a need to blame the other. Both were distressed that they had returned to such a destructive interpersonal pattern—blaming the other—because they had made a serious and successful effort to reduce such blaming tactics in our prior work together.

Directing them away from any unpleasant topics for the moment, I asked each to describe in detail what they had been doing since I had last seen them together. Cathy told me of the joys and trials of raising their infant daughter and of feeling tired much of the time, but added that for the most part she was content with their life. Her tiredness, she confessed, made her less interested in sex than usual, but she wasn't overly concerned about it. Phil eagerly described the growth of his business, which had required him to take on an assistant—a woman—and now had him looking for a building to purchase so he could move the rapidly expanding business out of their home. He also professed joy about being a father, and it was clear that he loved his daughter very much. He missed Cathy sexually more than she missed him, but said he could understand her fatigue and did not appear particularly angry at the diminished sexual frequency.

Since neither appeared to have a biological depression or to be unable to display interest-excitement in their descriptions of their separate lives, I asked if either felt that same interest in or around the other. Both said no. I inquired as to their current plan for spending any time together in "fun" activities. They had no such plans; when my question stimulated their thinking, they realized that for some months they had not set aside any time to be alone. I asked if either would mind engaging in some joint activities; neither did, so I set them the task of planning a few things together. Furthermore, I suggested that their current interpersonal dissatisfaction was complex and could only be made worse if they attempted to resolve these difficult issues by themselves. They, therefore, agreed to temporarily forego arguments over "significant" issues—except during therapy sessions.

The next session revealed only a slight amelioration in their negative emotional response to one another. However, they had gone to the local Rotary Club dinner together, and each displayed pleasure at the memory. Within several weeks of resuming regular therapy, they were spending significant amounts of time together and then spontaneously re-

sumed their sex life. Soon they reported that they had begun to ignore my instruction to avoid discussion of difficult topics. In a long heart-to-heart talk about Phil's new assistant, Phil had shared with Cathy his distress over several problems the assistant had caused with customers. Not only had Cathy been helpful to Phil but she had divulged her jealousy of this assistant—feelings she had previously been too embarrassed to disclose. Confessing his prior sexual feelings for the assistant, Phil confided that she need not be embarrassed by her accurate intuition. He went on to add that in the past several weeks he had seen the assistant in a new light that somehow made her much less appealing to him. Indeed, he had some real concern about whether certain mannerisms that upset his customers were too central to her personality for him to be able to expect change, in which case he would have to fire her.

As they related their discussion, they smiled at one another and Phil said he could not understand what had happened to him during the past few months that made him feel as if he didn't love Cathy.

Phil and Cathy had become caught up in the daily struggle of everyday life and did what so many young couples do—they forgot to continue to nourish their relationship. Because their inherent love for one another was strong and because neither suffered from any significant defect in the capacity for intimacy, it was relatively easy to help them reintroduce some interpersonal novelty. Affect theory teaches that novelty is the primary activator of interest–excitement. With the return of positive affect came the return of their sex life and the return of the relational resilience to handle situations that generate negative affect. Their case also demonstrates how the loss of the ability to maximize positive affect is one source of the inability to minimize negative affect—a topic to which our attention is now directed.

Failure to Minimize Negative Affect

Of the nine innate affects proposed by Tomkins, six are negative and experienced as inherently punishing—fear–terror, distress–anguish, anger–rage, disgust, dissmell, and shame–humiliation. Every child-caregiver dyad develops its own idiosyncratic set of interactions related to negative affect. The factors that determine the nature of such interactions are complexly interdependent on the temperament of the child, its moment-to-moment affective state, the scripts for negative affect learned by the caregiver, and the caregiver's current affective state. These factors promote variation in the methods used by a caregiver to handle negative affect in the child; nevertheless, most dyads settle into characteristic patterns of interaction that repeat with regularity. From these childhood patterns emerge the scripts that people use as adults to deal with negative affect in the self and in interactions with others. Those whose parenting provided inadequate relief from negative affect or too much negative affect are likely to experience failures of intimacy due to difficulty in minimizing negative affect.

For instance, in the earlier description of the first interpersonal script, it was shown how distress in the newborn signals the caretaker to take some action that relieves the distress and thereby triggers enjoyment–joy in both. Children who consistently experience enjoyment–joy when reliable caregivers relieve their distress learn two things. First, in this secure environment, they eventually become equipped to minimize negative affect in the self by learning self-soothing behaviors. Second, they learn to seek out and trust others to provide relief from negative affect when they are unable to soothe themselves. Alternatively, children whose distress is inconsistently relieved by another are less likely to learn satisfactory self-soothing techniques. When in distress, they may either withdraw from others, expecting little or no relief from interpersonal sources, or they may develop exaggerated or unrealistic expectations of how others should help them. In the latter case, they may learn to blame others when they experience negative affect. Blaming interactions increase the negative affect in a dyad by the principle of affect contagion, and the person who initially felt bad now feels worse and even more certain that the other is the cause of his or her pain. This is a common interaffective sequence in couples who fail to minimize negative affect.

When couples with difficulty minimizing negative affect seek professional help, they voice complaints like "We can't talk about anything without getting into a fight," "We never resolve disagreements," "He's always criticizing everything I do," or "She doesn't appreciate anything I do for her." Treatment of such couples is made more difficult by the contagious nature of their affect. They are usually stuck in a recursive pattern—similar to a computer frozen by a software program caught in a loop—where the negative affect in one triggers negative affect in the other triggers negative affect in the one and so on. This also triggers negative affect in everyone who comes in contact with them—not even the therapist is immune to affect contagion. While exposed to the affects released as the couple batter one another, therapists can become afraid, distressed, angry, disgusted, or experience shame or a dissmelling response to the couple. If the therapist is unable to minimize negative affect in the self, therapeutic errors can occur. Limit-setting is often necessary because uninterrupted fighting during therapy sessions simply reinforces the couple's hostility. I prohibit fighting in the office in order to create a safe therapeutic environment that teaches the couple appropriate limits. Couples whose problems result from a simple failure to minimize negative affect respect such limits.

When the couple cannot accept limits, a therapeutic impasse occurs. This suggests to the therapist that either a more deeply entrenched capacity for intimacy failure is present or a permanent loss of affection has occurred. Additional therapeutic strategies are necessary; these may include individual therapy or individual sessions as an adjunct to the couples therapy. It is critical that the therapist determine if enough interest in each other is present, for a person lacking such interest is usually insufficiently motivated to do the hard work that therapy requires. When the couple accepts limits on fighting, then the therapist can focus each partner on the negative affect being experienced within the self and demonstrate how to take responsibility for that affect. Hidden behind much of the chronic strife in couples who have difficulty minimizing negative affect is the belief that the other is responsible for the way one feels. No one can learn techniques for soothing one's own negative affect as long the belief persists that the other is responsible for the way one feels.

The example of Phil and Cathy demonstrates the role of shame in situations characterized by a failure to minimize negative affect. It was noted that in their first conjoint session, they were unable to look directly at one another while describing their anger. The therapist versed in affect theory pays very careful attention to the face because facial expression and its feedback to the CNS are integral components of the affect system. Even though Phil and Cathy were discussing their anger, the face of each was averted from the other by the hanging of the head characteristic of shame affect. Shame must be suspected in all failures to minimize negative affect. As Tomkins (1963) has noted, "If distress is the affect of suffering, shame is the affect of indignity, of defeat, of transgression and of alienation. Though terror speaks to life and death and distress makes of the world a vale of tears, yet shame strikes deepest into the heart of man" (p. 118). The effects of shame, as it turns off interest-excitement and enjoyment–joy, are deeply disturbing. Shaming interactions often result in anger, especially since anger helps one overcome the feeling of helplessness associated with shame. When the therapist is sensitive to the possibility that anger may be masking shame, it is much easier to help the couple limit fighting. Further techniques related to shaming interactions will be presented later in this chapter.

The couple with difficulty in minimizing negative affect usually projects many unfriendly thoughts onto one another. Tomkins (1992) defines projection as follows: "If a particular attitude of a significant other person in one's past history has been the unique activator of a particular response, then the later activation of this response in some other way can be expected to uniquely activate the expected 'cause'" (p. 221). If, while treating a couple unable to minimize negative affect, the therapist encounters significant projection, then exploration of childhood relationships is necessary. This encourages the couple to understand those responses to the other that are emotionally powerful and yet do not make sense intellectually. A patient once told me that he could not understand why on certain days he became so angry with his wife when she asked an apparently innocent question upon his arrival home from work. Later he remembered how angry he felt when his mother unleashed a barrage of questions when he came home from school each day. Without this insight he could not comprehend his negative reaction to a wife who was speaking to him only in friendly, interested tones. Furthermore, he also noticed that he only experienced this anger on days when he was overloaded at work, or the drive home was particularly harrowing, or when he was extremely hungry by the time he arrived home. Eventually, he concluded that his own distress would trigger a projective script that caused him to expect his wife to be just as annoying as his mother. This case demonstrates how a current experience of affect can resonate with an old script and become the basis of projection. From this quite ordinary example, one can easily extrapolate to the far more complex problems caused by here-and-now interaffective failures as they overlap with failures in the capacity of intimacy of a historical nature.

My five-part division of failures of intimacy is artificial because there are always elements from childhood that contribute to the interaffectivity of the present. All affective experiences are nested within complex and interrelated scripts. For this man, distress of the moment was projected onto his wife as the remembered attributes of his mother, causing a failure to minimize negative interpersonal affect in a clear example of the blending of past and present. By dividing failures of intimacy into simple and separate categories, the therapist gains a tool with which to help the couple deal with complexity. Effective therapy takes into account the fact that consciousness is a limited channel, governed by affect, and only one aspect of each problem may be approached at a time. Such simplification is necessary in order to take a step-like approach toward solutions for the complex problems inherent in failures of intimacy.

The negative affect experienced in interpersonal relationships is not necessarily destructive to intimacy unless the partners lack methods for its modulation or are ashamed of any expression of negative affect and, as a result, block intimacy by avoiding exposure of the inmost self.

Several therapeutic techniques can help reduce such shame, notably the assertion that few people enter a relationship with a natural ability to minimize negative affect; this is a skill that can only be learned as a relationship progresses. The uniqueness and complexity of each person dictate which techniques will work, and when. Nothing can prepare one for every idiosyncrasy in a given relationship. It is also important for the therapist to explain that negative interactions may provide wonderful possibilities for growth. In a new formulation of love utilizing the tenets of affect theory and script theory, Nathanson (1992) says:

> I believe that the nidus of love is the sequence that results when some infantile need has triggered negative affect and the caregiver provides solace by responding to that affect, determining its source, relieving the underlying need, and accepting the resulting positive affect. Love implies not a positive affect but a series of negative and positive affects linked together in sequence to form a scene. Built from the accumulated scenes of urgent need and solacing relief characteristic for each of us are the scripts that we will in adult life call love. (p. 244)

Important as positive affect may be to the warm, close, loving feelings of an intimate relationship, it is not enough. Intimacy is not possible unless one also knows for certain that one is loved even after the moments of intense negative affect that are inevitably experienced and expressed to the other. Intense anger surfaces at times in all successful relationships. Each must ultimately know that his anger is not held against him. Of course, unless partners learn to minimize this anger and convert it to positive affect, intimacy will remain beyond their reach. It is critical for such a conversion that one be able to assure the other that he is still loved despite having been angry. This leads the discussion to a consideration of the difficulties that can be encountered when one attempts to minimize a negative affect like anger without inhibiting affect. How does one express negative affect openly without harming the other, especially when that other seems to be the source of the negative affect? The answer should become apparent in the next section.

Failure to Minimize the Inhibition of Affect

The problems created in an individual who inhibits affect are described by Tomkins (1962) as follows:

> The inhibition of the overt expression of any affect will ordinarily produce a residual form of the affect which is at once heightened,

distorted and chronic and which is severely punitive. A chronic
negative affect is obviously painful. A chronic inhibited positive
affect is also painful, since it leads to chronic distress or anger by
the fact of inhibition or to chronic fear, shame, or self-contempt at
the ever present danger of disinhibition. (p. 330)

Scripts for affect inhibition may develop when an infant's distress is
too distressing for those around it. A caregiver who is already overloaded
and fending off distress may be pushed into anger when forced to resonate with the distress of an infant. Such inadvertent misattunement may
teach the infant that the expression of distress provokes anger in the
other, setting up scripts for wariness about affective openness. (That
such fear is warranted is too often proven by the horrifying news reports
about caregivers who shake their babies to death because they will not
stop crying.) As an adult, a person with such a script may too often
remain quiet when in distress. Her inmost self remains hidden from a
loved one, which may lead to a more general failure to minimize the
inhibition of affect within the couple. Since all relationships require
constant interplay and feedback in order for positive affect to be maximized and negative affect minimized, the inhibition of affect can be a
serious impediment to intimacy.

In general, the methods used by caregivers to modulate or socialize the
affects of their children generate the majority of the problems later
associated with the inability to express affect openly. All caregivers understand the importance of their role as teachers of modulation, especially the modulation of raw anger and distress, toward some other
expression that produces less anger or distress in the parent. Such socialization is necessary because the adult who displays raw negative affect
will be socially handicapped. Some of the methods used to teach socially
appropriate affect expression, however, can lead to overinhibition. The
child can be shamed or terrified by the process and learn that the free
expression of anger, distress, or any other negative affect will eventually
result in personal shame or terror at the response of others. Whatever
activates negative affect may then become something to be ashamed or
afraid of rather than something to be shared openly.

There are many other child-caretaker interactions that can lead to a
failure to minimize the inhibition of affect. A patient once described
herself as a "low-maintenance child." She had learned to force herself to
appear happy and without distress or fear because of her mother's
chronic unhappiness. She did everything possible to avoid increasing
her mother's pain. She became so successful at her low-maintenance
presentation of self that she seldom troubled her mother for anything.

As a result, her expression of negative affect was inhibited through her childhood and adolescence. She was so "good" that she did not even "act out" during her teenage years. She, therefore, never developed scripts for the open expression of negative affect to another. This pattern continued in her marriage, since she believed that it would be "selfish" to bother her spouse with her bad feelings.

Beavers (1985) emphasizes the advantage of selfishness in promoting a successful marriage when he says: "Only this (selfish) orientation can encourage openness, recognition of ambivalence, the evolution of responsible choice, and the clarification of personal boundaries" (p. 65). Although conventional wisdom suggests that selfishness precludes love for another, it is more accurate to state that appropriate selfishness fosters healthy care of the self. In this way we learn not to burden the other with caretaking functions and also become masters of our own negative affect. When the balance between positive and negative affect shifts dramatically toward the negative, the amount of positive affect one has to share with a loved one decreases to a level that makes a relationship unpleasant. Tomkins has shown how each of the nine innate affects operates as a separate mechanism, and that each affect is always available for prominence within the self. One who experiences distress from intense hunger or anger at the boss is less likely to be interested in interacting with a dearly loved partner until the distress is relieved by food or the anger is somehow diminished. Negative affect makes the inmost self less accessible; it must, therefore, be reduced to allow others into oneself. For Beavers, selfishness does not imply a narcissistic orientation; rather, it parallels Fromm's (1956) use of the term "self-love" (p. 60) and Wurmser's (1981) concept of "self-loyalty" (p. 256). True narcissism shuts out others in order to protect a damaged self. Healthy selfishness allows a temporary focus on the inmost self out of love and respect for the needs of the self and in order to enhance one's capacity for positive intimate interaction.

All close relationships require proximity that causes us to step on each other's toes. If, for whatever reason, one does not say "ouch" and communicate the distress experienced as a result of the other's actions, a complex dilemma is created. The need to disguise the distress causes the inmost self to be hidden from the other. The distress, if unrelieved, eventually triggers anger and resentment that must also be hidden. This causes further withdrawal and hiding of the inmost self. The other, perhaps not even aware of the offense, experiences feelings of rejection triggered by the withdrawal, without information adequate to allow reestablishment of the intimate bond. This now hurt other may also resort to withdrawal, thus setting in motion a recursive loop of rejection and

hurt. In such a stalemate, when only one partner has difficulty minimizing the inhibition of affect, the presenting complaints heard by the therapist are "I never know what he's feeling, he won't tell me" or "She never
gets mad, so I always feel like I'm the one who's wrong." If both partners
are unable to express negative affect, then the presenting problems are
more likely to include vague feelings that, even though the two people
care for one another, the marriage is stagnant and neither feels close to
the other. These couples often enter therapy because their sexual frequency has diminished to uncomfortably low levels. The following is an
example of such a couple.

*Bob was in therapy on and off for a number of years. He had been
raised in a lower-middle-class working family but had managed to complete college and two master's degrees. He was a hard worker who did
well at each level as he climbed the corporate ladder. He eventually
attained management level with a salary considerably higher than any
prior member of his family. His initial reason for entering therapy in his
early twenties was that he could not understand why he became so intensely angry at what were seemingly minor occurrences in his life. He
believed his anger was seldom warranted and thought himself defective
because of it. He would often ask, "Why can't I just control myself?"*

*His parents were also hardworking people. His father was a factory
worker whom Bob remembered as having a "gruff" personality and who
was for the most part a silent member of the family. His mother was
very loving and caring and the one who did the most for him and his one
sister. However, it was his mother who caused him to fear any display of
anger, for whenever he became angry or expressed any other negative
affect she reacted as if he had wounded her severely. This produced
shame, guilt, and the desire never to display negative affect. As an adolescent, his sexual fantasies involved scenes where he was whipped with a
leather belt by stern, cold women who were punishing him for being "a
bad boy."*

*During his first course of therapy, which lasted about three years, he
experienced a decrease in the intensity of his anger and felt less shame
when angry. Toward the end of this therapy, he terminated a relationship
with a woman who was in his eyes cold, hard, and untrustworthy, a
romance characterized by sequences of excitement, disappointment, and
rejection. It was soon after the breakup of this relationship that he began
dating Claudia, whose sweetness, thoughtfulness, dependability, and
empathic interest seemed the perfect antidote for his life experience of
chronic empathic failure. They married after two years of courtship.*

Bob returned to therapy after he and Claudia had been married for seven years. His presenting complaint was that the frequency of sexual intercourse had dwindled from an initial three to four times per month to about once a year. Six or seven months later, Claudia joined him in couples therapy. Both insisted that they were happy with the marriage, had not gotten involved in affairs (confirmed by each in individual sessions), and that they never fought. Both — Bob more intensely than Claudia — were puzzled and worried about the deterioration of their sexual frequency; they said that nothing they tried had improved it. I then met with Claudia individually for several sessions in order to obtain a more complete history.

Claudia has a twin sister, Ramona, and three older brothers. Her father was a blue-collar worker who supported the family well and cared for his alcoholic wife. Claudia remembers how her father would call before coming home from work to find out whether or not his wife had been drinking. She learned the same trick because she was so embarrassed by her mother's alcoholism that she feared bringing any of her friends to the house when her mother was drinking. The mother was not abusive, but Claudia frequently arrived home to find her passed out on the floor and never wanted one of her friends to observe such a scene. The entire family kept the secret of her alcoholism from the rest of the world. When I first met her, Claudia had not even told Bob about it.

Claudia's role in her family was a quiet one. Ramona was the noisy, bossy daughter who always got her way. Furthermore, she took care of Claudia. Once, when they were about 13, Claudia's teacher, a nun, slapped her across the face. Claudia told Ramona about the incident at recess, and after school Ramona came into the classroom and told the nun that if she ever touched Claudia again the entire family would unite against her. Claudia remembers being terrified as Ramona confronted the nun, certain that Ramona was going to be punished. However, the nun treated Claudia with respect for the remainder of the school year. In general, then, Claudia learned never to confront others because her twin would do it for her. She accepted the family's system of denial and became someone who never complained.

I used a didactic approach to present the concepts of affect theory so Bob and Claudia might see how affect is triggered in "normal" people. This was necessary to help them overcome the belief that negative affect was bad, even though it took many sessions for them to grasp this concept operationally. Once they understood it both intellectually and emotionally, I asked if they truly believed they could have lived together for seven years without having ever stepped on each other's toes. Both admitted that they could see things they had done that the other should have been angry about, but it took a while before either could admit anger at the other. Once this admission was made and accepted by both, a number of issues surfaced, exposing negative affect that had been present but disavowed for years. At first, they were both understandably fearful of such affect, but as time passed they became more comfortable that open expression of their feelings was not going to do irreparable damage to the marriage. When we then returned to the topic of their sexual relationship, each was able to be more open about what the other could do that would be more stimulating. Their sexual frequency increased in tandem with the degree of openness about their likes and dislikes.

Therapy for such couples is greatly enhanced simply by teaching the biology of the affect system, indicating that affect is innately present in all people. One advantage of this educational approach is that it provides a common language that encourages discussion and openness about affect but pressures neither to exhibit an affect about which he or she might have fear or shame. As was true in the case of Bob and Claudia, some people require many sessions to recognize that the expression of negative affect is healthy for a relationship and does not define one as an unloving, uncaring person. To force such people to express certain affects early in treatment only activates their learned shame response to negative affect, making them feel contemptible and encouraging them to resist or leave treatment in order to avoid such feelings. However, for treatment to be successful, the couple must master both the expression of negative affect to one another and the ability to recover from such moments.

As Bob and Claudia began to fight for the first time in their married lives, their interest in sex was rekindled. They had each been quietly experiencing a significant amount of negative affect about the other. The childhood inhibitory scripts that required them to suppress these negative feelings also suppressed interest–excitement. They settled into a quiet, uneventful, but overly controlled emotional pattern that closed each off from the other. Therapy allowed them to be more open in their expression of all affect — it minimized their inhibition of affect and allowed a better connection between their inmost selves. Such a connection thrives on the regular and clear expression of affect each time affect is triggered. The more open one is, the more the novelty of one's complex individuality — one's ever-changing minute-to-minute affective self — can activate interest–excitement in the other. With new interest–excitement available to link with the sex drive, the sexual life of this couple was enhanced. Their first fights were intense and thus distressing to them simply because they had no scripts for the healthy expression of anger. However, with continued therapy, they learned to express even low levels of anger. This is critical for the appropriately modulated expression of anger because it encourages graded expression, where anger of low intensity is expressed with low intensity and anger of high intensity is expressed with high intensity. Low intensity anger is much less contagious and usually less damaging than high intensity anger. Furthermore, much highly intense anger starts at a lower intensity and only builds up to high levels because it is not expressed and becomes what Tomkins (1991) describes as "backed-up" anger. Scripts that both minimize the inhibition of anger and minimize anger itself include knowing how to express anger in a graded fashion. People with such scripts can modulate their expression of anger and no longer feel the need to inhibit it. Nevertheless, as was mentioned in the case of Phil and Cathy, anger is often a surface manifestation of shame. In order to understand anger in couples, one must also understand the interpersonal dynamics of shame.

THE SPECIAL CASE OF SHAME

Shame-humiliation is the affect triggered whenever there is an impediment to ongoing positive affect. From an evolutionary standpoint, it makes sense to think of shame as a mechanism that evolved to direct attention to anything that blocks the inherently rewarding experience of positive affect. Only if attention is shifted to the source of that interruption can one make the adjustments necessary to regain the antecedent good scene. It also makes sense that to be effective this mechanism must be punishing; otherwise it would be experienced as another form of the positive state one was already enjoying. Shame is certainly a punishing negative affect. However, its cause and effects can produce confusion and misinterpretation if one is unaware of its mechanism of action.

Let us take as an example what happens to people in successful relationships. Everyone experiences a natural dimming of interest–excitement and enjoyment–joy as novelty declines. Without the distraction of falling-in-love, an intensely positive affect, each partner becomes more susceptible to prerelationship interpersonal scripts. Now interaffectivity will be dominated by biography because affect always resonates with its history. These historically based emotional responses control here-and-now interactions and, when outside of conscious awareness, produce confusion about the dynamics of these interactions. Coupled with the lessening of positive affect, a situation then develops where previously insignificant impediments trigger shame.

Any episode of shame activates each person's historically determined responses to shame. Anyone who has learned to defend against shame by using what Nathanson (1992) has called the *attack other* pole of the *compass of shame* will blame the other when shame is triggered by some impediment. To blame is to disavow shame. It also permits one to become angry — an affect that makes one feel more powerful and in control rather than weak and defective. Blaming forces the other into a posture of defense. Since most defensive maneuvers require denial of access to the inmost self, the attacker will experience further impediment to intimate interaction and, consequently, more shame. Soon a loop of shame and defense will be formed that can have disastrous consequences for the relationship. This is what happened to Cathy and Phil. Each ended up attacking the other because both were experiencing shame triggered because, although each was still interested in the other, that interest was impeded by their busy schedules. I interrupted the resulting shame loop by asking them to reintroduce novel interactions into their relationship, while prohibiting the *attack other* defense that functioned as an ongoing stimulus for shame. As soon as they removed the impediment to interest-excitement, the stimulus conditions for shame were gone, along with the *attack other* defense. Reciprocal exposure of the inmost self was now possible; this fostered even more interest–excitement and increasingly intimate interactions as they reconnected at this inmost level. Had I been unaware of the dynamics of shame, I might well have wasted a great deal of therapeutic time and effort by focusing on anger as the root of their troubles, probing their past to find the source of such anger in their early relationships with their caregivers. Although such an exploration is sometimes warranted, it can be extremely damaging if based on misunderstandings about affect, and thus lead away from the real problem. The therapist who does not understand affect dynamics will always produce shame when such probing defines one or both members of the couple as an "angry person."

Any couples therapist will find it useful to study Nathanson's compass of shame, which helps us identify the defensive styles that are indicative of underlying shame. In addition to the *attack other* pole mentioned above are the script libraries he calls *attack self, avoidance*, and *withdrawal*. Bob had learned to defend against shame by using *attack self*; for he could always find fault with himself before anyone else had a chance to demean him — his sexual fantasies reflected this masochistic orientation. *Attack self* is a compromise that does not prevent shame but instead allows one to control the amount of shame experienced by preempting others and shaming oneself before they can. Bob learned to do this in the context of his relationship with a mother whose shaming of him was subtle but pervasive. Anytime he exhibited any negative affect, she made him feel defective and somewhat stupid. He learned to act ashamed and to shame himself in order to avoid the far worse feelings evoked when she diminished him. Whereas this system works pretty well as protection from the original shaming other, friendlier people are often frustrated when frequent self put-downs keep the inmost self of that person at a distance. One hesitates before expressing anything negative to such a person for fear of hurting them or causing them to hurt themselves. This made it difficult for Claudia to let Bob know when his behavior bothered her.

Bob's defensive style negatively reinforced Claudia's, for she used avoidance to protect herself from shame. Such people act as if nothing bothers them so they do not have to confront anything that might trigger shame. It is difficult to connect with the inmost self of such people because they often make the other feel defective for showing negative feelings. For years, Bob was unable to convince Claudia that their once-a-year rate of sexual intercourse was symptomatic of a relationship problem and that it might be worthwhile for them to seek couples therapy. Bob's *attack self* defense and Claudia's *avoidance* defense made it more difficult for them to expose their inmost selves. As this impediment to positive affect triggered shame, each clung more intensely to their idiosyncratic defense against shame, and another type of shame loop was created. Therapy demonstrated to them that affect is a biological event triggered when the proper stimulus conditions are met, and as such neither a good nor a bad thing and nothing one need feel ashamed about. They were encouraged to express negative affect so that each could understand the self and other with greater clarity, and the pathway to their inmost selves could be reopened and made more available to the other. As they began to try this simple instruction, it was as if they each removed a defensive veil and the impediment with it. More interest–excitement then appeared in their relationship, an interest–excitement that extended to their sexual life.

These examples serve as a reminder that shame is the affect that makes people want to hide, to remove themselves from the presence of others who can see them. It is an affect that makes one seek privacy and wish to be distant from others. Tomkins's formulation about shame furthers one's appreciation of Erikson's (1963) description of *intimacy vs. isolation*, the sixth of the eight ages of man. Erikson wrote: "The counterpart of intimacy is distantiation: the readiness to isolate and, if necessary, to destroy those forces and people whose essence seems dangerous to one's own, and whose 'territory' seems to encroach on the extent of one's intimate relations" (p. 264). Phil and Cathy were struggling between intimacy and isolation. Therapy had to provide them with some mechanism through which they might move out of their isolation and onto more intimate ground. In the affect theory paradigm, the restoration of intimacy is not possible as long as positive affect is absent. I saw that their current lack of interest–excitement allowed only shaming transactions, and that in such withdrawn isolation, neither could be sufficiently open and vulnerable for interpersonal resolution and growth to occur. In other words, they could not feel the formerly warm connection between their inmost selves.

It is interesting to note that, while Phil and Cathy were developing "selfish" efficacy at their separate life tasks, they were blocked from being selfish around one another. Each would become either too angry or too frightened of the consequences of direct display of their own needs and wants — as signaled by the presence of negative affect — to communicate them to the other. This inability to communicate negative affect disabled the capacity of each to engage the other in his or her own self-caretaking tasks and made selfishness appear as a rejection of the other. Each, feeling hurt, lonely, and isolated from the other by the diminution in affective communication, began to project onto the other a deeply felt lack of interest in the relationship. Without a sense of security that the other is interested in one's existential dilemma, selfishness becomes an isolating and isolated act. One is then prevented from achieving the mature love described so concisely by Sullivan (1953b): "When the satisfaction or the security of another person becomes as significant to one as is one's own satisfaction or security, then the state of love exists" (pp. 42–43).

These examples indicate that shame must be suspected as *the* affect underlying a wide variety of problematic patterns of interaction. For instance, until proven otherwise, angry, blaming interactions should be regarded as representing the *attack other* defense against shame. Shame is an extremely compelling affect because it is so painful, and this makes it difficult for people to relinquish their defenses against it. However, for all practical purposes, shame within an intimate relationship usually *originates from impediments to ongoing interest-excitement and enjoyment-joy*. Nathanson (personal communication, 1995) described an observation made to him by Tomkins that "People with chronic shame are the most deeply loving in our society, for they have refused to give up their anticipation of a love that is always thwarted." This means that interest–excitement and enjoyment–joy frequently exist just below the surface of problematic interactions. Once the therapist has successfully directed the couple to detect and remove such impediments, interest-excitement and enjoyment-joy may recur without much more effort on the part of either couple or therapist. Tomkins (1991) describes this process as follows:

Because shame is evoked by and constitutes a partial interruption and reduction of positive affect, it readily lends itself to scripted reparative responses which return the scene to its positive quality. For this reason high positive-affect density is first of all vulnerable to damage by shame but also most readily repaired when this occurs in the midst of an otherwise primarily rewarding life. (p. 196)

The therapist must also be aware that there is a critical difference between the presence of shame in a couple's interactions and the presence of disgust. Disgust in either member of the couple earns a far more grave prognosis than does shame. Tomkins (1991) makes this distinction clear by saying "In shame there is every intention to return to the good scene, whereas in disgust the good scene has become unambiguously malignant and is to be spit out or vomited forth" (p. 196). This point is amplified further by Nathanson's (1992) suggestion that disgust is the primary affect operating in divorce.

Disgust is powerful because it creates intense conflict over our continued desire for what had appeared so tasty and has now become nasty. Disgust, then, is a good model by which to examine the phenomenology of divorce, in which people who have loved now turn against each other. The extraordinary force and tenacity of marital hate is dependent on the power of the preexisting marital bond, of the "drive" to be close, of the need for each other, of the warmth each once gave the other, of the degree of nurturance each represented to the other. In every moment, however brief, that an estranged person thinks of his or her partner, the affect of disgust will now intrude. (p. 128)

Disgust can be triggered by a variety of negative interactions, including those that create shame in either member of the couple. Whoever develops disgust has been the most shamed over the course of the relationship. To defend against that shame, one must extrude the once loved other from the inmost self through the mechanism of disgust. Relationships that have reached a stage where one or the other is experiencing significant disgust have little chance of reestablishing openness and closeness. No matter how hungry we may be, these powerful forces prevent us from eating food we have recently vomited.

CAPACITY FOR INTIMACY FAILURES

In the formulation suggested here, one's capacity for intimacy is found in the scripts related both to one's *desire* for intimacy and one's *ability* to be intimate. Capacity for intimacy failures can therefore involve the inability to expose the inmost self to another and/or a lack of desire, conscious or unconscious, to submit oneself to such exposure. In my experience, there are two general etiologies of the failure of the capacity for intimacy: (1) the lack of developmental acquisition; and (2) biological interference.

As may be seen in the case of attention deficit disorder (ADD), these two types of problems can coexist. Many children with ADD—currently recognized as an inborn biological condition—have difficulty with social interactions. They are often immature for their age, and if they have any friends, they are usually children who are two or three years younger. Furthermore, such children, especially if hyperactive (ADHD), can be so chaotic, difficult to control, noisy, and disruptive that their parents find themselves in chronic distress when the child is around. The parents may respond to such distress by distancing themselves from the child or by attempting to control the child with what often become angry interventions. The child of parents who distance themselves is robbed of the positive interaffectivity afforded by the affective resonance of inter-est–excitement and enjoyment–joy. This child does not learn that others find him interesting or enjoy his company. The child whose parents are often angry may seek to avoid interaffectivity because the affects involved are always punishing. Both groups of children, therefore, run the risk of growing up with a dearth of positive affective interactions with others and a corresponding deficiency in their capacity for intimacy. Substantial roadblocks to their inmost self result from their efforts to ward off the negative affect that always hovers around them. To make matters worse, such children are constantly bathed in shame because the coexisting learning disabilities, difficulty sitting still in the classroom, and other "primitive" behaviors draw attention to them as defective. By adolescence, their self-esteem has been damaged severely, interfering with their ability to develop the social skills normally acquired during the teenage years. The biologic flaw of ADD/ADHD can be a significant hindrance to the developmental acquisition of the capacity for intimacy. With this caveat in place—that biologic interference and developmental interference with intimacy can be interdependent—let us examine each condition as if they were separate entities.

Failure of Developmental Acquisition

This category of intimacy failures includes a wide spectrum of problems generated by childhood interactions with caregivers. Sullivan, for instance, called attention to the role of early interpersonal experience and the likelihood that it might produce *parataxic distortion*, which has been defined by Chapman (1978) as "all types of interpersonal events in which a person's feelings and behavior are warped by the effects of unhealthy relationships with close persons earlier in his life" (p. 115). The effects of these early relationships can be mild or so severe that the person experiencing them may neither be capable of nor wish to seek out intimate relationships. The milder end of this spectrum includes a number of situations in which the person simply never learned aspects of intimate interactions because none was in evidence during childhood. Phil's parents, for example, never fought. He could not remember ever seeing them angry at one another. On the other hand, Cathy's childhood experiences included seeing her parents express negative affect toward one another. As a result, Cathy was less disturbed than Phil when they fought. Phil worked very hard to contain his anger because he feared that each fight might be the one that ended their relationship; he lacked a script for managing interpersonal anger with his wife. He responded well to therapeutic maneuvers that increased his knowledge about the effects of negative interaffectivity, and eventually he learned how to express anger without the constant fear that he would ruin the marriage.

Phil's response is typical of people in therapy for mild developmental failures in their capacity for intimacy. Such people come to therapy because they *want* to change the way they relate to their significant other. They are relieved to learn that their problem is not caused by some major flaw deep within them, but rather by a simple lack of experience with certain easily mastered interpersonal scripts. This lessens their shame about being wrong or bad, and encourages them to learn new scripts.

At the more extreme end of the spectrum of failures of developmental acquisition are those people in whom the capacity for intimacy is limited by an almost complete absence of effective interpersonal scripts or by parataxic distortions of extreme severity. Many of the people with a *DSM-IV* Axis II personality disorder are included in this category. Such people have severe disturbances in their ability to expose their inmost self to others. Often they lack either the skills or the desire to connect with the inmost self of another. Take, for example, the following sentence from *DSM-IV* (1994): "Individuals with Narcissistic Personality Disorder generally have a lack of empathy and have difficulty recognizing the desires, subjective experiences, and feelings of others" (p. 659). It is also difficult to establish comfortable interaffectivity with a person suffering from paranoid personality disorder. The people with this diagnosis are depicted in DSM-IV as having " . . . a pattern of pervasive distrust and suspiciousness of others such that their motives are interpreted as malevolent" (p. 634). In other words, paranoid people believe they *already* know what is going on inside others.

In the paradigm for intimacy presented here, the refusal or inability by one to experience and connect with the inmost self of another produces an impediment to intimacy that cannot be overcome by the other. And since *DSM-IV* also says of the personality disorders that "The enduring pattern is inflexible and pervasive across a broad range of personal and social situations" (p. 633), couples therapy with such people is generally ineffective. I suggest that couples therapy is not the treatment of choice when one member of a couple has a personality disorder or some other condition characterized by massive failure in the developmental acquisition of intimacy. In my experience, such people do not enter couples therapy because they want to change. They may want an improved relationship, but they want the change to come from the significant other, whom they perceive to be at fault and in need of alteration.

Biological Interference

Physical disorders can also cause distortions or interference with one's capacity for intimacy. At the milder end of the spectrum of these disorders are temporary capacity-for-intimacy failures like those provoked by the common cold or the flu. When one is ill enough, interest–excitement is generally diminished, except for the desire to feel better or to be cared for by another. Distress–anguish is increased by illness, causing the sick person to want to avoid anything that might produce further distress. Tomkins (1962) describes this dynamic as "Low energy raises the threshold of positive affects and lowers the threshold of negative affects" (p. 303). Thus, one's inmost self becomes closed off to others as energy is limited and the primary need is for self-focus in order to heal. When all one wants is chicken soup and to be left alone, one's capacity for intimacy is limited biologically. If one is unaware that the other is sick, this can cause a variety of shame reactions. For instance, if on coming home from work one expresses an interest in sex but the other says, "Not tonight dear, I have the flu and am throwing up every hour," there will be a brief shame reaction triggered by the impediment to the sexual interest and experienced as a moment of rejection. However, upon recognizing that the loved one is sick, interest in sex will be replaced by an interest in taking care of the sick one, and the impediment is removed. Hence, these mild capacity-for-intimacy failures of a biological origin can usually be ameliorated by simple modifications in the couple's pattern of interaffectivity.

This is not true for those biologically induced capacity-for-intimacy failures at the severe end of the spectrum. Such disorders include many of the *DSM-IV* Axis I categories. Mental retardation, drug and alcohol addiction, and schizophrenia, for instance, can permanently reduce one's capacity for intimacy. Severe mental retardation and schizophrenia devastate the formation of the inmost self and leave one essentially unavailable for peer level relationships. And most couples therapists can recall more than one case where the addicted partner chose the addictive substance over a supposedly loved other.

The affective disorders also cause capacity-for-intimacy failures. The most prevalent of these are the so-called depressive disorders. Nathanson (1994) has suggested that the term "depression" fails to take into account which negative affect(s) the depressed person is experiencing. Is the unhappy person primarily in distress? Beset by constant fear, shame, or anger? Suffering from an inability to experience interest–excitement and enjoyment–joy? One might even have a combined affective disturbance, e.g., constant distress and an inability to find interest in anything. Whichever affect is at the heart of the "depressive" disturbance, interpersonal problems arise as the self is beset with unwanted, punishing negative affect. The more severe the depression, the more one's capacity for intimacy is reduced.

Segrin and Abramson (1994) reviewed two decades of research on interpersonal disturbances of depressed people, listing three common characteristics that cause difficulty in relating to others: lack of responsiveness, lack of politeness, and the failure to meet expected standards of social interaction. In the paradigm suggested here, these findings are clear indicators that the inmost self of the depressed person is closed to others. This breaks or prevents connection with others, thus producing an impediment to interest in the afflicted person. This impediment triggers shame that makes the nondepressed partner less interested in pursuing the relationship. Depressed people, therefore, have an impaired capacity for intimacy, and thus little hope of being able to relate intimately with others. Depression must be treated aggressively before asking someone to open up the inmost self in order to be intimate. Nor should the partner of a depressed person be forced to face rejection after rejection while attempting to get closer to someone whose inmost self is not available. In my experience, as long as one partner remains depressed, couples therapy must remain supportive and explanatory of the nature of depression. Anything else promotes greater dysfunction in the dyad by causing shame-based interactions that are doomed to fail.

Bipolar disorder presents another kind of impediment to intimacy. A manic person is caught in a state that is best described as an inability to shut off interest–excitement. The interest–excitement of a manic assembles with everything in its path. Such people are extremely interesting when one first meets them, at least until one realizes that the interest of the manic is generic and not specific to any one person or object. The affects in the inmost self of the manic are triggered, maintained, and controlled by chemicals in the brain that cause the illness rather than by external factors like the presence of another person. Even when positive affect is present, those close to a manic feel their efforts at relating to that person impeded. Furthermore, the longer interest–excitement cannot be shut off during a manic episode, the more that person experiences distress from unrelenting interest–excitement. After a while, this distress readily escalates to anger at even the slightest provocation. Nathanson (personal communication, 1995) also believes that high density interest-excitement leaves one preternaturally sensitive to impediment and, therefore, to shame. Manics and those who remain hypomanic for long periods of time suffer from a range of affective experience that reduces their capacity for intimacy, and their intimate relationships suffer accordingly. Couples therapy must focus both people on the illness in ways that allow greater understanding of how the illness interferes with intimacy; medication must be used to help the afflicted person control the illness.

Any physical disease can cause a failure in one's capacity for intimacy. It reduces one's ability to focus on another. This makes empathy difficult for both the sick person and loved one. At the same time, those who can remain connected feel an increase in intimacy as they struggle together to develop new scripts for relating to one another in the presence of negative affective states. In an instructive article on treating the interpersonal effects of illness, Rolland (1994) concludes:

> When illness or disability strikes a couples relationship, a number of significant structural and emotional skews are likely. A normative, preventive framework that addresses the special strains on couples can counteract dysfunctional relationship patterns and enhance opportunities for increased intimacy. Dealing with these skews can promote a couple's resilience by increasing the range of what they can discuss or handle in the face of loss. (p. 345)

Knowledge of affect theory and the ways affects guide the formation and maintenance of intimacy can give the couples therapist a framework for detecting and correcting "emotional skews."

SUGGESTIONS FOR THERAPEUTIC PROCESS

The definition of intimacy presented in this chapter and the categorization of failures of intimacy that derives from it provide clinicians with at least two additions to their therapeutic armamentaria. The first relates to the definition itself and addresses the most common technical problem faced by couples therapists. The majority of couples enters therapy locked in battle—some overtly angry and some more covert—about issues ranging from A to Z. These battles are waged with argument and counterargument, innuendo, accusation, rationalization, and the like, which cause the partners to feel distant and emotionally disconnected. Most such battles rely heavily on cognitive processes, each containing some modicum of truth in the eyes of the combatant. Except in cases involving physical danger to one of the partners, therapists struggle to avoid being drawn into these battles—no matter how much truth they see in an argument—in order to prevent themselves from becoming facilitators of further argument. The definition of intimacy as a process arising from the interplay of the inmost *affective* components of each person accords the therapist a procedure through which the couple may be distracted away from the cognitive elements of the battle and focused on what they want emotionally from the relationship. They can be directed to see how argument impedes intimacy by closing off the self from the other and produces negative affect—shame—as a result of being prevented from connecting with the inmost self of the other. It is easy for the therapist to slip beneath an argument and demonstrate that the person is really searching for affective resonance that produces warmth, tenderness, and a sense of acceptance by the other.

A relationship feels most intimate when people maximize positive affect and minimize negative affect. When they become lost in the superficial world of who is right and who is wrong, they cannot manage their interaffectivity. Sometimes they become lost in these illusions precisely because they are unable to manage interaffectivity. Nonetheless, in the midst of the most utterly recalcitrant impasse, even with each partner beseeching the therapist to take his or her side, couples can be redirected to the core feature of their intimacy by simple questions like "Which is really more important to you? Who is right or whether you feel the warm, tender, positive feelings created by the connection of your inmost selves?" If a couple prefers to know who is right, then therapy must be halted and their motives for being in therapy confronted and reevaluated. They may need a referee or a lawyer more than a therapist. Couples who are in therapy to change and to learn to be more intimate will always accept this question from the therapist as a message that they are off the path toward intimacy, and stop the battle. At that moment, the therapist can reach for whatever affect is vulnerable in each, and expose it to be shared with the other by saying "I think you were feeling hurt by what happened and reacted with an *attack other* argument to protect yourself. Isn't it true that all you really want is for the hurt feeling to go away?" A positive response to this question permits reopening of the inmost self of that person and simultaneously encourages the same process in the partner. This reopening of the inmost self of each causes an intimate reconnection that triggers both interest–excitement and enjoyment–joy. And it teaches the couple a much-needed script for turning negative affect into positive.

The second therapeutic tool emerges from the division into five categories of all failures of intimacy. These categories provide a flow chart from which a therapist can assess the level and efficiency of intimate functioning. Beginning with the evaluation, one can determine whether the couple is failing or succeeding at maximizing positive affect, minimizing negative affect, and minimizing the inhibition of affect. At the same time, the assessment helps determine to what degree failures of interaffectivity arise from developmental and/or biological flaws in each person's capacity for intimacy. In practice, most couples present for therapy because they are experiencing negative affect — usually the therapist is confronted first with descriptions of an unpleasant nature. It is my practice in the first session to give each person the chance to unburden himself of these angry, distressing, shaming, dissmelling, disgusting, or frightening thoughts in order to determine the strengths and weaknesses of his scripts for minimizing negative affect. I then ask questions about the positive aspects of the relationship — Do they experience interest–excitement and enjoyment–joy with one another? — to learn about their scripts for maximizing positive affect. Sometimes the first session will also give one an idea about the presence or absence of scripts for minimizing the inhibition of affect. But the second and third parts of the evaluation, which consist of one individual session with each partner, are usually more helpful in this regard because people are often less inhibited without their partner present. These individual sessions also offer the opportunity to probe more deeply and find out if either partner lacks sufficient interest–excitement in the relationship or expresses too much disgust for the other. In either case, as mentioned earlier, couples therapy cannot work. (It is still surprising to me how many people act interested in therapy in the first conjoint session but in the privacy of an individual session make it very clear that they have no real interest in continuing the relationship or exposing any vulnerability to the other.)

During this three-session evaluation, I am also engaged in the usual methods of diagnosing character pathology, affective disorders, and medical illnesses in each of the partners. As should be clear by now, any of these conditions requires specific action. Character disorders are rarely treated successfully in couples therapy; affective dysfunctions must be properly treated with psychopharmacological interventions; and physical conditions must be treated or understood properly so that their effect on the relationship can be managed.

It is beyond the scope of this chapter to describe an affect-based therapeutic process in detail. The brief case vignettes presented earlier provide examples of the utility of affect and script theories throughout the course of therapy. In each session I focus on the need to teach the couple how to learn the scripts necessary for maximizing positive affect, minimizing negative affect, and minimizing the inhibition of affect. This it true whether the issues being presented represent here-and-now problems or reflect parataxic distortions that are damaging the relationship. Every session also maintains focus on the degree of openness of the inmost self of each partner and attempts to remove any impediments to the transmission or reception of affective communication. Only when close attention is paid to the details of interaffectivity can intimacy be enhanced.

SUMMARY

The affect theory and script theory of Silvan Tomkins have led to a new lexicon for those interested in intimacy. From this fresh view of human motivation, we are informed as to how nine innate affects and the rules that govern them direct the formation of the scripts that guide interpersonal relationships. This chapter has reviewed prior definitions of intimacy and presented a new definition based on affect theory and script theory. The new definition has led to a categorization of the failures of intimacy. The five categories into which intimacy failures are divided provide a concise means by which the couples therapist can diagnose and treat relational problems and enhance the intimacy of people in disturbed relationships. They also help clarify which couples should not be treated conjointly. The therapeutic techniques presented in this chapter also provide new strategies with which the couples therapist can direct couples out of the impasses and rigidity created by content themes and toward the flexibility of emotionally based intimacy. This is especially easy once one is informed that the process of loving is rooted more in how we feel than what we think about that special someone.

REFERENCES

American Psychiatric Association (1994). *Diagnostic and statistical manual of mental disorders, 4th ed. (DSM-IV)*. Washington, DC.

Basch, M. F. (1983). Empathic understanding: A review of the concept and some theoretical considerations. *Journal of the American Psychoanalytic Association, 31*, 101–26.

Beavers, W. R. (1985). *Successful marriage: A family systems approach to marital therapy*. New York: Norton.

Chapman, A. H. (1978). *The treatment techniques of Harry Stack Sullivan*. New York: Brunner/Mazel.

Demos, E. V. (1980). Discussion of papers delivered by Drs. Sander and Stern. Presented at the Boston Symposium on the Psychology of the Self. Boston, MA.

Demos, E. V. (1982). Affect in early infancy: Physiology or psychology. *Psychoanalytic Inquiry, 1*, 533–74.

Erikson, E. H. (1963). *Childhood and society* (2nd ed.). New York: Norton.

Erikson, E. H. (1968). *Identity: Youth and crisis*. New York: Norton.

Fisher, M., & Stricker, G. (Eds.). (1982). *Intimacy*. New York: Plenum Press.

Fromm, E. (1956). *The art of loving: An inquiry into the nature of love*. New York: Harper & Row.

Harlow, H. F., & Zimmerman, R.R. (1959). Affectional responses in the infant monkey. *Science, 130*, 421–432.

Havens, L. (1989). *A safe place: Laying the groundwork of psychotherapy*. Cambridge, MA: Harvard University Press.

Kwawer, J. S. (1982). Object relations theory and intimacy. In M. Fisher & G. Stricker (Eds.), *Intimacy* (pp. 53–64). New York: Plenum.

Malone, T. P., & Malone, P. T. (1987). *The art of intimacy*. New York: Prentice Hall.

Nathanson, D. L. (1992). *Shame and pride: Affect, sex, and the birth of the self*. New York: Norton.

Nathanson, D. L. (1994). The case against depression. *Bulletin of the Tomkins Institute, 1*, 2: 1–3.

Rolland, J. S. (1994). In sickness and in health: The impact of illness on couples' relationships. *Journal of Marital and Family Therapy, 20*, 327–47.

Scharff, D. E., & Scharff, J. S. (1991). *Object relations couple therapy*. Northvale, NJ: Jason Aronson.

Segrin, C., & Abramson, L. Y. (1994). Negative reaction to depressive behaviors: A communication theories analysis. *Journal of Abnormal Psychology, 103*, 655–68.

Singer, J. A., & Salovey, P. (1993). *The remembered self*. New York: Free Press.

Stern, D. N. (1985). *The interpersonal world of the infant: A view from psychoanalysis and developmental psychology*. New York: Basic Books.

Sullivan, H. S. (1953a). *The interpersonal theory of psychiatry*. New York: Norton.

Sullivan, H. S. (1953b). *Conceptions of modern psychiatry*. New York: Norton.

Thoman, E. B., & Acebo, C. (1983). The first affections of infancy. In R. W. Bell, J. W. Elias, R. L. Greene, & J. H. Harvey (Eds.), *Texas Tech interfaces in psychology: I. Developmental psychobiology and neuropsychology*. Lubbock, TX: Texas Tech University Press.

Tomkins, S. S. (1962). *Affect, imagery, consciousness, Vol. 1: The positive affects*. New York: Springer.

Tomkins, S. S. (1963). *Affect, imagery, consciousness, Vol. 2: The negative affects*. New York: Springer.

Tomkins, S. S. (1991). *Affect, imagery, consciousness, Vol. 3: The negative affects: Anger and Fear*. New York: Springer.

Tomkins, S. S. (1992). *Affect, imagery, consciousness, Vol. 4: Cognition*. New York: Springer.

Tronick, E., Als, H., & Adamson, L. (1979). Structure of early face-to-face communicative interactions. In M. Bullowa (Ed.), *Before speech: The beginning of interpersonal communication*. New York: Cambridge University Press.

Wurmser, L. (1981). *The mask of shame*. Baltimore: Johns Hopkins University Press.

5

Script Theory and Human Sexual Response: A Glossary of Postulates, Corollaries, and Definitions

Donald L. Mosher

No one has done more than Donald Mosher to bring affect theory and script theory to bear on the problem of human sexuality. Long familiar with Tomkins's work, and indeed so close a collaborator that it was to him that Tomkins dedicated the fourth and final volume of *Affect, Imagery, Consciousness*, Mosher takes for granted a level of sophistication that may seem daunting to many. This chapter, a preview of what is to come in a long-awaited book on sexual scripts, is couched in the language of what Tomkins called "human being theory" and is dependent on the concept he called "minding."

As Tomkins stated in volume 4 of *AIC*, the human mind is made up of both cognitive and motivational subsystems–the former responsible for duplication and transformation of data, and the latter for the production of the urgency needed to make us do what is most important to the organism. The body consists of mechanisms that allow it to do (perform actions), to care (because affect makes it so), and, at this highest level of internal organization, to know. It is the system of minding that links knowing and caring, and it is in honor of this concept that the present volume is called *Knowing Feeling*, for such a linkage is what makes us truly human, truly sapient.

If there is any human function about which we care the most and know the least, it is our relation to sexuality. Most of our sexual activity, says Mosher, occurs during what he calls the "sexual trance," during which such matters as depth of involvement, ratio of positive and negative affect, and the nesting within our life history of the sexual activity of the moment become salient. Mosher's chapter sets up the vocabulary needed for the study of sexual interaction and offers an entirely new way of thinking about every aspect of sexual behavior. Like all new languages, it is best used to tell stories. After you have read it a few times, take any one of your own sexual experiences, or any supplied by a patient in therapy, and translate what you have always known into the system of analysis presented here. The effect is both startling and revelatory, for nothing will be the same again. –DLN

FROM THE PERSPECTIVE of Tomkins's script theory (1962, 1963, 1979, 1987, 1991, 1992), an analysis of human sexuality centers on sexual scenes as scripted by personality. Moreover, script theory can be extended to understand the interpersonal transactions in a sexual scene. This midrange of human minding about sexuality and human sexual interaction is located within the limits set, on the one hand, by the biology of sexual drive, affects, hormones, and reproduction, and, on the other hand, by the limits of a specific social system functioning within the historical context of a particular civilization.

Although a full presentation of a script theory of human sexuality would require a book, this chapter focuses on involvement and barriers to involvement within a sexual scene, resulting in a schema of steps in sex therapy. This chapter is limited to a listing of some key definitions, postulates, and corollaries. Although its abstractness saves pages, a fuller exposition — one in which that abstractness is particularized by example and discussion — might make it easier to understand.

ORIENTATION TO SCRIPT THEORY

UNITS OF ANALYSIS POSTULATE: The principal units of analysis in a script theory of sexuality are sexual scenes and sexual scripts.

DEFINITION OF SEXUAL SCENE: A *sexual scene* is a happening, consisting of transpiring events invested with erotic meaning; as a theoretical construct, its minimum definition must include as components at least one discrete affect invested in at least one sexual object (any psychological entity).

DEFINITION OF ELEMENTS OF SEXUAL SCENE: The *elements* of a sexual scene include a beginning, an ending, and its outcomes, for a cast of sexual actors interacting at a particular time and place, and with all of the sexual props, events, actions, affects, and psychological functions that create a specific and particular space-time gestalt that can be culturally characterized as a sexual episode.

DEFINITION OF OBJECTS: An *object* is any psychological entity, including all elements of the scene, such as persons, places, events, or props, but also other affects, drives, percepts, memories, fantasies, actions, and other psychological functions.

DEFINITION OF AFFECTS: *Affects* are sets of muscle and glandular responses located in the skin of the face and also widely distributed throughout the body that generate sensory feedback which is either inherently acceptable and rewarding or inherently unacceptable and punishing.

QUALIA COROLLARY: Discrete affects have *qualia* that are experienced, in general, as either inherently acceptable and rewarding or inherently unacceptable and punishing, and, more specifically, as the discrete positive qualia of interest–excitement, enjoyment–joy, the neutral quale of surprise–startle, and the negative qualia of fear–terror, distress–anguish, anger–rage, shame, disgust, and dissmell.

DEFINITION OF A SEXUAL SCRIPT: A *sexual script* orders information in a connected family of sexual scenes by rules for the prediction, production, enactment, interpretation, direction, management, control, defense, and evaluation of an unfolding sexual scene as an analog or a variant of that family of scenes.

DEFINITION OF A FAMILY OF SCENES: A *family of scenes* is a connected set of scenes sharing a family resemblance, resembling the family by sharing some degree of overlap within sets of contrasting (good versus bad scenes) and correlated distinctive features (elements within a scene) that identify a particular scene as a member of that family.

DEFINITION OF RULES: *Rules* are abstract but specific products of the system of minding that: (a) compress and store information about source, perceptual, affect, analyzer, memory, imaginative, response, target, and outcome processes, (b) order both afferent and efferent information, and (c) retrieve and expand information in the unfolding scene.

DEFINITION OF PSYCHOLOGICAL MAGNIFICATION: *Psychological magnification* is the process of script formation in which sexual scenes are connected as a family and are reamplified by fresh affect that is invested in the family and in the rules that order information within this family of interpreted, remembered, imagined, anticipated, and to-be-enacted scenes.

THE PRINCIPAL SCRIPT FACTOR POSTULATE: In sexual scripting, the principal script factor is repeated, dense changes in affects (including polar changes from positive to negative affect) within scenes or between connected scenes.

DEFINITION OF THE SYSTEM OF MINDING: Tomkins's general psychology of the human being is conceptualized as the *system of minding* that: (a) organizes cognitive and motivational subsystems by specifically linking "knowing" with "caring," and (b) is composed at a more elementary level of a multiply interactive, conversational society of media mechanisms that are "knowers," "carers," and "doers."

DEFINITION OF A MEDIUM: A *medium* is a mechanism for ordering information by representation (e.g., the eye, the hand, the neuron, the brain, the script).

MEDIA MECHANISM POSTULATE: A medium "conjoins and coordinates representation as isomorphic correspondence of source, structure, and product and re-representation as coherence and invention" (Tomkins, 1992, p. 28).

DEFINITION OF THE CENTRAL ASSEMBLY: The *central assembly* includes all units of the minding system functionally joined in a quantum of time, plus, as a permanent member, the *transmuting mechanism* that transforms some messages from the total set into conscious reports based upon the messages' relative density of neural firing.

MULTIPLE SEXUAL SCRIPTS POSTULATE: Each individual has a variety of sexual scripts that can be classified into a taxonomy with four broad classes: (a) Scripts of Orientation and Evaluation (e.g., Sexual Skill Scripts or Sexual Ideology Scripts), (b) Discrete Affect Scripts and Affect Focused Scripts (e.g., Sexual Excitement Scripts, Sexual Affect Management Script, Sexual Affect Control Scripts, or Sexual Affect Salience Scripts), (c) Affect Ratio Scripts (Affluent Sexual Scripts, Damage-Reparative Sexual Scripts, Limitation-Remediation Sexual Scripts, Contamination-Decontamination Sexual Scripts, and Toxic-Antitoxic Sexual Scripts), and (d) Change-Review Sexual Scripts (Sexual Love Scripts, Sexual Jealousy Scripts, or Dysfunction-Magnified Sexual Scripts).

ONTOGENESIS OF SEXUAL SCRIPTS POSTULATE: Sexual scripts organize modules from scripts learned earlier in life, including: (a) Discrete

Affect Scripts that order information about sensory pleasure (enjoyment and excitement) and the negative affects, (b) Relationship Scripts that order information about interpersonal intimacy and power, (c) Gender Scripts that order information about identity as male-female, masculine-feminine, gender conforming-nonconforming, (d) Affect Focused Scripts, based upon either the rewarding or punitive socialization of affects, that order information about the control, management, and salience of affect in sexual scenes, and (e) Ideological Scripts that order information about the nature of gender and sexuality in the human being and the norms of gender and moral sexual conduct.

THE VARIABLE RELATIONS POSTULATE: The abstract and general relations between affect and other modular components of the minding system are complex, because affects and their objects (any psychological entity) are related in various ways, in varying degrees, at various times; the relation between affect and sexual object can be: (a) *interdependent* (mutually influencing), for example, as in the resonance of affective sexual excitement with physiological sexual arousal, (b) *dependent* (one-way influence), for example, as when sexual arousal is dependent on a loved partner as the sexual object, or (c) *independent* (no influence), for example, as when excitement is about a nonsexual object, such as gaining money or establishing dominance, but a sexual activity is used as a means to obtain a nonsexual image.

THE COMPLEXITY COROLLARY: The complexity of the sexual scene — because of the modular structure of human minding, the degrees of freedom of affect, and the inventiveness of personality scripting — results from its many degrees of freedom; thus, understanding the complex living, minding, and social systems comprising human sexuality requires a theory matched to the complexity of nature.

THE UNDERSTANDING POSTULATE: The patterned sequences of affect activation, operation, interruption, and transformation to new affect are the principal dynamics to be understood in scenes; the patterned rules that order information in families of scenes are the principal dynamics to be understood in personality.

INVOLVEMENT THEORY AND AFFLUENT SCRIPTS

Mosher (1980) introduced a theory of depth of involvement in human sexual response that used some ideas from Tomkins's (1962) affect theory. The postulates of involvement theory are revised, refined, and extended to increase their conceptual coherence with script theory. Involvement theory focuses on scenes that people characterize as "having sex" or "making love."

DEFINITION OF HUMAN SEXUAL RESPONSE: Masters and Johnson's (1966) physiological definition of *human sexual response* as vasocongestion in the genitals, myotonia in the body, and orgasmic response is broadened to include concurrent psychological functions and interpersonal transactions, namely: (a) recruited or scripted sexual actions, (b) corresponding, coherent, and invented inner responses of recruited or scripted psychological functions, of which affect is the most significant, and (c) when the couple is the sexual unit, complementary or incompatible sexual and interpersonal transactions.

INNATE PLEASURE POSTULATE: The potential for experiencing sexual pleasure is innately scripted, since pleasure consists of inherently acceptable and rewarding: (a) sensations from the sexual skin and (b) the discrete affects of interest–excitement and enjoyment–joy that are invested in sexual objects.

ORGASM POSTULATE: Orgasmic response is triggered by a specific threshold of an accelerating density of neural firing that is conjointly potentiated by two sources of sexual pleasure: (a) an optimal density of physical sexual stimulation from sexual activities (e.g., kissing, touching, licking, sucking, stroking, and the like) engaging the sexual skin and (b) depth of involvement in the sexual scene.

DEFINITION OF SEXUAL SKIN: The *sexual skin* includes the corium of the entire body, but the sensitive and vascularized skin of the genitals; the face, lips, and tongue; the fingertips and hands; the breasts, thighs, and neck; and the perineum, anus, and buttocks have particular potential for becoming commonly eroticized within a sexual scene or script.

DEFINITION OF OPTIMAL DENSITY: *Density* is a function of the frequency, intensity, and duration of skin contact. Density of skin contact is *optimal* when: (a) it is interestingly novel, complex, or uncertain so that it follows the moderately accelerating gradient of neural firing that activates interest–excitement, rather than suddenly and steeply accelerating as in surprise–startle, steeply and rapidly accelerating as in fear–terror, or slowly losing acceleration as in boredom, and (b) it is repeated and familiar enough to elicit relaxed sensory and motor responses of enjoyment as it reduces excitement. Skin contact is: (a) nonoptimal when it is overly intense and prolonged, activating distress or anger, (b) nonoptimal but reparable when it temporarily interrupts excitement or enjoyment, triggering shame, and (c) nonoptimal and repellent when its source or target is nonappetitive, eliciting disgust or dissmell.

TEMPORAL CHANGE IN OPTIMAL DENSITY POSTULATE: The optimal density of physical stimulation shares an accelerating function — becoming proportionately more intense and frequent over time — with the conjointly accelerating objective sexual arousal and depth of involvement, which, after reaching a critical threshold, in turn: (a) increase the acceptable bandwidth of acceleration, incorporating fear, (b) mask the nonoptimal density affects of distress and anger, and (c) lower the threshold of appetitiveness of some sexual activities that now evoke less or zero shame, disgust, or dissmell.

ORGASM COROLLARY: The threshold for orgasmic response is causally triggered either by minimal or no physical sexual stimulation and deep involvement or by dense stimulation of the sexual skin and shallow involvement.

DEFINITION OF INVOLVEMENT: *Involvement* is the present state of psychological, affective, and sexual response within an unfolding sexual scene that results from feedback from: (a) overt sexual activities within the context of the sexual scene and (b) recruited internal responses — specifically including central feedback imagery about the degree of fit between the sexual image from an individual's sexual script and the unfolding events, activities, and transactions.

DEFINITION OF A SEXUAL IMAGE: A *sexual image* is a centrally generated blueprint for the feedback system that uses information about the achieved state to duplicate the predetermined state (desired outcomes in an image) through a sensory and memory matching feedback mechanism within the central assembly.

DEFINITION OF SEXUAL DESIRE: *Sexual desire* is a craving associated with sexual drive and a wish associated with a positive-affect-invested sexual image; as a wish, the sexual image is a special case of the general principle of forming an image in the central assembly and using a feedback system to duplicate it.

SEXUAL DESIRE POSTULATE: Sexual desire motivates entry into sexual scenes to achieve desired outcomes when (a) messages from three sources — (1) sensory signals of sexual drive, (2) affects associated with sexual objects, and (3) sexual images — (b) enter the central assembly, where they may or may not be transmuted into conscious reports, and (c) become the regnant image in the scene.

DEFINITION OF REGNANT IMAGE: An image is *regnant* when it is the image, among a set of potential images, that organizes the minding system for its duplication; an affect, image, or script is currently operating when it is regnant.

PURPOSE AND CONSCIOUSNESS COROLLARY: A sexual image is said to be a *purpose* when it is transmuted into a report (a conscious message) that serves as a conscious motive; but sexual activity may be nonconsciously motivated by messages from sexual drive, affect invested in sexual objects, or a sexual image that is regnant in the central assembly without being transmuted into a report of a purpose.

DEFINITION OF DESIRED OUTCOMES: The *desired outcome(s)* in a sexual scene—the sexual image as a central re-representation of a desired end state—may be conscious or unconscious, vague or clear, abstract or concrete, transitory or enduring, one or many, remembered as actual or imagined as possible, orgasmic or non-orgasmic in focus, and alternative or conjoint in its outcome criteria.

DEPTH POSTULATE: Taking the scene as a whole, the *overall depth of involvement* is a function of the goodness-of-fit of scene to sexual script; whereas *present depth of involvement* in an unfolding sexual scene is a function of the existing degree of match between the achieved state of involvement in the sexual scene and the desired predetermined state that is to be matched by a feedback system.

DEFINITION OF A FEEDBACK SYSTEM: A *sexual feedback system* is a mechanism for duplicating a centrally generated sexual image (the predetermined or desired state) that uses information from efferent, afferent, and central sources about the achieved sexual state and the desired state to reduce the difference to zero.

OVERALL RATIO POSTULATE: The overall ratio of positive to negative affect in a family of sexual scenes determines the predominant (the most frequently operating) Ratio Sexual Script; specifically, favorable ratios of positive to negative affect produce relatively stable Affluent Sexual Scripts or periodic Damage-Reparative Scripts, whereas unfavorable ratios of negative to positive affect produce relatively stable Toxic Sexual Scripts, or less toxic but potentially nuclear Contamination-Decontamination Sexual Scripts, or still less toxic but long-lived Limitation-Remediation Scripts.

DEFINITION OF AFFECT RATIOS: An *affect ratio* is the comparative proportion of two affects that is found by dividing the sum of the density of one affect by the sum of another since the total sum of affect experience is unity or one. In the general case, the *overall ratio of positive to negative affect*, which can be *favorable* or *unfavorable*, divides the sum of the density of positive affect scenes within the plot of a life by the sum of the density of negative affect within the plot of a life; in the special case, the differential magnification of any one affect into a predominant psychologically magnified script within the plot of a life decreases the potential for any other affect to become as strongly magnified. For example, the more distress has been magnified in the plot of a life, the less joy is open to magnification; if more anger is relatively and proportionally magnified, becoming the predominant affect in an individual's life, then any other negative affect, such as fear, cannot operate as frequently or be magnified for that person as strongly as rage.

DISCRETE AFFECTS IN RATIO SCRIPTS POSTULATE: In the subclasses of Favorable-Unfavorable Ratio Scripts, specific discrete affects are predominant: (a) interest–excitement and enjoyment–joy in Affluent, (b) shame in Damage-Reparative, (c) distress in Limitation-Remediation, (d) disgust in Contamination-Decontamination, and (e) terror, rage, and dissmell in Toxic-Antitoxic.

DEFINITION OF AFFLUENT SEXUAL SCRIPTS: *Affluent sexual scripts* are sets of self-fulfilling rules that order information within sexual scenes; these scripted rules produce, interpret, enact, direct, control, and evaluate an unfolding and rewarding sexual scene.

FAVORABLE RATIO COROLLARY: An Affluent Sexual Script develops when an individual has: (a) experienced a favorable ratio of positive to negative affects within a family of sexual scenes, (b) experienced graded doses of negative affect, and (c) learned scripted rules for repairing the damage of negative affect and for restoring positive affect and outcomes.

VARIANTS COROLLARY: The family of scenes governed by Affluent Sexual Scripts grows to include more members by the *principle of variants*—by finding a common core of unity or of similarity among the repetitions of different scenic elements in new and changing sexual scenes that continue to evoke similar positive affect sequences of alternating excitement and enjoyment.

AFFLUENT EFFECT POSTULATE: Through their compressed and expandable rules ordering information, Affluent Sexual Scripts facilitate an increasing state (or an overall deeper depth) of involvement in a sexual scene.

SCRIPT IDENTIFICATION POSTULATE: Affluent sexual scripts may be identified by specifying the rules ordering information in the family of sexual scenes about the preferred: mood; setting; cast; role expectations of self and partner; sexual style, techniques, and sequencing; sexual vocalizations and verbalizations; sexual fantasies; and the sexual image as desired consequences, as subjective experience of orgasm, as metaphor, and as the mundane or transcendent meanings of the enacted sexual scene.

IDENTIFIED AFFLUENT SCRIPTS POSTULATE: Mosher (1980) identified three specific affluent sexual scripts: (a) sexual role enactment, (b) sexual trance, and (c) sexual engagement with the partner, which were operationalized in the *Sexual Path Preference Inventory* (SPPI) (Mosher, 1988) by specifying the preferred variables in the elements of a sexual scene.

DEFINITION OF A SEXUAL PATH: A *sexual path* is a family of alternative plans that orders information about a set of preferred conditions and sequential steps in achieving the desired sexual image by specifying the preferred variables, functions, and alternative sequencing of compressed modular rules that are expanded to deepen involvement during the unfolding sexual scene.

DEFINITION OF PATH PREFERENCE: As measured by the SPPI, a sexual path is relatively *preferred* when an individual selects as elements in a desired sexual scene variables from that path as more preferred than variables from the other paths.

DEFINITION OF INVOLVEMENT POTENTIAL: As measured by the SPPI, *involvement potential* is the sum of the scores of the three paths that indicates the general potential for involvement in a variety of sexual scenes.

SCRIPT CHANGE COROLLARY: Because the rules of sexual scripts are: (a) selective in the number and types of sexual scenes that they order, (b) incomplete rules even within the scenes they attempt to order, and (c) accurate or inaccurate, in varying degrees, in achieving production, interpretation, evaluation, prediction, control, or evaluation of a given scene, scripted rules are continually reordered, potentially changing sexual scripts at varying rates.

REQUIRED AUXILIARIES COROLLARY: Because of the incompleteness of rules in all scripts, their enactment within an unfolding sexual scene requires auxiliary information from: (a) media mechanisms (e.g., vision, touch, kinesthesia, and the like), (b) movement and spoken or written language, and (c) the special auxiliary scripts of plots, maps, and theories.

RATE OF CHANGE COROLLARY: The rate of change in the rules of a script is a function of: (a) the type of script, (b) the type of disconfirmation of the rules, and (c) its magnitude.

EQUILIBRIUM COROLLARY: Affluent sexual scripts form a relatively stable equilibrium because: (a) there is a favorable ratio of positive affects, (b) their process of psychological magnification into affluent sexual scripts occurs in a context of a rewarding socialization of positive affects, and (c) the psychologically magnified set of rules favors: (1) dense—frequent, intense, and enduring—positive affect in sexual scenes, (2) the consciousness, display, vocalization, and verbalization of affect, and (3) flexible conditions for sexual behavior and response that produce self-fulfilling positive outcomes.

FLEXIBLE INSTANTIATION COROLLARY: Affluent sexual scripts demonstrate a flexible rather than a rigid conditionality and a wider rather than a narrower range of modular variables and of variables as alternatives.

DEGREE OF FIT COROLLARY: Within the sexual scene, feedback from media mechanisms organized as a feedback system will match or mismatch with varying degrees of fit: (a) the *conditions* (rules specifying certain preferred elements of a scene), (b) the *variables* (functions that can assume a specified range of values within a modular rule specifying a condition), and (c) the *variables as alternatives* (functions whose range of values depends upon auxiliary information from the scene and from special auxiliary scripts to further specify their conditionality).

THE MODULARITY POSTULATE: Scripts have the property of *modularity*, being variously decomposable, combinable, and recombinable.

PROFOUND INVOLVEMENT POSTULATE: When multiple, affluent, sexual and nonsexual scripts are aggregated and fused, depth of involvement will be profound; the scene is filled with dense affect and transcendent meaning.

AGGREGATED PATH PREFERENCES COROLLARY: The sexual scene elicits a peak experience when: (a) self and role have fused and responsiveness has become nonvolitional in the path of role-enactment, (b) the sexual scene has become so absorbing that it invests the actual and the possible with value until it has become the only reality in the path of sexual trance, (c) dense—frequent, intense, and enduring—love is focused on the personhood of the partner, and (d) these paths are aggregated or fused.

DRIVE, AFFECTS, AND SEXUAL RESPONSE

SEXUAL DRIVE POSTULATE: The *sexual drive system* provides concrete and specific *motivating information* derived from sensations of pleasure and pain in the consummatory site (the genitals) that is limited to *time, place, response*, and *object*—when and where to do what to what or whom to consummate the drive.

DEFINITION OF SEXUAL DRIVE: *Sexual drive* is a signaling mechanism of the motivational subsystem of the minding system that is organized by the living system's principle of reproductive ordering rather than by the representational principle of the minding system.

SEXUAL DRIVE COROLLARY: Simpler in organization than affect and cognition, sexual drive consists of signals from the genitals that motivationally inform of: (a) *time*, by increasing signals of drive deprivation from last consummation, (b) *place*, by signals of sensory pleasure in the genitals, (c) *response*, by enhancing sensory pleasure from any general response involving the genitals as the consummatory site, and (d) *object*, anything or anyone that produces effective touching of the sexual skin to induce consummation.

DRIVE-RESPONSE POSTULATE: From the perspective of the living system, sexual response, when defined as a reproductive, physiological response, is the sexual drive in operation as: (a) desire as drive deprivation, (b) arousal as drive activation and maintenance, (c) sexual activity as drive consummation, and (d) orgasm as drive reduction.

LIMITED FREEDOM OF DRIVE COROLLARY: Sexual drive can trigger affect and capture consciousness, but unless it does sexual drive lacks affect's urgency and amplification, its freedom of time, intensity, and object, and its freedom to invest in possibility.

PRINCIPAL MOTIVATOR POSTULATE: Affect is the principal motivator in the human being because it is both (a) sufficient, being more urgent than drives, pain, pleasure, and nonspecific amplification, and (b) general, possessing a freedom in time that permits flexible investments in intensity and density of affect, in objects and their substitutes, in possibility, in its instigation by multiple sources, in its reduction by multiple responses, and in its multiple matches with other components of the minding system.

AFFECT-INVESTED SEXUAL RESPONSE POSTULATE: Because of the modular assembly of affect with human sexual response, affect contributes its components to sexual response because affect is invested in human sexual response as an amplifying and correlating mechanism.

DEFINITION OF COMPONENTS OF SEXUAL RESPONSE: From the perspective of the minding system, the components of affect as a total complex or as subset also specify thirteen *components of human sexual response* that are posited to be conceptually and functionally distinct: (a) *innate sexual response programs*, (b) *innate sexual response program activators* (touching the sexual skin), (c) *learned sexual response program activators* (elements in the sexual scene) (d) *sexual response motor messages* (pelvic thrusting), (e) *sexual response motor, glandular, vasocongestive, and myotonic responses*, (f) *sexual response sensory feedback*, (g) *conscious sexual response sensory feedback*, (h) *sexual response memory traces*, (i) *retrieved sexual response memory images*, (j) *retrieved conscious sexual response images*, (k) *innate sexual response to retrieved memory images*, (l) *innate sexual response to transformed percepts*, and (m) *sexual response accretions*.

AFFECT PROPERTIES POSTULATE: Discrete affects are biological entities that are innately scripted as urgent, abstract, general, and analogic, while functioning as amplifying and correlating mechanisms.

DEFINITION OF AFFECT AS SEXUAL: To call an affect *sexual* implies only that it is a discrete affect that is currently invested in and amplifying sexual objects as its source or its responses to sexual objects or to the affect itself as targets; like all affects, affect in a sexual scene remains abstract, requiring the individual to particularize the affect as sexual in its meaning by investment within the context of the sexual scene.

DEFINITION OF URGENCY: An activated affect makes the individual care urgently (a) because it amplifies all ongoing and recruited psychological processes, making them "more so," and (b) because of affect's high density of neural stimulation and Tomkins's principle of maximal density of stimulation in his model of selection into consciousness (Tomkins, 1992, p. 307), affect is frequently transmuted into a conscious report that gains additional amplification by awareness of its discrete rewarding or punishing qualia.

DEFINITION OF ABSTRACT: As innate biological programs, affects are abstract, in the specific sense of possessing a characteristic profile of onset, pattern of neural firing while in operation, offset, and a discrete qualia as an element of this innate pattern; if a discrete affect is activated by a learned sexual object, it still must match the programmed profile of an innate activator. Affect remains abstract—conceived apart from specific or potential objects, concrete or actual instances—until it is particularized by specific sources and targets as it is made actual in the scene. For example, the rate of the rising gradient of neural stimulation associated with excitement makes it abstractly urgent that more neural stimulation from a source (in this instance, a sexual source rather than, say, the excitement engendered by mathematics or basketball) continue to be maximized at that exciting rate in the sexual scene, but it is the scripted individual who particularizes the choice, selection, and attention to multiple sexual images and to their re-representation as coherent and invented sexual stimuli and meaning.

DEFINITION OF GENERAL FREEDOMS: The affect system has innate structural properties that are general, including both the general ability to combine as a module with other components of the minding system within a central assembly and the general degrees of freedom of affect specified by Tomkins (1962): (a) freedom in time (rather than the rhythmic specificity of the drive system), (b) freedom of intensity, (c) freedom of object, (d) freedom of density, and (e) freedom to invest, combine, intensify, modulate, suppress, or reduce other affects.

DEFINITION OF ANALOGIC AMPLIFICATION: *Analogic amplification* refers to affect's property of making any ongoing psychological process "more so" by being similar to, but also different from, its source; affect amplifies by analogy: (a) by increasing awareness of it source through compelling affect receptors that are analogs of whatever arouses terror, rage, or joy, and that impart the discrete qualia of terror, rage, or joy, and (b) by the similarity in time of the affect's profile of activation, maintenance, and decay to its source. For example, excitement and enjoyment invested in sexual drive and arousal are analogic amplifiers, in which one affective bodily response, primarily located in the skin of the face, amplifies other bodily responses primarily located in the skin of the genitals. Just as pain is an analog of injury, "sexual" excitement is an analog of aroused genitals in their shared acceleration of neural stimulation and "sexual" joy is an analog of orgasm in its rapid deceleration of neural stimulation. By being analogous to the quality of feelings from its specific affect receptors, as well as in its profile of activation, maintenance, and decay, affect in sexual scenes amplifies and extends the duration and urgency of the outer or inner, innate or learned, sexual stimuli that trigger excitement and enjoyment (cf. Tomkins, 1991, p. 7).

DEFINITION OF CHANGE-AMPLIFYING MECHANISM: To survive, the human being must be oriented toward changes in the world; as the principal motivator, affect is triggered by changing densities of neural firing that are a function of changing sources of neural stimulation. Affect is a mechanism to amplify *change* as an abstract and general source of affect and to amplify the responses to that source of change and to amplify the affect itself.

DRIVE-AFFECT AMPLIFICATION POSTULATE: To function as an urgent motivator, sexual drive must be amplified, typically by these discrete affects: (a) distress in the drive deprivation aspect of desire and by interest–excitement in the anticipatory aspect of sexual desire, (b) either interest–excitement or enjoyment–joy and their sequential alternation during consummatory sexual activity, (c) predominantly interest–excitement during arousal and plateau, and (d) predominantly enjoyment–joy during orgasmic release and reduction.

INNATE AFFECT ACTIVATORS POSTULATE: Affects have innately stored affect programs, whose profiles are described by the model of density of neural stimulation, that are triggered by any inner or outer source that produces: (a) specific non-optimum levels or (b) specific accelerating or (c) decelerating gradients of neural firing, which are the specific causal triggers of discrete affects.

DEFINITION OF THE DENSITY PRINCIPLE: Innate activators of affect have general characteristics that are described by a single principle: *changes in the density (the number of neural firings per unit of time) of neural firing or stimulation*, with three distinct classes as variants of this principle—stimulation acceleration, stimulation deceleration, and nonoptimal levels of stimulation.

GENERAL FUNCTION OF AFFECTS POSTULATE: Since discrete affects evolved by promoting inclusive fitness and have general functions, specific affects in the sexual scene have general functions that can be described abstractly for positive affect as making a good scene "more so," including amplifying human sexual response, and, for negative affect, as making a bad scene "more so," including attenuating human sexual response.

FUNCTION OF SURPRISE–STARTLE COROLLARY: When activated by a critical bandwidth of extremely rapid, accelerating neural firing, the inherently somewhat negative startle response is an interrupter mechanism that clears the central assembly during the sexual scene; attention is refocused on the source of surprise; surprise is ancillary to every other affect, since its ordinarily neutral qualia will be positive or negative as a function of: (a) turning attention to the interrupting source and the interpretation of that source in a sexual scene, and (b) the discrete affect that is instigated following surprise, such as excitement or fear or anger.

FUNCTION OF FEAR COROLLARY: When fear–terror is activated by any relatively rapid, accelerating inner or outer source within a sexual scene, the major function of fear's toxicity and urgency is to motivate the reduction of the toxic state as quickly as possible by: (a) avoidance, experienced as frozen immobility in terror, which keeps the person from moving closer to danger, and (b) escape and flight from the source of danger if or when the terror is transient, abating to fear.

FUNCTION OF INTEREST–EXCITEMENT COROLLARY: When interest in sexual objects is activated by any relatively slowly accelerating inner or outer source, it motivates entry into a sexual scene; the function of excitement within the sexual scene is to amplify and make more urgent the already intense sexual stimulation in the scene, often by shifting the exciting focus of attention from sexual sensations to sexual perceptions, to sexual motor movements, to sexual conceptions, to sexual imagery, memories, and fantasies in a *changing* sampling of the exciting sexual object.

ACCELERATING GRADIENTS COROLLARY: Because surprise–startle, fear–terror, and interest–excitement are each activated by accelerating gradients of neural firing, there is an unstable equilibrium among them, creating familiar sequences such as startle, quickly beginning and ending, followed by fear that is longer lasting, and then by interest or excitement that can be maintained still longer in a sexual scene.

THE INNATE FUNCTION OF JOY COROLLARY: Given that any relatively steep deceleration of neural firing produces joy, whereas any gradual reduction of stimulation produces a neutral state or indifference, then a sudden and steep reduction of sexual pleasure and excitement, as in orgasm, innately activates the smile of joy, but a gradual reduction of sexual pleasure and excitement produces a neutral state or indifference; sudden relief from pain, fear, and distress will elicit a smile of joy as a smile of relief within a sexual scene.

THE LEARNED FUNCTION OF JOY COROLLARY: Within a sexual scene the function of enjoyment–joy, when modularly linked with the minding system, is to activate inherently acceptable and rewarding enjoyment by: (a) serving as a *name* (a message sufficient to retrieve a memory from a specific address in a neural store) of stored feedback of components of affective and sexual response (including the smile of joy, but also memories and motor patterns of familiar sensual pleasure) that translates such awarenesses into motor messages (the smile or patterns of touching or movement) that expand and match the stored compression; (b) serving as an inherently rewarding amplifier of enjoyment whenever any anticipation or recollection, first, triggers sufficiently intense excitement, and second, then is suddenly reduced by recognition that what is novel and of interest is also familiar as a recurrence or anticipated denouement, triggering the smile of joy; and (c) serving to elicit a bonding mutuality of shared smiling and social satisfaction that is both similar to and different enough from the enjoyment created by sexual intercourse to amplify sources of sensory pleasure that are also inherently social in providing satisfaction simultaneously for both other and self through shared sociosexual activity.

THE HABITUATION COROLLARY: Affects activated by accelerating (surprise, fear, excitement) or a decelerating gradient (enjoyment) of neural stimulation *habituate* (demonstrating a decreased responsiveness, with generalization and spontaneous recovery) following massed and repeated activation by the same source; whereas affects activated by nonoptimal level of dense neural firing (distress and anger) fail to habituate to repeated, massed exposures to the same source.

THE FUNCTION OF DISTRESS COROLLARY: Distress–anguish functions to make a sexual scene one that is filled with unpleasantly dense and ongoing neural stimulation from a variety of inner or outer sources (such as fatigue, pain, unrelieved sexual drive deprivation, and anticipation of loss) that trigger the cry of distress: (a) communicating to the actor and to the alter that all is not well in the sexual scene, and (b) motivating both the self and partner to reduce the crying response, but with a degree of toxicity that is tolerable for both. Distress may attenuate sexual pleasure, but accelerating sexual excitement can also mask distress, and orgasm can reduce accumulated excitement and distress, thereby producing both smiles and tears or mixed cries of sexual relief.

THE FUNCTIONS OF FEAR–DISTRESS COROLLARY: Whereas fear–terror is a toxic affect that is triggered by great risk of danger and at great cost and that requires immediate emergency responses of avoidance of or escape from danger, distress–anguish is a less toxic affect that speaks to the ubiquity of human suffering from any source that triggers a nonoptimal, high level of dense neural firing; distress permits the human being to cope with and solve disagreeable problems, without habituating, but also without the high level of psychic risk and biologic cost of fear–terror.

THE FUNCTION OF ANGER COROLLARY: Because of its social consequences, anger–rage is the most socially problematic and toxic of affects
within a sexual scene. Its problematic nature arises both from the innate
nature of anger and from minding (as knowing and caring) about its
nature and consequences. The social toxicity of anger and rage stems
from a conjunction of several innate characteristics of anger: (a) it has
an innate high intensity; (b) the total density of nonoptimal neural firing
is doubled because the high intensity activator is summed with the high
intensity affective response; (c) the summated intensity may be endlessly
sustained and prolonged; (d) the responses to anger are innately imprinted with the doubled intensity of the activator and the affect; (e)
both the imprinting of the doubled intensity of the neural firing of
summed activator and anger on the response to anger *and* the sustained
duration of the anger response increase the difficulty of controlling both
anger and aggression (an overt response intended to produce injury in
others that is sometimes dependent on anger, sometimes independent of
anger, and sometimes interdependent with anger); (f) the expression of
either anger or aggression or both is innately contagious; and (g) the
innate contagion of anger from actor to alter is innately capable of
escalating both anger and aggression in sequential steps. Also, (a) anger
and aggressive acts within a sexual scene may produce lasting damage
to the relationship or to the victim; (b) any expression of anger or aggression is regarded as a threat to the social relationship or to the
social order; and (c) highly developed societies ideologically monopo-
lize the use of violence as acceptable only when used by legitimate authority.

DEFINITION OF AUXILIARY AFFECTS: *Auxiliary affects* are supplementary affects, still in the process of evolving, that are subsidiary to
either drives (disgust and dissmell) or other affects (shame) in their
development and activation; these drive or affect auxiliaries serve both
self-motivating and other-signaling functions of rejection.

THE SHAME COROLLARY: Operating only after interest–excitement
or enjoyment–joy have been activated in a sexual scene, the innate activator of shame is the incomplete reduction of excitement and joy; such a
barrier may attenuate the intensity of these positive affects sufficiently
to end the sexual scene or may be only temporary and be overcome
within the sexual scene. The innate affect of shame is signaled by the
lowering of the eyelids, of the tonus of muscles in the face, and of the
head and is experienced as feedback primarily from the skin of the face;
this affect program may be centrally assembled with different sources,
targets, responses, and consequences that produce variables as alternatives to the theoretical construct of shame (or patterned variants of the

innate affect program for the shame response), including: shyness over the strangeness of the sexual act or object, shame as sexual inferiority, shame as sexual discouragement, shame as anticipated failure, shame as sexual loss, and shame as anticipated sexual guilt or remorse over moral transgression.

DEFINITIONS OF DISGUST AND DISSMELL: *Disgust* and *dissmell* (a word coined by Tomkins) are innate defensive responses that are auxiliary to the hunger, thirst, and oxygen drives, but also highly generalizable to learned stimuli. Dissmell, which is signaled by the lifting of the upper lip, the wrinkling of the nose, and withdrawal of the head, is an early-warning system that the sexual object or response is aversive as bad smelling; disgust, which is signaled by the lowering of the jaw, the protrusion of the tongue, and the head moving forward, is an innate defensive response to a sexual object or a sexually overt or recruited response that has been contacted, tasted, or ingested. Digital contact with bodily fluids, or kissing, licking, or sucking, or fellatio, cunnilingus, anilingus, and coition that elicit learned disgust create stimulus or symbol generalization, which may include the sexual alter as the source of disgust.

THE DISGUST COROLLARY: When disgust is activated in sexual scenes, it interrupts overt sexual activity or attenuates human sexual response, or both, either temporarily or permanently, with complete rejection of activity or object increasing over time if the disgust continues to be activated; disgust, however, may be either: (a) *attenuated* by proportionally more dense excitement, or (b) *habituated* when the attractiveness of alter or the love of alter succeeds in maintaining the contact in spite of the initial disgust until the disgust attentuates, the appetitiveness of activity or object increases, and excitement is released from attenuation and further amplified.

THE DISSMELL COROLLARY: When dissmell is activated in sexual scenes, the sexual partner or sexual activity itself is rejected, with the actor attempting to maintain a permanent distance, given his or her dissmelling alienation from the object.

TOXICITY OF SHAME-DISGUST-DISSMELL COROLLARY: As invested in sexual objects, shame is briefer and less toxic than disgust or dissmell; disgust is a relatively toxic and frequently implicated affect in sexual scenes, but it remains neglected in the treatment of sexual dysfunction and in discord among sexual partners; dissmell is still more toxic than disgust in sexual scenes, creating loss of sexual desire, personal alienation, divorce, prejudice, and hatred toward the alien other. When dissmell is combined with rage, it creates the sexual hatred of some men whose rage produces disorganized lust murders but whose dissmell prevents penile penetration but permits masturbation.

THE DISTANCE AND TIME COROLLARY: Tomkins conceptually distinguished shame from disgust from dissmell along dimensions of *distance* and *duration* of rejection of objects. In sexual scenes: (a) shame is an interruption and partial attentuation of exciting or enjoyable close contact and is only a temporary barrier to the return to the communion of mutually shared excitement and enjoyment, (b) disgust is ambivalent in direction, involving both a taking in and an ejecting of objects, and is intermediate in its duration of rejection of the object and variable in its dynamics of distance, and (c) dissmell involves a permanent rejection at a great distance from the object.

THE GENERALITY OF AFFECT INVESTMENT COROLLARY: Although the positive affects of interest–excitement and enjoyment–joy are the discrete affects most commonly associated with sexual desire, experience, and action, any affect, any combination of affects, or any affect complex — affects that are joined with cognitions about source, response, and meanings — could be invested in sexual objects.

BARRIERS TO DEPTH OF INVOLVEMENT

BARRIERS TO INVOLVEMENT POSTULATE: Within an unfolding sexual scene, some events, activities, or transactions that mismatch — a poor degree of fit — the sexual image may serve as a temporary or permanent barrier to deepening involvement in the sexual scene.

DEFINITION OF BARRIERS: A *barrier* to deepening involvement in a sexual scene is any event, activity, transaction, or recruited inner response that: (a) mismatches the regnant sexual image or regnant sexual script, and (b) triggers negative affect.

PERMEABILITY OF BARRIERS COROLLARY: Permeable barriers delay human sexual response, instituting a search for alternatives; impermeable barriers produce consequent failure to reach desired outcomes.

DUPLICATION POSTULATE: Because the individual is motivated to duplicate the sexual image, mismatched feedback directs an increasing hierarchical search from *responses* to *tactics* to *strategies*; thus, duplication may require: (a) new overt and recruited responses attempting to minimize the differences to zero, (b) tactical changes in plans designed to achieve the same image by the same or alternative paths, and (c) strategic changes in scripts designed to achieve alternative images, whether sexual or not.

DUPLICATION OUTCOME COROLLARY: Given a barrier to depth of involvement, the ability to duplicate any desired sexual image in the scene is a function of: (a) the density and toxicity of the negative affect that is triggered, (b) scripted resources to cope with barriers and to repair damage to the scene, and (c) competition for regnance from other scripts, including Dysfunction-Magnified Scripts.

DYSFUNCTION-MAGNIFIED SCRIPTS: A script that results from psychological magnification of scenes containing acquired sexual arousal or orgasmic failures resulting from an unexpected barrier to involvement. A typically good sexual scene has suddenly turned bad and is momentously bad for the future.

NEGATIVE AFFECT POSTULATE: Negative affect that is activated by a barrier attenuates human sexual response by both: (a) directly attenuating sexual arousal, and (b) indirectly amplifying both the barrier as a source of negative affect and the responses to that source and to the affect itself.

TOXICITY OF AFFECTS POSTULATE: The toxicity of negative affect is directly proportional to its biological urgency and inversely proportional to its relative frequency of activation.

RANKED-TOXICITY COROLLARY: Among the discrete negative affects, toxicity is ranked into four grades of potential toxicity: (a) extremely toxic: fear–terror, anger–rage, and dissmell, in that decreasing order, (b) highly toxic: disgust, (c) moderately toxic: distress–anguish, and (d) mildly toxic: shame (Tomkins, 1991, pp. 195–196).

ACTUAL TOXICITY COROLLARY: The actual degree of toxicity experienced in the sexual scene would be a function of (a) the specific frequency, intensity, and duration of specific negative affects, given their relative levels of toxicity, (b) the psychological magnification and dysfunctionality of scripts associated with the affect, and (c) the *resonance*—mutual amplification through time—of affect and ideology.

UNFAVORABLE RATIO POSTULATE: A relatively toxic sexual script develops when an individual has: (a) experienced an unfavorable ratio of negative to positive affects within a family of sexual scenes, (b) experienced dense and ungraded doses of a specific negative affect, and (c) learned no scripted rules for repairing the toxicity of negative affect and for restoring positive affect and outcomes.

ANALOGS COROLLARY: The members of the families of scenes in relatively toxic sexual scripts proliferate by the *principle of analogs*—imposing similarity on scenic elements in new and changing sexual scenes that might be different yet seem somehow similar (unconsciously analogous) to the old scene that evoked negative affect or positive-to-negative affect sequences.

IMPERMEABLE BARRIERS POSTULATE: Impermeable barriers in sexual scenes evoke specific negative affects that (a) attenuate, prevent, or completely inhibit sexual response and coping responses, and (b) motivate escape or avoidance responses.

AFFECT AS CHANGE-AMPLIFYING POSTULATE: Affect is a mechanism that: (a) amplifies *change* in a sexual scene as an abstract and general source of the affect, (b) amplifies sexual responses to any source of change that triggers positive affect, and (c) amplifies the affect itself as well as any ongoing or recruited responses.

AFFECT AS CORRELATING POSTULATE: Affect in sexual scenes connects source and response by imprinting the response with the same profile of amplification and discrete qualia that it imprints on its activator; this is a structural correlation.

AMPLIFYING-CORRELATING COROLLARY: Positive discrete affects invested in sexual objects as source and target amplify both source and responses, making the source more sexy and the responses more sexual, and thus both more similar to one another as erotic and sexually correlated.

AMPLIFICATION COMPARED TO MAGNIFICATION POSTULATE: Since affect is organized by abstract and general innate scripts, its capacity to amplify change and to correlate source and response is limited in comparison to the minding system's freedom to connect and reamplify through magnification the consequential change in affect dynamic within a family of scenes.

MAGNIFICATION AS CHANGE-OF-CHANGE POSTULATE: Magnification is the change-of-change, a reamplifying of already once amplified change by fresh affect invested in the rules that order information about that change; according to Tomkins (1991, p. 176), "Magnification is to amplification as acceleration is to velocity."

SCRIPT CHANGE COROLLARY: Changing personality must center primarily on changing scripts, with their psychologically magnified rules for ordering changing information in connected families of scenes, because magnification, as the change of change, is a more potent dynamic operator than amplification.

MAGNIFIED SEXUAL DYSFUNCTION SCRIPTS

SCRIPT DYNAMIC OF SEXUAL DYSFUNCTION SCRIPTS POSTULATE: Any good sexual scene turned bad — positive sexual affect that is suddenly interrupted and transformed to negative affect — creates a dense change in affects, that, if repeated — by finding recurrent analogs in actual scenes, or in anticipated possible future scenes, or in remembered past bad scenes, or in remembered scenes that are now prophetic analogs of the recent bad scene — begins the process of psychological magnification: (a) connecting good-scenes-turned-bad by rules ordering information in that family, and (b) reamplifying those scenes and their rules with fresh negative affect that is not necessarily the same affect that was triggered in the original scene.

GROWTH OF MAGNIFICATION POSTULATE: The rate of growth in potential magnification of a Sexual Dysfunction Script is a function of: (a) the types of the individual's scripts, (b) the type of disconfirmation of the rules, and (c) the magnitude of disconfirmation of the rules.

SEX-NEGATIVE SCRIPT'S EFFECT COROLLARY: When either predominant or regnant, all Sex-Negative Scripts (such as those above): (a) create barriers to increasing the state (or an overall greater depth) of involvement in a sexual scene, (b) trigger negative affect, and (c) attenuate or prevent sexual responses.

RECRUITED SCRIPTS IN MAGNIFIED-DYSFUNCTION COROLLARY: The modularity of scripts and their capacity for decomposing and recombining increase the potential for psychological magnification of a sexually good-scene-turned-bad by potentially recruiting: (a) a Sexual Change-Review Script (e.g., "My sex life will never be the same again, because" " . . . I'm too old to get an erection," or "My husband has never loved me," (b) a Sexual Affect Control Script (in which sexual affect is controlled by shame, guilt, disgust, or fear), (c) a Sex-Negative Ideological Script (e.g., Jehovanist Ideology Script), and (d) a dominant Sexual Ratio Script.

TYPES OF DISCONFIRMATION COROLLARY: The type of disconfirmation is a function of: (a) the discrete affect that is activated and amplifying the source of change in the scene, and (b) recruited perceptual, analyzer, and memory responses that interpret and evaluate the meanings of the source and the responses to the source and to the affect according to multiple criteria of correspondence, coherence, and invention.

MAGNIFICATION OF DISCONFIRMATION POSTULATE: The magnitude of disconfirmation is a function of: (a) the density and toxicity of the activated affect, and (b) the dynamic operator that is disconfirmed.

DEFINITION OF A DYNAMIC OPERATOR: Affect invests value in objects; the magnitude of the increase in value is a function of four specific *dynamic operators*: (a) *amplification* makes object "more so," (b) *magnification* makes object "more so through time," (c) *idealization* makes object "most so through time," and (d) *sacralization* consecrates object as timeless and supreme in value.

SOCIAL AND SEXUAL DYNAMICS IN COUPLES

THE CO-CREATION POSTULATE: An interpersonal sexual scene is co-created by two (or more) individuals, each with his/her own sexual scripts that represent a desired sexual image that governs each individual's scripted effort to produce, predict, interpret, direct, manage, defend, or evaluate the unfolding scene.

THE NEGOTIATION COROLLARY: The specific sexual transactions — who will do what, when, and to whom — are seldom verbally negotiated, but when they depart from an individual's acceptable range of anticipated social sexual scripts, the individual will commence negotiations with the partner.

DISTINCT MEANINGS COROLLARY: The co-created sexual scene may produce distinct interpretations, meanings, consequences, and evaluations for each actor.

DISTINCT OUTCOMES COROLLARY: The outcome for each actor in the co-created sexual scene is distinct from the outcome of the other since it is a function of the degree of fit of the expanded scene to each individual's sexual image; outcomes of sexual images, however, may be scripted as relatively independent of, dependent on, or interdependent with the partner's outcomes.

THE SEXUAL INCOMPATIBILITY POSTULATE: Partners are sexually incompatible: (a) within a scene, if their sexual images are mismatched, if their interpersonal responses are noncomplementary, or if their contexts for the scene are mismatched; (b) within a relationship, if their sexual and interpersonal scripts are mismatched or noncomplementary.

PATH INCOMPATIBILITY COROLLARY: The actors' preferred sexual paths and corresponding images may or may not be compatible or reconcilable; incompatibility can result from the general and relative preference for the path of role-enactment by men and for the path of partner-engagement by women.

CONTEXT COROLLARY: The present sexual scene with this partner is nested in a space-time context: (a) through recruited memory of both the immediate and remote past, within: (1) a family of both sexual and nonsexual scenes involving this partner, and (2) a family of both sexual and nonsexual scenes with past sexual partners; and (b) through anticipation of the immediate and remote, sexual and nonsexual, possible futures (1) with this partner, and (2) with others.

DEFINITION OF CONTEXT: In the minding system, a scene is a level that is embedded within a meta-level as: (a) a *description* is to a *point of view*, (b) a *picture* is to a *frame*, and (c) *meaning* is to *context*; the context of any unfolding scene is provided by the family of connected immediate and remote, past and future scenes.

NESTED INVOLVEMENT POSTULATE: Although involvement is experienced subjectively as a state in the here and now, *involvement* is also: (a) as a construct, sequentially unfolding within the quantum of the unfolding scene as hear-and-now moments, and (b) as the product of a script, nested in the space-time of a life as history and possibility.

TIME-INTEGRATION COROLLARY: Coherent sampling and integration across time of conversational, transactional, and sexual interactions by both parties must occur in the sexual scene if the intended meaning of the partner's transactions are successfully communicated (have their intended effect).

SELF-FULFILLMENT POSTULATE: Affluent sexual scripts permit frequent sexual self-fulfillment since they increase the number of alternative plans within alternative paths and the set of interpersonal and sexual skills needed to achieve complementarity with the partner; relatively toxic sexual scripts make positive outcomes less likely.

SELF-VALIDATION POSTULATE: Unfavorable Ratio Sexual Scripts produce more self-validation than self-fulfillment, proving to the self that the rules of the script have once again predicted (and produced) an analog scene that is interpreted and evaluated as expectedly negative in a particular and familiar way.

ASSIMILATION-ACCOMMODATION COROLLARY: To achieve sexual and self-fulfillment, an individual may need either (a) to assimilate the partner's actions and events to the script, or (b) to accommodate to the scene as much as the scripted degree of conditionality permits.

DEFINITION OF ASSIMILATION: *Assimilation* is the process of transforming the interpretation and evaluation of events in the sexual scene to fit the sexual script; using imagination, fantasy, or denial, the actual scene is made congruent with the desired sexual image.

DEFINITION OF ACCOMMODATION: *Accommodation* is the process of transforming the variable functions in the sexual script to fit events in the sexual scene or of altering the sexual plan or path so that the expectation of the desired image is realigned with what is possible in the unfolding scene.

ORGANIZING PSYCHOSEXUAL THERAPY

In brief, the following overlapping steps organize sex therapy from the perspective of script theory:

1. Create a playful and creative therapeutic context.
2. For each partner, assess the Sexual Dysfunction Scene, using a present-centered approach to the landscapes of action and consciousness.
3. For each partner, assess the Preferred Sexual Scene to identify goal changes in conditions and variables.
4. Assess path preferences using the *Sexual Path Preferences Inventory*.
5. Using information from the SPPI and the Preferred Sexual Scene, develop strategies and tactics for deepening involvement in the preferred path and for increasing an optimal density and sequencing of sexual activities.
6. Search for points of overlap in partners' preferences and negotiate to reduce incompatibility in paths and images.
7. Note all barriers to deepening involvement and eliminate or reduce these sources of negative affect.
8. Examine the pattern of rules in all sex-negative scripts for possible reordering of rules.

THE POTENTIAL OF SCRIPT THEORY

Script theory promises a mother lode to any psychotherapist who seeks and discovers its wealth of nuggets. Tomkins's theoretical genius spawned a grand theory of affect, minding, and personality. My own tasks are to help systematize the theory, to translate faithfully the constructs into measurable variables, and to apply the theory to the phenomena of gender and sexuality. But the prospecting has just begun. Tomkins's theory of addiction can clarify the so-called sexual addictions. Tomkins's view of plurideterminism is crucial in understanding the psychosexual trauma of sexual abuse and rape. Some of the purest ore to be mined by script theory awaits the prospector who seeks to typify various forms of sexual pathology through the personological study of individuals.

If you like what you read in this chapter and book, then read and study Silvan Tomkins's four volumes on *Affect, Imagery, Consciousness*; your scholarship will reward you with excitement and joy at the esthetic beauty of this golden theory.

REFERENCES

Masters, W. H., & Johnson, V. E. (1966). *Human sexual response*. Boston: Little, Brown.

Mosher, D. L. (1980). Three dimensions of depth of involvement in human sexualresponse. *The Journal of Sex Research, 16*, 1–42.

Mosher, D. L. (1988). Sexual Path Preferences Inventory. In C. M. Davis, W. L. Yarber, & S. L. Davis (Eds.), *Sexuality-related measures: A compendium* (pp. 225–227). Lake Mills, IA: Graphic Press.

Tomkins, S. S. (1962). *Affect, imagery, consciousness, Vol. 1: The positive affects*. New York: Springer.

Tomkins, S. S. (1963). *Affect, imagery, consciousness, Vol. 2: The negative affects*. New York: Springer.

Tomkins, S. S. (1979). Script theory: Differential magnification of affects. In H. E. Howe, Jr., & R. A. Dienstbier (Eds.), *Nebraska Symposium on Motivation*, Vol. 26. Lincoln, NE: University Press.

Tomkins, S. S. (1987). Script theory. In J. Aronoff, A. J. Rubin, & R. A. Zucker (Eds.), *The emergence of personality*. New York: Springer.

Tomkins, S. S. (1991). *Affect, imagery, consciousness, Vol. 3: The negative affects: Anger and fear*. New York: Springer.

Tomkins, S. S. (1992). *Affect, imagery, consciousness, Vol. 4: Cognition*. New York: Springer.

6

Empirical Studies
of Shame and Guilt:
The Internalized Shame Scale

David R. Cook

One of the most difficult problems facing the student of emotion is bridging the difference between innate affect and its adult manifestations. Historically, the importance of infantile affect display as the precursor of adult emotion had been overlooked, largely because infants are unable to describe in adult language the feeling states that accompany these patterns of display. Similarly, the importance of facial display in the adult was ignored because everyone knew how easy it was to dissemble, to fake the display of an affect one did not really feel. In general, studies of emotion involved parameters that could be studied with ease, like pulse rate, respiration, and the intensity of sweating as measured by the galvanic skin response, or the verbal forms through which adults expressed their feelings.

When a graduate student asked Dr. Cook how to go about measuring the importance of shame experience in the formation of an individual's personality, this professor with a career-long interest in cognition turned suddenly into a rapt student of emotion. Previous shame scales had been based on analysis of the frequency with which shame-related words appeared in the conversation or writing of an individual, or on the reaction of those being tested to specific situations thought to involve shame and standardized as the responses of normal college students.

Recognizing that certain shame experiences seemed more painful than others, and that for each person the degree of such pain seemed consistent, Cook went about the problem quite differently. Working from clinical examples provided in the work of psychologist Gershen Kaufman and psychoanalyst Léon Wurmser, he culled from their case descriptions statements that seemed to convey these intense forms of shame. Using affect theory as an overall description of human emotion, Kaufman had introduced the idea that the degree of psychopathology was roughly proportional to the degree to which shame affect had become internalized within the personality. Thus, Cook called his new test "The Internalized Shame Scale."

Tinkering with the ISS as new information about shame appeared in the literature, he ended up with the 30-item questionnaire now used widely throughout our field. An actor in local community theaters and a gifted clinician, Cook, like all of us who have studied shame, began to see it everywhere. In this chapter, he compares the ISS to other published shame scales and shows how his own understanding of his test has changed as he has mastered affect theory.   –DLN

OF ALL THE INNATE AFFECTS, shame is the most ubiquitous in clinical populations. As the affect that is triggered when there is an impediment to the continuation of either of the positive affects, shame would seem to be implicated in practically all disorders for which people seek treatment.

Although the empirical study of shame in a clinical population can be traced back at least to Helen Lewis's (1971) work, until quite recently there has been a dearth of research on shame. The lack of a sound psychometric instrument to measure shame has been a primary impediment to this research. This appears to be changing with the publication in the past few years of a number of studies reporting on measures of both shame and guilt (Harder, Cutler, & Rockart, 1992; Harder & Lewis, 1987; Hoblitzelle, 1987; Kugler & Jones, 1992; Tangney, 1990; Tangney, Wagner, & Gramzow, 1992).

My own measure, the Internalized Shame Scale (ISS) (Cook, 1987, 1994), is the only measure of shame that has been used extensively with clinical populations where issues of shame are most salient. Although relatively little of the research involving the ISS has been published in professional journals, the scale has been introduced in one book (Harper & Hoopes, 1990) and has been used in about a half dozen published articles and over 30 doctoral dissertations either completed or in progress. The scale has been requested for use in research and clinical work in a number of countries, including England, Portugal, Germany, Slovenia, Poland, Australia, and China. It has been translated into Chinese and used in one published study by a Chinese psychologist. Unfortunately, most of the studies to be reviewed here were carried out without knowledge of the ISS. Nevertheless, they provide considerable comparative data that contribute both to our understanding of adult shame and to the validity of the ISS as a measure of internalized shame.

In this chapter I review some empirical studies addressing shame, guilt, and pride—the so-called "self-conscious" emotions. I place the development of the ISS in a context that includes data from these studies. The general frame of reference for most of these studies is the hypothesized relation of shame and guilt to psychopathology. While there is a remarkable convergence in the data to be reviewed here, the theoretical framework underlying the previous work is inadequate.

Few empirical studies of shame utilize Tomkins's affect theory as the basis for hypotheses and the interpretion of data. One result of this is the failure to understand guilt as a variant of shame. Instead shame and guilt are treated as independent enough emotions to warrant separate measurement constructs in the investigation of psychopathology. (Similarly, an empirical study of pride reviewed below fails to consider its relation to the positive affects of excitement and joy.) Psychologists who use a cognitive approach to the understanding of emotions place shame and pride later in development and believe that they are triggered by self-evaluation that requires a level of cognitive development that comes about some time after infancy.

In my opinion, the investigation of guilt as a separate construct is an empirical dead-end for the study of psychopathology. The focus should be on the one primary emotion of shame. As we will see in the following pages, research on shame, especially the ISS, has implications for clinical assessment and practice.

SHAME, GUILT, AND PRIDE

Cognitively-based emotion theorists consider shame, guilt, and pride to be the so-called "self-conscious emotions" (Tangney & Fisher, 1993). As such, these emotions cannot manifest themselves until the individual has developed cognitive capacity sufficient to allow for self-evaluation. They are, in other terms, "secondary" emotions, presumably not "hardwired" into our biology as are the "primary" emotions. This viewpoint is difficult to square with infant-based emotion theory and accounts for the confusion resulting in and from research that assumes that shame and guilt are two separate and distinct emotions.

The difficulty with these constructs is readily resolvable once the distinction between an *affect* and an *emotion* is understood. Shame, as a primary affect, is meaning-free and triggered by anything that impedes the continuation of interest or enjoyment. The characteristic facial expression that is part of the biological script for shame involves the lowering of the eyelids, head turned down, gaze averted, and the blush. With development comes the "software" of life experiences that ensure the modulation of all the primary affects and their differentiation and coassembly in ever more complex relations.

The core affect of guilt, embarrassment, shyness, discouragement, and humiliation is shame, but the coassembly of perceptions, cognitions, and intentions into any of these emotions can be vastly different. "Try as we might," says Nathanson (1992), "we have been unable to find a physiological mechanism, an innate affect, that would explain guilt in any way other than its relation to shame" (p. 144).

Guilt involves a moment of discovery or exposure of what one might wish to hide, this need itself a certain sign that shame is involved in guilt. But if the infant can experience shame affect from birth, the experience of guilt requires that " . . . the child must *know* that s/he has *performed an action* and that this action has *caused harm* to *another person*. . . . This series of cognitions is possible only quite late in development, considerably later than the period at which innate shame develops and with it the elements from which adult shame is assembled" (Nathanson, 1987, p. 46, emphasis in original).

Guilt, according to Nathanson, results from the coassembly of shame with fear of reprisal or punishment. The fear of punishment, of course, stems from the recognition that one has violated some rule, standard, or boundary. The shame experience is much more about the failure of the self. This is a widely agreed-upon phenomenological distinction. Nonetheless, the sense of shame as a failure of the self is itself the result of appraisals of shame affect that become possible with cognitive development. In fact, our concept of shame emotions is so intertwined with the idea of the self that it is difficult to understand the significance of shame as a biologically based affect, present in infants and meaning-free, as are all the primary affects.

Nathanson (1987) suggests:

To find the origin of guilt one must determine at what point in development the infant is able to understand the object is also a person with a self, and that this person is capable of experiencing discomfort much as does the infant. If we are to accept that the reference standard for guilt is the ideal relationship, then guilt cannot appear in development until the child masters the concept of a relationship. (p. 46)

At the positive end of the affect spectrum, cognitively oriented psychologists consider pride to be a distinct and later appearing emotion because it is triggered by the evaluative function of recognizing that a goal has been successfully achieved. From the perspective of affect theory, pride is the affect of enjoyment–joy released under three conditions: (1) a goal-directed intentional activity is undertaken under the influence of interest–excitement; (2) the activity is successful in achieving the goal; and (3) the achievement of the goal releases the individual from the preceding effort, triggering enjoyment–joy (Nathanson, 1992). When affects are studied from the perspective of infants, these so-called "self-conscious" or "self-evaluative" emotions can be observed much earlier than cognitive theorists find them. Nathanson cites references suggesting that pride can be observed easily in the three-to-four-month-old infant, or whenever a baby is old enough to try something "on purpose."

If children can set standards and goals at very early ages, then they can experience guilt and pride at very early stages – well before the development of the capacity for a full cognitive appraisal of their actions. Michael Lewis (1992), a cognitively oriented psychologist, reports observing highly goal-oriented behavior in a one-year-old. He cites research suggesting that by age three children will already have their own sets of standards, rules, and goals, and will show "distress" when they violate them.

Lewis reports a laboratory experiment with two-and-one-half-year-old children in which an experimenter leaves a room after informing the child not to look at a very attractive toy that has been placed behind him/her. Most of the children looked at the toy when alone and at least 65% of these children told the experimenter upon his return that they did not look. Videotapes of the children's faces just after they looked reveal "indications of guilt: a lowering of the eyes, no smile, and a certain tension in the body" (p. 68). This expression waned by the time the experimenter reentered the room and was replaced by a more "neutral or innocent" expression. The "guilty" expression reveals the coassembly of shame (lowered eyes) with fear (tension in the body) that Nathanson has hypothesized as characteristic of guilt.

Lewis, Alessandri, and Sullivan (1992) cite the studies of shame and pride in children aged two to five years conducted by Heckhausen and his associates. Based on facial and bodily action, Heckhausen observed both shame and pride in children as early as 27 months. Pride was indicated by raising of the eyes, a smile, and a look of triumph. Proud children sat straight up and threw their arms up in the air as if to inflate themselves. The shame reaction was defined as, "their bodies collapsing, the lowering of their heads, their eyes and hands become motionless and stay on the blocks. This coupled with tense general posture and a kind of Duchenne smile" (Geppert & Heckhausen, 1988, p. 1, quoted in Lewis et al., 1992). These reactions followed success or failure in a task, respectively.

Lewis and his colleagues extended Heckhausen's research to examine the occurrence of shame and pride in relation to the difficulty of a task and to the gender of their 33–37-month-old subjects. The presence of shame or pride was determined from scoring videotapes for the defined indicators. Shame was defined as "body collapsed, corners of the mouth are downward/lower lip tucked between teeth, eyes lowered with gaze downward or askance, withdrawal from task situation and negative self-evaluation (i.e., 'I'm no good at this')." Pride was defined as "erect posture (i.e., shoulders back and head up), smile — either open or closed mouth — eyes directed at parents, points at outcome or applauds, and positive self-evaluation (i.e., 'aah!' or 'I did it!')" (Lewis et al., 1992, p. 632). These definitions are in accord with the facial expressions associated with shame and enjoyment–joy, although the definition for shame also includes some indication of distress (corners of the mouth downward), with which shame is often coassembled.

The findings indicated that pride was never shown when subjects failed, and shame was never shown when subjects succeeded on a task. There was significantly more shame when failing the easy rather than the difficult tasks, and significantly more pride when successful in the difficult than the easy tasks. Pride at success was exhibited more often than shame at failure. Overall, females showed more emotion than males. However, while girls and boys exhibited equal amounts of pride, girls showed significantly more shame than boys, especially when failing the easy task.

The relation of task difficulty to expressed emotion indicates that by the age of three children are able to discriminate task difficulty, at some level, and are able to evaluate their behavior in terms of this factor. The researchers concluded that their findings supported their hypothesis that children's evaluative processes influence their emotional response.

From the perspective of affect theory, however, the influence of the so-called "evaluative processes" on the emotional response is more apparent than real. The novelty of the various tasks (easy and difficult) in the experiment would have been a trigger for interest (all tasks were done with a parent present, alternating mother and father). To the extent that the child became invested in succeeding at the task (perhaps increasing the gradient of intensity to "excitement") the "competence pleasure" of succeeding would be an ample trigger for joy exhibited as pride. The tasks were such that there was much more success with the easy than with the difficult tasks.

The shame reaction is more complicated. If shame is triggered when interest is incompletely reduced, then failure on any of the tasks could have impeded the continuation of interest and triggered shame affect. But why would more shame experiences be observed in the condition of failing the easy as opposed to the difficult task? One consideration bears on the coding system for arriving at the occurrence of either shame or pride. For an emotion to have "occurred," three out of five of the defined behaviors had to be observed within 30 seconds of task completion. Affects occur over a range of intensity (e.g., interest–excitement, enjoyment–joy). The intensity of shame affect is proportional to the intensity of the positive affect that is impeded. Thus, the more interest triggered by the task, the greater (i.e., more evident) would be the shame that is triggered when the interest was impeded by failure.

What remains beyond the triggering of the affect are all the "software"-mediated reactions to the shame affect. The fact that there were gender differences typical of the different ways boys and girls are socialized around emotions, even at this early age, suggests that what the observers were noting was the reactive phase of the shame experience, which involves a cognitive process, but is not itself a trigger for shame affect. Memories of previous experiences of success and failure at tasks could also be associated with the intensity of triggered shame or pride. But the capacity to modulate affect display, already developed in a three-year-old, would account for at least some of the variance in the coding of the occurrence of shame or pride, which were treated as all-or-nothing categories in the analysis.

The results of this study say a lot more about the socialization of emotions at an early age, particularly along gender lines, than they do about how learned self-evaluative cognitions "influence" or trigger emotion display at certain stages of development. While such variants as pride and guilt (deriving from enjoyment and shame) clearly require a development to appear, they are still rooted in the primary, "hardwired" affects identified by Tomkins. The software of development adds to the great complexity of emotional expression but does not change the basic biological substrate of emotions.

A study by Ferguson, Stegge, and Damhuis (1991) examined the understanding of guilt and shame in children between seven and twelve years old. Based on previous studies, they hypothesized that children would not be able to differentiate guilt from shame in their verbal reports until approximately ten or eleven years of age. Two studies were conducted. In the first, fifth-grade boys and girls were given various scenarios and asked a series of structured questions about them. Some of the scenarios were intended to promote reports of shame (social blunders, uncontrollable in nature), and some were moral transgressions of a controllable nature, intended to elicit reports of guilt. One finding indicated that the children responded with guilt significantly more often when the event was a transgression rather than a blunder, but they responded equally often with shame to both transgressions and blunders. Thus, these children feel ashamed both when they transgress a moral norm and when committing a faux pas, an outcome that confirms the overlap of shame with guilt.

Other results of this study convinced the researchers that ten-to-twelve-year-old children understand many of the distinctions that adults have been shown to draw between guilt and shame. Children were also able to differentiate guilt and shame, seeing guilt as related to violation of moral norms and shame as involving other people's knowing about the misdeed and possibly reacting negatively. This is clearly in keeping with Nathanson's (1987) definition of guilt as a combination of shame (wanting to hide the misdeed) and fear (of punishment for the transgression).

A second study by Ferguson et al. included second graders as well as fifth graders. The children were asked to sort statements descriptive of shame and guilt into boxes labeled "guilty," "ashamed," "guilty and ashamed," and "neither of these two." Results indicated that guilty feelings are associated by eight-to-twelve-year-olds with doing something wrong, regret, self-directed anger, and making amends. Both age groups associated shame with a fear of ridicule and feelings or facial expressions of embarrassment. Younger children showed a relatively greater concern with how others might react to them by associating both the shame and guilt statements with a desire for the behavior to remain undetected, not to confess, not to approach others, and not being able to control the emotions themselves (Ferguson et al., 1991).

These researchers raise an interesting question about the importance of learning to discriminate guilt from shame, recognizing that even psychologists do not always distinguish them. They see the importance of this differentiation as a response in which an adaptive level of guilt

> flag(s) a momentary break with our obligations to others and informs us to maintain our interpersonal relationships through approach and reparative action. Adaptive shame, in contrast, bears a different message involving at least temporary interpersonal with-

drawal and a rethinking of our actual abilities and attributes compared to how we would ideally like to be or behave. (p. 837)

Ten-to-twelve-year-old children appear to understand these adaptive implications and also to perceive shame as an emotion that significantly influences one's feelings of self-worth. Younger children, in contrast, are much more concerned with the reactions of others toward them in conditions of both guilt and shame.

From the way that guilt and shame are differentiated in the literature, it seems clear that the reparative possibilities for expiating guilt are much more direct and available to the individual than the reparative opportunities for ameliorating shame. Indeed, this is one reason why guilt and shame become confounded in those who are subjected to an excess of shame-triggering experiences. It also explains why shame experiences are more likely to be associated with psychopathological disorders than are guilt experiences (reliably resulting from controllable transgressions).

APPROACHES TO MEASURING SHAME AND GUILT

Several different approaches have been used to measure shame and/or guilt. One of the earliest methods was a quasi-projective measure developed by Gottschalk and Gleser (1969). In this method subjects are asked to speak for five minutes about some dramatic event in their life. Each clause of the verbal record is then scored for one of six types of anxiety. "Shame anxiety" is scored for clauses containing references to ridicule, inadequacy, shame, embarrassment, humiliation, overexposure of deficiencies or private details, or threat of such experience. This approach and a similar approach developed by Binder (1970) have also been applied to content from an "early memories test" developed by Mayman (1968) as a measure of shame or guilt. Harder and Lewis (1987) included these measures in their early research. They reported test-retest reliabilities (two weeks and five weeks) of .75 and .69 for the Binder approach and .24 and .14 for the Gottschalk report. Harder and Lewis also found that these approaches had inadequate construct validity. Ursu (1984), in her dissertation, also found that the Gottschalk method applied to the early memories test as a measure of shame failed to yield any construct validity. This approach to measuring shame has been pretty much discarded.

Perlman (1958) and Beall (1972) have generally been identified as the original developers of a large pool of items designed to measure shame.

Perlman's scale consisted of one-sentence items judged by experts to be descriptions of shame- or guilt-inducing situations. Subjects were asked how anxiety-provoking they believed each described situation would be for "most people." Beall's original test consisted of 103 items that were judged to stimulate either shame or guilt. Most of the items were situations (e.g., "You are criticized in front of your peers") to which respondents rated how "upset" they would be if they found themselves in that situation. A subset of these items, however, was descriptive of traits or characteristics (e.g., "I keep secrets and worry that they might be discovered"); respondents were to rate how characteristic each statement was of themselves. These two forms for items—situational or trait-related—were the forerunners for most of the scales developed subsequently.

Tangney's (1990) Self-Conscious Affect and Attribution Inventory (SCAAI) follows the situational format. The SCAAI consists of a series of negatively and positively valenced scenarios with multiple response options, two of which are representative of "shame-proneness" and "guilt-proneness." The scale was designed for a young adult college population, so a typical situation is the following: "A professor whom you admire asks a question in class. You raise your hand and give the wrong answer." The shame response is "You have the feeling that everyone is looking at you." The guilt response is "You feel annoyed with yourself for raising your hand and vow to study more for the next class."* The inventory yields scores for each of these response categories based on the scale rating for each.

Subsequent to this, Tangney developed the Test of Self-Conscious Affect (TOSCA), a revised version of the SCAAI constructed from subject-generated scenarios and responses. The two scales are considered "equivalent" by Tangney, though the TOSCA may be more "psychometrically sound."

A modified "trait" approach to measuring shame and guilt involves the use of adjectives as items. Hoblitzelle (1987) adapted a shame/guilt test (ASGS—Adapted Shame/Guilt Scale) first developed by Gioiella (1981), which consisted of a series of adjectives that were identified as either guilt words, shame words, or filler words. Through factor analysis, Hoblitzelle obtained an adapted version of 12 guilt words (e.g., condemned, immoral, delinquent, indecent, unscrupulous) and ten

---

*Nathanson has pointed out (personal communication) that both these responses represent shame. Guilt requires the idea of punishment, but in the case of the "guilt" response, shame is motivating the student to further study. Such subtle failures to distinguish shame from guilt probably account in part for the consistent overlap between the two types of measures.

shame words (bashful, mortified, shy, humiliated, abashed, embarrassed, depressed, chided, reproached, and ashamed). Items were rated
on a 7-point scale.

Harder's (Harder & Lewis, 1987) Personal Feelings Questionnaire
(PFQ) is a modified version of the adjective format. Shame items included the following: embarrassment; feeling ridiculous or laughable;
feeling humiliated, "stupid," or "childish"; feeling helpless or paralyzed;
feelings of blushing. A subsequent revision of this scale (PFQ2) expanded the original scale to the following items: embarrassed, feeling
ridiculous, self-consciousness, feeling humiliated, feeling "stupid," feeling "childish," feeling helpless/paralyzed, feelings of blushing, feeling
laughable, feeling disgusting to others (Harder & Zalma, 1990, p. 734).
Similar items were used to measure guilt.

The items on the ISS (Cook, 1987, 1994) were based on phenomenological descriptions of the shame experience. The items on the ISS followed the "trait" approach and were all couched in the intensely negative
language that characterizes descriptions of shame experiences (see Table
6.1). Subjects rate these items on a 5-point scale based on the frequency
of experiencing, from *never* to *almost always*.

One question that arises from the existence of a potentially large pool
of items purporting to measure shame and guilt is whether there is a
multiplicity of factors involved. One early investigation of this was Novak's (1986) dissertation. Novak administered to each of 310 college
undergraduates a 129-item scale consisting of items from the Beall and
Perlman scales as well as 33 items from a pilot version of the ISS.
Using both an exploratory and a confirmatory factor analysis, Novak
identified four basic clusters of items, which he labeled "situational
shame," "fear of exposure," "embarrassment," and "inferiority." All the
items in the situational shame cluster were from the Beall and Perlman
scales and described situations in which subjects indicated their degree of
anxiety. All the fear of exposure items were from the part of the Beall
item sample scaled according to how characteristic each statement was
of the respondent (e.g., "I worry about giving myself away"). All the
items on the embarrassment and inferiority clusters (except one) were
from the pilot version of the ISS.

Situational shame correlated .49 with fear of exposure, .28 with embarrassment, and .26 with inferiority. The intercorrelations among the
latter three clusters, however, were .64, .76, and .77. Situational shame
appeared to be a measure of "state shame," while the other three clusters
were more similar to "trait shame." The correlations suggested that there
was more to experiencing the shame state than could be accounted for by
high trait shame (i.e., internalized shame).

TABLE 6.1
Internalized Shame Scale (ISS)

NAME: _____ DATE: _____

DIRECTIONS: Below is a list of statements describing feelings or experiences that you may have from time to time or that are familiar to you because you have had these feelings and experiences for a long time. Most of these statements describe feelings and experiences that are generally painful or negative in some way. Some people will seldom or never have had many of these feelings. Everyone has had some of these feelings at some time, but if you find that these statements describe the way you feel a good deal of the time, it can be painful just reading them. Try to be as honest as you can in responding.

Read each statement carefully and circle the number to the left of the item that indicates the frequency with which you find yourself feeling or experiencing what is described in the statement. Use the scale below. DO NOT OMIT ANY ITEM.

SCALE

0	1	2	3	4
NEVER	SELDOM	SOMETIMES	OFTEN	ALMOST ALWAYS

SCALE

0 1 2 3 4   1.   I feel like I am never quite good enough.

0 1 2 3 4   2.   I feel somehow left out.

0 1 2 3 4   3.   I think that people look down on me.

0 1 2 3 4   4.   All in all, I am inclined to feel that I am a success.

0 1 2 3 4   5.   I scold myself and put myself down.

0 1 2 3 4   6.   I feel insecure about others' opinions of me.

0 1 2 3 4   7.   Compared to other people, I feel like I somehow never measure up.

0 1 2 3 4   8.   I see myself as being very small and insignificant.

0 1 2 3 4   9.   I feel I have much to be proud of.

0 1 2 3 4   10.   I feel intensely inadequate and full of self-doubt.

0 1 2 3 4   11.   I feel as if I am somehow defective as a person, like there is something basically wrong with me.

0 1 2 3 4   12.   When I compare myself to others I am just not as important.

(Continued)

TABLE 6.1
Continued

SCALE

0	1	2	3	4
NEVER	SELDOM	SOMETIMES	OFTEN	ALMOST ALWAYS

0 1 2 3 4   13. I have an overpowering dread that my faults will be revealed in front of others.

0 1 2 3 4   14. I feel I have a number of good qualities.

0 1 2 3 4   15. I see myself striving for perfection only to continually fall short.

0 1 2 3 4   16. I think others are able to see my defects.

0 1 2 3 4   17. I could beat myself over the head with a club when I make a mistake.

0 1 2 3 4   18. On the whole, I am satisfied with myself.

0 1 2 3 4   19. I would like to shrink away when I make a mistake.

0 1 2 3 4   20. I replay painful events over and over in my mind until I am overwhelmed.

0 1 2 3 4   21. I feel I am a person of worth at least on an equal plane with others.

0 1 2 3 4   22. At times I feel like I will break into a thousand pieces.

0 1 2 3 4   23. I feel as if I have lost control over my body functions and my feelings.

0 1 2 3 4   24. Sometimes I feel no bigger than a pea.

0 1 2 3 4   25. At times I feel so exposed that I wish the earth would open up and swallow me.

0 1 2 3 4   26. I have this painful gap within me that I have not been able to fill.

0 1 2 3 4   27. I feel empty and unfulfilled.

0 1 2 3 4   28. I take a positive attitude toward myself.

0 1 2 3 4   29. My loneliness is more like emptiness.

0 1 2 3 4   30. I feel like there is something missing.

Novak concluded from his analysis that there was no higher order factor, such as "malignant shame," associated with these three intercorrelated clusters, but that the higher order factor itself was "inferiority." Of all the theoretical pathways explored by Novak to explain the interrelation of these factors, the only one that made theoretical sense began with the experience of a deep sense of inferiority. The items tapping this dimension and that of embarrassment (extreme self-consciousness) were from the ISS pilot scale.

Kugler and Jones (1992) addressed the issues of trait vs. state emotions with regard to measuring guilt. Their Guilt Inventory assessed the domains of "trait guilt" (e.g., "Guilt and remorse have been a part of my life for as long as I can recall"); "state guilt" (e.g., "At the moment I don't feel particularly guilty about anything I have done"); and "moral standards" or subscribing to a code of moral principles (e.g., "I believe in a strict interpretation of right and wrong"). Since their aim was to develop a "pure" measure of guilt, they correlated their three guilt measures with other measures of guilt and shame (including an early version of the ISS), as well as with Izard's Differential Emotions Scale (Izard, 1977). Subjects in this research were college students (n = 832) and non-college adults (n = 209). Kugler and Jones found that both state guilt and trait guilt were significantly related to every measure of *guilt and shame* with which they were compared with the exception of "sex guilt." I will return to some of the specific data from this study later, but the important finding for this discussion was stated by the authors:

> Although the theoretical reasons for distinguishing guilt and shame remain, . . . strong empirical evidence supporting the conceptual distinction was not obtained in the present study using these instruments designed to measure shame and guilt. Instead, it was clear that just as for state and trait guilt, the two are strongly related. (Kugler & Jones, 1992, p. 324)

This analysis of the different approaches to the measurement of shame suggests some clear conclusions. If shame is a primary human emotion, then one or another situation will trigger shame in everyone. "Situational" items to measure shame or guilt can only assess the self-reported expectation that shame (or guilt) will be experienced in particular situations and how likely that is to happen at what intensity. The "trait" approach to measuring shame or guilt (which includes the adjectival item types) gets at the more enduring or chronic results of frequent shame experiences over a lifetime. The trait approach to the measurement of guilt cannot be differentiated reliably from similar measures of shame.

For example, the trait guilt measure of Kugler and Jones correlated .72 with the ISS.

As the data to be reviewed will show, state and trait approaches to measuring shame are only modestly correlated with each other (Harder et al., 1992) and very differentially correlated with other measures of psychopathology. While the two methods clearly share some common variance, the measurement approach makes a significant difference when we are studying the relation of shame to psychopathology.

How does this theoretical framework change the way we might approach the measurement of adult shame and guilt? Guilt, by definition, requires cognitive appraisal of a situation in which shame is triggered. Guilt involves the perception that one has violated a standard, done harm to someone, crossed a boundary somehow. It would follow that it is not possible to measure guilt without reference to hypothesized guilt-inducing situations. Thus, the situational item form as used in Tangney's SCAAI/TOSCA guilt measure is most appropriate.

The forms of shame that come to clinical attention involve ideoaffective complexes more profoundly associated with the failure or inadequacy of the total self. While there are many social situations that can trigger "embarrassment" without guilt, the deeply painful aspects of shame emotion most likely to be related to psychopathology are not bound to specific situations. Moreover, shame affect can be triggered without an interpersonal situation, as has been noted in infant observations (Broucek, 1979, 1982). Like guilt, shame can also be triggered as a result of neurotransmitter malfunction without regard to any specifically "shaming" situations (Nathanson, 1987, 1992).

It follows from this that the experience of shame in adults cannot be measured adequately by the situational item form. Shame emotions that become implicated in clinically significant symptomatology are the product of many "shame scenes" experienced over time and "internalized" as an aspect of the self-concept, perhaps influential in the development of a personality style. For a measurement approach to tap into this phenomenology would require items more globally related to the self. Adjective-based scales tap but weakly into this experience. All of the ISS items are drawn from intense levels of the shame experience, and as such are likely to measure the greatest possible variance in "trait shame" that can be obtained in the self-report format.

It also follows from this perspective that any valid measure of guilt will have variance in common with any valid measure of shame (Kugler & Jones, 1992), since guilt is a variant of shame. While the presence of shame affect does not demand cognitive capability, the experience of guilt does, making guilt an important social and psychological phenomenon worthy of study in relation to such issues as conscience, social control, and morality. Nevertheless, in matters of psychopathology, mental health assessment, and treatment, shame is the dominant emotion requiring our attention. "Guilt-loaded" shame may be diagnostically important (see chapter 8 on psychopharmacology), but guilt per se or guilt-proneness is not as significant as shame for the assessment and treatment of emotional disorders.

RELIABILITY AND VALIDITY OF THE ISS AND RELATED SCALES

The ISS, as briefly described here, is the fifth revision of a scale that began (in 1984) with a pool of 90 items drawn from phenomenological descriptions of the experience of shame. The current version has been in use since 1989. A detailed description of the developmental history of the ISS is contained in the manual available from the author (Cook, 1994).

The ISS consists of 30 items, six of which are positively worded "self-esteem" items. The "shame score" is based entirely on responses to the 24 negatively worded "shame items." The main purpose of the positively worded items is to reduce response set, but the score of those six items, which correlates about .70 with the shame items, can be used as an independent estimate of "self-esteem." Item selection emphasized the contribution of each item to the total score. Items with low item-total correlations were dropped, as were items that reduced the alpha coefficient. A factor analysis of the ISS items did not yield factors that were sufficiently independent of each other, thus reinforcing the unidimensionality of measured shame, which has been confirmed in large-scale studies by Novak (1986) and Chang (1988).

Reliability data for the ISS were obtained from both nonclinical and clinical samples. The nonclinical sample consisted of 645 undergraduate and graduate students at a midwest university (68% females). The mean age of these subjects was 24 (SD = 8; range = 17–63). Almost 75% of the sample were single. Eighty-six percent were white, 10% were Native American, and the rest other minorities. A one-way ANOVA indicated that there was no significant difference in the means (31.9 vs. 33.7) of the males and the females (F = 1.9; p = .17). These subjects, from a number of classes, volunteered to complete the ISS.

A number of different clinical samples were combined for the purposes of obtaining reliability data. Data were collected from subjects in several different chemical dependency treatment programs, with the most typical diagnosis being alcohol dependence. In addition, two inpatient and two outpatient samples of psychiatric patients were included in this data set. The most common diagnosis of these subjects was depression or dysthymia; other diagnoses included eating disorders, PTSD, anxiety, and adjustment disorders. The total clinical sample consisted of 370 subjects (54% females). The mean age was 38 (SD = 11; range = 15–79). Thirty-one percent were single, 27% married, and the remaining 42% were divorced, widowed, or cohabiting. Seventy-nine percent of these subjects were white, 13% African-American, and the remaining 8% Hispanic or Native American. As with the nonclinical data set, the means for the males and females (51.5 vs. 52.2) did not differ (F = .09; p = .75).

For the 24 shame items, the item-total correlations for the nonclinical group ranged from .56 to .73, with a median correlation of .63. For the clinical group, the range of item-total correlations was .52 to .82, with a median correlation of .70. The alpha reliability coefficients of .95 and .96 indicate that these items are very high in internal consistency. As would be predicted, the item means and item variability were greater for the clinical than the nonclinical sample. On a one-way ANOVA, all item means for the two groups were significantly different at <.0001. Only two item variances were nonsignificant.

A subset of 44 graduate students from the nonclinical data set was retested on the ISS after an interval of seven weeks. The test-retest correlation for the shame items was .84. Since there is greater variability in the scores of clinical samples and treatment would be expected to have an impact on levels of internalized shame, stability coefficients for clinical subjects were not obtained. While comparative reliability data on other shame and guilt scales are adequate, none has as high internal consistency as the ISS with both clinical and nonclinical samples.

A significant aspect of the development of the ISS was the express intent to use it as a tool for studying shame in clinical populations. This is in contrast to the expressed intent of Tangney to develop the SCAAI for a college population and as part of a "family of measures for assessing self-conscious affective style across the life span" (Tangney, 1990, p. 104). Likewise, Harder and his colleagues report data only for college students and Hoblitzelle's original study with the ASGS included only college students. Indeed, it would appear that the ISS is the only measure of shame that has been used extensively with clinical samples, despite the fact that both Tangney and Harder were interested in the relations among shame, guilt, and psychopathology.

The express intent of studying shame and guilt as separate constructs is the expectation that they will be differentially related to each other and/or to other measures of psychopathology and related constructs (e.g., self-derogation, self-consciousness, etc.). The Tangney and Harder studies reveal the confounding problem of both the theory base and the measurement methods.

Table 6.2 shows how the three measures of shame and guilt correlate with one another, as well as the correlation of the ISS with all but the ASGS scales. The subjects in all the studies cited for these data were

TABLE 6.2
Comparative Correlations of Measures of Shame and Guilt

	ISS	SCAAI Shame	PFQ Shame	ASGS Shame	SCAAI Guilt	PFQ Guilt	ASGS Guilt
SCAAI-S	39/52[e]	—	42[c]	54[a] 34/43[c]	43–48[a]	—	21/38[a]
PFQ-S	49/63[e]	42[c]	—	.61[b]	08ns/ 04ns[e]	52[b]	43[b]
ASGS-S	—	54[c] 39/43[a]	42[b] 61[c]	—	17[c]	46[b]	39[b]
SCAAI-G	10ns/ 07ns[e]	43–48[a]	17ns[c]	24ns[c] 09ns/ 29[a]	—	04ns[c]	10ns/ 21[a]
PFQ-G	47/64[e]	28/42[e]	52[b]	46[b]	04ns[c]	—	30[b]
ASGS-G	—	21–38[a]	43[b]	39[b]	10ns/ 21[a]	30[b]	—
Hostility Guilt	24[d]	22/36[a]	—	—	37/47[a]	—	—
Morality Guilt	58[d]	23/37[a]	—	—	31/39[a]	—	—
Sex Guilt	15[d]	—	—	—	—	—	—
Total Guilt	32[d]	—	—	—	—	—	—

Note: Unless noted (ns) all correlations significant at < .05; decimals omitted; r–r = range of 3 or more studies; r/r = two studies
[a]Tangney, 1990 [b]Harder & Zalma, 1990 [c]Harder et al., 1992 [d]Lighty, 1990 [e]McFarland, personal communication: Male/Female correlations with TOSCA

drawn from a college population. The n's in the various studies ranged
from 58 to 301 (four of seven datasets were over 200 each).

The corresponding shame and guilt scales for the SCAAI, the PFQ,
and the ASGS correlated .43–.48, .52, and .39 respectively. These correlations all shared method variance. The SCAAI shame scale, using a
situational item format, correlated at about the same level with the other
two adjectival format shame scales (.39 to .54). The two adjectival
shame scales (PFQ and ASGS) correlated from .42 to .61. When the
guilt scales were compared with each other, however, there was a dramatic drop in the correlation between scales with different methods. The
SCAAI situational guilt scale essentially did not correlate with the more
global scales (.04 with PFQ and .10/.21 with ASGS), while the two
global guilt scales correlated .30 with each other.

The Mosher Guilt Scale (Mosher, 1979) uses a quasi-situational format. A stem provides the situational element, and respondents must
choose between two responses (e.g., If I robbed a bank: a) I should get
caught. b) I would live like a king. Masturbation: a) is wrong and a sin.
b) is a normal outlet for sexual desire.). Tangney (1990) views the Mosher scale as "an undifferentiated index of both guilt and shame" (p. 109).
The significant correlations of both the SCAAI shame and guilt scales
with the Mosher scales for Hostility and Morality Guilt support this
view. The ISS also correlated significantly with the Mosher scales,
though the correlation with sex guilt was negligible. The substantially
higher correlation of the ISS with Morality Guilt (.58) would support
Tomkins's formulation: "Shame is experienced as guilt when positive
affect is attenuated by virtue of moral normative sanctions experienced
as conflicting with what is exciting or enjoyable" (Tomkins, 1987).

McFarland (personal communication)* administered the ISS and the
TOSCA and PFQ shame and guilt scales to a sample of 72 college males
and 146 college females with an age range of 20–47. The correlations
with the ISS are shown on Table 6.2. The ISS correlates significantly
with both shame scales and the PFQ guilt scale (common method variance that taps into shame). With the situational guilt scale (TOSCA/
SCAAI), however, there is no correlation with the ISS. The correlations
with the PFQ scales were substantially higher than with the TOSCA due
to the shared method variance of the ISS and PFQ. McFarland provided
correlations with the TOSCA Shame and PFQ Guilt (significant –
.28/.42), indicating the shared variance attributed to shame, and be-

---

*Kenneth R. McFarland, a doctoral student in the Department of Psychology,
University of Oregon, Eugene, OR, provided these unpublished data to the
author.

tween the TOSCA Guilt and the PFQ Shame (nonsignificant), suggesting that situationally measured guilt does not tap into any variance in "global shame."

These data lead to some important conclusions about these two constructs. The assertion that guilt is essentially a variant of shame is supported by the significant, if modest, correlation between shame and guilt measures (with the exception of McFarland's data for TOSCA Guilt and PFQ Shame). All the measures of shame that were intercorrelated overlapped with one another to about the same extent, regardless of method. However, the situational (i.e., "state") measure of guilt (SCAAI) did not correlate with the more global (i.e., "trait") measures of guilt, which correlated with each other.

This differs from the findings of Kugler and Jones (1992) who reported that "there was virtually no evidence from these analyses for supporting the distinction between trait and state guilt" (p. 325). However, their work supports the measure of "state guilt" as outperforming the measure of "trait guilt." Even so, they concluded that there was only scant support for distinguishing between guilt and shame on the basis of the measures used in their study, which included the ISS, SCAAI, and PFQ.

RELATION OF SHAME AND GUILT
TO PSYCHOPATHOLOGY

It is in relation to psychopathology that measures of shame and a specific concern for the emotion of shame become most relevant. I assume that all forms of psychopathology are basically emotional disorders with shame a common component in each. Based on Tomkins's affect theory, this would be true whether the etiology of the disorder was primarily biological or psychosocial. The construct validity of a measure of shame will depend largely on the extent to which it correlates with various valid measures of psychopathology.

Harder and Lewis's (1987) approach to establishing the construct validity of the PFQ scales was to correlate them with measures of self-derogation, low self-esteem, instability of self-concept, external locus of control, social anxiety, shyness, anxiety, depression, hostility, and regression defense. Both the PFQ shame and guilt scales correlated significantly with each of these variables (range = .30–.55). The lack of any significant difference between these sets of correlations can be attributed to the overlap of shame and guilt when measured by the common "global trait" method.

Table 6.3 shows comparative data drawn from several different studies in which measures of shame and guilt, including the ISS, were correlated with the same measures of psychopathology derived from the SCL-90 (Derogatis, 1983, 1992). Taken together, these studies strongly support the hypothesis that shame, but not guilt, is the significant emotional component in psychopathology. Moreover, the data also support the superior validity of the "trait" approach to measuring shame as best exemplified by the ISS. Specific analyses of these studies follow.

Harder et al. (1992) reported on two studies, one of which included data from all three shame and guilt scales, the SCAAI, PFQ2, and ASGS. All three shame scales correlated significantly with measures of depression, self-derogation, social anxiety, and shyness. The correlations tended to be highest for the ASGS shame scale. The PFQ2 guilt scale correlated significantly with depression (.39) and self-derogation (.50),

TABLE 6.3
Comparative Correlations of Shame and Guilt Measures
With the SCL-90 Scales

SCL-90	ISS	SCAAI Shame	ASGS Shame	SCAAI Guilt	PFQ2 Guilt
Depression	71[a]	32–43[b]	38[c]	15–24[b]	34[c]
Somatic	45	14–27	34	11ns–18	42
Obsessive-Compulsive	61	31–38	50	19–22	38
Interpersonal Sensitivity	74	42–56	47	21–29	48
Anxiety	62	24–36	31	18–25	33
Hostility	51	13–20	02ns	01ns–03ns	24
Psychoticism	72	25–39	37	11ns–23	40
Phobic Anxiety	55	25–32	35	01ns–18	29
Paranoid Ideation	61	23–40	23ns	08ns–17	25
GSI	77	—	44	—	45

Note: Unless indicated (ns) all correlations significant at < .05; decimal omitted; r–r = range for three studies
[a]Akashi, 1994 [b]Tangney et al., 1992 [c]Harder et al., 1992

but the SCAAI guilt scale did not, a finding that Harder et al. felt went "against the weight of theoretical and clinical evidence linking character-istic guilt dispositions with these two conditions" (p. 592). However, the PFQ2 guilt scale also correlated significantly with social anxiety (.29), shyness (.29), and public self-consciousness (.28). The authors stated: "Our data add to questions of the PFQ2 Guilt scale's discriminant valid-ity, because the data produce a correlation pattern uncomfortably simi-lar to what would be expected of a valid shame measure" (p. 592). The PFQ shame and guilt scales correlated .52.

These data confirm the confounding of shame and guilt. While the SCAAI guilt scale is appropriately in the form of situations, the PFQ scales use the more trait oriented approach of adjectives. When the more valid situational guilt measure is used, there is no correlation with related measures of the stigmata of shame (e.g., depression, self-derogation). When the more global trait measure of guilt is used, the overlap with shame accounts for the correlations with the shame related variables.

The second study reported by Harder et al. selected the ASGS Shame scale and the PFQ2 Guilt scale as the best measures of those constructs to correlate with the SCL-90, the data shown in Table 6.3. The only nonsignificant correlation was with ASGS Shame and Hostility–anger. When each variable was partialled for the other, a few of the correlations fell below significance levels but the pattern remained essentially the same. Again, these two scales share both method and construct variance and were correlated (.46).

In contrast, the data reported by Tangney et al. (1992), as shown in Table 6.3, showed a clearly differentiated pattern between the measure of shame and the measure of guilt. When Tangney et al. parceled out guilt from shame, only three of the 27 correlations with guilt were signifi-cant and only one of the 27 correlations with shame was not significant. When guilt is measured appropriately by situational items, it does not correlate with psychopathology. Shame, even when measured by situa-tional items, apparently will account for enough variability in shame emotion to correlate with every form of psychopathology measured by the SCL.

Harder et al. (1992) were aware of Tangney's findings and described the negligible role of guilt in psychopathology as a "wholly unexpected possibility" (p. 594). Even so, they cite Tomkins's position that guilt is the "physiological equivalent to shame" (p. 594), a statement that does not adequately reflect the complexity of Tomkins's discussion of shame and guilt. In any case, they interpret their results with the PFQ2 Guilt scale as evidence that guilt " . . . is, indeed, associated with the entire range of symptomatology observed among college undergraduates and that its influence on such symptoms is at least equal to that shown by shame" (p. 601). They go on to assert that "guilt is much more involved with symptomatology than the current clinical and theoretical emphasis on shame would imply" (p. 601).

The theoretical edifice that suggests guilt plays a significant role in psychopathology is drawn from outdated psychodynamic theory that, from Freud forward, has neglected (with few exceptions) the study of shame in particular and affect in general. This has also contributed to the development of guilt measures that are based on the assumption that guilt is an emotion separate and distinct from shame and can be measured as a kind of "trait" similar to the global nature of shame emotions; as has been pointed out, shame references the entire self while guilt is trigged by specific acts. The common variance shared by the PFQ2 Guilt measure and the SCL-90 scales can be accounted for by a measurement method that taps into shame as much as guilt. When guilt is measured in relation to situations, however, this overlap with psychopathology disappears. Contrary to Harder's conclusions, the focus in studying the emotional content of psychopathological symptomatology should be shame and not guilt.

Both Tangney and Harder point out the subjectively greater emotional pain associated with shame as opposed to guilt. Tangney et al. (1992) point up this distinction and its implication for psychopathology in their statement:

> Shame is a painfully devastating experience that, at least temporarily, leads to a crippling of adaptive self-functions. Thus the tendency to experience shame across a range of situations may render people more vulnerable to a variety of psychological disorders because of repeated disruptions in self-functioning. (pp. 475–476)

Both Harder and Tangney recommend studies with clinical populations.

From the beginning of its development the ISS has been administered to both clinical and nonclinical samples. The data shown in Table 6.3 for the ISS were obtained by Akashi (1994) in conjunction with her dissertation. These data were not reported in her dissertation proper, which involved a much more complex analysis of the relation between shame and psychological distress (to be discussed below).

Akashi obtained her sample from 336 adult psychotherapy outpatients between the ages of 19 and 67 attending 23 clinics in the Columbus, Ohio area. The psychopathology variables were obtained from administering the Brief Symptom Checklist (Derogatis, 1992), a 50-item version of the SCL-90. The reliability and validity of the brief version are comparable to the SCL-90 and the scales are identical (Derogatis & Melisaratos, 1983).

These data clearly confirm the pervasive role played by shame emotions in the psychopathology of a clinical population. The correlations (.45–.74) are also the highest reported in any of the empirical literature on shame and measures of psychopathology. Because the items on the ISS come much closer to the phenomenological experience of adult shame emotions, the ISS is a much more sensitive measure of the internalization of shame than are the adjective-based scales and the situation-based scales. While there is considerable convergence in the data from these various studies using four different measures of shame and guilt, the ISS comes closest to providing a clinically useful measure of internalized shame.*

THE SHAME-PSYCHOPATHOLOGY CONNECTION

Shame, as Tomkins (1963, 1987) has described, is auxiliary to the positive affects and triggered whenever the flow of positive affect is attenuated but the trigger for postitive affect remains active. At its most basic, biological level, shame is the affect triggered whenever positive affect is impeded. This biological "script" comes to be nested within a lifetime of developmental experiences, and the emotional system clearly becomes a complex coassembly of different primary affects associated with different situations and memories. Shame may be coassembled with any of the other affects, but it is most salient as the affect relating to sociability and the sense of self because of its built-in connection to positive affect.

If shame is triggered often across childhood and adolescence, with infrequent or inadequate reparation of those experiences, the individual typically develops a defensive script to enable the management of the painful emotions associated with the triggering of shame. The resulting defensive "affect management scripts" can take many forms and are analogous to the various symptoms described in Axis I disorders or in the personality styles/disorders of Axis II. Nathanson has described these scripts as the "compass of shame" in the opening chapter of this book and in his 1992 book.

---

*The data from the ISS in Table 6.2 should be compared cautiously with data from the other measures because the ISS sample were adult outpatients and the other samples were college students. Also, a different version of the SCL-90 (SCL-50) was administered to the ISS sample. Although the ISS correlations are substantially higher than for the other scales, it is not known if the differences might have resulted from sampling differences.

Given the biological script for shame, it is logical to expect to find shame implicated to some degree in any disorder or problem accompanied by "negative affect." In fact, the existence of a common thread of "negative affect" that cuts across diagnostic categories has been noted in a number of studies, primarily in relation to depression and anxiety.

Watson and Kendall (1989), for example, have pointed out the presence of negative affect in both anxiety disorders and depression; they suggest that it accounts for the fact that in many patients symptoms of one disorder overlap with those of the other. For this reason, a "tripartite model" of anxiety and depression has been proposed that differentiates depression and anxiety according to the presence of low or high "positive affect" in relation to the presence of high "negative affect" (Clark & Watson, 1991).

In a related study, Zinbarg and Barlow (1992) factor analyzed a large number of instruments administered to 156 patients admitted to the Center for Stress and Anxiety Disorders who met criteria for a principal diagnosis of one of the anxiety disorders, as well as 32 normal controls. They found a "higher order factor" common to all the diagnostic categories of anxiety, which they labeled "negative affect." On this factor the clinical groups did not differ from each other, although they did differ from the "no mental disorders" control group.

Akashi (1994) investigated the relation of attachment, measured by the Parental Bonding Instrument (Parker, 1983), and shame, as measured by the ISS, to "psychological stress" as measured by the Brief Symptom Checklist (Derogatis, 1992). Using a structural equation model, Akashi tested the general hypothesis that shame is an intervening variable between attachment and psychological stress. In the sample described above, she tested three models related to this hypothesis.

In the first model, the direct effect of attachment on psychological stress was tested and found to have a statistically significant negative effect with an error term of .868, indicating the amount of psychological stress not accounted for by attachment. The second model tested the effect of attachment on shame and of shame on psychological stress. Both relations were significant and predicted a negative effect on psychological stress. The error term of .343 indicated the amount of variance in psychological stress not accounted for by shame.

The third model tested was designed to examine what effect attachment would have on psychological stress when the effect of shame was left in the equation. In this model, the previously significant relation between attachment and psychological distress seen in the first model disappeared. No statistically significant variance was explained by attachment with shame in the model. These results clearly confirmed that attachment (i.e., childhood experience with parents) only affects psychological stress through internalized shame (the second model).

The data reviewed here support the conclusion that the "negative affect" that cuts across so many Axis I and Axis II diagnostic categories is shame, internalized and often coassembled with one or more of the other primary negative affects. Shame is the affect triggered whenever positive affect is impeded. This biological script, along with developmental experiences that can trigger shame in an endless variety of ways, readily accounts for the ubiquitous appearance of shame in all forms of psychopathology.

SHAME AND DYSPHORIA

Nathanson (1994) argues that depression is a "wastebasket term" and should eventually be discarded in favor of a more accurate notation of the active negative affects involved. From the standpoint of affect theory, "depression" is a disparate collection of dysphorias with varying symptom patterns. The fact that there are nine different "mood disorders" (i.e., depression) and 11 different anxiety disorders specified in *DSM-IV* supports this assertion. The research referred to above on the overlap of depression and anxiety is further evidence for the plethora of ways in which disorders or disturbances of affect have become categorized. If assessment and treatment focused primarily on the affects involved in the disturbance, assessment and treatment would become much more systematic.

Consider the links between shame and depression. Helen Block Lewis (1987) has provided one of the most extensive reviews of the literature on shame and depression. In her own early studies, Lewis (1971) collected data that supported the hypothesis that gender differences in field-dependence and field-independence were related to differences in the incidence of depression for men and women and for the prominence of shame in field-dependent depressed women and guilt in field-independent men who had a tendency more toward paranoia than depression. In a more recent study, Izard and Schwartz (1986) stated that their data on children, college students, and adults demonstrated that the common core of emotions in depression included shame or shyness in addition to sadness and inner-directed hostility. As Nathanson (1992) has pointed out, "inner-directed hostility" is a remnant of drive theory, better conceptualized as the *attack self* pole of the compass of shame. In this light, Izard and Schwartz's work confirms Nathanson's comment that classical depression references the affects shame and fear, while atypical depression is about shame and distress.

Empirical research with the ISS substantiates this overlap of shame with symptoms of depression. The most widely used clinical scale for depression is the Beck Depression Inventory (BDI) (Beck & Steer, 1987). Studies conducted by myself and other researchers have correlated the BDI and the ISS. It is clear from these correlations that there is substantial convergent validity between the ISS and depression as measured by the BDI for both clinical and nonclinical samples. These correlations ranged from .59 to .79 with a mean of .69 and median of .67.

In order to see more clearly how the ISS relates to the BDI in a clinical sample, the BDI scores were used to create four categories of depression for a sample of 185 psychiatric subjects from outpatient and inpatient treatment settings. The subgroups were based on score levels specified in the BDI manual (Beck & Steer, 1987). Scores of 0–9 are asymptomatic, 10–18 mildly depressed, 19–29 moderate to severely depressed, and 30 or above extremely depressed. Table 6.4 shows the results of an ANOVA comparing the ISS scores for these four groups.

These data suggest substantial criterion validity for the ISS as a measure of the negative affectivity known to be associated with depression. Within this clinical population, the subjects reporting the highest levels of current depressive symptoms also had the highest levels of internalized shame. The post hoc test (Newman-Kuels) indicated that all the symptomatic categories were differentiated from the categories below them on the ISS. For the "moderate to severe" group, the 95% confidence interval for the mean was 57.2 to 65.0, and for the "extreme" group, this interval was 64 to 73.9.

TABLE 6.4
Comparisons of ISS Scores for Four Levels
of Depression on the BDI

BDI Category	N	M	SD	SE	F	Prob
1. Asymptomatic	40	29.1	13.2	2.1	65.54	.0000
2. Mild Depression	46	41.6	15.1	2.2		
3. Moderate–Severe	57	61.1	14.8	1.9		
4. Extreme	42	68.9	15.9	2.4		

Post hoc test (p = < .05) Group 2 > 1; Group 3 > 1, 2; Group 4 > 1, 2, 3

Regardless of diagnosis, almost every clinical sample that has been tested with the ISS has yielded a group mean of 50 or higher. Based on these results, scores on the ISS of 50 or above are considered to be indicative of painful or problematical levels of internalized shame. Based on the data in Table 6.4, scores of 60 or above are very likely to be accompanied by multiple symptoms of depression.

The role of shame in depression and the utility of the ISS in the diagnostic assessment of shame is a complex matter that is just beginning to be studied. Of particular interest are patients diagnosed with "atypical depression." Nathanson regards this group of depressed patients to be particularly "shame loaded" and "characterized by such typical stigmata of shame as social phobia, rejection sensitivity, hysterical features typical of shame conflict, and withdrawal characterized by hypersomnia" (1987, p. 48).

In contrast to the atypical group, the "endogenous depressed" are regarded by Nathanson as more "guilt loaded." These latter patients he has found respond better to tricyclic antidepressant medication, whereas the atypical patients (i.e., shame loaded) seem to do better on the MAOIs or the newer SSRI drugs, fluoxetine, sertraline, and paroxetine.

Given that the ISS is highly correlated with the BDI, regardless of diagnosis, we can hypothesize, based on Nathanson's observations, that patients diagnosed with "atypical" depression will have higher scores on the ISS than will patients diagnosed with major or bipolar depression (i.e., "endogenous"). Given that the typical depressive symptomatology of these two groups would be expected to be similar, we would hypothesize that the groups will not differ on the BDI. Moreover, since the BDI can be divided into two categories of symptoms, cognitive and somatic, we would predict that the atypical group would have higher scores on the cognitive items and lower scores on the somatic items and the reverse would be true for the endogenous group.

It was possible to make this test with the data available from the private psychiatric practice of a psychiatrist trained by Nathanson in affect theory. These data are shown in Table 6.5.

Each of the patients in this sample had been given a *DSM-III-R* diagnosis of atypical depression, dysthymia, major depression, or bipolar disorder. The latter two diagnoses constituted the "endogenous" group (typically distinguished by significant anhedonia), and the former two categories were represented in the "atypical" group.

The results tentatively support the hypothesis that the atypical patients' shame scores will be higher. There was a substantial difference in the mean scores (10.9 points), and the significance level was just slightly greater than the .05 level considered acceptable for rejecting a null hy-

TABLE 6.5
Comparison of Two Diagnostic Groups on the ISS and BDI

SCALE/Group	N	M	SD	F	Prob
ISS					
Endogenous	18	41.0	21.6	3.80	.0550
Atypical	61	51.9	20.5		
BDI TOTAL SCORE					
Endogenous	18	19.0	13.1	0.01	.9245
Atypical	59	19.3	11.5		
BDI COGNITIVE ITEMS					
Endogenous	18	11.7	9.1	0.52	.4730
Atypical	59	13.4	8.7		
BDI SOMATIC ITEMS					
Endogenous	18	7.3	4.9	1.66	.2017
Atypical	59	5.9	4.0		

pothesis. Detecting differences when the sample size of one group is disproportionately small accounts for the tentative nature of these results despite all the differences being in the hypothesized direction.

An examination of the ISS means themselves, as well as the variances, further substantiates the significance of this finding. The group mean for the atypical patients was at the low end of the score range considered problematic from testing large clinical samples (e.g., 50), while the mean for the endogenous group was considerably below that cutoff. The maximum score for the endogenous group was 67, compared to the maximum score of 90 for the atypical group. A much smaller standard error of measurement for the atypical group (2.6 vs. 5.1) suggests that the range of error variance in their scores was much smaller, though that difference might disappear with a larger endogenous sample.

As predicted, there was no difference in the total score on the BDI. The differences on the cognitive and somatic items of the BDI were in the predicted direction, but did not reach statistical significance. However, the differences between the two groups on the somatic items was relatively large (1.4 points, or greater than the standard errors for each group—1.1 and 0.5 respectively) and the probability level (.20) approached significance. These results certainly warrant more careful investigation with larger groups of depressed patients.

CLINICAL IMPLICATIONS

Affect theory allows us to make much more sense of clinical data than was possible on the basis of traditional psychoanalytic theory. Various contemporary theories of psychotherapy show a remarkable convergence in providing an explanation for personality development and behavioral problems. But affect theory allows us to see and understand more than ever before. It is a complex and comprehensive theory.

The ISS, though not originally developed on the basis of affect theory, has found a theoretical home in the work on shame of Tomkins and Nathanson. The data reviewed here, from a variety of studies using several different shame scales, substantiates the greater validity of the ISS. In turn, data from studies using the ISS are beginning to provide considerable empirical support for hypotheses regarding shame derived from affect theory.

No single scale for measuring any affect is likely to be able to do justice to the complexity of our affects, especially as our life experiences overlay the biology of our affects. Nevertheless, the ISS provides clinicians with a quick and simple way to assess the salience of internalized shame in an individual patient and to make it possible to begin to address shame directly in treatment.

The manual for the ISS (Cook, 1994) contains some detailed suggestions for using the ISS. Protocols are being developed that will enable the responses to particular ISS items to be linked to the cognitive phase of shame reactivity, as well as to the compass of shame.

At present, a useful rule of thumb for assessing a patient with the ISS is to take any score of 50 or higher as an indication that shame is prominent in the presenting issue. The likelihood is that such an individual has developed a *withdrawal* or *attack self* mode of defense. Depending on other diagnostic indicators based on an understanding of affect theory, such a score may also indicate consideration of a course of medication, for chronic and persistent shame pathology often responds best to a combination of psychotherapy and SSRI treatment.

The following case study illustrates how the ISS can be used in conjunction with other psychometric instruments to help focus and evaluate treatment.

Helen was a 35-year-old, single, professional woman. Her presenting issue was a difficult relationship with a married man with whom there was no prospect of any future. In addition, she complained of depression and suicidal thoughts. At intake her score on the ISS was 83, but the

BDI score was only 11 (very mild symptoms) and her score on the Beck Anxiety Inventory (BAI) was zero. This suggested an unusual psychometric picture in which internalized shame appeared to be highly prominent but without any indication of anxiety symptoms or significant depressive symptoms.

Three weeks into treatment she completed the MCMI-II. She had a significant Axis I scale score for Dysthymia and predominant Axis II scales on Avoidant and Self-Defeating. Both of these personality styles can be associated with the rejection sensitivity often seen in atypical depression. The fact that a difficult relationship issue motivated her to seek therapy is also typical of this type of client, although in Helen's case the rejection was not overt but implicit in the man's refusal to consider leaving his wife for her. Such patterns of behavior fit into the attack self *script library and may be regarded as part of a stable personality style.*

The first four sessions dealt with the crisis over breaking up with her lover. She carried this off very well, feeling empowered by this success, but continued to struggle with depressed moods in which a nagging inner voice told her she was "scum" and that she should die. Review of her early childhood revealed no abuse to account for this self-image, although she characterized her parents as "emotionally neglectful" and provided anecdotes illustrating how they seemed uninterested when she felt wronged. She was a woman with many artistic talents and accomplishments who was also reasonably successful in her professional position and with a number of friends. But a theme of nothing ever being "good enough" kept emerging as we tried to focus on the significance of these accomplishments. Another theme was the idea that she was not able to fill up the empty void herself but needed someone else to do that.

At the seventh session a structured interview assessment (SCID) indicated a diagnosis of dysthymia. At the eighth session I recommended that she obtain a prescription for Prozac from her family doctor. Between sessions nine and ten she made a suicide gesture by swallowing some pills but took herself to the hospital and was all right, though shaken by the experience. She also began taking Prozac between these two sessions. She agreed to remove all razor blades from her house, though not before scratching herself a bit.

At the 11th session she took the Beck Hopelessness Scale (BHS) and scored 15, indicating severe hopelessness and a high suicide potential. Her ISS score taken at that point was 66, still high but down from the score of 83 at intake. The 12th session was two weeks later and about four weeks after she began the Prozac. Her BHS score had dropped to six, a "safe" level for suicide indications. Two weeks later, at the 13th session, her BHS score was eight (still low) and her ISS had dropped to

57. She was reporting a dramatic improvement in her mood state, which she (grudgingly) attributed to the Prozac.

A few weeks later, when her mother was visiting, we had a conjoint session that enabled her to share some of her childhood pain and confusion with her mother. Her mother's perspective on what had happened proved to be more benign than Helen had supposed. Her mother was also very good about listening to her and accepting her feelings.

The total period of treatment was about four months and consisted of 15 sessions. The suicidal ideation ceased completely. While the final ISS score was still in the "high" range (57), the drop from the initial level of 83 indicated a significant change, which was confirmed in her self-report. Follow-up was possible for this client. She discontinued the Prozac after less than six months, continued to experience a stable, generally positive mood state, and within the year met a man, fell in love, and married him! She now has a baby and is still doing quite well.

This case probably illustrates the problem of shame as a "hardware" dysfunction that the Prozac was able to correct. While the "cloud" of shame and suicidal ideation was largely relieved by the Prozac, the therapy helped this client to solidify these changes in her life and to trust them as "real." At the outset of treatment the ISS called dramatic attention to the importance of shame in her emotional discomfort, despite the relative absence of any typical symptoms of "depression." The fact that this client responded well to Prozac in the absence of standard symptoms of depression substantiates the salience of shame as the key to her dysfunction. The fact that Helen was able to discontinue the Prozac after a relatively short period and maintain her gains indicates that, at least in some cases, the "hardware" problem does not need continuous long-term maintenance treatment with medication.

REFERENCES

Akashi, A. (1994). *Investigation of attachment, shame and psychological stress in outpatient psychotherapy clients*. Doctoral dissertation, Ohio State University.

Beall, L. (1972). The shame-guilt test. The Wright Institute, 2728 Durant Ave., Berkeley, CA 94704.

Beck, A. T., & Steer, R. A. (1987). *Beck depression inventory manual*. San Antonio: The Psychological Corporation.

Binder, J. (1970). *The relative proneness to shame or guilt as a dimension of character style*. Doctoral dissertation, University of Michigan.

Broucek, F. (1979). Efficacy in infancy. *International Journal of Psychoanalysis, 60*, 311–316.

Broucek, F. (1982). Shame and its relationship to early narcissistic developments. *International Journal of Psychoanalysis, 63*, 369–378.

Chang, S. (1988). *The measurement of shame and its relationship to other personality traits*. Doctoral dissertation, Michigan State University.

Clark, L. A., & Watson, D. (1991). Tripartite model of anxiety and depression: Psychometric evidence and taxonomic implications. *Journal of Abnormal Psychology, 100*(3), 316–336.

Cook, D. R. (1987). Measuring shame: The internalized shame scale. *Alcoholism Treatment Quarterly, 4*(2), 197–215.

Cook, D. R. (1994). *Internalized shame scale: Professional Manual*. Menomonie, WI: Channel Press (Available from author: E5886 803rd Ave., Menomonie, WI 54751).

Derogatis, L. (1983). *SCL-90-R manual*. St. Petersburg, FL: Clinical Psychometrics.

Derogatis, L. (1992). *Brief symptom inventory: Administration and scoring, and procedures manual–II*. Baltimore: Clinical Psychometric Research.

Derogatis, L. R., & Melisaratos, N. (1983). The brief symptom inventory: An introductory report. *Psychological Medicine, 13*, 595–605.

Ferguson, T. J., Stegge, H., & Damhuis, I. (1991). Children's understanding of guilt and shame. *Child Development, 62*, 827–839.

Geppert, U., & Heckhausen, H. (1988). Self-related and self-evaluative emotions: Embarrassment, shame, guilt, and pride. Paper prepared for the Conference on the Development of Shame and Guilt, Pacific Grove, CA.

Gioiella, P. P. (1981). *The relationship of relative shame/guilt proneness to the attribution of responsibility under no shame and shame arousal*. Doctoral dissertation, New York University.

Gottschalk, L. A., & Gleser, G. (1969). *The measurement of psychological states through the content analysis of verbal behavior: Text*. Berkeley: University of California Press.

Harder, D. H., & Zalma, A. (1990). Two promising shame and guilt scales: A construct validity comparison. *Journal of Personality Assessment, 55*(3&4), 729–745.

Harder, D. W., Cutler, L., & Rockart, L. (1992). Assessment of shame and guilt and their relationships to psychopathology. *Journal of Personality Assessment, 59*(3), 584–604.

Harder, D. W., & Lewis, S. J. (1987). The assessment of shame and guilt. In J. N. Butcher & C. D. Spielberger (Eds.), *Advances in personality assessment* (pp. 89–114). Hillsdale, NJ: Erlbaum.

Harper, J. M., & Hoopes, M. H. (1990). *Uncovering shame*. New York: Norton.

Hoblitzelle, W. (1987). Differentiating and measuring shame and guilt: The relation between shame and depression. In H. B. Lewis (Eds.), *The role of shame in symptom formation* (pp. 207–235). Hillsdale, NJ: Erlbaum.

Izard, C. E. (1977). *Human emotions*. New York: Plenum.

Izard, C. E., & Schwartz, G. M. (1986). Patterns of emotion in depression. In M. Rutter, C. E. Izard, & P. B. Read (Eds.), *Depression in young people: Developmental and clinical perspectives* (pp. 33–70). New York: Guilford.

Kugler, K., & Jones, W. H. (1992). On conceptualizing and assessing guilt. *Journal of Personality and Social Psychology, 62*(2), 318–327.

Lewis, H. B. (1971). *Shame and guilt in neurosis*. New York: International Universities Press.

Lewis, H. B. (1987). Shame and the narcissistic personality. In D. L. Nathanson (Eds.), *The many faces of shame* (pp. 133–161). New York: Guilford.

Lewis, M. (1992). *Shame: The exposed self*. New York: Free Press.

Lewis, M., Alessandri, S. M., & Sullivan, M. W. (1992). Differences in shame and pride as a function of children's gender and task difficulty. *Child Development, 63*, 630–638.

Lighty, G. A. (1990). *Dimensions of shame: The construction and validation of a measurement of shame*. Doctoral dissertation, California School of Professional Psychology, Fresno Campus.

Mayman, M. (1968). Early memories and character structure. *Journal of Projective Techniques and Personality Assessment, 31*, 303–316.

Mosher, D. L. (1979). The meaning and measurement of guilt. In C. Izard (Ed.), *Emotions in personality and psychopathology* (pp. 105–129). New York: Plenum.

Nathanson, D. L. (1987). A timetable for shame. In D. L. Nathanson (Ed.), *The many faces of shame* (pp. 1-63). New York: Guilford.

Nathanson, D. L. (1992). *Shame and pride: Affect, sex, and the birth of the self.* New York: Norton.

Nathanson, D. L. (1994). The case against depression. *Bulletin of The Tomkins Institute,* 1:2, 9-11.

Novak, W. (1986). *The measurement and construct of shame.* Doctoral dissertation, Michigan State University.

Parker, G. (1983). *Parental overprotection: A risk factor in psychological development.* New York: Grune & Stratton.

Perlman, M. (1958). An investigation of anxiety as related to guilt and shame. *Archives of Neurology and Psychiatry, 80,* 752-759.

Tangney, J. P. (1990). Assessing individual differences in proneness to shame and guilt: Development of the self-conscious affect and attribution inventory. *Journal of Personality and Social Psychology, 59,* 102-111.

Tangney, J. P., & Fisher, K. W. (Eds.). (1993). *The self-conscious emotions: Shame, guilt, embarrassment and pride.* New York: Guilford.

Tangney, J. P., Wagner, P., & Gramzow, R. (1992). Proneness to shame, proneness to guilt, and psychopathology. *Journal of Abnormal Psychology, 101*(3), 469-478.

Tomkins, S. S. (1963). *Affect, imagery, consciousness, Vol. 2: The negative affects.* New York: Springer.

Tomkins, S. S. (1987). Shame. In D. L. Nathanson (Ed.), *The many faces of shame* (pp. 133-161). New York: Guilford.

Ursu, M. W. (1984). *An investigation of the construct validity of several measures of proneness to shame.* Doctoral dissertation, University of Minnesota.

Watson, D., & Kendall, P. C. (1989). Understanding anxiety and depression: Their relation to negative and positive affective states. In P. C. Kendall & D. Watson (Eds.), *Anxiety and depression: Distinctive and overlapping features* (pp. 3-26). San Diego: Academic Press.

Zinbarg, R. E., & Barlow, D. H. (1992, November). *The construct validity of the DSM-III-R anxiety disorders: Empirical evidence.* Paper presented at 26th Annual Meeting of AABT.

7

Implications of Affect Theory for the Practice of Cognitive Therapy

Shelley F. Milestone

One of the problems facing the student of psychotherapy is the simple observation that most systems of therapy work. That they work best in the hands of their inventor suggests that some quality of art is involved; that they can be taught at all suggests that there is a body of knowledge that can be imparted and from which a newcomer can achieve at least some competence until experience allows the lurching efforts of beginners to smooth into some sort of personal art. Eventually, each of us develops a highly individual style of doing psychotherapy, a way of living out our part of the contract to enable change in those who ask for our assistance in finding more comfort with their emotions.

My own style is anecdotal. Often, when I sense that the flow of therapeutic interchange has gotten stuck, I am impelled to tell my patient some story, joke, or personal experience that has been brought to mind by the material we are discussing, taking care that such information is introduced only when I know that it is directly analogous to the situation at hand. The success of such a style is dependent on my observation that no one is defended against an anecdote (jokes hit their target long before the listener realizes their "significance"), but that interpretations can be spotted a mile away.

Early in my career, a senior colleague pointed out that the function of an interpretation is to close off a path in order to alter the flow of associations to the matter under investigation. An analogue activates whole scripts (with all the experiences they contain) and brings them into therapeutic focus; I am comfortable with the complexity so engendered.

Every once in a while I encounter a patient who is made distinctly more uncomfortable by my pattern of therapy, however carefully I limit these intrusions that are so characteristic of my work. For such patients, anything that veers from the specific chain of thought, the particular image or construct that represents "the problem," is experienced as a digression and a waste of valuable time. Except in those specific situations where I know I am using "glue" techniques to reduce associations and decrease ambient affect, I work best when I can show that the problem at hand is itself an analogue of some larger pattern of affect modulation. Therapists, like patients, have both character structures and some assemblage of innate talents and abilities. What mode of treatment best suits patients who seem allergic to the kind of extension I find interesting? Dr. Milestone offers one possibility.

Dr. Milestone demonstrates how the cognitive therapist identifies the ideoaffective complexes that produce the uncomfortable associations called "automatic thoughts." She teaches the patient to examine such thoughts in order to figure out the specific links between those thoughts and whatever triggered them so that, by working together like scientists, patient and therapist can build new chains of response to these triggers. Often, when such treatment is successful, an individual learns to block one realm of thought by the intentional introduction of another. A solid understanding of affect theory makes cognitive therapy all the more comprehensible for us as scholars and effective for us as clinicians.   –DLN

A s we interact with our patients, what captures our interest and attention tends to match our theory of psychotherapy, psychopathology, and the human being. Cognitive therapy (CT) has gained wide acceptance over the past two decades as an effective treatment for a growing range of clinical disorders (Freeman, Simon, Beutler, & Arkowitz, 1989). It is a system based on logical and easily taught processes. Therapist and patient collaborate to form a concept of the patient's problem and to structure the therapeutic session toward maximum therapeutic efficiency.

There is a continuing move to formulate models that explain how environment, affect, cognition, and action all become synthesized into that remarkable gestalt we call the person (Lazarus, 1989; Wright & Thase, 1992). The writings of Silvan Tomkins (1962, 1963, 1982, 1991, 1992) and Donald Nathanson (1987, 1992) offer new ways to integrate the modern concept of affect into cognitive therapy. Affect and cognition make up a mutually interacting system. Affect theory and CT may be linked in three realms: the formal conceptualization of the patient, the nature of the therapeutic relationship, and the form of the therapeutic process.

CONCEPTUALIZATION

Patients come to us in hope that we can do something to remove or alter the thoughts and feelings that have made their lives difficult. For each category of symptom, the cognitive therapist attempts to find a belief that underlies or seems to power a whole group of thoughts. Depressed patients tend to exhibit what Beck (Beck & Rush, 1989; Beck, Rush, Shaw, & Emery, 1979) calls "the cognitive triad" of negative view of self, negative view of the future, and negative interpretation of ongoing events and experiences. Similarly, in anxiety, the patient sees the world as a dangerous place, overestimates the probability of risk in any situation, and discounts internal and external rescue factors (Beck, Emery, & Greenberg, 1985).

Integral to each major personality disorder is some systematized group of assumptions that can be determined with the aid of careful questioning to identify the patient's systematic pattern of thinking (Beck, Freeman et al., 1990). The case conceptualization consists of hypotheses about the patient's conditional assumptions ("if I work hard I will be successful") and/or unconditional beliefs or schemas about self, others, and the world ("the world is against me") (Persons, 1989; Young, 1990).

What Guidano and Liotti (1983) call a developmental analysis may be understood as a method of determining the importance of early experiences with innate affect, which functions both as the primary motivational system and as the basic communication system used by infant and caregiver (Tomkins, 1982). In taking a history, we focus on such matters as the patient's recollection of the affective tone of the early environment, inquiring as to how each parent responded to the patient's expressions of distress, anger, fear, and excitement. Affect theory directs our attention to patterns on a microlevel, leading to consideration of facial and vocal expressions. Affective interactions in early childhood can lead to the development of beliefs that assume great importance in adult life.

Consider for a moment the implications of this simple observable interchange between a mother and her toddler. The toddler, as he struggles to learn to walk, will invariably fall. Frequently a fall that does not result in harm will produce a startled expression on the child's face, at which time he will look to his mother's face. If she smiles, he will smile; if she exhibits fear, distress, anger, or any other negative affect, the toddler may look frightened for a moment and then begin to cry. All of us have witnessed such scenes.

The affective reactions of this mother might further intensify the child's negative affect were she to maintain her own expression of negative affect rather than help the child modulate the negative affect she herself unwittingly triggered in him. But consider what might happen if this mother had earlier suffered considerable anguish over a prolonged period of infertility, then gave birth to premature twins who died of a viral infection contracted in the hospital, and finally succeeded in delivering this little boy. She is primed to respond to much of her toddler's exploratory behavior with the face and exclamations of fearful alarm. Her son will assemble a collection of many scenes in which his initiatives or moves toward autonomy produce a strong fear response from his mother.

Contrast this child's experience with one whose mother consistently responds to his explorations with applause and smiles. According to studies by Stern (1991), by three months, infants have begun to set up representations of what to expect from significant others. Of the two toddlers just described, one is forming representations that link developing competencies with approval and support, while the other links experimentation with disapproval. Nathanson (1992) suggests that the affects of shame and fear occur in a child whose moves toward self-reliance are greeted with negative affect.

This example highlights how our very earliest experiences with innate affect form the basis of our adult experience of emotion. If repeated often enough, these early scenes serve as the beginnings of what Tomkins (1991) calls scripts, and are similar in structure to what cognitive therapists identify as schemas. Scripts are rules for predicting, interpreting, and responding to similarly affect-laden scenes that have been connected by cognition—a combination Tomkins has called psychological magnification. In the language of affect theory, cognitive therapy attempts to change psychological magnification by restructuring associations to a triggered affect and thus changing emotion and "remembered" biography. Just as a script or a schema is the product of both affect and cognition, the treatment offered in cognitive therapy alters these structures by interfering with the combination of affect and cognition that had existed earlier.

Sometimes it is less the patient's beliefs about the subjective experience than the expression of affect that is at issue. Boys are taught that "only wimps feel afraid" and girls are told that "nice girls don't get angry." Dysfunctional families often send the message that "it's not okay to talk about feelings." After an interaction with her husband, one patient reported intense feelings of hopelessness and irritability, lasting over a day. When, that night, she awoke her husband because she felt she couldn't swallow, he told her not to worry because this symptom was only a manifestation of her imagination. During the initial interview she was asked what had gone through her mind at the time; she replied that she had thought "He's not validating my feelings."

It turned out that this was a recurring theme from childhood; often she had been told that she was "too emotional." The patient understood that because of some rule that had evolved between her and her family, a rule that had grown to the significance of a script or schema, she was not *allowed* to feel.

The cognitive therapist uses a technique called "the downward arrow" (Burns, 1980), through which we take such a statement and ask over and over again "if this (the current statement) is true, what does this mean?" until patient and therapist have reached some irreducible core. In the case of the patient described above, the downward arrow revealed the beliefs that (1) "It is useless to express feelings to anybody," (2) "No one believes me," and (3) "I am not important." It is this latter belief that operates as her core schema. Each of these three statements involves negative affect that has been incorporated into a concept of self and other.

THERAPEUTIC RELATIONSHIP

Within CT, affect theory has important implications for the therapeutic relationship. Take, for example, the automatic thoughts and images that occur within the stream of consciousness, often involving subjective appraisals of current situations. When the process of evaluation determines the presence of automatic thoughts, a cognitive therapist might tell the patient, "We will be like scientists together, detecting these thoughts, evaluating them, and correcting them." By this statement we shift attention from the person as a whole to the conclusions drawn by that individual; this defines the therapeutic relationship as a collaborative one, which reduces the imbalance of power and status often present in interactions between one who is defined as "sick" and one who is "well." Such an approach significantly reduces the patient's experience of shame.

Adopting an active, open, exploratory approach characterized by the willingness to share one's own feelings helps minimize shame. A therapist who, as a matter of principle, refuses to share at the affective level may well be replicating scenes from a family environment in which childish inquiries were met with silence or disapproval. No child is capable of understanding that these maneuvers were designed to protect the parent from the shame of exposure. Rather, the child "hears" such refusal as messages about personal disclosure ("it's not okay to talk about feelings or problems") or self-worth ("you're not worth listening to"). The developing child has been robbed of an opportunity to learn affect modulation and has been placed in a situation where emotional expression is linked with shame. Therapists must be aware that their facial expression and voice tone will be analyzed by patients in the language of their own upbringing.

The discipline of CT produces a therapeutic relationship quite unlike that of most other treatment settings. Since patient and therapist are joined as scientists studying the relation between thoughts and feelings, any thought or feeling that emerges during the therapeutic interaction may be studied as if it were an object of great interest. It is this therapeutic attitude that characterizes CT. Thoughts accompanied by intense negative affect will be assessed immediately; never will the patient be subjected to the sort of therapist inaction that might allow unintentional worsening of such distress. The active approach of the cognitive therapist defines and delimits the affective and cognitive linkage under investigation.

So it is that a cognitive therapist might ask a patient questions almost unthinkable for one trained in psychodynamic theory. I have found that asking "How did you know you were loved?" frequently triggers strong emotion. Should the patient respond with distress, anger, fear, or any other negative affect, I will then ask about the thoughts that accompanied the intense unpleasant feeling. By my explicit assurance that we are interested in the automatic thoughts responsible for such feelings, and through my own demeanor, I teach the patient that any emotion, no matter how powerful, can be broken down into pieces capable of analysis and change.

At all times patient and therapist aim for a collaborative relationship (Beck et al., 1979). While it is true that certain patients, notably borderlines, may find any shared enterprise beyond their capabilities, the therapist's constant return to the language of collaboration provides a significant decrease in anxiety and shame. Hypnotic intervention requires the operator to be active and the subject passive; a patient in psychoanalysis will talk much more than the analyst. When a cognitive therapy session is going well, patient and therapist will talk equally; this is another realm of therapeutic collaboration. Within such an environment it is possible for any emotion to be unearthed, examined, detoxified, and reduced to its component innate affects and interacting cognitions.

THERAPEUTIC PROCESS

All cognitive therapy is modeled on the observation that emotions and behavior are determined not by our actual experience of the world but by the way those experiences are structured (Beck, 1976; Kelly, 1955). As described above, it is through the process of case formulation and conceptualization that the therapist forms an understanding of the reaction patterns typical for any patient (Persons, 1989). Associated with any emotion must be some constellation of cognitions; an emotion powerful enough and intrusive enough to bring someone to treatment will always be associated with a group of thoughts that have been taken for granted by the patient. These cognitions, often in telegraphic form, occur spontaneously on the periphery of consciousness and are frequently accepted as fact (Beck & Rush, 1989). The early phase of cognitive therapy is spent teaching the patient to tune in to this involuntary automatic thinking.

Here we see another link between the cognitive theories of Beck and the affect theory of Tomkins. The healthy individual works with an affect system that is remarkably flexible, not locked into any particular group of thoughts. But emotional illness is characterized by the obligatory association between an affect and some recurring cluster of cognitions; the cognitions come to act as stimuli for the affect, which then calls forth more of the same cluster of thoughts. Treatment aims to break into this automatic and destructive pattern, seen so clearly in the global thinking of the depressed or chronically anxious patient.

The therapist might begin treatment by asking the patient to describe some disturbing event that has taken place or some scene witnessed and experienced. With care, the therapist will demonstrate that the story being told is not really a matter of facts, but a mass of appraisals, thoughts, and interpretations colored by some affect. I'll explain that a fact is something that has actual existence, something about which 1,000 out of 1,000 people would agree. It helps to explain that feelings are not facts — that they may be based on facts, but they are different from facts. Here is where it is important for the patient to learn the names of the nine innate affects, the feelings associated with each, and the basic rules of the affect system. Affect, of course, is a part of our normal bodily equipment; the thoughts that so disturb the patient must be identified as entities quite apart from the affects with which they have come to be experienced.

Many patients come into therapy believing that their feelings are "bad." A basic understanding of the affect system helps them grasp the nature of emotion, counters the cognitive distortion that we call "emotional reasoning," and interferes with the erroneous conclusion that "if I *feel* this way, it must be so." CT teaches the patient to test the cognitive component of emotion, for emotions are greatly influenced by what we tell ourselves about a particular feeling.

Over the course of therapy, patients are taught to *detect* self-defeating automatic thoughts, *evaluate* and question them, and then *correct* these thoughts toward new, rational views that are more objective, adaptive, and capable of providing solutions for the problems of the moment. Patient and therapist devise experiments and assign homework that will allow the patient to *know experientially* the effects of the new cognitions and beliefs. To drive home the connection between processes involved, I offer the handy acronym DECK: Detect, Evaluate, Correct, Know.

"Cognitions coassembled with affect," says Tomkins (1992, p. 7) "become hot and urgent. Affects coassembled with cognitions become better informed and smarter. . . . The amplified information of the motivational system can be and must be transformed by the cognitive system and the transformed information of the cognitive system can be and must be amplified by the motivational system." Change is most likely to occur if the therapist can identify, access, and test hot cognitions (Beck, 1987).

Sometimes we will ask the patient to *imagine* a scene in which the target affect and accompanying automatic thoughts are likely to occur; by this process of imagery one is encouraged to *experience* a scene in the safety of the therapeutic environment. Similarly, patient and therapist may play roles, experimenting with feelings and thoughts. Affect theory helps us devise experiments that will elicit emotion. In this way emotions are brought into the therapeutic interchange, so they may be detected, evaluated, and corrected.

Let's take the example of a patient who views the world as a dangerous place and describes her mother as anxious and overprotective. For one such patient I would act as a frightened mother, staring somewhat to the side, my voice trembling as I exclaimed, "Oh my god, don't touch that!" or "Come back here, don't go over there, you'll fall and kill yourself!" Once the patient reported that my mimicry was accurate, I would then ask how a child might have felt in the presence of the mother I had just portrayed, what thoughts might have come to that child's mind, and what messages the child might have received about the world.

Similarly, if a patient described his father as hypercritical, I might conjure a scene in which a child had just spilled a glass of milk. With my face and voice displaying disgust, shame, and anger, I would exclaim, "How could you *do* that?!" and then check for the patient's thoughts and feelings. Such vignettes are based on the words and affects used by patients to describe their own parents, but are colored by my own developing hypotheses of the patient's central views about self, others, and the world at large.

So powerful is the affective impact of role-playing and imagery work that the cognitive therapist must be firmly grounded in a conceptualization, lest the purpose of the intervention become lost in the tides of emotion so produced. Done properly, such activity within the therapeutic interaction will produce hot cognitions that lead further into the patients' central schemas. Knowing, for example, that any interruption of the positive affects interest–excitement or enjoyment–joy can trigger shame, I might devise experiments intended to elicit shame. Such experiment would be attempted only with the express permission of the patient, and only when a working collaborative relationship had been established.

This technique is helpful for a patient who, in session, reports thoughts without feeling. In the spirit of such an experiment, I once asked a patient to tell me about a recent movie she seemed to enjoy, after which I responded, "You liked that? I *hated* it!" Her eyes and head dropped immediately; she stuttered for an instant, and then began to respond in ways characteristic of her relationship with a highly critical father. It was easy for us to determine from this experiment that the hot cognitions "I'm not good enough" and "I never know what's right" represented the *attack self* pole of Nathanson's compass of shame and could be treated by techniques of reframing and reattribution.

For this purpose, we then devise an alternative view that counters what Beck et al. (1979) call the personalization distortion of attributing a negative outcome to a defect in the self. The view we construct is, "Her opinion is different. This does not mean mine is invalid. Everyone is allowed his or her own perspective." This provides a cognitive model through which the toxicity of shame may be decreased. Next we try to ascertain whether this new way of thinking may be useful in other circumstances known to trigger shame.

In another case, I asked a fashion-conscious woman to compliment what I was wearing, after which I then discredited the requested compliment by saying, "Oh, this old thing? It's way out of style now." For this patient, the experiment triggered thoughts of her own stupidity, also demonstrating effectively how her husband might feel when she rejected his compliments.

On occasion, after explaining carefully what I am about to do, I will address the patient by the wrong name, noticing the thoughts that accompany the brief moment of shame so produced. These techniques can also be considered a form of desensitizing exposure for the "rejection sensitive" patient.

CONCLUSION

Given the same patient and the same expression of emotion, a therapist with a background in psychoanalytic theory will operate quite differently from one trained in cognitive therapy. Proper psychodynamic technique might encourage the development of associations to any thought, memory, or idea, associations made in response to the affects that amplify them and that range far and wide from their starting point. A cognitive therapist will forestall such wide-ranging digression from whatever thought or feeling has been expressed, attempting instead to examine this particular combination of cognition and affect as an example of a class of similar thoughts.

The informed cognitive therapist believes that affect, intentional behavior, and neocortical cognition are interconnected, and that they influence one another reciprocally. Cognitive therapy involves a focused attempt to identify and correct faulty information processing, maladaptive assumptions, and early negative schemas in order to alter the emotional aspects of experience, thus opening the way for new behavioral responses. These, in turn, will reciprocally influence the cognitive realm. Affect theory provides the essential link between cognition and the biology of emotion.

REFERENCES

Beck, A. T. (1976). *Cognitive therapy and emotional disorders*. New York: International Universities Press.

Beck, A. T. (1987). Cognitive therapy. In J. Zeig (Ed.), *The evolution of psychotherapy*. New York: Brunner/Mazel.

Beck, A. T., Emery, G., & Greenberg, R. L. (1985). *Anxiety disorders and phobias: A cognitive perspective*. New York: Basic Books.

Beck, A. T., Freeman, A., & Associates. (1990). *Cognitive therapy of personality disorders*. New York: Guilford.

Beck, A. T., & Rush, A. J. (1989). Cognitive therapy. In H. I. Kaplan, B. J. Saddock

(Eds.), *Comprehensive textbook of psychiatry: Vol. 5.* Baltimore, MD: Williams & Wilkins.

Beck, A. T., Rush, A. J., Shaw, B. G., & Emery, G. (1979). *Cognitive therapy of depression.* New York: Guilford.

Burns, D. D. (1980). *Feeling good: The new mood therapy.* New York: Morrow.

Freeman, A., Simon, K. M., Beutler, L. E., & Arkowitz, H. (1989). *Comprehensive handbook of cognitive therapy.* New York: Plenum Press.

Guidano, V. F., & Liotti, G. (1983). *Cognitive processes and emotional disorders.* New York: Guilford.

Kelly, G. (1955). *The psychology of personal constructs.* New York: Norton.

Lazarus, R. S. (1989). Constructs of the mind in mental health and psychotherapy. In A. Freeman, K. M. Simon, L. E. Beutler, & H. Arkowitz (Eds.), *Comprehensive handbook of cognitive therapy.* New York: Plenum Press.

Nathanson, D. L. (Ed.). (1987). *The many faces of shame.* New York: Guilford.

Nathanson, D. L. (1992). *Shame and pride: Affect, sex, and the birth of self.* New York: Norton.

Persons, J. B. (1989). *Cognitive therapy in practice: A case formulation approach.* New York: Norton.

Stern, D. N. (1991). *Infancy: Relationships represented in the mind: A developmental perspective.* Paper presented at the 144th annual meeting of the American Psychiatric Association, New Orleans, LA.

Tomkins, S. S. (1962). *Affect, imagery, and consciousness, Vol. 1: The positive affects.* New York: Springer.

Tomkins, S. S. (1963). *Affect, imagery, and consciousness, Vol. 2: The negative affects.* New York: Springer.

Tomkins, S. S. (1982). Affect theory. In P. Ekman (Ed.), *Emotion in the human face* (pp. 353–395). Cambridge, UK: Cambridge University Press.

Tomkins, S. S. (1991). *Affect, imagery and consciousness, Vol. 3: The negative affects: Anger and fear.* New York: Springer.

Tomkins, S. S. (1992). *Affect, imagery, and consciousness, Vol. 4: Cognition.* New York: Springer.

Wright, J. H., & Thase, M. E. (1992). Cognitive and biological therapies: A synthesis. *Psychiatric Annals, 22,* 451–458.

Young, J. E. (1990). *Cognitive therapy for personality disorders: A schema focused approach.* Sarasota, FL: Professional Resource Exchange.

8

Affect Theory and Psychopharmacology

Donald L. Nathanson

James M. Pfrommer

Therapists who understand the affect system are unlikely to spend much time debating the difference between mind and body or arguing whether it is wrong to use medication for what seems like a psychological problem. It is through their effect on the body that the affects make themselves known. Facial display is dependent on an intricate web of nerve fibers carrying instructions to delicate muscles nested within a microcirculation that can be altered rapidly to change our experience of each pattern of muscle contraction and relaxation. The rate of breathing and the rate and intensity of cardiac contraction are influenced by affect. These are very much matters of the body even though they are experienced as significant parts of our emotional responses to mental phenomena.

How can something go wrong with the circuitry for innate affect? The simplest example, of course, is our universal experience with ingested substances like caffeine and alcohol, which have profound effects on what and how we feel. In this chapter, James Pfrommer and I suggest that every drug that alters our emotions can only do so by working through the affect system. We suggest that psychopharmacology is nothing more alarming than an extension of what we have always sensed about the relation between body and emotion.

It is clear that one can alter the experience of innate affect by manipulation of the biochemical environment. What about those situations in which an individual experiences an affect, with all its somatic and cognitive concomitants, in the apparent absence of any known stimulus for innate affect? One reasonable hypothesis is that an acquired or inherited defect of the biochemical sequences responsible for the expression or maintenance of any affect produces ideoaffective complexes that present to us as clinical conditions quite refractory to verbal therapeutic techniques.

As we begin to think about each psychiatric medication in terms of the affects it turns down and/or allows to be turned up, it becomes clear that careful investigation of which affects are most important in each of the major diagnostic categories and which treatments best allow normalization of affective experience would reap major benefits. –DLN

IN THIS PAPER we will show how affect theory, introduced by Silvan S. Tomkins (1962, 1963, 1991, 1992), can influence our practice of psychopharmacology. Biology, psychology, and descriptive psychiatry are linked by their relation to the affect system; such an understanding allows greatly increased sophistication in our efforts to ameliorate certain unpleasant affective states.

THE FUNCTION OF AFFECT

Tomkins (1962) stressed that each affect functions as an amplifier that calls attention to anything with which it becomes associated or "coassembled." There are nine of these nonspecific amplifiers, and therefore nine different ways that affect can, by this amplification, increase the likelihood that the information with which it has been assembled will be used by the organism. Interest–excitement and enjoyment–joy, the two positive affects, are counterbalanced by six decidedly negative affects (fear–terror, distress–anguish, anger–rage, dissmell, disgust, and shame–humiliation), all of which may be halted instantly by surprise–startle, an affect that is too brief to have either a positive or a negative flavor. By their effects on bodily structures that evolved for other reasons (heart rate, voice, facial musculature, sweat, etc.) these nine innate affects call attention to their triggering source in nine quite different ways.

Important things *feel* important because they have been amplified by affect. Amplification provides both the power to cause awareness and the motivation to make us take action. Yet these *psychological* qualities of the affect system are completely dependent on the gestalt formed by the *biological* effects triggered at what Nathanson (1988, 1992) has called the sites of action for each mechanism. Although the circulatory system did not evolve so that the heart might thump harder in excitement or fear, the affect system evolved to act on or influence circulatory function in highly specific ways. Similarly, the mechanisms for the control of sweating, breathing, and a wide range of voluntary muscles may be placed momentarily under the command of the affect system.

All of these sites of action for innate affect are quite ordinary biological mechanisms set off by well-known groups of neurotransmitters. Since these sites of action can be triggered under the control of affect programs, we infer that one of the properties of the affect system is to direct the release of neurotransmitters. If some aberration of neurotransmitter metabolism causes things to happen at the sites of action normally associated with one or another innate affect, we humans are likely to mistake the pattern of actions so released as the gestalt normally associated with a normal affect. In such situations, the psychopharmacologist looks for medication that normalizes affect physiology.

As Nathanson (1992) has suggested with his computer analogy for the division of affect-related information, affective disorders may result from malfunctions of hardware, firmware, or software. Psychopharmacological treatment may be indicated for defects occurring at the hardware or firmware levels, or in those special circumstances when problems in living push the software of affect management into realms that overload cognition.

The first goal of psychopharmacologic evaluation is to ascertain whether the patient's affects are serving as a source of information for living or are in some way interfering with effective living. Often patients will assume that only illness brings negative affect, or that negative affect has no value and should be eliminated. By its nature, negative affect is unpleasant and motivates us to "turn off" whatever has triggered it; it is only logical to expect that some people might wish to get rid of the affect mechanism itself rather than use it to locate whatever potential danger it is amplifying.

Nevertheless, just as we would be at risk were we to lose our ability to sense pain, our ability to live in the world is assisted by the information given us through unpleasant emotional experience. In many ways, the affects are analogous to the gauges on the dashboard of a car. A temperature gauge that reads in the red provides information that is neither pleasant nor welcome—yet it is of no use to ignore, blame, rage at, or be ashamed of the gauge. Many people fail to process the subtle data provided by the affect system; they seem unable to learn how to make use of the information so amplified. Recognition and acceptance of affect is central to competent human performance.

Much of our work as psychotherapists requires a solid understanding of innate affect. Yet the patients who are referred to a psychopharmacologist often experience affect at levels of intensity and over durations that cannot be explained by the normal range of physiological affect mechanisms. In such cases, affect provides information that misleads or that takes over consciousness to an untoward degree.

DISORDERS INVOLVING AFFECT

Who is sent to the psychopharmacologist? Some people are sent to us simply because the primary therapist has given up. Stubborn, recalcitrant, difficult patients are referred for medication in hope that *something* will shock their system into readiness for change. Even though we may try one or another kind of medicine, here the real need is for change in the paradigm on which treatment has been based (Kluft, 1992).

It is our responsibility to determine whether the patient's emotionality comes from memory that has been repressed, ignored, or forgotten, from obligatory interaction with family members whose contribution to one's daily life has been overlooked, or from a flawed or faulty system of cognitive processing. A switch to family therapy, psychoanalysis, cognitive-behavioral therapy, or hypnotic intervention involves the software of human emotion rather than its hardware.

Most of the time, however, patients come to use because they seem locked in one emotion or another. All of us get stuck every once in a while; the competent adult knows how to take a break, go to a movie or sporting event, drink a modest amount of alcohol, or find some other way of shifting our affect away from the subject of the moment. On occasion, psychiatric medication will be needed to modulate an affect that we cannot handle any other way. Low-dose phenothiazines and benzodiazepines are excellent medications for the acute relief of uncontrollable, high-density fear–terror or distress–anguish. The best among us may get overloaded occasionally and need the kind of momentary relief available by taking a milligram or so of trifluoperazine (Stelazine), or a modest amount of alprazolam (Xanax).

On the other hand, the persistent distress–anguish of a weeping dysthymic disorder, the rampant fear–terror of panic disorder, the polarity of inappropriate interest–excitement and the counterbalancing inability to trigger positive affect seen in bipolar affective illness seem to represent true disorders of affect mechanisms. We assume that some defect of neurotransmitter metabolism has altered normal affect physiology, and we try to repair the hardware defect with medication that returns this physiology toward normal.

Certainly it is easy enough to spot the patient whose complaints fit into one of the classical symptom patterns mentioned above. Bruce J. Berg (personal communication, 1993) has suggested that each of the affect programs has evolved as patterns of effects involving many neurotransmitters, while the best known affective disorders are more likely experienced as the gestalt of the effects of single neurotransmitter action. While the patient assembles the data provided at the various sites of action as if it represented an ordinary innate affect, we recognize instead the more limited action of an aberrant neurotransmitter system. The psychopharmacologist is faced with patients who complain about unpleasant symptoms that fall into subtle patterns that both resemble innate affect and differ from it. Our search for affective experience that is of greater-than-normal intensity and/or duration is also aided by a clear understanding of normal affect.

PATTERN RECOGNITION AND AFFECT DYNAMICS

Innate affect is always associated with a triggering event. For the affect shame–humiliation, this involves any impediment to the continuation of the positive affects interest–excitement or enjoyment–joy. But physiological shame affect is not what we have been brought up to think of as the emotion shame. The model elaborated by Nathanson as the compass of shame (1992) suggests that any such impediment to positive affect may initiate one of four distinctly different patterns of behavior — *withdrawal, attack self, avoidance*, and *attack other*. Experienced by the individual or witnessed by outsiders, the events associated with shame affect may therefore include actual withdrawal, masochistic submission to the will of others, narcissistic avoidance of shame, or actual attack on the person of others. In the adult, shame may be triggered when the interpersonal bridge is broken (Kaufman, 1985), when something has been revealed that we would have preferred kept private, or when we fail.

Guilt seems to have developed as a subset of shame. Our studies of the developmental pathways for guilt (Nathanson, 1987) suggest that the mature emotion involves two affects — shame at the discovery of one's action, and fear of reprisal. In brief, we are ashamed when something hidden is exposed, and guilty when improper actions have been revealed.

The normal operation of the hardware, firmware, and software of emotion would explain any moment of shame or guilt brought on by such triggers.

Yet there are many clinical situations characterized by shame and guilt of far longer duration and far greater intensity than would make sense in this model. Few of us would be puzzled by a patient who complains ceaselessly about guilt for which no reasonable cause may be ascertained. We understand unremitting guilt as part of the pattern of symptoms associated with classical depression; treatment with tricyclic antidepressants (TCAs) is usually quite effective.

Klein, Gittleman, Quitkin, and Rifkin (1980) described patients with one subtype of depression that included atypical vegetative signs such as hypersomnia, increased appetite, a great deal of anxiety, and the triad of chocolate craving, rejection sensitivity, and applause hunger — symptoms that all tended to respond poorly or incompletely to the TCAs but rather well to the monoamine oxidase inhibitor antidepressants (MAOIs). These "atypical" depressions, which we now also treat with the selective serotonin reuptake inhibitor antidepressants (SSRIs), have been described by Nathanson (1987) as characterized by unremitting shame affect.

Social phobia and the avoidant personality disorder, both surely less about fear than shame, may also be understood and treated as highly patterned conditions associated with shame experience that has been triggered by abnormalities of neurotransmitter function, and that also respond well to SSRI or MAOI treatment.

The psychopharmacologist looks for averted gaze, downcast eyes, and the stammer or moment of acute discomfort that so often accompanies shame affect. We learn sensitivity to the brittle anger associated with the *attack other* form of shame response, as well as flashes of defensive narcissism and masochism. Much of the symptomatology seen in the borderline syndrome involves shame affect displayed as bursts of anger, "narcissism," and the well-known oscillation between overvaluation and devaluation of the significant other; these features of the borderline spectrum respond to treatment with the SSRIs fluoxetine, sertraline, and paroxetine. Even when the borderline patient's unusual sensitivity to shame has been ameliorated by such pharmacologic intervention, much psychotherapy is needed to help normalize the patient's relation to affect.

Because each affect appears as a specific pattern of bodily responses, we outsiders may suspect the presence of an affect even when the patient doesn't know one has been triggered. Among the motor movements we study are facial expressions, as well as the pace, tone, and volume of speech. The crying patient may display anger in the motor pattern of reaching for tissues or the steady whining tone of voice.

In addition to these physiological patterns, we also note the associated cognitions — the paranoid patient who says he feels people are watching him and laughing at him for being overweight is dealing with shame, while the apparently equally paranoid patient who claims the CIA is plotting against him because he is a threat to world security is dealing with fear and anger. One might treat the former patient with drugs like the SSRIs, which reduce or detoxify shame experience, and the latter with phenothiazines, which decrease fear.

Each class of medication deals with different neurotransmitter systems and may be associated with different innate affects. We think of the benzodiazepine tranquilizers as antianxiety agents that are involved with the neurotransmitter gamma-aminobutyric acid (GABA); now we must begin to wonder whether GABA is what Nathanson (1988, 1992) calls a biochemical mediator of the affect fear–terror. Above we noted a group of clinical conditions characterized by what appears to be an abnormal relation to shame affect and a certain responsiveness to medications that increase the amount of serotonin available in the central nervous system. While it is possible that this neurotransmitter may be involved in the mediation of both physiological shame affect and the type of shame seen in these disorders, the best we can say at this time is that the correction of serotonin abnormalities reduces shame hypersensitivity. (Just because something acts as a remedy does not mean that its absence caused the condition in question.)

Snider, Fisher, and Agranoff (1987) have linked phosphoinositide (part of the "second messenger system") to a host of clinical disorders, including bipolar affective illness. The affect theorist wonders whether the normal expression of interest–excitement might be related to any of the fifteen neuroreceptors (including muscarinic, cholinergic, α-adrenergic, and 5-HT$_2$) that have been associated with phosphoinositide. It is generally assumed that abnormalities in the manufacture, transport, or metabolism of specific neurotransmitters may be responsible for specific classes of psychiatric illness. Affect theory may explain the clinical presentation of these biochemical defects and offer new ways to study the neurobiology of normal emotion.

Take, for instance, the mildly hypomanic patient whose interest–excitement is triggered not by the sort of data influx gradient normally called novelty, but by the biochemical illness itself. Our life experience of normal sequences of source and affect leads us to believe that any particular moment of affect has been triggered by its normal source. All our lives we have been excited only when some triggering event has fulfilled Tomkins's criteria for the release of the preprogrammed innate affect mechanism. Yet if we are hypomanic, something else has released the neurotransmitters (and therefore stimulated certain sites of action) normally associated with excitement. We experience interest or excitement in the absence of this normal sequence because we have deduced erroneously the presence of the normal sequence of source and affect.

Were the sites of action stimulated too few, or were they stimulated in a pattern unrecognizable to us as part of an innate affect, we might fail to register or "think about" the effect of this neurotransmitter. The sweat gland is a minor site of action for the affect fear–terror; drugs that cause sweating are unlikely to make us think we are afraid. But when enough of the pattern associated with an innate affect has been triggered, we act as if an affect had been triggered by its normal sequence of events, and scroll through our experience in an attempt to explain this apparent affect. This is the reason hypomanic patients seem interested in or excited by nearly anything. The affect precedes its "assigned" trigger.

This is our model for classical depression. Whatever neurotransmitter dysfunction is responsible for the persistent distress-anguish associated with that syndrome, it makes the patient think about life events that are steady-state and of higher-than-optimal intensity. Whatever pattern of neurotransmitter malfunction is responsible for classical depression may also trigger something that the patient can only interpret as guilt, which must then be explained in terms of one's life experience of improper actions.

One whose guilt is completely and permanently relieved by confession and/or penance has suffered this emotion for reasons associated with normal neurochemistry. One who in therapy confesses and "works through" crime after crime with scant relief of the underlying guilt is more likely dealing with some pattern of affective experience brought into consciousness by something wrong with neurotransmitter biology. All emotional experience is a matter of the biology of affect and the psychology associated with our life history. It is the job of the psychopharmacologist to recognize the patterns into which symptoms may be grouped, and to use these patterns to diagnose and treat any persistent affective state that is due to aberrations in the biology of affect.

Nevertheless, even a patient with a known disturbance of neurotransmitter physiology (a biological defect responsible for a persistent affect state) is capable of experiencing a normal affect when the trigger for that affect is actuated. A hypomanic patient may still experience profound excitement when exposed to something truly novel, just as a borderline or social "phobic" patient may be embarrassed in ways indistinguishable from normal. It is essential that we instruct patients in the language and range of normal affective experience in order that they learn to distinguish the normal from what is part of their illness. A clear understanding of affect theory will allow the clinician to answer the question so often asked by patients: "Is my illness psychological or biological?"

A 40-year-old lawyer had spent 12 years in psychotherapy for diffi-culty making, forming, and maintaining intimate relationships, and the sense that he rarely if ever "had a good time" anywhere. The apparent normality of his self-image, thoughts, and feelings about the future, his ability to work effectively, and his involvement in recreational activities had always convinced both him and the treating therapist that he was not "depressed." On the premise that his symptoms were caused by a rela-tively constant shame state unassociated with triggers that could be found in his present or past life, pharmacologic treatment was initiated with sertraline in doses ranging from 25–50 mg/d.

Within a few days of starting this regimen he reported significant improvement in his general state of well-being and began to laugh with pleasure at ideas and comments that earlier he would have ignored. Much as if he were in the caboose of a train, viewing his life prior to the institution of this medication, he now began to describe a history of shame experiences of such constancy that he called them the "atmo-sphere" of his life. Over a period of two months he began to learn how to live without this painful affective state, how to enter a new situation without his (previously denied) expectation of inadequacy, incompe-tence, failure, "stupidity," or ungainliness.

Of particular interest during his subsequent psychotherapy were the moments when he was embarrassed for reasons that might have caused shame for anyone, and that responded to previously ineffective psycho-therapeutic techniques. "I still get embarrassed," he said, "but the 'hang time' of the feeling is much shorter."

This case demonstrates how a subtle disorder of mood can become so thoroughly integrated with the development of an individual's personal-ity that the relief of such a disorder requires or makes possible massive revision of one's concept of self.

A 38-year-old salesman had smoked marijuana at least twice each day since his 12th birthday. Adolescence requires us to develop scripts for the management of sexuality, increased body strength, and a host of interpersonal tasks. For this patient, all of these developmental mile-stones had been achieved through a haze of drug-induced dissociation. Unless so protected, he tended to handle the experiences of intense ex-citement, anger, distress, and fear by exploding in rage. Each of his previous attempts to stop using marijuana had been terminated by a rising tide of negative affect for which he had no skills of modulation. Treatment aimed at the identification of each innate affect and the devel-opment of techniques of affect modulation allowed him to become who

*he might have been had these life tasks not been influenced by his drug
history.*

Just as a biological illness may produce the equivalent of an innate
affect that must be explained and handled like affect triggered in the
normal ways, an exogenous substance can influence affective development. The chronic use of adrenergic substances taken for the treatment
of allergic rhinitis or asthma can have as much influence on our ability
to understand our emotional environment as the presence in the blood-
stream of too much or too little thyroxin. Sophisticated treatment must
take into account the relation of such substances to the affect system.

Although subtle neurotransmitter defects may be responsible for some
cases of substance abuse, it is of perhaps equal importance to recognize
that those whose use of marijuana and alcohol has begun in early adolescence are the most likely to have been reared in families that provided
inadequate psychosocial systems for the modulation of innate affect.
Successful pharmacologic intervention will often necessitate a prolonged
period of psychotherapy that fosters the integration of this new affective
climate.

It would be misleading and inaccurate to explain real life as characterized by long periods of calm (during which no affect is triggered) punctuated by bursts of stimuli that trigger discrete episodes of innate affect
that blend gracefully into the preexisting calm. So much is going on at
any moment that there are lots of stimuli capable of triggering affect and
therefore gaining amplification and consequent entry into consciousness.
Sources of affect give way to one another constantly, producing the ebb
and flow of feeling that color waking experience. Tomkins (1962) has
codified all 19 of the possible interrelations and sequences of innate
affect in his chapter "Affect Dynamics," work that holds up well even in
this era of attention to affect analogues produced by the disorders of
biology that require pharmacotherapy.

MEDICATION RESPONSE

The therapist skilled in the recognition of innate affect and affect dynamics often finds our diagnostic nomenclature cumbersome and inadequate. It would be so much easier were illnesses classified by the affects
responsible for the symptoms expressed and experienced. The pleomor-
phic group of "depressions" is characterized by varying mixtures of all
the negative affects — only the chronicity of the resultant assemblage
validates the umbrella term "depression." Let us examine very briefly

some of the otherwise puzzling reactions to medication seen in this group.

By the time they are referred for medication, many depressed patients seem so frozen that they are nearly unable to express any emotion. Some of these patients exhibit swings of affect that have puzzled many clinicians. The anergic, nearly immobile patient who begins to cry some weeks after starting an antidepressant is not getting worse, despite the fears of family and friends. In these cases, whatever has blocked the expression of affect has been released enough that distress–anguish may peep through. Often this is a sign that the drug really is working!

The affect interest–excitement can be inhibited by social rules that prohibit its expression; people who are forbidden to look or act excited will be seen as depressed. Anything that encourages a broader range of affective expression will produce a release of previously restricted positive affect. The phenomenology of the cocktail party is dependent on the common observation that modest doses of alcohol encourage the appearance of conviviality and boisterous sociality when positive affect has been held in check by work-related (shame- and fear-based) rules for affect modulation.

Klein et al. (1980) have suggested that it is useful to segregate dysphoric patients on the basis of their ability to respond with pleasure to normal stimuli. In the language of affect theory, anhedonic patients seem to have either primary dysfunction or massive suppression of the affect interest–excitement, whereas mood-reactive patients make and maintain enough of this positive affect that its acute reduction can trigger enjoyment–joy. To the degree that one cannot generate interest, a major substrate for the other positive affect is lost; it is this combination of affective inhibitions that we describe as anhedonia.

Early in the development of an intimate relationship, a lonely and lovelorn individual may feel wonderful to the point of mild grandiosity, require less sleep than usual, and greet the world with far more "energy" than before. Love gives permission for exuberant positive affect that is quenched and daunted when the relationship fails. The therapist who has counseled a patient through several sequences of apathy, excitement, loss, and a return to apathy may well wonder whether these mood swings should be treated with lithium salts as a variant of bipolar affective illness.

These patients turn out to be exquisitely vulnerable to shame; success in love provides external validation of their personal adequacy and produces temporary lysis of their chronic shame state. Affect theory provides a novel explanation of what is often called "extreme mood reactivity." Tomkins (1962) has stated that complete resolution of chronic and enduring shame will produce intense enjoyment–joy, while incomplete resolution will produce excitement. An understanding of the complex equilibrium between shame and the positive affects fosters radical alterations in psychotherapy. Many of these patients, long suspected to harbor a mild form of bipolar affective illness that may some day require treatment with lithium salts, are actually responding to the lysis of chronic shame. Similarly, patients who seem literally to burst into excitement when released by TCAs from chronic depression may be expressing the normal dynamics of affect rather than a subtle form of bipolar illness.

Describing this group of patients in a different frame of reference, Klein et al. (1980) have stated that the MAOIs damp the swings of such moods; the SSRIs may be even more effective in such situations. It is important to realize that directly proportional to the suddenness of one's release from any chronic inhibition of positive affect will be the magnitude and intensity of the positive affect released. Both the released positive affect and the preexisting mood are misunderstood by the patient in terms of associations to past personal events, rather than the more important dynamics of innate affect.

Whereas Freud saw all excitement as intrinsically connected to the sexual drive, Tomkins maintains that the two mechanisms are entirely separate despite the avidity with which they coassemble. Nathanson (1992) suggests that the stimulus gradient provided by the rising tide of sexual arousal is a perfect trigger for interest–excitement, the drive and its amplifying affect then forming a mutually reinforcing, apparently unitary pair that all of us know as "sexual excitement." The loss of libido so frequently associated with depressive anhedonia, as well as the loss of appetite for food, may be understood as failure of the affective amplification necessary for normal function.

No matter what the cause, any difficulty in the generation or maintenance of interest–excitement will be experienced as problems with the *functions normally amplified* by that affect — memory, concentration, motivation, or decision-making. Patients do not complain about any specific problem with affect. Instead, they describe their situation as the loss of the entire gestalt of triggering stimulus and its analogic amplification: "There isn't anything interesting in my life anymore"; "I haven't seen a good movie in months"; "He just isn't as sexy as he used to be." It is the clinician who must determine that affective amplification is lacking (as in the case of anhedonic depression) or over-much (as in the case of shame affect in "atypical depression" and interest–excitement in hypomania).

A 45-year-old woman was referred for evaluation. She said that she could not get over the feeling that she had failed to produce a son for her husband. She was no longer able to enjoy her daughters, and had lost interest in work, marriage, and all other aspects of life. This major depression responded rapidly and completely to a course of treatment with a tricyclic antidepressant. With the return of her normal range of positive affect, she found it hard to believe how she could ever have felt guilty about something as removed from her personal control as the gender of her children.

Many of the older debates in clinical psychiatry can be resolved by an understanding of the biological nature of the affect system. No one would quibble with the psychoanalyst who prefers that the analysand experience "anxiety" adequate to pry significant memories loose from storage in the unconscious. Yet as Nathanson (1992) has explained in his chapter "Overload: Affect Beyond the Level of Tolerance," both psychosocial interaction and biological illness are capable of magnifying affect to levels of intensity that can only be handled by methods inimical to uncovering therapy. In such situations, judicious use of medication can normalize the biology of affect and augment the efficacy of previously ineffective therapeutic techniques.

THE SHAME OF PSYCHOPHARMACOLOGY

Although systems of psychotherapy have always been based on the relationship between patient and therapist, psychopharmacology has been dominated by a medical model characterized by gross asymmetry of the therapeutic relationship. The laboratory-based physician often comes to see the patient as little more than the vehicle within which are stored certain mechanisms in need of repair, and expresses displeasure when therapeutic recommendations are seemingly ignored. Often a case seems to be "in trouble" not because the medication chosen has turned out to be incorrect, but because the patient feels defective or inadequate when offered a diagnosis that refers to a biological defect.

Such confusion between the shame associated with an attribute of the person and shame of the entire self is easy to understand. Of even more significance is the possibility that biological illnesses characterized by aberration of the physiology of the innate affect shame-humiliation may magnify to literally toxic proportions the patient's affective reaction to our offer of treatment. Central to good psychopharmacologic practice is this understanding that anybody who is asked to take chronic psychiatric medication will experience the therapeutic interaction as intensely shaming. We must remain in good empathic contact with the patient to whom we offer medication.

CONCLUSION

Most of our current diagnostic categories and therapeutic concepts must be revised in terms of this new understanding of human emotion. Nowhere is this more critical than in the realm of psychopharmacology, which seeks to normalize neurobiology so that an individual can experience innate affect at an intensity that allows optimal information-processing, and only when triggered by the innate triggers for which it has evolved.

REFERENCES

Kaufman, G. (1985). *Shame: The power of caring* (2nd ed.). Cambridge, MA: Schenkman Books, Inc.

Klein, D. F., Gittleman, R., Quitkin, F., & Rifkin, A. (1980). *Diagnosis and drug treatment of psychiatric disorders: Adults and children.* Baltimore, MD: Williams & Wilkins.

Kluft, R. P. (1992). Paradigm exhaustion and paradigm shift: Thinking through the therapeutic impasse. *Psychiatric Annals, 22,* 502–508.

Nathanson, D. L. (1987). A timetable for shame. In D. L. Nathanson (Ed.), *The many faces of shame.* New York: Guilford.

Nathanson, D. L. (1988). Affect, affective resonance, and a new theory for hypnosis. *Psychopathology, 21,* 126–137.

Nathanson, D. L. (1992). *Shame and pride: Affect, sex, and the birth of the self.* New York: Norton.

Snider, M. R., Fisher, S. K., & Agranoff, B. W. (1987). Inositide-linked second messengers in the central nervous system. In H. Y. Meltzer (Ed.), *Psychopharmacology: The third generation of progress.* New York: Raven Press.

Tomkins, S. S. (1962). *Affect, imagery, consciousness, Vol. 1: The positive affects.* New York: Springer.

Tomkins, S. S. (1963). *Affect, imagery, consciousness, Vol. 2: The negative affects.* New York: Springer.

Tomkins, S. S. (1991). *Affect, imagery, consciousness, Vol. 3: The negative affects: Anger and fear.* New York: Springer.

Tomkins, S. S. (1992). *Affect, imagery, and consciousness, Vol. 4: Cognition.* New York: Springer.

9

Image-Oriented Psychotherapy Using Drawings as a Feedback Mechanism

Jeanette Wright

That music, art, and dance may be used to communicate emotion comes as no surprise. What may be a bit more difficult to discern is the modality through which any of these nonverbal forms can manage to act as a medium of affective expression. Music may be the easiest to explain in terms of affect theory: individual sounds occur at rates that increase, decrease, or stay the same, and they vary in intensity or loudness at rates that increase, decrease, or stay the same. Sequences of sounds can trigger affect simply because these sequences fulfill the characteristics of any other stimulus for innate affect. The funeral dirge evokes distress–anguish because it is of constant density sustained for long periods of time; the tonalities involved produce coloration that offers little excitement or relief. The music chosen as accompaniment to motion pictures is a precise mirror and therefore amplifier of the action taking place in the drama, whether the unrelenting, unpleasant increase associated with fear, the optimally increasing cadences associated with excitement, the steady drone of distress, or the loud, raucous, steady noise that parallels (is an analogue of) and therefore triggers anger.

As we go through life, certain of these sequences may become known to us as reliable and replicable symbols for particular events.

In addition to their function as triggers for innate affect, they come to convey large amounts of information by association. Thus, the fanfare of trumpets is exciting not only because of its stimulus qualities in terms of the affect system but also because by the time we have reached adult status we have heard so many such fanfares that we know a great deal about what will happen next.

Many of us tend to move our bodies in ways that are influenced by music, and the art associated with this combination is called dance. The dancer can mimic any of the bodily actions associated with innate affect–the droop of distress, the chest thrust forward and up in pride, the whoop of joy–and also trigger affect in us as watchers by moving at a rate or intensity that fulfills the criteria for the release of any of the innate programs for affect. The tap dancer can trigger affect through both musical and dance modalities. There is a language of gesture that works to evoke feeling in the viewer by referencing such ideoaffective complexes.

Color, too, can become a signifier of mood. The bright yellow of sunshine, the dull gray of fog, the darker blacks of night–by the time we are old enough to have seen these hues and learned to associate them with specific situations, they have taken on the function of symbols. Yet steady bright sunlight can trigger distress when we are provided no opportunity for the relief that can be brought by the dark of night. Everything that can be produced as graphic art can be a source of affect by both symbolic, memorialized triggers and innate triggers.

In this chapter, Jeanette Wright demonstrates that when patients in therapy agree to draw as part of their attempt to communicate their inner life, what they draw can be understood both as symbolic representations of the experiences that need to be discussed and also as depictions of the affects associated with those moments. Wright shows that there are many patients who are able to show us their affects through what they draw even though they may be nearly mute if asked to talk about their feelings. The more you know about the facial displays associated with innate affect, the more you are likely to ask patients to draw when they seem unable to talk.
–DLN

IMAGE-ORIENTED PSYCHOTHERAPY is grounded in the tenets of psychoanalytic self psychology with the powerful added dimension of visual representation. It is my method for assisting patients in the graphic representation of their inner landscape, so they may see what they think and feel, what they know or almost know, and what they have disavowed or forgotten. By studying the faces they draw, patients learn to identify affective experience; further, in studying the rest of the figure, as well as the background of the drawings, they learn to recognize those biographical scenes that influence their current experience of affect. According to Basch (1983), the shared affect present in an interaction is the core of empathy. To this I would add that remembering what had to be forgotten is the beginning of a new sensitivity for oneself.

In the past 25 years of my own self-analysis, and in my work as a psychotherapist, I have been struck by the capacity of the drawn image to bring into consciousness that which words alone were unable to express. The image, as well as the creative interplay with the image, has become of central importance in my interaction with patients; consequently, I call my method of working "image-oriented psychotherapy." Using this approach, patients are not held to any universal symbol system but are assisted in finding the words that best describe the images they have made. Visual images often escape the mind's censor more readily than words. Therefore, when the drawn image precedes the words, a deeper level of meaning can be achieved.

When people draw or doodle, they often find faces in their markings. Building on Darwin's (1872/1979) work, Tomkins's (1962) study of the face as the locus of affect display brings reliability to image-oriented work. While the artwork is symbolic — and, therefore, subject to changing interpretations — the affects are not symbolic; they are more constant and more reliable. Affects may register on the face for a matter of seconds. However, affects displayed in a drawing create a record that can be looked at again and again. Tomkins found affect in the faces of people and in photographs of people. My work with patients demonstrates that affect can also be found in people's *drawings* of faces. Nathanson (1992), as the major translator of Tomkins's work on affect theory, has been a catalyst for the application of Tomkins's theories in my work as a psychotherapist.

Intrinsic to image-oriented psychotherapy is a tacit agreement between patient and therapist that each other's creativity is of value to the therapy and can be joined in the treatment. According to Tomkins, consciousness is a function of affect, and it is for me a rather profound experience to be present with patients as both consciousness and affect achieve translation in their imagery.

The drawn image further appears to me as a translation of preconscious and unconscious symbolic process made by the eye and the hand. Lawrence Kubie's (1958) work on the neurotic distortion of the creative process describes three concurrent streams of symbolic processes — the unconscious, the preconscious, and the conscious symbolic systems—that he believes operate in both the creativity and the psychological illness of the human being. He postulates further that the flexibility of symbolic imagery is made possible by the "free, continuous and concurrent action of preconscious processes" in contrast "to the rigid, repetitive and idiosyncratic imagery of unconscious processes." In using free association and free drawing, patients are working with preconscious symbolic processes, and old data becomes assembled in new patterns. I introduce free drawing into therapy in much the same way as I bring in free association.

Often, however, the drawings and the associations are not free and are bound to unconscious processes. The incorporation of free drawing with free association is a useful and even powerful technique through which to connect patients to their preconscious symbolic processes. I see the effects of this technique when patients express surprise about what they have drawn or said. Individual patients may have little or extraordinary talent; regardless, the creative process is the same. My purpose is to join basic principles of psychotherapy with the creative aspects of the personality.

Everyday I encounter patients who are reenacting and reliving what they cannot bear to remember. As a consequence, their emotions are not available to them as a source of information. They have yet to learn that emotions can provide a useful link to the source of their pain. There are many reasons for this phenomenon. For some, emotions are numbed through alcohol, drugs, and other self-destructive behaviors. Others fear emotion itself, as in posttraumatic stress disorder, which is so often characterized by the dread to repeat. Some, as in alexithymia, are unable to describe emotional experience and instead may endure severe somatic symptoms, and others have divided the affects among internal, alternate part-selves to end up with dissociative identity disorder. Whatever the variation, the theme for the patient seems to be the same: emotions are perceived as disturbing and overwhelming; they must be blocked.

When there is a disorder of emotion, experience can lose its context, the past can collapse into the present, and the individual can feel overloaded. The automatic response at that time may be to shore up the false self, shut down, attack others, or switch to an alternate personality. Our hope is that, through therapy, patients can learn new ways of "doing emotions." However, I have found that such patients must be highly motivated to undertake this task. One particular patient, embattled by thirty years of PTSD sequelae and now in her fifth year of therapy, has been strongly motivated to learn new tools for recognizing and modulating affect states. She recently said, "PTSD is like an albatross—if it hangs around your neck all these years, it's bound to stink." It is this "albatross factor" that often stimulates patients to consider my challenge that they learn how to "do emotions" differently.

For those patients who accept this challenge, I begin by creating structures with them that assist in the organization and reassociation of experience. Such structures are characterized by a shift from a problem-solving therapy to a treatment process focused on recognizing, under-standing, modulating, and visually representing emotions in order to link those emotions to biographical scenes and create new meanings. I explain that negative affect states are like an abscessed tooth that must be drained to obtain relief. The use of drawing during emotional upheavals can often modulate the emotions, give symbolic representation to trig-gering events, reduce the impetus to act out, and further permit patients to become participants in, observers of, and self-authorities over their own experience.

In volume 4 of *Affect, Imagery, Consciousness*, Tomkins (1992) refers to the "Image" as a blueprint for the primary feedback mechanism. Image-oriented psychotherapy utilizes drawing as an application of this principle. Tomkins further postulates the following:

- There exists a centrally-controlled reporting mechanism.
- Human beings achieve their purposes through a feedback mecha-nism.
- Such purpose is primarily a conscious purpose, i.e., to produce a centrally emitted blueprint that Tomkins calls the Image.
- Sensory data become conscious as imagery.
- Memory data must be translated into imagery.
- Both sensory- and memory-based images are the consequence of mechanisms that employ the feedback mechanism.
- A sharp distinction exists between the operation of imagery in sen-sory and memory matching and the Image as the blueprint for the primary feedback mechanism.
- The feedback system is a duplicating system, and what is duplicated is a centrally generated Image.

Informed by these principles, I have come to understand patient draw-ings as outcomes and evidence of psychotherapeutic change. The drawn image captures the current stimuli organized by the individual's internal image, and produces the central blueprint that makes conscious the past and the anticipated future. The drawings presented in this chapter came from an intersubjective process between patient and therapist as mediated by a piece of drawing paper; this process altered the central blue-print.

While functioning as a feedback mechanism for the patient, the drawing is also a message to the therapist that, of all the matters occupying the mind of the patient, whether verbalized or not, whatever is of most importance to the patient at this moment in time may be located in the drawing. At that point, I see my task as noticing this image and assisting the patient in discovering its meaning.

After a period of listening to verbal presentation of problems and concerns, I take a psychoeducational approach and introduce the patient to the language and basic principles of affect theory. It has proven useful to:

1. Point out that human beings are born with nine innate affects: two positive affects: interest–excitement and enjoyment–joy; one neutral affect: surprise–startle; six negative affects: fear–terror, distress–anguish, anger–rage, disgust, dissmell, and shame–humiliation. The preponderance of negative affects somewhat explains why it can be such a struggle to maintain equilibrium.

2. Refer to affects as preprogrammed biological information-processing systems. This helps me identify a person's inability to learn from experience as part of a more general failure to learn how to use emotions as signals to and information about oneself. In the effort to protect oneself from a hostile environment, some may focus on what others do, but have little awareness of how they themselves are being affected.

3. Emphasize that the affects are experienced on a continuum of intensity. If it appears that their lives are being lived at the extreme end of human emotion, they may have had to devise ways to protect themselves from emotional overload. Inquiry then follows to identify their particular pattern: How do they block or override emotional experience? Do they shut down all emotions? Do they numb emotions through drugs or alcohol? Do they fear emotion itself? Do they lack words to convey moods or feelings? Do they compartmentalize and divide emotions among alternate part-selves?

4. Explain that when their affects get triggered, whether by internal or external events, they may feel rage, rather than anger, terror rather than fear. I try to make it clear that it is possible for them to learn how to tolerate and contain milder levels of negative affect, and to avoid or interrupt the extreme forms.

5. Explain that affects only last a few seconds, but that moods can be

sustained for days, months, or years. I tell them the reward for learning to understand their emotions is that they can shorten the amount of time they feel depressed, agoraphobic, self-destructive, out of control, or whatever it is that disables them.

6. Refer to affects as biological and emotions as biographical. Nathanson (1992) has been particularly helpful to persons who feel as though they are "damaged goods" for having been sexually abused (p. 50). I explain that they may have absorbed the evil perpetrated upon them and are locked into a shame-based view of themselves. In coming to understand the affects as biologically driven, they begin to let go of their image of themselves as disgusting for also having experienced sexual pleasure.

7. Teach them to recognize their own physiological and behavioral responses to particular affects and then work with them to develop affective management protocols to use when these affects get triggered.

Each of the points above is incorporated into a method of image-oriented psychotherapy through which I attempt to elicit a patient's drawings of affects experienced during the session. Patients are also encouraged to draw at home when negative affect gets triggered and to bring the drawings to their next therapy session.

AFFECT PROCESSING:
PROTOCOLS AND STRUCTURES

Affect protocols are defined as documents developed by the patient and me that identify that patient's unique signs and symptoms for a specific affect. These protocols include step-by-step tasks the patient agrees to follow when "hit" by this affect.

The signs and symptoms are identified by the patient in response to such questions as "How does your body know when it is afraid?" and then written down in rank order parallel to the density of the affect. Tomkins (1962) placed the affects on a continuum (e.g., fear-terror) to show movement from the mildest form to the most intense presentation. The patient's signs and symptoms are similarly ranked. Many of my patients experience their bodies as separate from themselves, and once these patients are able to recognize that their bodies are sending them a message, I ask them to undertake four tasks designed to bring about modulation of affect, restore equilibrium, and begin to understand what is going on.

Patients are advised to be alert to their earliest warning signs. In the case of Ms. D (Figure 9.1), when she becomes aware of increased heart rate, dry mouth, or shallow breathing, she is (Task #1) to recognize that she is being "hit" by an affect and is experiencing fear. At the same time (Task #2) she is to take six slow, deep breaths to calm herself. Then (Task #3) she is to draw or write about what is going on inside/outside, and (Task #4) bring the drawing/writing to her next therapy session, where we will explore more fully what is in the drawing and what it means to her. Working together, we discover the source and nature of the affect, work I call "affect-processing."

Often, when relief is experienced through the recognition of affective experience (Tasks #1 and #2), patients are tempted to halt their attention to affect-processing. However, they soon discover this relief is quite temporary, which gives me an opportunity to reemphasize the connection between drawing and the understanding of their emotions.

I suggest that emotions are part of an inner landscape and often require some means of transformation before they can be sufficiently understood and integrated into the conscious self. At this juncture in the process, drawing becomes a pivotal component. As persons use line, color, shape and space, they come to see what is preoccupying their thoughts, what they almost know, how they feel, what they have forgotten, and what they have dissociated. They learn to use drawings as feedback mechanisms from one part of the self to another.

Utilizing drawings as feedback mechanisms is also a way of referencing the memory. However, it seems that a referencing of the past must be guided in some way. Parkin (1987) quotes the psychologist William James, who writes "Suppose I am silent for a moment and then say . . . Remember! Does your memory obey the order and reproduce any definite image from your past? Certainly not. It stands staring into vacancy and asking, what kind of a thing do you want to remember?" (p. 31). The drawings presented throughout this chapter were done by patients who have asked themselves James's question: What kind of a thing do they want to remember? These are determined individuals who have adopted an attitude of wanting to make sense out of their current suffering and learned to turn to drawing and writing to guide them in the referencing of their past.

Terr continues to make major contributions to the growing body of research on trauma and memory. Her studies present careful and compelling data on how childhood trauma is forgotten and how and why such memories return in adulthood. She reminds us that memories are essential for an understanding of self, and if memories are absent, it may at times be important to search for them. Terr (1994) writes:

Our thoughts come from our word and association centers, but our memories come from every part of the cerebral cortex. They come not only from the frontal lobes, where we feel old motor movements and rethink old thoughts, but also from the temporal lobes, where we register the sounds, balance sensations, and emotions accompanying memory; from our parietal lobes, where we apprehend physical sensations; and from our occipital lobes, for accompanying visual information, metaphors, and colors. Many parts of the cortex fire simultaneously, as our memories come to us — more parts than are necessary simply for thinking (p. 105)

In my experience, when a person working within the context of self-understanding allows the eye and hand to produce graphic images, memory fragments from all parts of the cortex are being gathered up, so to speak. As a result, the memory becomes more complete and understandable.

Image-oriented psychotherapy allows the drawn image to become integrated into the interplay of words and behaviors between patient and therapist and often determines the focus of the session. The assumption is made that, with the elicitation or the presentation of a drawing, something important is coming into awareness. The act of drawing can interrupt/stop affective amplification. If patients can draw when an affect hits, they can represent on a piece of paper what otherwise might be acted out in destructive ways. During an affective experience, so much is happening nonverbally, intrapsychically, and physiologically that linear functioning is very difficult. People may be able to think more clearly when somewhat angry, but they are less likely to think clearly if the anger grows into rage. Turning to nonlinear activity, i.e., line, color, shape, and space, to externalize these internal/external events taps into a more "like-minded" system of symbolization. Also, a record of these nonlinear events can now be seen by the therapist.

Often, "talk" is not sufficient if radical new learning is to take place. For this reason, I have also developed written structures for patients to work on at home. One of these is called "A Structure for Understanding Emotions Using Breathing, Writing, and Drawing." I write out this piece of affect-processing in linear form while at the same time recognizing that emotions and creativity have a life of their own that may or may not be linear. With this structure to guide them in writing or drawing their way through affect-processing, patients are more likely to produce the information necessary to understand what is going on.

The following instructions are given to keep patients focused while engaged in their own individualized creative process:

1. Begin with six slow, deep breaths.
2. Place the feelings you are having within the current scene by writing and/or drawing about where you were and what was going on when you became aware that an affect had hit.
3. Recall your physical symptoms and let these tell you which affect(s) you are experiencing.
4. Write or draw about other scenes from your storehouse of memories that resemble the scene in which you currently find yourself.
5. Bring this material to your next therapy session.

It is the creative interplay between patient and therapist that produces powerful images of affect and generates "maps for healing," as defined by Stone (1993). This material allows me to assist patients in changing their self-image and correcting misperceptions. Now that the scripts have reached a more conscious level, patients and I understand jointly which scripts are perpetuating their disabling view of themselves. Also, exploration of the drawing as a feedback mechanism provides an opportune moment for me to aid patients in decision-making. Nathanson (1992) asks, "Can patients adjust their self-image, . . . or must they continue to defend against their experience by the repetition of scripted methods of behavior?" To this I would add, "Can patients also accept what the affectively-released graphic image is showing them?" It is at this point I might say to the patient, "Now you have a decision to make."

Patients tend to experience negative affects as unwanted body experiences. Initially, they learn that these body experiences are affects with a range of intensity; later, they are able to see the positive benefits. Instead of being subjected to the extreme ends of human emotions (anguish, terror, rage, humiliation), patients become aware that the milder forms of distress, fear, anger, and shame are messages that help them understand experience. In time, the threatening quality of negative affect itself becomes less of a threat, and mild experiences of negative affect bring insight rather than overload. Through the use of these protocols, patients come to think of the negative affects as "messages and choices" rather than "symptoms" of unwanted affects.

When affect-processing is complete, biological and biographical experiences have been reassociated, memories have acquired new context, and the patient has gained a fuller perspective of life experience. Trauma research by Van der Kolk (1993) and others indicates that, during a traumatic event, experience is not processed and integrated and often continues for the person as visual image or physical sensation. Unless affect-processing occurs in therapy, traumatized individuals often remain victims of recurring mental and physical pain.

EXAMPLES OF AFFECT-PROCESSING:
PROTOCOLS AND STRUCTURES

Alexithymia: Lisa

Lisa is a 50-year-old patient in treatment for alexithymia who is using therapy to learn how to recognize body sensations as signals to herself and to heal the dissociation of mind, body, and emotions. Lisa has struggled with anxiety attacks most of her life and is now learning to connect these attacks with her particular signs of fear-terror. She completes the protocol (Table 9.1) by representing the experience in a drawing (Figure 9.1), which was further explored in her next therapy session.

Lisa's verbal response was: "I ask myself, what is triggering this? Then I remember my sister and I were once visiting my father, and we had to share a bedroom. My sister had a dream that I was chasing her with a knife and was now afraid to sleep with me. I had been a substitute mother to my sister growing up and realize how much a part of me she has been for 43 years. I wonder if I have absorbed her anxiety image of the knife. I suddenly realize that our relationship isn't anything I imagined it to be. It's like I have been living with these extremities, and I've just discovered they aren't mine. They are artificial limbs and I wasn't even aware of it. How do I get my own limbs?"

In this drawing, Lisa represents herself as a torso with the facial display of fear–terror (frozen stare) and blind thoughts (no pupils in eyes). Stacked up beside her are truncated images of arms and legs. The drawing and verbal associations give evidence of patient's newly formed realization that she loses connection with herself when matters arise that include her sister. As she traced the onset of the anxiety attack to being home in bed when an image of knives flashed in her mind, she was able to reassemble pieces of a lifetime pattern in which she would dissociate

TABLE 9.1
Fear–terror Affect Protocol: Lisa

Signs and Symptoms	Tasks
Heart races (fear)	Recognize I am experiencing feel-
Dry mouth (fear)	ings of fear terror
No voice (fear)	Take six slow, deep breaths
Feels insecure (terror)	Write or draw about what is going
Feel I'm slipping away from	on using structure for under-
reality (terror)	standing emotions
	Bring to therapy

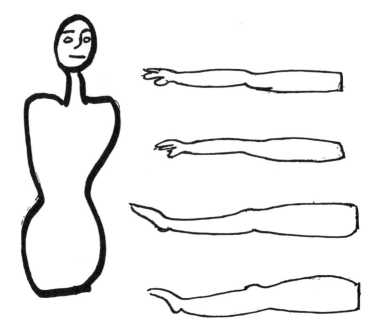

Figure 9.1 Lisa as torso with display of fear–terror.

her own emotions and absorb the emotions of members in her family of origin and later in her nuclear family as well. The image of herself as a torso with extremities stacked separate and next to her highlights a lack of mobility and calls to mind Tomkins's (1992) reference to consciousness as an ability to move about in space and handle and predict rates of change. Now Lisa is able to make a decision. The drawing provided this patient with feedback of how she viewed herself: immobile and numb. She showed a readiness to adjust her self-image when she asked the question, "How do I get limbs of my own?"

Shame–humiliation Affect Protocol as Developed in Session: Dr. Ross

Dr. Ross, a 40-year-old male physician, is in treatment for depression. He is using image-oriented psychotherapy to access emotional experience currently available to him only at an intellectual level. When he arrives saying he feels unfocused and disconnected, I ask if he could draw what it is like inside of him at this time. He draws Figure 9.2, commenting, "There's a black thing and a not so black thing and a dark red blot on

Figure 9.2 Dr. Ross: "There's a black thing and a not so black thing and a dark red blot on top of it."

top of it." I ask him what it would feel like to be inside this picture and he replies, "It would feel lost, like fighting smoke. There is no 'where' to go. . . . All the shapes could extend forever, and you're just lost."

While we discuss the drawing, Dr. Ross shifts sideways in the chair so that we no longer face each other across the desk, and I wonder if he is embarrassed about drawing in my presence. So I inquire as to how he knows when he is feeling shame. Dr. Ross identifies his shame-humiliation affect protocol (Table 9.2).

TABLE 9.2
Shame–humiliation Affect Profile: Dr. Ross

Signs and Symptoms
Turns body crosswise and physically crosses   some part of his body Turns head away Feels warm . . . might blush Becomes unfocused and disconnected

I ask him to take six slow, deep breaths; then I call his attention back to the drawing and ask what is it like for him to be an accomplished physician and have no "where" to go, to have this feeling of ontological insecurity. He says, "That's when I regard myself as a nothing . . . as the mote in my childhood twilight sleep . . . insignificant, unworthy to change anything." Exploration further revealed Dr. Ross's dread of repeating the loss of his right to be angry. He says, "If I'm too successful at controlling, recognizing, and dealing with my anger, then I'll lose my right to be angry." I suggest that this fear of losing his right to be angry has already happened growing up in a home that forbade the expression of emotion, and I encourage the use of the protocols to assist in repairing and changing his way of experiencing emotion.

Dr. Ross is also beginning to identify his longtime habits of clenching his jaw and chewing on the inside of his mouth with the affect anger-rage, and while shame affect remains largely disconnected, he is developing a language for connecting physical behaviors with their emotional counterparts (see Table 9.3). Tomkins (1962) called such gestures as clenching and chewing on inside of the cheek "miniaturization" of affect, in which the gesture replicates one part of the affect and comes to replace it as its symbolic expression. Nathanson (personal communication) views my work as a method for expanding the miniaturized affect by calling attention to other realms of data compression and storage.

The collage in Figure 9.3 was done by Dr. Ross duringing this same session. It represents the facial display of anger-rage embedded in strips of red and black construction paper torn in anger. Black strips of paper cover a red face that has a black eye and a red eye. A large black "X" spreads across the face, crossing out the nose and portraying the patient's contempt toward himself for being angry. A set mouth in black conveys the clenched jaw of anger.

The protocols, and the paper I write them on, seem to function as transitional objects that patients use as affect modulating auxiliary aids

TABLE 9.3
Anger-rage Affect Protocol: Dr. Ross

Signs and Symptoms	Protocol
Making hand into a fist	Take six slow, deep breaths
Clenching jaw	Recognize feelings of anger–rage
Chewing on inside of mouth	Draw/write about what was going on when the affect hit you
	Bring to next therapy session

Figure 9.3 Dr. Ross's black and red collage representing the facial display of anger–rage.

when they are not in a therapy session. Patients tell me they carry the protocols with them in their purse, their pocket, their backpack; they put them on the nightstand, take them on trips. One patient even shrunk and laminated them. This is consistent with Nathanson's (1992) observation that the transitional object is a symbol of the caregiver's ability to provide modulation for the intense negative affect experienced by the child.

Visual Representation of Disgust and Dissmell: Margaret

Margaret, a 43-year-old artist in treatment for a dissociative disorder, discovered that she had encoded childhood and adolescent experiences of severe sexual abuse into nursery rhymes and artwork. During her course of psychotherapy, she integrated each of the negative affects that had been divided among part-selves. This woman struggled with doubts about the veracity of her memories until she learned to identify affect in the faces of countless numbers of her drawings. The facial display of affect in these drawings was sufficient proof for her to accept her experience of extreme forms of human emotion: humiliation, anguish, rage, terror, disgust and dissmell.

Figure 9.4 is an example of the integration of disgust and dissmell. It is a double image of a face *and also* a historical record of disgusting and dissmelling experiences representing the smells and the tastes of years of sexual abuse. The patient began this drawing intending to record a series of major traumatic events in her life. Only three years later did Margaret see that she had preconsciously arranged these events in the form of a face, a face that was reeling from the smells and tastes of dehumanizing experiences. But she wasn't sure it was a face until she used tracing paper over the original drawing to pull out the forms in more detail. While working on this drawing, she would become nauseated; she could only work for about 15 minutes without throwing up. She says, "The feeling of disgust was coming up into my body, but I hadn't yet fully connected it until in a therapy session when I held my face in the shape of the face in the drawing—then I connected the feeling to dissmell. The tracings proved to me I was not making up what I was seeing. This happened to me and I have the feelings that connect with this image. I found my face. I found my feeling of disgust."

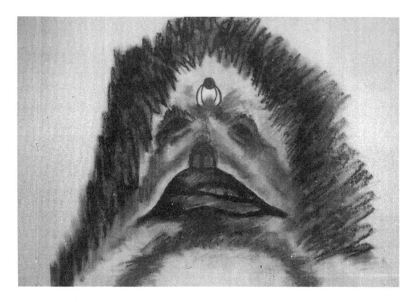

Figure 9.4 Margaret's double image of a face integrating disgust and dissmell.

Figure 9.5 Margaret's screen memory.

Although details are quite clear in the original drawing but less so in this reproduction, the biographical scenes in the double imagery link trauma with facial affective display and read as follows:

Image #1. A baby comes forth from her body and forms the knitted forehead.

Image #2. The "old woman" alter who guards against overwhelming affects sits before a black hole and forms the flared nostrils and nose.

Image #3. A child lies on a burial mound, forms the upper lip and symbolizes the death of emotions.

Image #4. A terrified ghost of a child lies in the ring below the mouth and forms the throat (not shown in this reproduction). Margaret says, "The terror is in the throat—the silent

scream never came out—and all those other images and
scenes are stacked upon it."

Margaret also drew Figures 9.5, 9.6, and 9.7. Figure 9.5 symbolizes a
screen memory and visually represents a composite drawing of four affects. The eyebrows are up (distress–anguish), the face is cold and blue,
and the hair is standing on end (fear–terror). There is blush on the face
(shame–humiliation), and the jaw is clenched (anger–rage). The figure
has neither hands nor feet, is helpless, and looks like someone's hand
puppet. Margaret believes that when she draws the eyes shut, she doesn't
want to see the sights around her.

Figure 9.6 represents exposure of the screen and revelation of the

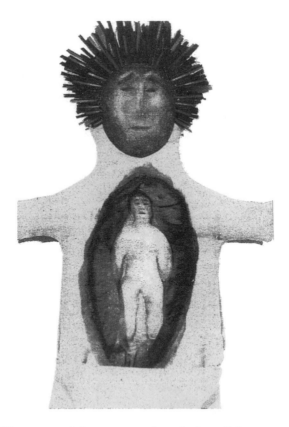

Figure 9.6 Exposure of the screen and revelation of the memory.

Figure 9.7 Visual representation of anger–rage.

memory. The patient states, "You take down the clothing and that's the memory of me in the hole being peed on, but others inside kept covering it up, and this doll sculpture is the only way I could figure out how to represent that experience. When I went to the fabric store, I knew I had to find a disgusting color. Only later did I realize that I was representing the smell and feel of urine on the body." (The body of the figure is a bright yellow-green.)

Figure 9.7 is a visual representation of anger–rage, which can be seen in the frown and clenched jaw.

Patients with dissociative disorders are masters at hiding affect from themselves and from me. Figure 9.8 shows a mask used by Margaret to cover feelings she couldn't show as a child and that, into adulthood, were available to her only in a dissociated state. The masks were her bridge from dissociated to nondissociated affect.

Margaret brought the drawings of this mask and several others to therapy five years ago, but at that time neither she nor I was looking sufficiently closely at the faces. We now understand what she was trying to tell me—she didn't *feel* the way she *looked*. Margaret said, "Jeanette, the feelings weren't there *for* you to see." We now understood that she and I had been replaying mother's failure to understand Margaret's sig-

Figure 9.8 One of Margaret's masks.

nals, interference in Margaret's ability to signal distress as a child, and her subsequent withdrawal into an internal world of part-selves. Figure 9.8 is Margaret's mask for rage. The color blue covers and "cools down" the red face underneath; terror is seen in the fixed stare, erect hair and anguish in the arched eyebrows.

Figure 9.9 is the face of Margaret's 13-year-old part-self Willow, represented in a watercolor painting 30 years later. Having learned to recognize affect in the faces that she draws, Margaret could see the combination in this watercolor of four dissociated affects: the arched eyebrows of distress–anguish, the averted eyes of shame–humiliation, the erect hair of fear–terror, and the pursed lips of anger–rage.

In studying the background in this watercolor Margaret also discovered biographical scenes of disgust and dissmell. The name "Willow" encodes references to dissociated grief and utter despair each time her body was violated. The triangular form of this image and the salmon and red colors led the patient to believe she had drawn an embedded

Figure 9.9 Margaret's 13-year-old part-self Willow.

image of a sore and swollen vulva, bringing back memories of the birth of her baby thirty years earlier when she was 13. The yellow-green colors brought back further memories of dried blood and urine. The aqua colors in the background brought back memories of sitz baths and relief from the pain. Abandonment, despair, and self-loathing were reassociated as the patient remembered: (1) the rawness of her vulva following the childbirth, (2) the rawness of her vulva after acts of sexual exploitaion, (3) having mastitis and infections following childbirth and feeling mother was too disgusted by her to give her physical care, and (4) getting her menstrual period back after the birth of the baby with the fear and rage that she "might get pregnant again."

Catching the Mood: Marlon

Marlon, a 41-year-old man in treatment for bipolar affective illness, uses drawing to "catch" and express rapid mood changes. In the quick sketch shown in Figure 9.10 he portrays distress–anguish with arched eyebrows and mouth drawn down. The head thrown back communicates his burden of self-dissmell.

Figure 9.10 Marlon's quick sketch catches distress–anger.

There are times when a person is simply inconsolable, and our at-tempts to explore negative affect yield only shame and self-disgust. Mar-lon puts into words and pictures (Figure 9.11) the dilemma experienced by many of my patients during similar periods of despair: "In Vietnam (and all wars, really) conquering soldiers were not just satisfied with beating an enemy, there is some primal need to humiliate him as well. Often, after a foe is vanquished his body would be propped up against a wall or tree in a humiliating pose and the jubilant soldier might literally shit upon the head of his victim; the ultimate act of defiling one's oppo-nent. A mocking piss in the face, a denial of the opponent's worthiness as an equal on the battlefield. This is me, the dead and weak soldier. Unworthy; in a world of shit. Unworthy to compete, to travel in harm's way. A fool, an incompetent bungler.

"Affects? Burning stomach, debilitating anxiety attacks, rivers of sweat, a feeling that death is just around the bend. For what? For just attempting to do a job I've done before; a bit of work employing skills

Figure 9.11 Marlon: "This is me, the dead and weak soldier. . . . A fool, an incompetent bungler."

I've taught others who have gone on to be at least moderately successful. I have no memory. NONE!!

"Things I've done and been good at in the past don't stick, every day alive is like the first time. Who the fuck can exist at this level of stress??? It's being an eternal trainee, wearing a big badge that screams, 'FOOL — LOOK OUT!' on my chest. I feel like a 41-year-old virgin, always ready to make the same mistakes, again, again, again, and again. The internal program is strong and deep. The AFFECTS never, never, never, ever, EVER CHANGE!!! The oldest feelings I can recognize, the only ones I know. Give me sleep, sleep, deep and long and quiet."

Flashback to Abuse: Laura

Laura is a 41-year-old woman in therapy for dissociated experience of sexual and physical abuse at the hands of her mother. This patient's denial of sexual and physical abuse has broken down as she has pieced together the various flashbacks. Figure 9.12 is a flashback view of a patient in a depersonalized state looking down on the bathtub and the figure of herself crawling across the floor of the bathroom. It was a

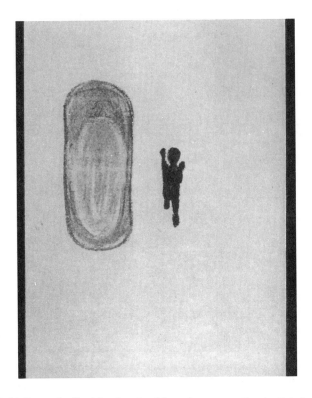

Figure 9.12 Laura's flashback—looking down on the bathtub and the figure of herself crawling across the floor of the bathroom.

particular ritual in which her mother would make her crawl back and forth across the floor as long as the mother deemed necessary.

Figure 9.13 is a flashback of Laura huddled on the floor and mother standing next to her with a belt.

Figure 9.14 is a "mother-child portrait" drawn by Laura three years after the flashbacks. She struggled for months to complete this image and was distressed that it looked so flat. There were no shadows, she says, so she couldn't figure out where the light source was in the picture. When she realized there wasn't any light source in the picture, the relationship with her mother became crystallized for her. I commented that if positive affect between a mother and child is lacking, altered, or obliterated by sexual exploitation, then perhaps what she was representing in this portrait was the absence of her mother as a source of light for her as a child. Laura is filled with self-disgust and self-dissmell. She said this

Figure 9.13 Laura's flashback — huddled on the floor with mother standing next to her with a belt.

image came to her following my asking if she knew where her mother ends and she begins. Her response can be seen in this joining of the skulls where the brown deadness of the one flows into the brown deadness of the other. Here we can see the child's absorption of mother's emotional deadness. The mother has no arms, and the child holds onto mother with anxious attachment. The flat, midnight blue background further represents biographical scenes of loneliness in the absence of mother's love. For this woman it appears that there was no internalization of mother as a light source. She has had to learn about herself from the absence of mother-daughter love rather than from its presence.

SUMMARY

The work of Tomkins and his followers persuades us that regardless of culture, race, gender or economic circumstance (1) all human beings are

Figure 9.14 Laura's "mother–child portrait."

born with nine innate affects, and (2) these affects are the primary
motivators of behavior.

The artist Paul Klee once wrote that he painted so that he wouldn't
cry. In image-oriented psychotherapy, patients often draw to undo the
forgetting. They allow themselves an attitude of creativity, realizing that
often words are not enough if they are to make sense out of their suffering. They work very hard to discover the sets of circumstances under
which they had to disavow or dissociate unbearable feelings that severely
altered their emotional life. My task is to guide the patients in the restoration of a full range of affective experience as they make visible and
conscious the rage and grief that had to be forgotten.

A therapy that focuses on assisting individuals to "do emotions" differently is in itself an affect-triggering experience. Reflecting, reconstructing, and remembering are tasks that trigger shame, fear, distress, anger, disgust, and dissmell. This type of therapy is not only more intense but often lengthier than many problem-focused therapies. So how is it that patients sustain such a difficult work? The answer is complex. I've observed this process for over twenty years, and in studying affect theory, I believe I've come closer to an understanding. While image-oriented psychotherapy certainly triggers negative affects, it also triggers the positive affects of interest–excitement and enjoyment–joy. What I have witnessed through the years is not just patient despair but also the joy and excitement that come with their self-discovery. Pain and joy accompany the birth of a self just as they greet the arrival of a new life. It is the positive affects that enable the patients to endure, because without them their lives have no meaning. Patients are further sustained in this affect-triggering therapy by the therapist, whose presence assures that intense affect will be modulated. The therapist's presence in the interaction means that a new script is being formed.

It takes time to exchange a depersonalized or posttraumatic stress state for life in the present, and often there is a sense of time running out. But without sufficient time in therapy, the losses of a traumatic childhood are not likely to become fully conscious and sufficiently mourned. These individuals are amazed and saddened when they discover that not everyone grows up in the shadow of extreme cruelty and deprivation. They struggle to claim what they had to dissociate and did not even have a language to describe. It takes time for grown men and women to bear the realization that as children they were not safe in the presence of their own mothers and fathers. It takes time for patients to realize they may have also absorbed the depression, the despair, and the shame of their parents even though indications of absorption and affect contagion appear over and over in the transference and in their drawings. Their imagery is evidence of their effort to give conscious form to losses experienced all alone and never spoken. It takes time to heal ongoing revictimizations—to sort out the "me" from the "not me."

When patients are encouraged to use creativity, to turn to imagination, to symbolize, they reconnect with the healthiest and strongest parts of themselves. It is the return of the positive affects that sustains the search for just the right material, color, shape, or word, forming that which has been absent or invisible and bringing order out of chaos. These graphic and literary accomplishments bring rich moments of interest–excitement and enjoyment–joy to my patients.

Throughout these years, I have found that many patients deepen their connection to beauty, truth, and spirituality. It is one of my joys to be present for personal discoveries of what the philosophers and poets teach: that beauty and personal truths, harsh and gentle, come forth in imagery, music, art, poetry, dance, theater, and nature as a reflection of that which is within. Slowly, patients begin to reconcile and settle into their own personal reality. It all takes time.

When my patients draw, they are putting themselves in a receptive state for something new to come forth. They come to realize that the disavowed or dissociated emotions are being made visible and that they are learning how to live with feelings they can't help having. Nathanson (1994) writes, "Normal emotion (which includes everything we have ever considered as motivated behavior) cannot be said to have occurred until something happens inside the brain, goes outside the brain to the face, and then comes back into the brain for further analysis and processing" (p. 1). That is just what happens. During image-oriented work I watch as affect reaches outside to the face and goes back into the brain for the reassociation of cognition and affect.

Bringing imagery and affect into the therapeutic relationship provides a frame of reference that bridges the gap between the patient and a therapist whose experiences may otherwise be vastly different. Being a part of such a therapeutic relationship is a privilege for me, and I thank those patients whose imagery and affect are displayed in this chapter.

REFERENCES

Basch, M. F. (1983). Empathic understanding: A review of the concept and some theoretical considerations. *Journal of the American Psychoanalytic Association, 31*, 101–26.

Darwin, C. (1872). The expressions of the emotions in man and animals. Reprint. New York: St. Martin's Press, 1979.

Kubie, L. (1958). *The neurotic distortion of the creative process.* Toronto: McGraw-Hill Tyerson Ltd., pp. 1–52.

Nathanson, D. L. (1992). *Shame and pride: Affect, sex, and the birth of the self.* New York: Norton.

Nathanson, D. L. (1994). Editorial. *Bulletin of the Tomkins Institute, 1*(1), 1.

Parkin, A. (1987). *Memories and amnesia.* Oxford, UK: Basil Blackwell Ltd.

Stone, A. M. (1993). Trauma and affect: Applying the language of affect theory to phenomena of traumatic stress. *Psychiatric Annals, 23.*

Terr, L. (1994). *Unchained memories.* New York: Basic Books, p. 105.

Tomkins, S. S. (1962). *Affect, imagery, consciousness, Vol. 1: The positive affects.* New York: Springer.

Tomkins, S. S. (1992). *Affect, imagery, consciousness, Vol. 4: Cognition: Duplication and transformation of information.* New York: Springer, p. 323.

Van der Kolk, B. (1993). The body keeps the score: Memory and the evolving psychobiology of post traumatic stress. *Video Tapes.* Boston, MA: Massachusetts General Hospital: Trauma Clinic. Harvard Medical School.

10

The Affective Life of Infants: Empirical and Theoretical Foundations

Julie Abrams Faude

C. Wayne Jones

Michele Robins

When you've been up all night with a screaming baby who has a fever and doesn't begin to grab at her ear until dawn, you don't think much about the history of antibiotic research on the way to the pediatrician. All you want is a prescription for today's version of penicillin and the opportunity for a nap. When the police drag a raging, hallucinating, psychotic patient into your emergency room, you place the patient in restraints, take a history, and (like as not) reach for some injectable tranquilizer. You are unlikely to muse about the fact that Thorazine, the first modern tranquilizer, was developed as part of the *cocktail lytique* meant to reduce the body temperature of patients undergoing heart surgery in Paris. And few of us who enjoy increased efficacy as psychotherapists because we know how to partition emotional discomfort into combinations of six negative affects ever think about the generations of research that made it easy for us to develop new clinical techniques.

One of the issues that occupied Tomkins early in his study of innate affect was the observation that sciences grow and thrive according to fashion. In the days of Skinner and behaviorism, emotion was considered unworthy of study by anyone of importance. Infant and child study by researchers imbued with psychoanalytic theory focused on early psychosexual development, while psychopharmacologists often ignored our descriptions of the range of normal emotion in their desire to repair the abnormal. ("Is there a biology of normal emotion?" replied one best-selling psychiatrist-author when asked about affect theory by a radio interviewer.) For many years, the study of emotion was simply out of fashion, and the study of the face a nearly laughable endeavor.

In this chapter, Faude, Jones, and Robins have summarized some of the major areas of research that have drawn attention to the importance of innate affect as both the means through which caregiver and preverbal infant communicate, and the single most important factor in the development of personality.—DLN

LITTLE FRANCIE, an energetic and interested four-month-old, eagerly turns her face toward her approaching father and giggles excitedly. Her father talks to her in a soft, soothing voice, with Francie cooing back in rhythm, wildly kicking her feet and waving her arms, as if engaged in a very important dialogue. The father suddenly becomes distracted by the doorbell, however, and interrupts the pattern. Francie stops moving, frowns, and her voice becomes higher pitched, showing increasing signs of distress until her father re-engages.

Such interpersonal exchanges are commonplace in the daily lives of most infants and their families. For infant researchers, it is through the study of the subtle complexities involved in these routine parent-infant exchanges that we find important clues regarding the foundations of emotional development. Most current infant researchers (e.g., Izard, Hembree, & Huebner, 1987; Lewis, Alessandri, & Sullivan, 1989; Stern, 1985) would identify Francie's expressive behavior as clearly reflective of infant affective experience. There would likely be disagreement, however, regarding what is most important about Francie and her father's behaviors.

Bowlby (1969) and Ainsworth and Bell (1970) would describe Francie's behavior in terms of its communicative importance in the growing infant-caregiver relationship, focusing on how the responsive cooing, giggles, and crying serve as "built-in" signals to promote physical closeness and bonding. Other researchers (Brazelton, Koslowski, & Main, 1974; Fogel, 1982; Stern, 1974; Tronick, Als, & Brazelton, 1980), who analyze the complex face-to-face exchanges between infants and caregivers, would stress the manner in which Francie's expressive behavior serves to regulate her father's behavior. Demos (1988) and Tomkins (1962, 1963) would focus on the motivational information contained in Francie's behavior, which provides clues about her and her father's subjective experience. Beebe and Lachmann (1988) would discuss Francie's affective exchanges with her father in terms of its implications for the development of empathic capacities.

Within the last decade, there has been an explosion of research on the significance for human development of early affective states. The overarching theme of this research is that the process of organizing and making sense of affective experience begins at birth. Most of this research has taken a relational view of infant development, given that infants are so dependent upon their caregiving environments for the opportunity to develop completely. Clinical developmentalists, such as Greenspan (1992), have constructed an integrative, comprehensive model of social-emotional development based on these assumptions. Greenspan highlights the centrality of affect and the relational context in the growth of other developmental capacities, such as cognition, language, and motor skills. How infants and toddlers organize their affective experience is posited to both inform and to be informed by the unfolding of other developmental capacities within the context of the caregiving environment. We assume that as the child grows and develops, affective experience is organized and handled in a progressively complex manner.

Many of the clinical discussions in this book rest on the notion that affect exists from the beginning of life and that affect is the linchpin to understanding how people function and change. This chapter focuses on the empirical and theoretical foundations for such an assumption. To address this assumption, we must explore the world of infant affect. In this chapter, we will introduce several of the key researchers and theoreticians involved in the study of infant affect. We will present their basic premises and the data that have driven their thinking.

INFANT AFFECT: AN OVERVIEW

General recognition and acceptance of infant affect are relatively recent phenomena. Historically, in this country, we have tended to view infants as either passive and at the mercy of their environments (e.g., Skinner, 1974) or as active but within a passive environment (e.g., Piaget, 1952). In both of these views, the infant's interactions with the environment are one-way and non-interactional. Within both of these perspectives, the affective life of the infant has received little attention, as if expressive behavior in infancy were random and disconnected from true feeling states.

Kagan's (1984) work sheds some light on this historical American trend. According to Kagan, infant affective displays have become a perfect screen for the projection of our cultural beliefs. He argues that as adults we ascribe to infants characteristics that are undeveloped or even opposite to the values that we prize. For example, the Japanese, who tend to value a highly intertwined social connectedness and interdependency, view their babies as possessing a unique autonomy by nature. Kagan's research suggests that Japanese mothers see their infants as needing to be wooed into the dependent role; therefore, they are more likely than parents from other cultures to rush to soothe a crying infant, to talk vigorously to a babbling baby, and even to sleep in the same bed to solidify and encourage mutual lifelong bonding.

In sharp contrast, American parents tend to encourage autonomy and individualism to help infants and young children overcome their more dependent, passive natures. There is a body of research evidence to support Kagan's ideas (e.g., Ujiie & Miyake, 1984) comparing infant-mother interaction patterns in Japan and in the U.S. Generally, Japanese mothers were more accepting of their infant's proximity-seeking behavior than American mothers; they were more likely to pick up their babies and hold them longer after a separation.

While there has been a clear shift in perspective toward attributing more human qualities to infants (Mahler, Pine, & Bergman, 1975), the inclination to disqualify infant affective expressions as indexing true differentiated emotion states can still be seen. This is partly due to the tendency of theorists to subordinate emotion to cognition. The general idea is that "genuine" affects do not occur before requisite cognitive milestones have been achieved. Malatesta, Izard, and Camras (1991) explain that this view arises because infants are unable to attach a verbal label to their affect. This downplays the emotional significance of other earlier modes of cognitive representation, such as sensorimotor (e.g., Piaget, 1952) or imagistic (Horowitz, 1972). This in itself may represent a cultural bias of sorts. Another issue is the apparent lack of specificity between elicitor events and expressive responses, which perpetuates the impression that infant affective expression is random and unorganized. Moreover, the observation that infants tend to respond to physical as opposed to psychological aspects of stimuli seems to further the notion of affective discontinuity in development (Camras, in Malatesta, Izard, & Camras, 1991).

In support of the notion that "genuine" affects exist in infancy, the differential emotions theorists suggest that human expressions appear to be morphologically and functionally continuous with adult expression (Malatesta, Culver, Tesman, & Shepard, 1989). Their findings, which will be explored in more detail later in this chapter, suggest that expressive behaviors in early infancy occur in the same contexts and index corresponding feeling states as those of the adult affective expression.

Malatesta-Magai (1991) argues that there is a regular correspondence in the social world between social displays and their feeling states and that it would be chaotic if we could not trust these displays. Infants' expressive behaviors are functionally relevant as adaptations and not meaningless random events. Malatesta and Izard (Malatesta et al., 1991) argue further that the perception that they are random arises from our difficulty perceiving continuities in structure, function, and process.

Demos (1988) suggests that we should as readily accept the relation between the internal experience and behavioral expression of infants as we do with older children and adults, assuming that infant facial expressions and vocalizations are indications of an internal affective state. Recent advances in the recording of physiological changes that occur in concert with infant facial expression (e.g., Ekman, Levenson, & Friesen, 1983) provide more scientific justification for this position. Demos (1988) argues that it is not an inferential leap to assume that a crying infant is experiencing something far more negative and punishing than simple "distress," the vague and imprecise term often assigned to infant affective expressions. She reasons that perhaps the affective experience of the infant may be at times more specific and defined, such as anger. At other times, an infant's cry may be signaling a more generalized discomfort, such as hunger or tiredness.

There are few theorists today who seriously challenge the notion that affective experience can be independent of any learning or interpretive activity. Some confusion over terminology may account for the occasional disagreement related to this point. Researchers and theoreticians have tended to use the terms emotion, affect, and feelings interchangeably. In this chapter, as elsewhere in this book, the work of Tomkins (1962, 1963) is used to define affect as a brief but powerful physiological reaction to certain conditions of neural stimulation. Affect, therefore, is the biologic substrate of emotion, or the constellations of physiologic responses that form the basis of the individual's emotional experience. Emotion involves our memory of previous experiences of an affect or our associations to an affect. With the biologic substrate of affective response as a template, a person's memories, cognitions, and associations can accrete to become what we see as mature emotions. Awareness of these affects and emotions is referred to as a capacity for feelings (Basch, 1976).

Just as breathing comes naturally to an infant and involves an interaction-with-the-world to which the infant is predisposed, affect and its communication to others also seem to come naturally to humans. The range and interaction of affects allow us to explore the dynamics of the relations between affect and action, affect and cognition, affect and experience (Stone, 1993). In the remainder of this chapter, we will present studies representative of research on the affect system of infants and the various roles or functions that this system seems to play in general development. Most of the studies we describe were done within the context of the parent-child relationship, one within which the affect system seems to function optimally.

Following a brief discussion of temperament and its relation to the affect system of the infant, we will discuss four major themes that have emerged in the study of infant affect. These themes are organized along the different hypothesized roles or functions of infant affect: the punctuation of certain experiences as important and meaningful; the facilitation of attachment with caregivers; the provision of a foundation for regulated self- and other-representations; and the opportunity for empathy or sharing another's emotional world.

INFANT AFFECT AND TEMPERAMENT

No presentation of infant affect would be complete without a discussion of temperament. In fact, studies of infant affect would be more difficult to interpret without an understanding of temperament, a constitutional variable posited to influence thresholds for affective response and the intensity with which an affect will be experienced. In part, studies of temperament have dramatically furthered the shift from thinking about infants as passive, blank slates to seeing them as highly active participants in their own growth and experience. Leading infancy researchers White, Field, Meltzoff, and Kagan (1987) have named as two of the most important discoveries about infancy to emerge in the past 20 years (1) the active role infants play in structuring their world from birth and (2) the enduring nature of the infant's temperament.

As Stern (1985) noted, "the capacities that permit the infant to yoke his diverse experiences of the social world are to an enormous extent constitutionally—that is, genetically—determined" (p. 188). Individual differences in emotional capacity, tone, and style of emotional expression may explain differential responsivity to social interactions from the first days of life. Both parents and researchers have recognized that all infants are not alike; these differences can be measured with reasonable reliability (Berger, 1985; Buss & Plomin, 1975; Campos, Barrett, Lamb, Goldsmith, & Sternberg, 1983; Dunn, 1980). It is clear that infants differ in their propensity for irritability, activity level, interest in the world around them, and in the amount of soothing it takes to calm them. The temperamental properties most often studied are activity, fussiness, fearfulness, sensitivity, attentiveness, and vigor of reaction (Kagan, 1984). Measures of temperament often predict later emotional and behavioral disorders (e.g., Rutter, Birch, Thomas, & Chess, 1964; Thomas & Chess, 1979) across many contexts (e.g., Graham & Stevenson, 1986).

Emotional reactivity, which appears to have fairly direct neurobiological correlates, is an important dimension thought to underlie individual differences in infant temperament. In fact, temperament is currently most often conceptualized as a psychobiological construct (e.g., Izard et al., 1991). In a recent review of research on temperament, Rutter (1987) included "emotional reactivity" as an example of a temperamental attribute that shows substantial heritability and stability over time and is included by virtually all researchers.

More generally, recent studies have stressed the relation between physiological response patterns and the development of individual differences in temperament. The majority of this work focuses on physiological changes involving the heart. Under normal, relaxed circumstances, the heart rate cycles in accordance with respiration; shortly after inspiration the heart rate rises, and shortly after expiration the heart rate decreases. The influence of respiration on heart rate has been termed respiratory sinus arrhythmia (RSA) (e.g., Porges, McCabe, & Yongue, 1982). RSA is variability in heart rate (HR) that occurs at the same frequency as breathing. The vagus nerve (a major trunk of the parasympathetic system) mediates the decrease in heart rate. When a child is concentrating on a difficult task, the affect of interest–excitement can inhibit the vagal control of the heart rate; the heart rate then rises and becomes more stable. Under relaxed conditions, heart rates are lower but are also more variable. Children who tend to have faster and more stable heart rates (i.e., showing low vagal tone and low RSA) when tending to challenging tasks are considered more physiologically aroused (or "emotionally reactive"). In infants studied at three, six, and nine months, moderate to high intercorrelations were found in the cardiac measures indexing heart-rate variability (i.e., vagal tone, heart-period variance, and heart-period range) (Izard et al., 1991). Temperamental features appear to be related to heart rate, heart rate variability, vagal tone, and RSA.

Findings from longitudinal research studies (e.g., Thomas & Chess, 1979) suggest that temperamental differences, especially at the extremes, are quite enduring and that individual differences in physiology play an

important role in temperament. Two of the most enduring temperamental traits appear to be inhibition and lack of inhibition to nonthreatening
but unfamiliar events. Kagan has been able to identify autonomic responses, such as heart rate patterns, that might index a temperamental
vulnerability analogous to the clinical concept of anxiety-proneness. Kagan and Moss (1962) found that shyness and sociability in infants were
preserved throughout childhood and adolescence. Behavioral timidity in
unfamiliar situations and fast heart rates (which were correlated) were
the best preserved qualities of children from 3 to 29 months old (Kagan,
Kearsley, & Zelazo, 1978; Plomin & Rowe, 1979).

In two longitudinal research studies, children at 21 months who were
classified as extremely shy or sociable were again observed at 4, 5.5, and
7.5 years of age. At four years of age, the 22 subjects inhibited at 21
months were more socially inhibited in interactions with an unfamiliar
peer than those identified as uninhibited children. They also displayed a
higher and more stable heart rate (i.e., low vagal tone, low RSA), were
more reluctant to guess at difficult problems, and showed more frequent
heart rate accelerations when listening to a story (i.e., more aroused or
reactive) than the uninhibited children (Kagan, Reznick, Clarke, Snidman, & Garcia-Coll, 1984). There was a moderate inter-age, average
correlation of inhibited and uninhibited styles from 21 months to 7.5
years. Three-fourths of the children retained their expected classification
from 21 months to 7.5 years of age. Although half of the sample showed
modifications of their extremely inhibited profiles, only a few of these
children were as spontaneous and sociable as the uninhibited subsample.
About 10% of the uninhibited group at 21 months were shown to be shy
at 7.5 years old. More of the inhibited subjects in the eighth year of
life showed a greater sympathetic reactivity (i.e., behavioral differences
associated with peripheral physiological variables) than the uninhibited
subjects. It is possible that inherited variation in arousal thresholds contributes to shyness and social avoidance. However, a third longitudinal
study (Kagan, Reznick, & Gibbons, 1989) suggests that constructs of
inhibited and uninhibited refer only to those children who fall at the
extremes (top and bottom 15%) of a phenotypic continuum from shyness to sociability.

Kagan posits that the relation between heart rate variability and behavioral inhibition may be due to a decrease in RSA (i.e., a decrease in
HR variability) in unfamiliar situations because the inhibited child must
engage in more mental work to assimilate discrepant or uncertain events.
Other studies support this hypothesis. For example, Richards and Cameron (1989) found a consistent positive correlation for three testing
groups (ages 14, 20, and 26 weeks) between levels of RSA and the ap-

proach subscale of the Infant Temperament Rating Scale. Infants with high levels of RSA (slow and variable heart rates or high vagal tone) were more likely to approach novel situations. In addition, Fox (1989) found that infants selected at 14 months for having high vagal tone (slow and variable heart rates, high RSA) tended to spend less time close to their mothers, were more sociable, and displayed more approach behavior toward strangers than the other group of infants. This is akin to Kagan's uninhibited children. Interestingly, Fox also found that the 5-month-olds with high vagal tone (more HR variability, high RSA) were actually more responsive to both positive and negative events as well as better able to regulate their distress than the low vagal tone children. These low vagal tone (and in this case less behaviorally reactive) 5-month-olds tended to develop into 14-month-olds who were more wary of novel situations. The author posits that these 5-month-olds may have already learned a passive mode of responding to mildly stressful situations. Although there was a passive behavioral response, the physiological data show clear physiological arousal in the form of high heart rate accompanied by low variability.

Studies relying on heart rate analyses, however, have not always produced consistent results. For example, Healy (1989) found that 11- to 35-month-old children who were rated as more negative in mood (i.e., highly reactive to environmental events), difficult in temperament (i.e., more sensitive to mildly aversive events), and more hesitant to approach a novel toy had slower tonic heart rate and higher estimates of heart rate variability compared with children rated as easy in temperament. Healy states that the difference in results may be due to sampling and methodological differences between studies. In a contradictory study, Izard et al. (1991) found that measures of heart rate variability over the first 9 months of life (which were generally consistent) were significant predictors of an index of security at 13 months. They found that the greater the infants' HR variability (associated previously with uninhibited children), the higher their attachment insecurity scores. Based on other research findings cited above, one would have expected insecure children to be more physiologically aroused and therefore to have more stable heart rates (showing low vagal tone). More research in this area is needed to clarify the meaning of these findings.

Despite the inconsistencies in heart rate studies, there is ample evidence regarding the enduring nature of temperament. For example, Lamb, Hwang, Bookstein, and Broberg (1988) observed 144 Swedish-born children at 16 months and again one year later (28 months). Along with high family socioeconomic status and high quality of home care, a major determinant of personality maturity was having an "easy" temperament. In another Swedish longitudinal study of 149 children (MacEvoy, Lambert, Karlberg, & Karlberg, 1988), early affective, temperamental antecedents of Type A behavior were explored. Liveliness, sociability, and poor appetite during infancy and childhood were positively related to adult Type A irritability and hurried behavior clusters. Cummings, Zahn-Waxler, and Radke-Yarrow (1984) studied 24 children for 9 months, beginning at 10, 15, or 20 months of age and again for 3 months between the ages of 6 and 7 years old, focusing on changes in responses to anger and affection in the home. Individual patterns of responding with distress (i.e., crying, distressed facial expression, verbal expression of concern, shutting out) and/or anger (i.e., hitting, pushing, scolding, or yelling) to naturally occurring as well as simulated incidents of anger showed continuity across the 5-year span of the study. These individuals' emotionality may be viewed (as Buss and Plomin, 1975, would posit) as a "temperamental disposition to arousal, reactivity, or excitability in reaction to threatening, annoying or frustrating situations" (Cummings et al., 1984). Interestingly, responses to affection were not correlated with responses to anger. This supports Buss and Plomin's view that emotionality as a dimension of temperament functions in response to unpleasant rather than pleasant stimuli.

Studies of temperament indicate clearly that any consideration of infant-caregiver interactions from either a clinical or a research point of view must take infant individual differences into account. An infant with a low tolerance for stimulation or a poor capacity to regulate arousal may show more difficulty than one with more resilient temperamental features. This is borne out in studies of infant-caregiving mismatching and maternal depression, to be discussed later in this chapter.

INFANT AFFECT AS PUNCTUATION
OF EXPERIENCE

In our review of the important functions of infant affect, we begin with a model that posits affect to be the result of neurological patterns of arousal. Different sets of complex neurologic activity result in one of a few primary affects. This is the basis of affect theory. We begin with this micro-level analysis of affect and build up to more inferentially based models. In this section we focus on the motivational function of affect in the developing infant, as we review research that posits affect as an amplifier of particular patterns of stimulation, thus producing feedback to self and other. That is to say, important things feel important because they have been amplified by affect. Amplification in turn gives rise to some level of awareness and stimulates action for both caregiver and child. Tomkins (1962, 1963) has asserted that the affect system is the primary motivational system in the personality and has presented a model to explain how these inherited affects are activated, how discrete events relate to their activators, and how the correlated sets of responses (affects) are experienced subjectively. Affect is viewed as present from the moment of birth and perhaps before, and is viewed as the core of the neonate's capacity for inner awareness.

Demos (1988) upholds the work by Tomkins and suggests that affective communication is important because we assume it contains motivational information about the other person or about oneself. Just as fear or alarm cause an adult to swat away a buzzing bee, infant affect propels the infant into action. Tomkins (1962, 1963) builds on the work of Darwin (1872), which conceptualizes affect as a biologically inherited system controlling facial muscle responses, autonomic blood flow, respiratory, and vocal responses. These correlated sets of responses define the number and specific types of primary affects. Tomkins presented evidence for nine primary affects and described the inherited set of patterned responses for each affect. This functionalist, developmental evolutionary theory furthermore assumes that underlying feeling states are pre-wired (Eibl-Eibesfeldt, 1979; Issacson, 1982; Panksepp, 1982), pre-adapted propensities and that they operate flexibly in adaptation and development.

Tomkins argued that the face is the primary site of affect and takes the lead in establishing and creating an awareness of an affective state, with the other avenues of expression coming into play later in development. Tomkins claims that the affect program causes a change in the vasculature and musculature of the face. Specifically, the vascular changes make the muscular actions much more salient. There is a different pattern of contraction and relaxation for each affect. So completely does the infant get taken over by this action, as well as by associated changes in cardiovascular, respiratory, postural, and exocrine systems, that the infant learns to associate the triggering stimulus with the gestalt of these activities. In essence, the facial component of the gestalt is the analogue of the whole affect and is enough to represent the affect. This is why Tomkins places such emphasis on the face. Tomkins's emphasis on the face was followed up by Ekman (1972, 1978) and Izard (1971), who independently explored the validity of facial expressions. Their work demonstrated that these expressions were produced, recognized, and given similar meanings in a wide range of Western and non-Western cultures.

First Tomkins and then Ekman and Izard have produced detailed anatomically-based coding systems for analyzing facial expressions. At present our understanding of affective phenomena is sophisticated and precise. For instance, Ainsworth's "strange situation" assessment of attachment used global ratings and averaged responses over time. The presence or absence of distress was determined by whether or not the child cried at any time during the experimental procedure. By contrast, recent studies have recorded the sequence and details of the child's reactions and report a variety of responses to strangers. The more precise and sophisticated the methodology, the more complex our understanding of the phenomenon becomes.

There is a growing body of data on infant facial expression that consistently confirms that all of the possible facial components of affect may be displayed on the face of the young infant and that these components are structured into the innate affect patterns (Ekman, 1982; Field, 1982; Oster & Ekman, 1978). Each expression is associated with distinctively different motivational goals and feeling states. This theory is in opposition to the James-Lange (1890) theory of emotion, which posits that one first becomes aware of a global visceral response, which, when given a cognitive interpretation or label, is experienced as an affective state. Tomkins's theory has also received some confirmation from neurological studies reported by Pribram (1980), who states that the evidence from his laboratory indicates that the autonomic nervous system is involved in stabilizing emotional states already set in motion.

According to Tomkins, affect functions as an amplifier for associated events and serves to punctuate the complex messages that are broadcast and received by parent and child. Affects, and responses to them, have both innate and learned determinants and so can be influenced and modified by experience. For example, the facial and vocal expressions of affect are managed and influenced according to social, cultural, and familial "display rules" that specify who can show what emotion to whom, and in what context affect can be expressed (Ekman & Friesen, 1969).

These various postulates have led Tomkins to conclude that discrete affects are present at birth and that development consists of the gradual construction of affect complexes or of ideoaffective organizations. This view is in contrast to much current work on infant affect. Sroufe (1979) and Emde (1980), for example, both argue that affective expressions in early infancy represent precursors to true affect, reflecting merely physiological tensions, and that only later, when the infant can become cognitively engaged with a stimulus, can one speak of psychophysiological tension and therefore of affect.

Psychoanalytic writers on affect, such as Brenner (1974, 1982) and

Arlow (1977), argue that there are only global states of pleasure and displeasure in infancy; gradually, these become differentiated into discrete affects as ideas become associated with experience. Tomkins is alone in asserting that affect and cognition can vary independently of each other and that cognition need not be involved in activating or in prolonging an affective state. Demos (1988) claims that according to Tomkins the "cry of the hungry neonate and the smile of the cognitively engaged three-month-old are both manifestations of the same innate affect mechanism, which in the first instance is not coassembled or connected with cognition. Over time, the neonate will gradually connect her experiences of a particular dysphoric state (e.g., hunger) with a variety of causes and with a variety of consequences. These ensuing affect complexes will gradually begin to guide her behavior" (p. 35). The argument calls for viewing the entire interaction process through a developmental lens.

The work of Stern suggests that salient perceptual phenomena are largely prestructured and thus do not have to be learned bit by bit. Rather, the infant responds to higher order variables that span across sensory modalities and not to specific sensory variables. Perception is organized so as to detect invariants in stimulation. As described more completely in our review of attachment studies, the young infant is a highly competent perceiver, able to recognize the common temporal structure present in auditory and visual events and to extract information across sensory modalities. Demos (1988) claims that the young infant is capable of experiencing the full range of primary affects. Positive and negative affective states will prime the infant to respond in a corresponding manner. For example, the interested baby will focus intently, hold his limbs still and scan the surroundings for novelty (Stechler & Carpenter, 1974; Wolff, 1965). By contrast, a distressed infant will produce a rhythmical cry with the corners of the mouth pulled down and the inner corners of the brows drawn up. These specific affective states are important aspects of the infant's early experience because they create the core experiences for infant motivation to act and for caregivers to respond.

With this formulation, Demos (1988) proposes a question critical in understanding the infant's development of self: How is affect allied to learning? The intensity dimension of affect is an important aspect of the infant's early experience. In a model such as that of Tomkins, where affect is seen as an adaptive biological system, it is assumed that the occurrence of negative affect is inevitable or unavoidable. For example, an experience of distress or anger that combines intensity with duration may produce an increase in negative affect. This means that, as an analogue of its stimulus profile, an affect is therefore capable of triggering more of the same affect. The infant therefore has the following options: The experience may compel the infant to retreat or to avoid such punishing escalation in the future by overcontrolling the expression of distress or anger, or the infant may constrict activities to avoid the eliciting stimulus or situation. Multiple experiences with ineffective negotiation of affect will have future clinical implications. In either case, the infant is unable to remain in the situation and strives to develop adaptive skills or strategies for dealing with the causes of the distress or anger. At the other extreme, if the infant's experiences of affect are too mild or brief, then the infant's motivation to act will be diminished and opportunities to develop adaptive responses will not occur. Interestingly, Freud (1923) also theorized that most infant learning occurred in the time between feeling distressed and being soothed.

THE ROLE OF INFANT AFFECT IN ATTACHMENT

Attachment can be considered from many different perspectives. It can be defined as a set of infant behaviors, a motivational system, a relationship between mother and infant, a theoretical construct, and a subjective experience of the infant. It is beyond the scope of this chapter to review the voluminous literature on human attachment and the multiple perspectives taken by those who have worked in this area. Rather, to frame the role that affect plays in attachment and communication, we will review studies on the origins and development of attachment relationships and continue with an account of recent work focusing on how infants are "wired" to communicate with their caretakers. Ultimately, the value for clinicians of this research lies in the extent to which it can genuinely affect and inform sensitivities in the immediate therapeutic interaction with children and their families.

There has been considerable research on the significance of early affective states for attachment in particular and for development in general. The relation between affect and attachment is comprised of several important features, many of which are key to motivational theorists. As we have described above, affect serves as a valuable signaling (communicative) function within the attachment system long before the acquisition of language. Affect cues the caregiver to the infant's subjective experience. That is, visual expressions, vocalizations, and movements all work in concert. The caregiver gives coherency to this rich and varied force, and typically is motivated to act in response.

Infant affect pulls a parent into the infant's world, compelling him or her to respond to the infant's needs. Infant affect serves to keep a caregiver present, an important evolutionary feat, since infants cannot survive otherwise. Infants express their needs through the expression of affect, and caregivers are able to help; affect therefore draws both closer. From an adult's point of view, the compelling feeling of being able to alleviate an infant's anguish or other strongly expressed affect is quite powerful. That is, to know (or believe) an infant is crying for one's arms, or searching out one's eyes for the sense of well-being that only a known, beloved, and trusted caregiver can provide supports attachment in both parties.

John Bowlby (1959, 1969, 1973, 1980) was one of the first psychoanalytic researchers to move from historical reconstruction ("top-down") to observational ("bottom-up") research modes and to link these two perspectives. Bowlby drew from the ethological perspective because it offered him a wide range of concepts that were yet undeveloped in the psychological literature, especially those related to the formation of intimate social bonds. Bowlby and his colleagues studied the affective response of infants to prolonged separation from their mothers in inadequate institutional care in the post-World-War-II era.

Bowlby pointed out that the mother-infant subsystem has a long evolutionary history in which the behaviors of both members have evolved toward mutual regulation. Stern (1985) notes that Bowlby was also ahead of his time when he suggested that attachment is "a perspective on evolution, on the species and on the individual dyad, it is also a perspective on the subjective experience of the infant in the form of the infant's working model of mother" (p. 25). That is, infants internalize their experiences with attachment figures. In time, these internalizations provide an emotional center around which later relationships congeal.

Bowlby was also attuned to the interactive dance in which *both* partners are involved. His research showed that both caregiver and infant behaviors work to maintain proximity. Despite a number of variations (e.g., age, previous home environment, type of institution, length of time away from home, and health), there was remarkable uniformity in the response of infants to separation. Once a child reached six months, typical sequences of responses became evident. Initially, there came a "protest," with the infant showing strong distress behavior (crying, shaking, throwing, and looking eagerly for mother). By the second stage, "despair" and hopelessness began setting in. The infant became withdrawn, inactive, and made little or no demands on the caretaker. Finally, the infant became "detached" from nurses and mothers on their visits. With further prolonged separation, when the infant had become transiently attached to a number of nurses, the infant acted as if contact with humans did not hold much significance for him or her at all. When nurses changed or left, the child did not react. As such, early experience of loss or deprivation had devastating effects on at least some features of the infant's development.

In sum, Bowlby posited that infants are born with an innate need for social interaction, a need that becomes focused on one special person shortly after birth, a view much in line with the ethologist Konrad Lorenz (1966), who studied critical "imprinting" periods in animals. Proximity-seeking was seen as having evolutionary survival value. Bowlby posited that the infant uses any means available to communicate with the caregiver in order to remain close to her. Bowlby's perspective celebrates the centrality of affectional relationships, and his research provided early support for the significance of the love relationship between an infant and a caregiver.

Ainsworth (1967, 1979) and her colleagues (e.g., Ainsworth & Wittig, 1969), studied the *kinds* of relationships that babies form with their mothers, examining the strength and quality of the attachment. Ainsworth, Blehar, Waters, and Wall (1978) defined attachment as an affective bond characterized by "strong emotions, not only security, anxiety, and anger, but also love, grief, jealousy, and, indeed, the full spectrum of emotion and feeling" (p. 23). Ainsworth developed the standardized "strange situation," in which a child's reaction to separation from the parent, to the introduction of a stranger, and to the reunion with the parent could be studied formally. Three types of attachment were seen: secure, avoidant, and resistant. Ainsworth's work also pointed to how infant and mother influence or regulate one another's behavior. The most securely attached infants negotiated the strange situation best, suggesting that a well-attuned mother-child relationship helps produce a more capable and emotionally resilient infant.

Some longitudinal studies found that the quality of attachment at one year predicts styles of relating up through five years of age. The securely attached infant seems to develop the most mutually satisfying relationships. Resistant attachment patterns at 12 months have been found to be predictive of psychopathology in boys at age six (Lewis, Feiring, McGuffog, & Jaskir, 1985). It should be noted that attachment patterns are culture-bound, with different attachment patterns and different outcomes in North German babies (Lutkenhaus, Grossman, & Grossman, 1985) and Japanese children (Miyake, Chen, & Campos, 1985). Blehar, Lieberman, and Ainsworth (1977) found that securely attached one-year-olds had shown more looking, smiling, and excitement in social play when they were two to four months of age. In contrast, resistantly attached one-year-olds had shown more looking away, fussing, and un-responsiveness at four months of age.

Both Bowlby (1959) and Ainsworth (1979) viewed attachment as a specific developmental task of a particular life phase. In the past decade, researchers have recognized that attachment (viewed as a quality of relatedness) extends far beyond the mother/infant bond and stretches across the entire life span. Nevertheless, this early research on styles or patterns of attachment demonstrates how some early experiences show continuity across developmental periods.

Many recent studies portray how exquisitely evolved newborns and caretakers are for mutual communication of affect. As part of the Brazelton Neonatal Behavioral Assessment Scale, three-day-old infants normally turn their heads to track a colored object or the sound of a bell. Then the infant is picked up by the experimenter and held under its head and bottom. Both the experimenter and mother call out the baby's name. Most babies, after two to three calls, turn to their mother's voice, as if they already recognize the mother's voice. This can be an emotionally exhilarating experience for the mother (as cited in Cramer, 1992). Newborn sucking rates increased in response to the sounds of the human voice in comparison to other sounds of the same pitch and loudness (Friedlander, 1970), suggesting that the newborn prefers the human voice (Siqueland & DeLucia, 1969). Three-day-old newborns placed on their backs turned toward a breast-pad soaked in their mother's milk rather than toward a different nursing mother's breast pad, regardless of which side the breast pad was placed (MacFarlane, 1975).

At two months, babies enter a period that lasts until seven to eight months of age. During this stage, social responsiveness increases along with direct eye-to-eye contact, smiling, cooing, quick learning, better motor patterns, and the stabilization of sleep and activity cycles. These changes are generally agreed upon by all observers of (especially parents). At two to three months of age, infants will smile at many face-like configurations, yet will stare longer at a drawing of a human face than at one in which the elements of the drawing—eyes, nose, mouth—are mixed up (Gewirtz, 1965). Infants are attracted to visual complexity. Walton, Bower, and Bower (1992) found that eleven of twelve newborns (12–36 hours old) preferred an image of their mother's face as opposed to an image of a stranger's face!

Infant senses are also perfectly fitted to promote communication and attachment. Newborns see best at a distance of about nine to ten inches, which is the distance between the eyes of a nursing baby and the mother's face. Infants only four to five months old can recognize a stimulus presented for as little as one to two minutes two weeks later (Cohen & Gelber, 1975). Infant hearing is also highly developed, with the greatest response to sounds at about 40 to 60 decibels, the range of a normal speaking voice (cited in Cramer, 1992).

Infants can make many discriminations by two months. One of the most acute discriminations is between the sounds of human speech. They can respond to a minimal sound contrast, such as the difference between "pa" and "ba" (Eimas, Siqueland, Jusczyk, & Vigorito, 1971). Even infants' physiognomy (large head in relation to the body, large eyes compared to other facial features, delicate skin, short limbs, large torso, and tiny hands) makes then physically attractive to adults and stimulates a response (Brazelton & Cramer, 1990). The communication of affect seen in mutual gazing, mutual smiling, and social play in the first four months predicts cognitive measures at one and two years (Alper, 1982; Cohen & Beckwith, 1979; Crockenberg, 1983).

Infants also have the amazing ability to synthesize senses (sounds and visual images) (e.g., Bower, 1967). That is, if a visual image is dislocated from its auditory component, infants experience negative affect (Meltzoff, 1990). In one study, four-month-olds were shown two films at the same time, about three inches apart. One showed a peek-a-boo game and the other showed a hand beating a drum. When the two films were shown with a single auditory soundtrack, the baby looked at the film that would match the sound (i.e., hearing the drum, the baby would look at the drum movie). Clearly, the baby understands which sound goes with which picture, relating the two senses. This is called cross-modal equivalence.

Meltzoff and Moore (1977) investigated the imitative capacity of 12- to 17-day-old newborns and showed that newborns can imitate both facial and manual gestures. Such behavior cannot be explained in terms of conditioning or innate releasing mechanisms. Newborns have been shown to imitate lip protrusions, mouth openings, tongue protrusions, and sequential finger movements (Meltzoff & Moore, 1983). This amazing capacity to imitate suggests that neonates can equate their own behaviors with gestures they observe others doing. Again, this implies active intermodal matching of proprioceptive and visual modes.

Why is cross-modal transference important to attachment and communication? If an infant did not have this capacity to synthesize, how would he know that the face and voice of a soothing mother were part of a single entity? How would he make the connection between the experience of drinking from the breast and attachment to the whole person? An infant "knows" that the sound of the mother's voice is just one part of the full reality he knows as mother. Infants are able to experience and construct a single image of mother, an image that is integrated and unitary, rather than multiple and fragmented, as might be expected were all the isolated acts and feelings left in their original form (as has been described in autistic children, who have great difficulty with attachment).

AFFECTIVE REGULATION IN SELF-
AND OTHER-REPRESENTATIONS

One of the main developmental feats in infancy is learning how to modulate, endure, and tolerate affective experience in order to benefit from the adaptive function of affect. The social environment is important in fostering the infant's self-regulatory capacities. Although infants have some capacity to modulate their affective states, they are largely dependent upon their caretakers to soothe and maintain them at more moderate or optimal levels. Healthy adaptation allows the infant to be an *active* agent in the regulation of affect and has implications for the ability to "coassemble" or integrate information.

Let us turn to the context in which affect is expressed and the phenomenon of interactive regulation. By self-regulation we mean organization of behavior to achieve desired states or goals. We focus on how affect is regulated within the relational context because a strong case has been made by major theorists in the field (e.g., Malatesta & Wilson, 1988) that adult capacities to manage one's emotional life (i.e., sexual desire, ambivalence, narcissistic injury, shame, etc.) are grounded in the cycling of emotional arousal in infancy. Optimally, during these early years, the infant incorporates what was other-regulated into a process of self-regulation. Infant and caregiver play active roles in modulating affect. At times, a sensitive caregiver increases pleasure, curiosity, surprise, etc., in the infant and at times she decreases it. Each subtle shift is made up of a seamless and only recently-studied treasure trove of looks, movements, touches, and signals. What follows is a description of this fascinating body of research.

We are interested in vocal, visual, and kinesic "matching" (or mirroring) of affective direction between infant and caregiver. Observations of infants as they sustain or disrupt face-to-face encounters have led to the development of a scale describing the levels of engagement—the various ways infants combine their orientation to the mother, their visual attention to her, and subtle variations in their facial expressiveness (Beebe & Gerstman, 1980; Beebe & Stern, 1977). This scale has been influenced by the concept that nuances of affective quality occur on a continuum rather than as discrete on/off categories. At the neutral midpoint of the scale, the infant is oriented toward the mother, visually engaging her face. At the high end one sees a full display of mouth opening and widening, which may be accompanied by thrusts of the head toward mother and by positive vocalizations. The general impression is that this is an expression of delight. At the low level of the scale there is a loss of visual regard, with the head and gaze averted from the mother. There is also a loss or inhibition of responsivity, in that the infant maintains a limp, motionless head-hang (which Tomkins would identify as innate shame) regardless of the mother's attempts at engagement.

A compelling set of research evidence highlighting the importance of attunement between caregivers and infants comes from studies that have examined infant-caregiver interactions in which affective resonance is missing or askew. Here we see the potentially profound detrimental effects of misattunements on the functioning of the infant. For example, Cicchetti, Ganibon, and Barnett's (1991) work with high-risk infant populations sheds some light specifically on the maternal role in affect regulation. Three- to four-month-old infants of clinically depressed mothers (including those with post-partum depression) were found to be less content, less responsive to the environment, and fussier. Similarly, Cohn, Matias, Tronick, Connell, and Lyons-Ruth (1986) found that 6- to 7-month-old infants of unipolar depressed mothers showed little positive affect, were socially withdrawn, expressed a limited range of affect, and lacked a sense of contingency. Field (1989) found that maternal depression influences an infant's interaction and attachment. During play, these infants were less positive, less vocal, less spontaneous, and more physically aroused (a sign of negative affect) than infants of non-depressed mothers. The parenting was more disengaged and intrusive than positive.

In studies of maltreated children, Gaensbauer, Mrazek, and Harmon (1980) described four patterns of affect differentiation: (1) developmentally and affectively retarded, (2) depressed, (3) ambivalent and affectively labile, and (4) angry. Different types of maltreatment yielded different affective patterns. For instance, physically abused infants showed negative affect (anger, sadness), while emotionally neglected infants showed more blunted affect (Gaensbauer & Hiatt, 1984). Unfortunately, these interactive styles generalized to interactions with other adults (Field et al., 1988).

Stern (1971, 1977) documented differential interactional styles between infant and caregiver, observing that mothers tend to gaze steadily, whereas it is the infant who "makes" and "breaks" the visual contact. Infants have control over the looking, looking away, and closing the eyes that "allow the infant by two to three months a subtle instant by instant regulation of social contact" (Stern, 1977, p. 502). Mothers and their normal infants were studied at three to four months. They were seated face to face, with the infant in an infant seat in an otherwise bare room, while videotape cameras produced a split-screen view of the interactions. This research paradigm specifically examined only the purely social exchange during periods of the affect interest-excitement or alert attention.

Yet by three to four months the extensive range of interpersonal affective display may be seen.

The multidimensional nature of the infant's positive expressiveness, based on head movements and mouth opening and closing, as well as increments in the smile display (mouth widening and narrowing), gives the infant a remarkable capacity to communicate slight changes in intensity and quality of mood without necessarily changing orientation or visual regard (Beebe, 1973). Facial mirroring studies show that both infant and mother influence the partners' direction of affective engagement. Beebe's (1973) review suggests that some kind of mirroring, matching, and imitation is a central aspect of the mother-infant interaction in the early months of life. However, using the statistical technique of time series analysis to track the interactions (Gottman, 1981), it was found that both mother and infant were mutually responsive.

Several researchers have considered the nature of matching in mother-infant play at four months and evaluated whether this matching is mutually regulated (Kroner, 1982). Using the engagement scales described above, the affective content (or levels of engagement) were examined. Mothers and infants were found to match the direction of affective change, despite each having a different placement on the scale. That is, mother and infant tended to increase or to decrease engagement together, but they were rarely at the same level of engagement. Microanalysis of filmed interactions between mother and infant show that levels of engagement shift so rapidly that the temporal relations between infant and caregiver occur in split-second mutual adjustments (Beebe, 1982). Beebe proposes that the representations of self and object matched both in the direction of affective change and in various temporal patterns provide a foundation for the later ability to share subjective states with another (Beebe, 1982; Stern, 1985).

We'll now talk about temporal matching in vocalization. An adult dialogue model of vocal congruence (Jaffe & Feldstein, 1970), in which adult partners match both pauses between vocalization and cycles of vocalizations and pauses, has been applied to infants and their caregiver partners. Interpersonal pauses or switching pauses are measured to mark the boundaries of turn-taking from the first to the second speaker's turn. Switching pauses between mother and infant have been found to match at four months (Beebe, Alson, Jaffe, Feldstein, & Crown, 1988). At nine months (Jasnow, 1983) it appears that matching is mutually influenced and that each partner influences the duration of the other's behavior to become more like his/her own. Since turn-taking can be considered the fundamental temporal structure of dialogue, the function of switching pause matching seems to be the regulation of turn-taking in a manner that is similar to adult speech (Beebe, Jaffe, Feldstein, Mays, & Alson, 1985). Interpersonal pause matching may be a subtle index of attunement in the mother-infant dyad.

We will now explore the matching of temporal patterns in mother-infant kinesic interactions. Here kinesic refers to movement or changes in orientation, gaze, and facial expression. Studies (e.g., Zelner, 1983) have aimed to explore the interpersonal timing of these frequent affective exchanges. A kinesic turn is comparable to a vocal turn, in that sequences of interaction are recorded as a member completes one unilateral move and then the other member's unilateral movement occurs. The study of temporal pattern matching consists of examining "holds," which are considered the functional equivalent of "vocalization" in the study of vocal matching. A hold is the stationary posture of the interactants or behavioral silences between kinesic turns; these kinesic turns are generally comprised of a single movement with a subsequent hold. Mothers and infants tend to match the duration of movements and holds (Beebe et al., 1985). Unlike vocal matching, time series analysis suggests that there is inverse kinesic matching, such that as one partner's movement becomes longer, the other shortens that movement (or vice versa). This compensatory matching (Beebe, 1982) may be interpreted to mean that the two partners work together to maintain a fairly constant dyadic activity level in the service of maintaining a "homeostatic negative feedback" system.

Each partner enacts the rhythm alternatively, so that together they carry out the unbroken rhythm (Jaffe, Anderson, & Stern, 1979), described below as the dance of attunement. The infant comes to view self rather than other (e.g., caregiver) as the agent in modulating affect. When the infant has made this causal connection (or coassembled experience) over time, he or she has an early positive experience in building an internal memory of self as a self-monitor. This might allow an infant to initiate self-modulating behavior earlier, rather then wait for the external modulating action of a caregiver. In such a situation, the infant may experience less frustration because of difficulties with temporal matching between self and primary caretaker, an ability perhaps of use when negotiating with other people later in life.

The role played by the matching and timing of vocal interactions and temporal patterns in the subsequent development and regulation of more complex emotional states (such as having a stable time sense, handling a range of shifting emotional states, tolerating needs and waiting for them to be met) has been exquisitely studied by Daniel Stern (1977, 1985). Stern (1985) writes that research discoveries "of developmental psychology are dazzling, but they seemed doomed to remain clinically sterile unless one is willing to make inferential leaps about what they might mean for the subjective life of the infant" (p. 5). However, Stern's "inventions" of what the interpersonal world of the infant feels like to an infant are a direct result of well-designed and rigorous research studies.

Stern and his colleagues videotaped hundreds of mother-infant pairs. One camera tracked each partner's movement, after which the two images were placed on a single monitor to compare and relate the effects of minute changes in one partner on the other. Mother-infant pairs were observed at two, four, six, nine, eighteen, twenty-four, and thirty-six months, either at home or in child-friendly laboratories. Mothers and infants spent about 10–15 minutes playing together. Attunement was measured by parental matching of absolute intensity, intensity contour (changes in intensity over time), temporal beat (a regular pulsation in time), rhythm (a pattern of pulsations of unequal stress), duration (a time span), and shape (some spatial feature of a behavior). Then the parent would look at the videotape and answer questions about their matchings, i.e., why did she do what she did, when she did it, and how she did it. The researcher joined the parent as a collaborator and was a partner in the inquiry. Stern believes this "research-therapeutic alliance" was crucial to the quality of their results.

Stern (1983) describes three "self-with-other" schemata (as distinct from a self-representation or an other-representation): state sharing, state transforming, and state complementing. These "process" experiences are viewed as innate constitutional endowments that make the infant by nature responsive to others. Many of the discrete and social capacities reviewed in the previous sections are the building blocks of these experiences. Stern observed that many of these self-experiences are regulated by others, including arousal, affect intensity, security of attachment, affect categorizing, attention, curiosity, cognitive engagement with the world, and somatic states.

Over time and with multiple repetitions, Stern hypothesized that these "lived episodes" become "generalized episodes of interactive experience" that later on become part of mental representations. Repeated episodes of an infant with a self-regulating caregiver can go on to form what Stern calls RIGs — representations of interactions that have been generalized. Beebe and Lachmann (1988) also argue that "the expectancies the infant has of characteristic interaction structures and their distinctive features summarize into generalized composites or prototypes at the point in the first year when the ability to abstract information develops" (p. 311). Stern's work helps clinicians and developmental theorists better comprehend both the subjective world of the infant and how core emotional experiences translate into the representational world of adults.

Optimally, mothers and babies follow a rhythmic pattern of synchro-nous mutual engagement and withdrawal. This phenomenon can be de-scribed as an interactive dance. Babies will react to variations on these interactive sequences, just as a dance partner who changes abruptly from a two-step to a cha-cha will get a funny look from his partner. If the variation is too abrupt or unexpected, the baby will respond with some degree of negative affect. As described below, the "still-face" procedure capitalizes on this reaction in studies of infant affect.

Stern (1985) utilized a more refined procedure in his studies of nine-month-olds. In order to create naturalistic perturbations of attunement, mothers watched videotapes of play interactions and identified likely-to-recur attunement episodes specific to that pair. The mothers would re-turn to the observation room, play with their infant, and when the ex-pectable attunement behavior arose, perform the expected perturbation. For example, one infant banging a toy and flailing about on his stomach got a vigorous jiggle on his bottom from his mother, at about the same rate and intensity of his body movements. This qualified as an attune-ment and the baby had no reaction. Another attuned response took place with no reaction. Soon after, the mother was instructed to do the same thing, but misjudge the baby's level of joyful animation, pretending the baby was less excited, and to jiggle accordingly. This time the baby turned around and looked at the mother, as if to say, "what's going on?" The infants consistently noticed and reacted to these mismatches, which then disrupted their play. As in other studies reported in this chapter, Stern found that infants develop an expectation of being matched.

What are the results when an infant's timing or behavior is not matched? Beebe and Stern (1977) looked at six-minute videotape play sessions of mother-infant pairs at four months. What they found was that in some pairs the mother seemed to "chase" the infant while the infant actively "dodged" her—an example of a misattunement. These mother-infant pairs showed a marked lack of the positive affect and mutual gazing common to this age group. The mother would follow the infant's head and body movements by pulling him, picking him up, repositioning him and even forcing his head in her direction. Yet the infant "dodged by moving back, ducking his head down, turning away, pulling his head from her grasp, or by becoming limp and unresponsive. The infant exercised a virtual 'veto power' over her attempts to engage him in a face-to-face encounter" (Beebe & Lachmann, 1988, p. 324). The researchers make clear that going limp or "playing possum" is an active coping mechanism, rather than one of tuning out because of the respon-sivity and vigilance involved. Infants are active agents in shaping their response to the environment.

Statistical analyses of the taped sessions revealed predictable mutual influences, e.g., a looming maternal head was followed by a defensive head movement away and back by the infant. This then would stimulate the mother to chase the baby further. Some striking "dodges" were 90-degree head turns by the baby or shutting of the infant's eyes through the center when moving the head side-to-side. The authors note that these physical and visual aversions "and limp, motionless states can be seen as a series of increasing visual-spatial boundaries in relation to the mother" (p. 324).

It seems likely that multiple experiences like these would affect a child's feelings of attachment and an infant's sense of "efficacy" (i.e., when an infant is able to produce a desired effect). Unfortunately, in these misattuned situations, the baby is seeking to reduce stimulation and these actions instead produce heightened intensity, leading to the development of the sense that the only way to feel good is to do it for yourself. The infant is getting help neither in the regulation of personal arousal nor in building secure attachment to a soothing other. Clinicians might consider how these kinds of early attachment experiences might affect the transference relationship in adulthood.

Interestingly, Malatesta et al. (1989) found that contingency of maternal facial response to infant expressions predicted only increases in positive affect and expressivity for the middle range of intensity. High levels of maternal contingent response were associated with negative infant affect; the level of stimulation was too high for the infant and then triggered distress–anguish or even anger–rage. In most cases, mothers in face-to-face play with their infants moderated the emotional expression of their infants, contingent upon the infants' ongoing emotional behavior.

Ongoing misattunements may also have consequences in the development of self-representation. As Stern (1985) points out, early mental representations are seen as interactive, such that an infant is storing patterns of actions-of-self-in-relation-to-the-world. In this process model of early representation, both self and object are conjointly and simultaneously represented. If interaction structures organize the infant's experience, one can posit that the chase and dodge pattern will affect later adaptations, defenses, representations, and subjective experiences. These infants do not have the multiple experiences of state-sharing that are key to subjective intimacy (Stern, Barnett, & Spieker, 1983). Many of these clinical manifestations will be explored in later chapters of this book.

Young children's observations and perceptions of the emotional responses of others are used to modulate emotional arousal and to guide their own behavior. Researchers emphasize the importance of emotional interpretations of the referenced other. This phenomenon has been called "social referencing" and, at times, "emotional referencing" (Campos & Sternberg, 1981; Klinnert, Campos, Sorce, Emde, & Svejda, 1983). Social referencing can be viewed as an important component of attachment, self-regulation, and contingency perception.

Vygotsky (1978), the highly influential Soviet psychologist, posited "the zone of proximal development," by which he described how infants make use of social objects to acquire deep and necessary knowledge of the world. Although research on social referencing is not often seen in the light of Vygotsky's work, these areas of inquiry seem highly related. In Vygotsky's research, mothers were seen to target their interactions to a developmental challenge just beyond the baby's current level, yet within the baby's reach. For example, an infant who is learning to walk will be guided gently by a caretaker's hand, yet will not be held up. The infant needs to find his own balance, yet the caregiver will not allow him to become overly frustrated or hurt. In this way the caregiver provides "scaffolding" for the child's sense of security during developmental transitions. This safety net functions quite similarly to the modality of social referencing.

A demonstration of infants' understanding of feelings states in others was seen in studies by Sternberg, Campos, and Emde (1983). They found that by the end of the first year children look to their mother's emotional expressions in order to understand and respond in situations of uncertainty. For instance, eight-and-one-half-month-old infants used their mother's expression to navigate a "visual cliff" (i.e., a sheet of glass over which the baby crawls, which appears midway to have no bottom). The infant repeatedly looks back, almost instinctively. The baby is surprised, but still attracted to a toy on the other side. When mothers displayed fear, no infant crossed the "cliff," yet when mothers showed joy or interest, 75% crossed. Several researchers have found that both normal and impaired infants scrutinize their caretaker's face, read the signals, and integrate this information into their own feeling states (e.g., Sorce, Emde, & Frank, 1982).

Infant-caregiver interactions serve to regulate emotional exchanges with the external world, and in turn prime the child to experience the beauty of a secure attachment bond. The baby learns from the mother's face to feel brave or defeatist. What a clear example of the powerful mirror the parental role involves! The implication is that babies are emotionally dependent upon the caregiver's state of mind as revealed to them by the facial display of innate affect. Multiple experiences of social referencing influence a child's sense of self and later on, identity.

INFANT AFFECT AND EMPATHY

The many ways that mother and infant regulate and match the timing and affective direction of behavior "provide each a behavioral basis for knowing and entering into the partner's perception, temporal world, and feeling-state" (Beebe & Lachmann, 1988, p. 320). One of the many implications of this research (and research by others, i.e., Basch, 1983; Nathanson, 1986) is that early affectively charged experiences may provide a foundation for our capacity to empathize with others. These clear-cut examples of the matching of affective direction, temporal patterns, and specific facial expression suggest ways that we learn to participate in the subjective state of the other, a core component of empathy. As Demos (1988, p. 27) stated, "Affect is thought to play an essential role in empathic exchanges, to be the primary medium of communication between infants and caregivers, and to remain an important nonverbal element in all communication throughout life."

Empirical investigations of early empathy suggest that young children are capable of empathic feelings that guide and possibly motivate their behavior. Hoffman (1975) addresses the ontogeny of empathy, positing that infants involuntarily experience another person's distress, which he calls "empathetic distress." From his perspective, young children are motivated to aid another in order to decrease their own negative feelings. Around 18 months, with the development of person permanence, distress in the emerging self becomes differentiated from the distress of the other. However, the child assumes the other feels the same way as the child feels. Hoffman (1975) explains that with the development of "sympathetic distress" there is a "gradual emergence of a sense of the other as distinct from the self, the affective portion of the child's global empathic distress—the feeling of distress and desire for its termination—is extended to the separate self and other that emerge" (p. 114).

Hoffman (1982) considers empathic arousal (e.g., feeling bad as a result of someone else's discomfort) as key to the emergence of early moral development. Infants and toddlers are sensitive to the emotional states of important others; yet their empathic response appears to be dictated by associated cognitive skills (Ungerer et al., 1990).

Research on empathy has a long history involving a great variety of investigative tactics and phenomena studied. Although there are varying opinions (i.e., Basch, 1983; Nathanson, 1986) on the definition of empathy (especially in investigations of the very young child), it can be viewed most usefully as a multidimensional construct having at its definitional core the experience of another's affective or psychological state, with significant cognitive and emotional components occurring later in development (Zahn-Waxler & Radke-Yarrow, 1990).

Researchers have studied the emotional aspects of empathy by measuring, at one extreme, the extent to which children can display a perfect vicarious match of another's distress to more simply measuring facial expressions of concern, sympathy, or compassion for another in distress. Usually, the emotional response considered important to empathy is sharing the "general emotional tone" of another rather than an identical affective match (Thompson, 1987, p. 123). Considering Beebe and Lachmann's discussion of matching studies, there are many similarities with what we see in infants and how we index empathy in children and adults. With both infants and adults, feeling states are expressed in behavior, perceived by another, and then matched in some way (i.e., timing, affect, direction, etc.). The actual imitation or matching of the other's experience may generate a similar emotional state in the person, which can then be defined as experiencing empathy (see Ekman, 1983; Zajonc, 1985).

Empathy and sympathy have been conceptually differentiated; however, it is more difficult to validate this difference empirically. Eisenberg and Fabes (1990) consider empathy to be an other-oriented "emotional response that stems from another's emotional state or condition, [and] is congruent with the other's emotional state or condition, and involves at least a minimal degree of differentiation between self and other." Sympathy is seen as a more complex cognitive skill involving the "other-oriented desire for the other person to feel better and is not the same as merely feeling what the other person feels" (p. 132). Sympathy involves the added component of feeling sorrow for another.

In yet another conceptual distinction important to an understanding of empathy in both adults and young children, Batson (1987) differentiates feelings of empathy for another in distress (e.g., concern) from feelings of "personal distress." As in the above definitions, empathy and sympathy are seen as other-oriented responses, whereas personal distress in response to another's suffering evokes an aversive emotional reaction (e.g., anxiety, fear, or distress) and is therefore more self-oriented. His work suggests that under some conditions (and/or due to individual differences) prosocial behavior may be truly empathically based, whereas under other conditions (and/or for other individuals) altruistic behavior may emanate from efforts to reduce personal distress. Those individuals who become more personally distressed in response to another's suffering may assist them only if it is the easiest way to alleviate their own unpleasant feelings. On the other hand, those who respond more empathically may help another even at great personal costs, as the motivational basis for their behavior is other-oriented. Batson's studies of adults have led to an appreciation of the pluralistic motives for altruistic behavior.

Ungerer et al. (1990) sought to determine if self-regulatory skills at four months of age predicted primitive empathic response at twelve months of age in a sample of 45 first-born children. The focus was on individual differences in empathic response (i.e., why some one- to two-year-olds ignore distressed peers while others express concern or become agitated). They found that 15 one-year-olds showed a personal distress reaction (indexed by sucking on a part of the body, clothing, or object) to a videotape of a peer fretting and crying, whereas 30 showed no reaction. These 15 one-year-olds did not differ from the other 30 on a measure of physiological maturation (using sleep-activity records) at four months.

The two groups were also compared on results of the "still-face" procedure at four months. This is a research methodology in which the mother faces the baby and has a normal playful interchange. She then stops all movements, vocalizations, and imitations. Normally, the baby becomes surprised, then tries to get her attention, and can get distressed and even apathetic (which could be viewed as shame). Those 15 one-year-olds who showed the personal distress reaction to the tape at twelve months had distinctly less well-regulated responses to the interactive stimulus of the still-face procedure (at four months) than the 30 children who did not show personal distress to the tape. During the still-face procedure these 15 infants showed more self-comforting behaviors — seen as a sign of poorer self-regulation — than the other 30 subjects. This behavior is considered to be a self-oriented response that distances the infant from interactive involvement with others in the environment. These infants' emotional response is seen as too difficult to handle, and therefore they disengage from the stressful event and their surroundings as well. Whether one agrees with the perspective that self-soothing behavior is a sign of poor self-regulation, these results do suggest some stability of individual differences in the capacity to self-regulate in the face of distressing social stimuli from four to twelve months of age.

Although the following study involves children older than we have been discussing so far, we include it in our review because it suggests how early congruence of feelings states gets differentiated into actual prosocial behavior. In a nine-month, naturalistic study of the origins of altruism, Zahn-Waxler and Radke-Yarrow (1982) found that, as subjects aged from one to three years, they experienced increasingly less personal distress and more sympathetic concern in response to others' distress. While an "orienting" response was elicited by 26% of the younger group

(9 to 14 months), along with distress cries by one third of this group, the highest percentage of prosocial acts was observed in the 15- to 24-month-old group. They postulate a major developmental shift in the second year from "global distress" responses to constructive, other-focused, sympathetic, and helping responses. Before a child can nurture and care for another out of true empathic concern, he or she must be able to modulate and handle "global distress" (i.e., aversive arousal). This implies a certain level of physiological maturity. During the second year of life, children's overall social-emotional life becomes increasingly integrated, organized, and emotionally regulated (Cicchetti & Schneider-Rosen, 1986). With respect to empathy, they may become both more self-regulated and other-oriented as they further differentiate self from other in the second half of the second year.

SUMMARY

Since infants do not possess the language to explain the connection between internal states and facial and behavioral displays, research on affective development in infancy necessarily differs in methodology from research carried out at other life stages. Until the recent past, researchers did not include infants in studies of affect because of their hesitancy to interpret the meaning of infants' behavioral displays. As is evident in the studies described above, technological advances have created new opportunities to measure subjective events in the very young child. For example, measures of psychophysiological arousal (heart rate and skin conductance response), affordable infra-red lighting, and high-resolution video equipment now allow for microchronological tracking of internal and external emotional displays without self-report. For infants, the focus is on observed affective response in the context of the social environment. Interpreting the cognitive and emotional meaning (or developmental sequelae) of these indices has led to several new theories of early affective development.

The studies reported in this chapter have maintained a developmental perspective. The researchers have attempted to refrain from evaluating infant affect by standards more appropriate for evaluating older children's or adult affect. Malatesta, Izard, and Camras (1991), for example, note that in the past researchers tended to hold infants to standards that we do not impose on adults, such as requiring only one affect in response to an event, rather than allowing for rapid emotional oscillations. How affect is manifested and the meaning it has are indexed by different behaviors in different age groups, yet the functional significance of these behaviors may be quite similar. For example, an "empathic" response of a eight-month-old may be manifested by the sucking of fingers with the purpose of calming down. At age two, the response may be a sad expression combined with moving toward the mother's leg for reassurance, asking "What happened?" or even staring in a concerned way. By age three, the child may use words to cheer up a friend by explaining that his or her mother will be back or by trying to explain what happened. In general, the goal of most developmentally based studies of infant affect is to discover when functionally related behaviors first appear (however immature their forms) and to ask about conditions of their acquisition, maintenance, and developmental sequence.

Taken as a whole, the studies reviewed in this chapter provide substantial evidence to support the notion that right from the start affect plays a primary role in organizing, motivating, and sustaining behavior. The research of Tomkins, Demos, and other affect theorists provides a very strong case for the existence of innate affects that provide the biological substrate for all human experience. The healthy infant comes well-equipped with a complete repertoire of facial and kinesic displays that serve to punctuate certain experiences as more important than others, both for infants and for their caregivers. The affective displays of infants contain high demand value for caregivers and others, thereby automatically pulling for some type of caregiving response. The research of Bowlby, Ainsworth, and other attachment theorists provides a very strong case for the powerful communicative role of early affective displays in fostering emotionally sustaining infant-caregiver relationships. The implication of this work is that human beings are wired to become social because they are endowed with an affect system.

As much of the research above implies, considerable individual differences in the activation and display of affect are shaped by interactive, environmental forces. According to Malatesta-Magai (1991), affective development occurs within the individual but emerges as a product of mutually influential interactions within a particular kind of social ecology. At this juncture a clinical developmental theory, such as that proposed by Greenspan (1992), can be useful in translating research into efforts to understand development that is off-course and to plan how to modify it.

As part of Greenspan's clinical approach to strengthen the infant-caregiver relationship and to help infants develop optimally, he coaches caregivers and educators in the process of "floortime." Central to this work is the "opening and closing of circles of communication" (Greenspan, 1992), a process that very much resembles the research described earlier on infant-parent matching of affective responses (Beebe & Stern,

1977). For example, in the process described by Greenspan, the caregiver expresses an interest in the child (opening a circle), and the child responds with a gestural reaction (closing the circle). Opening and closing multiple circles encourage development and provide an opportunity for the sharing of affect. Greenspan utilizes infant affect to help parents and children relate to one another. His sensitivity to the influence of the child-caregiver interaction, the child's unique adaptive capacities, and environmental factors is a central component of his clinical-developmental theory (Greenspan, 1992) and makes his work valuable for clinicians attempting to apply infant research findings to their clinical work.

REFERENCES

Ainsworth, M. D. S. (1967). *Infancy in Uganda.* Baltimore: Johns Hopkins University Press.

Ainsworth, M. D. S. (1979). Attachment as related to mother-infant interaction. In J. B. Rosenblatt, R. H. Hinde, C. Beer, & M. Bushnell (Eds.), *Advances in the study of behavior* (pp. 17–57). New York: Academic Press.

Ainsworth, M. D. S., & Bell, S. M. (1970). Attachment, exploration and separation: Illustrated by the behavior of one-year-olds in a strange situation. *Child Development, 41,* 49–67.

Ainsworth, M. D. S., Blehar, M. C., Waters, E., & Wall, S. (1978). *Patterns of attachment.* Hillsdale, NJ: Erlbaum.

Ainsworth, M. D. S., & Wittig, B. (1969). Attachment and exploratory behavior in one-year-olds in a stranger situation. In B. M. Foss (Ed.), *Determinants of infant behavior.* New York: Wiley.

Alper, R. (1982). *Mother-infant interaction and infant cognitive competence.* Unpublished doctoral dissertation, Yeshiva University, New York.

Arlow, J. A. (1977). Affects and the psychoanalytic situation. *Journal of Psychoanalysis, 58,* 157–170.

Basch, M. F. (1976). The concept of affect: A re-examination. *Journal of the American Psychoanalytic Association, 24,* 759–777.

Basch, M. F. (1983). Empathic understanding: A review of the concept and some theoretical considerations. *Journal of the American Psychoanalytic Association, 31,* 101–126.

Batson, C. D. (1987). Prosocial motivation: Is it ever truly altruistic? In L. Berkowitz (Ed.), *Advances in experimental and social psychology* (Vol. 20, pp. 65–122). New York: Academic Press.

Beebe, B. (1973). Ontogeny of positive affect in the third and fourth months of the life of one infant (Doctoral dissertation, Columbia University, 1973). *Dissertation Abstracts International, 35:*2, 1014b.

Beebe, B. (1982). Micro-timing in mother-infant communication. In M. Key (Ed.), *Nonverbal communication today: Current research* (pp. 169–195). New York: Mouton.

Beebe, B., Alson, D., Jaffe, J., Feldstein, S., & Crown, C. (1988). Mother-infant vocal congruence. *Journal of Psycholinguistic Research, 17:*3, 245–259.

Beebe, B., & Gerstman, L. (1980). The "packaging" of maternal stimulation in relation to infant facial-visual engagement: A case study at four months. *Merrill-Palmer Quarterly, 26,* 321–339.

Beebe, B., Jaffe, J. Feldstein, S., Mays, K., & Alson, D. (1985). Interpersonal timing: The application of an adult dialogue model to mother-infant vocal and kinesic interactions.

In T. Field & N. Fox (Eds.), *Social perception in infants* (pp. 217-247). Norwood, NJ: Ablex.

Beebe, B., & Lachmann, F. M. (1988). The contribution of mother-infant mutual influence to the origins of self- and object representations. *Psychoanalytic Psychology, 5*:4, 305-337.

Beebe, B., & Stern, D. (1977). Engagement-disengagement and early object experiences. In N. Freedman & S. Grand (Eds.), *Communicative structures and psychic structures* (pp. 35-55). New York: Plenum.

Berger, M. (1985). Temperament and individual differences. In M. Rutter & L. Hersov (Eds.), *Child and adolescent psychiatry: Modern approaches* (2nd ed.). Oxford: Blackwell Scientific.

Blehar, M. C., Lieberman, A. F., & Ainsworth, M. (1977). Early face-to-face interaction and its relation to later mother-infant attachment. *Child Development, 48*, 182-194.

Bower, T. G. R. (1967). Phenomenal identity and form perception in infancy. *Perception and Psychophysics, 2*, 74-76.

Bowlby, J. (1959). The nature of the child's tie to his mother. *International Journal of Psychoanalysis, 39*, 350-373.

Bowlby, J. (1969). *Attachment and Loss*, Vol. 1. New York: Basic Books.

Bowlby, J. (1973). *Attachment and Loss*, Vol. 2. New York: Basic Books.

Bowlby, J. (1980). *Attachment and Loss*, Vol. 3. New York: Basic Books.

Brazelton, T. B., & Cramer, B. G. (1990). *The earliest relationship.* Reading, MA: Addison-Wesley.

Brazelton, T. B., Koslowski, B., & Main, M. (1974). The origins of reciprocity: The early mother-infant interaction. In M. Lewis & L. Rosenblum (Eds.), *The effect of the infant on its caregiver.* New York: Wiley.

Brenner, C. (1974). On the nature and development of affects: A unified theory. *Psychoanalytic Quarterly, 43*, 532-566.

Brenner, C. (1982). *The mind in conflict.* New York: International Universities Press.

Buss, A. H., & Plomin, R. (1975). *A temperament theory of personality development.* New York: Wiley-Interscience.

Campos, J. J., & Sternberg, C. R. (1981). Perceptory appraisal and emotion: The onset of social referencing. In M. E. Lamb & L. R. Sherrrod (Eds.), *Infant social recognition.* Hillsdale, NJ: Erlbaum.

Campos, J. J., Barrett, K. C., Lamb, M. E., Goldsmith, H. H., & Sternberg, C. (1983). Socioemotional development. In M. M. Haith & J. J. Campos (Eds.), *Infancy and developmental psychobiobiology. Volume 2 of Mussen's handbook of child psychology* (4th ed.). New York: Wiley.

Chen, S. J., & Miyake, K. (1984). Japanese vs. United States comparison of mother-infant interaction and infant development: A review. *Research and Clinical Center for Child Development, 82-83*, 13-26.

Cicchetti, D., & Schneider-Rosen, K. (1986). An organizational approach to childhood depression. In M. Rutter, C. Izard, & P. Read (Eds.), *Depression in young people: Clinical and developmental perspectives.* New York: Guilford.

Cicchetti, D., Ganibon, J., & Barnett, D. (1991). Contributions from the study of high risk populations to understanding the development of emotion regulation. In J. Garber & K. A. Dodge (Eds.), *The development of emotion regulation and dysregulation.* Cambridge: Cambridge University Press.

Cohen, L., & Gelber, E. (1975). Infant visual memory. In L. Cohen & P. Salapatek (Eds.), *Infant perception: From sensation to cognition* (Vol. 1, pp. 347-403). New York: Academic.

Cohen, S., & Beckwith, L. (1979). Preterm infant interaction with the caregiver in the first year of life and competence at age two. *Child Development, 50*, 767-776.

Cohn, J. F., Matias, R., Tronick, F. Z., Connell, D., & Lyons-Ruth, K. (1986). Face to face interactions of depressed mothers and their infants. In E. Z. Tronick & T. Fields (Eds.), *Maternal depression and infant disturbances.* San Fransisco: Jossey-Boss.

Cramer, B. G. (1992). *The importance of being baby.* New York: Addison-Wesley.

Crockenberg, S. (1983). Early mother and infant antecedants of Bayley skill performance at 21 months. *Developmental Psychology, 19,* 727–730.

Cummings, E. M., Zahn-Waxler, C., & Radke-Yarrow, M. (1984). Developmental changes in children's reactions to anger in the home. *Journal of Child Psychology and Psychiatry and Allied Disciplines, 25,* 63–74.

Darwin, C. (1872). *The expression of emotion in man and animals.* Chicago: University of Chicago Press, 1965.

Demos, E. V. (1988). Affect and the development of the self: A new frontier. In A. Goldberg (Ed.), *Frontiers in self psychology: Progress in self psychology* (Vol. 3, pp. 27–53). Hillsdale, NJ: Analytic Press.

Dunn, J. (1980). Individual differences in temperament. In M. Rutter (Ed.), *Scientific foundations of developmental psychiatry.* London: Heineman Medical.

Eibl-Eibesfeldt, I. (1979). Human ethology: Concepts and implications for the science of man. *Behavioral and Brain Sciences, 2,* 1–57.

Eimas, P. D., Siqueland, E. R., & Friesen, W. J. (1969). Pan-cultural elements in facial displays of emotion. *Science, 171,* 303–306.

Eimas, P. D., Siqueland, E. R., Jusczyk, P., & Vigorito, J. (1971). Speech perception in infants. *Science, 171,* 303–306.

Eisenberg, N., & Fabes, R. A. (1990). Empathy: Conceptualization, measurement, and relation to prosocial behavior. *Motivation and Emotion, 14*:2, 131–150.

Ekman, P. (1972). Universal and cultural differences in facial expression of emotion. *Nebraska Symposium on Motivation, 19,* 207–283.

Ekman, P. (1978). *Manual for the Facial Affect Coding System.* Palo Alto, CA: Consulting Psychologists Press.

Ekman, P. (1982). Personal communication, as reported in "Affect in early infancy," E. V. Demos, *Psychoanalytic Quarterly, 1*:4, 533–574.

Ekman, P. (1983). Autonomic nervous system activity distinguishes among emotions. *Science, 209,* 1140–1141.

Ekman, P., & Friesen, W. (1969). The repertoire of nonverbal behavior: Categories, origins, usage, and coding. *Semiotica, I,* 49–98.

Ekman, P., Gaensbauer, T. J., & Harmon, R. J. (1976). *Emotional expression in infancy.* New York: International Universities Press.

Ekman, P., Levenson, R., & Friesen, W. (1983). Autonomic nervous system activity distinguishes among emotion. Science, 221, 1208–1210.

Emde, R. N. (1980). Toward a psychoanalytic theory of affect: II. Emerging models of emotional development in infancy. In S. I. Greenspan & G. Pollock (Eds.), *The course of life: Psychoanalytic contributions toward understanding personality development. Vol. I: Infancy and early childhood.* Washington, DC: National Institutes of Mental Health.

Emde, R. (1988). Development terminable and interminable I and II. *International Journal of Psychoanalysis, 69,* 283–296.

Field, T. (1982). Discrimination and imitation of facial expressions by neonates. *Science, 218,* 179–181.

Field, T. (1989). Maternal depression effects on infant interaction and attachment. In D. Cicchetti (Ed.), *Rochester Symposium on Developmental Psychopathology.* Vol. 1 (pp. 139–163). Hillsdale, NJ: Erlbaum.

Field, T., Healy, B., Goldstein, S., Perry, S., Bendell, Schankey, S., Zimmerman, E. A., & Kuhn, C. (1988). Infants of depressed mothers show "depressed" behavior even with non-depressed adults. *Child Development, 59,* 1569–1580.

Fogel, A. (1982). Affect dynamics in early infancy: Affective tolerance. In T. Field & A. Fogel (Eds.), *Emotion and early interaction.* Hillsdale, NJ: Erlbaum.

Fox, N. A. (1989). Psychophysiological correlates of emotional reactivity during the first year of life. *Developmental Psychology, 25*:3, 364–372.

Freud, S. (1961). The ego and the id. In J. Strachey (Ed. and Trans.), *The standard edition* of the complete psychological works of Sigmund Freud (Vol. 19, pp. 3–66). New York: Norton. (Original work published in 1923)

Friedlander, B. Z. (1970). Receptive language development in infancy. *Merrill-Palmer Quarterly, 16*, 7–51.

Gaensbauer, T. J., Mrazek, D., & Harmon, R. (1980). Affective behavior patterns in abused and/or neglected infants. In N. Frude (Ed.), *The understanding and prevention of child abuse: Psychological approaches.* London: Concord Press.

Gaensbauer, T. J., & Hiatt, S. (1984). Facial communication of emotion in early infancy. In N. A. Fox & R. J. Davidson (Eds.), *The psychobiology of affective development* (pp. 207–230). Hillsdale, NJ: Erlbaum.

Gewirtz, J. L. (1965). The cause of infant smiling in four child-rearing environments in Israel. In B. M. Foss (Ed.) *Determinants of infant behavior*, Vol. III. London: Methuen.

Gottman, J. (1981). *Time series analysis.* Cambridge: Cambridge University Press.

Graham, P., & Stevenson, J. (1986, September). *Temperament and psychiatric disorder: The genetic contribution to behavior in childhood.* Paper presented at the Child and Adolescent Psychiatry Section of the Royal Australian and New Zealand College of Psychiatrists.

Greenspan, S. I. (1992). *Infancy and early childhood.* Madison, CT: International Universities Press.

Greenspan, S. I., & Porges, S. W. (1984). Psychopathology in infancy and early childhood: Clinical perspectives on the organization of sensory and affective-thematic experience. *Child Development, 55*, 49–70.

Healy, B. T. (1989). Autonomic nervous system correlates of temperament. *Infant Behavior and Development, 12*, 289–304.

Hoffman, M. L. (1975). Developmental synthesis of affect and cognition and its implications for altruistic motivation. *Developmental Psychology, 11*, 607–622.

Hoffman, M. L. (1982). Affect and moral development. In D. Cicchetti & P. Hesse (Eds.), *New directions for child development: Emotional development.* San Francisco: Jossey-Bass.

Horowitz, M. J. (1972). Modes of representation of thought. *Journal of the American Psychoanalytic Association, 20*, 793–819.

Issacson, R. L. (1982). *The limbic system.* New York: Plenum.

Izard, C. E. (1971). *The face of emotion.* New York: Appleton-Century-Crofts.

Izard, C. E., Hembree, E., & Huebner, R. (1987). Infants' emotional expression to acute pain: Developmental changes and stability of individual difference. *Developmental Psychology, 23*, 105–113.

Izard, C. E., & Malatesta, C. Z. (1987). Perspectives on emotional development: I. Differential emotions theory of early emotional development. In J. D. Osofsky (Ed.), *Handbook of infant development* (2nd ed., pp. 494–554). New York: Wiley.

Izard, C. E., Porges, S., Simons, R. F., Haynes, O. M., Hyde, C., Parisi, M., & Cohen, B. (1991). Infant cardiac activity: Developmental changes and relations with attachment. *Developmental Psychology, 27*:3, 432–439.

Jaffe, J., Anderson, S., & Stern, D. (1979). Conversational rhythms. In D. Aronson & R. Rieber (Eds.), *Psycholinguistic research* (pp. 393–431). Hillsdale, NJ: Erlbaum.

Jaffe, J., & Feldstein, S. (1970). *Rhythms of dialogue.* New York: Academic.

James, W. (1890). *Principles of psychology.* New York: Dover.

Jasnow, M. (1983). *Temporal accommodation in vocal behavior in mother-infant dyads.* Unpublished doctoral dissertation, George Washington University, Washington, DC.

Kagan, J. (1984). *The nature of the child.* New York: Basic Books.

Kagan, J., Kearsley, R., & Zelazo, P. (1978). *Infancy: Its place in human development.* Cambridge, MA: Harvard University Press.

Kagan, J., & Moss, H. A. (1962). Birth to maturity. New York: Wiley.

Kagan, J., & Reznick, R. S. (1984). Task involvement and cardiac response in young children. *Australian Journal of Psychology, 36*:2, 135–147.

Kagan, J., Reznick, R. S., Clarke, C., Snidman, N., & Garcia-Coll, C. (1984). Behavioral inhibition to the unfamiliar. *Child Development, 55*, 2212–2225.

Kagan, J., Reznick, R. S., & Gibbons, J. (1989). Inhibited and uninhibited types of children. *Child Development, 60*:4, 838–845.

Klinnert, M. D., Campos, J. J., Sorce, J. F., Emde, R. N., & Svejda, M. (1983). The development of social referencing in infancy. In R. Plutchik & H. Kellerman (Eds.), *Emotion in early development. Vol. 2. of Emotion: Theory, research and experience.* New York: Academic Press.

Kroner, J. (1982). *Maternal facial mirroring at four months.* Unpublished doctoral dissertation, Yeshiva University, New York.

Lamb, M. E., Hwang, C. P., Bookstein, F. L., & Broberg, A. (1988). Determinants of social competence in Swedish preschoolers. *Developmental Psychology, 24*:1, 58–70.

Lewis, M., Allesandri, S., & Sullivan, M. (1989). *Expectancy, loss of control and anger expression in young infants.* Unpublished manuscript.

Lewis, M., Feiring, C., McGuffog, C., & Jaskir, J. (1985). Predicting psychopathology in six-year-olds from early social relations. In S. Chess & A. Thomas (Eds.), *Annual progress in child psychiatry and child development, 1985* (pp. 496–519). New York: Brunner/Mazel.

Lichtenberg, J. (1983). *Psychoanalysis and infant research.* Hillsdale, NJ: Analytic Press.

Lorenz, K. (1966). *On aggression.* New York: Harcourt, Brace, Jovanovich.

Lutkenhaus, P., Grossman, K. E., & Grossman, K. (1985). Infant-mother attachment at twelve months and style of interaction with a stranger at the age of three years. *Child Development, 56*:6, 1538–1542.

MacEvoy, B., Lambert, W. W., Karlberg, P., & Karlberg, J. (1988). Early affective antecedents of adult type A behavior. *Journal of Personality and Social Psychology, 54*:1, 108–116.

MacFarlane, J. (1975). Olfaction in the development of social preferences in the human neonate. In M. Hofer (Ed.), *Parent-infant interaction.* Amsterdam: Elsevier.

Mahler, M., Pine, F., & Bergman, A. (1975). *The psychological birth of the human infant: Symbiosis and individuation.* New York: Basic Books.

Malatesta, C. Z., Culver, C., Tesman, J. R., & Shepard, B. (1989). The development of emotion expression during the first two years of life. *Monographs of the Society for Research in Child Development, 54*(1–2, Serial No. 219).

Malatesta, C. Z., Izard, C., & Camras, L. A. (1991). Conceptualizing early infant affect: Emotions as fact, fiction, or artifact? In K. Strongman (Ed.), *International Review of Studies on Emotion.* New York: Wiley.

Malatesta, C. Z., & Wilson, A. (1988). Emotion/cognition interaction in personality development: A discrete emotions, functionalist analysis. *British Journal of Social Psychology, 27*, 91–112.

Malatesta-Magai, C. (1991). The development of emotion expression during infancy, In J. Garber & K. A. Dodge (Eds.), *The development of emotion regulation and dysregulation.* Cambridge: Cambridge University Press.

Meltzoff, A. N. (1990). Towards a developmental cognitive science: The implications of cross-modal matching and imitation for the development of representation and memory in infancy. *Annals of the New York Academy of Sciences, 608*, 1–37.

Meltzoff, A. N., & Moore, M. K. (1977). Imitation of facial and manual gestures by human neonates. *Science, 198*, 75–78.

Meltzoff, A. N., & Moore, M. K. (1983). The origins of imitation in infancy: Paradigm, phenomena, and theories. *Advances in Infancy Research, 2*, 265–301.

Miyake, K., Chen, S. J., & Campos, J. J. (1985). Infant temperament, mother's mode of interaction, and attachment in Japan: An interim report. *Monographs of the Society for Research in Child Development, 50*:1–2, 276–297.

Nathanson, D. L. (1986). The empathic wall and the ecology of affect. *Psychoanalytic Study of the Child, 41*, 171–87.

Oster, & Ekman, P. (1978). Facial behavior in child development. *Minnesota symposia on child psychology*, Vol. II. Hillsdale, NJ: Erlbaum.

Panksepp, J. (1982). Toward a general psychobiological theory of emotions. *Behavioral and Brain Sciences, 5*, 407–468.

Piaget, J. (1952). *The origins of intelligence in children.* New York: International Universities Press.

Plomin, R., & Rowe, D. C. (1979). Genetic and environmental etiology of social behavior in infancy. *Developmental Psychology, 15*, 62–72.

Porges, S. W., McCabe, P. M., & Yongue, B. G. (1982). Respiratory-heart rate interactions: Physiological implications for psychophysiology and behavior. In J. Cacioppo & R. Petty (Eds.), *Perspectives in cardiovascular psychophysiology* (pp. 223–264). New York: Guilford.

Pribrim, K. (1980). The biology of emotions and other feelings. In R. Plutchik & H. Kererrman (Eds.), *Emotion: Theory, research and experience.* New York: Academic Press.

Richards, J. E., & Cameron, D. (1989). Infant heart-rate variability and behavioral developmental status. *Infant Behavior and Development, 12*, 45–48.

Rutter, M. (1987). Temperament, personality and personality disorder. *British Journal of Psychiatry, 150*, 443–458.

Rutter, M., Birch, H., Thomas, A., & Chess, S. (1964). Temperamental characteristics in infancy and later development of behavioural disorders. *British Journal of Psychiatry, 110*, 651–661.

Sander, L. (1980). New knowledge about the infant from current research: Implications for psychoanalysis. *Journal of the American Psychological Association, 28*, 181–198.

Siqueland, E. R., & Delucia, C. A. (1969). Visual reinforcement of non-nutritive sucking in human infants. *Science, 165*, 1144–1146.

Skinner, B. F. (1974). *About behaviorism.* New York: Knopf.

Sorce, J. F., Emde, R. N., & Frank, M. (1982). Maternal referencing in normal and Down's syndrome infants. In R. N. Emde & R. J. Harmon (Eds.), *The development of attachment and affiliative systems* (pp. 281–292). New York: Plenum.

Sroufe, L. A. (1979). The ontogenesis of emotion in infancy. In J. Osofsky (Ed.), *Handbook of infant development.* New York: Wiley.

Stechler, G., & Carpenter, G. (1974). A viewpoint on early affective development. In J. Hellmuth (Ed.), *The exceptional infant, Vol. 1: The normal infant.* Seattle: Special Child Publications.

Stern, D. N. (1971). A microanalysis of the mother-infant interaction. *Journal of the American Academy of Child Psychiatry, 10*, 501–507.

Stern, D. N. (1974). Mother and infant at play: The dyadic interaction involving facial, vocal and gaze behaviors. In M. Lewis & L. A. Rosenblum (Eds.), *The effect of the infant on its caregiver.* New York: Wiley.

Stern, D. N. (1977). *The first relationship.* Cambridge, MA: Harvard University Press.

Stern, D. N. (1983). The early development of schemas of self, other, and self-with-other. In S. Kaplan (Ed.), *Reflections on self psychology* (pp. 49–84). New York: International Universities Press.

Stern, D. N. (1985). *The interpersonal world of the infant.* New York: Basic Books.

Stern, D. N., Barnett, R. K., & Spieker, S. (1983). Early transmission of affect: Some research issues. In J. D. Call, F. Galenson, & R. L. Tyson (Eds.), *Frontiers of infant psychiatry.* New York: Basic Books.

Sternberg, C., Campos, J., & Emde, R. N. (1983). The facial expression of anger in seven-month-old infants. *Child Development, 54*, 178–184.

Stone, A. (1993). Trauma and affect: Applying the language of affect theory to the phenomena of traumatic stress. *Psychiatric Annals, 23*:10, 567–576.

Thomas, A., & Chess, S. (1979). *Temperament and development.* New York: Brunner/Mazel.

Thompson, R. (1987). Empathy and emotional understanding: The early development of empathy. In N. Eisenberg & J. Strayer (Eds.), *Empathy and its development.* New York: Cambridge University Press.

Tomkins, S. S. (1962). *Affect, imagery, consciousness, Vol. 1: The positive affects.* New York: Springer.

Tomkins, S. S. (1963). *Affect, imagery, consciousness, Vol. 2: The negative affects.* New York: Springer.

Tronick, E., Als, H., & Brazelton, T. B. (1980). Monadic phases: A structural descriptive analysis of infant-mother, face-to-face interaction. *Merrill-Palmer Quarterly, 26,* 3–24.

Ujiie, T., & Miyake, K. (1984). Responses to the strange situation in Japanese infants. *Research and Clinical Center for Child Development, 1983–84 Annual Report,* 27–36.

Ungerer, J., Dolby, R., Waters, B., Barnett, B., Kelk, N., & Lewin, V. (1990). The early development of empathy: Self-regulation and individual differences in the first year. *Motivation and Emotion, 8*:2, 93–106.

Vygotsky, L. (1978). *Mind in society.* Cambridge, MA: Harvard University Press.

Walton, G. E., Bower, N. J., & Bower, T. G. (1992). Recognition of familiar faces by newborns. *Infant Behavior and Development, 15*(2), 265–269.

White, B., Field, T., Meltzoff, A., & Kagan, J. (1987). Baby research comes of age. *Psychology Today, 21*:5, 46–47.

Wolff, P. (1965). The development of attention in young infants. *Annals of the New York Academy of Sciences, 118,* 815–830.

Zahn-Waxler, C., & Radke-Yarrow, M. (1982). The development of altruism: Alternative research strategies. In N. Eisenberg-Berg (Ed.), *The development of prosocial behavior.* New York: Academic Press.

Zahn-Waxler, C., & Radke-Yarrow, M. (1990). The origins of empathetic concern. *Motivation and Emotion, 14*:2, 107–130.

Zajonc, R. B. (1985). Emotional and facial efference: A theory reclaimed. *Science, 228,* 15–22.

Zelner, S. (1983). *The organization of vocalization and gaze in early mother-infant interactive regulation.* Unpublished doctoral dissertation, Yeshiva University, New York.

11

Affect and Defense

Michael Franz Basch

During the past 20 years, Dr. Basch has written a number of books and articles that have become essential reading for any student of our field. His work combines an extraordinary erudition in the history of psychoanalytic thought with a deep recognition of the importance of what goes on between the participants in any healing exchange. Although he is widely and correctly credited as the intellectual source of most of the concepts known now as self psychology, he has taken care to explain and validate those contributions of Sigmund Freud that remain valuable in this era of explosive interest in biological psychiatry.

In this brief and incisive chapter, Basch reaffirms Freud's primary interest in the nature of emotion, and demonstrates that all of what we call the mental mechanisms–every way we defend against some form of mental content–is actually a defense against affect. Reading this chapter, one becomes all the more interested in how the affective significance of a thought or action can be separated from our memory of the event itself. Much of uncovering therapy, he explains, may be seen as the effort to alter affect management scripts, so that memories and experiences that have been separated may be united in a way that permits reevaluation of experience by a stronger and more centered individual.

257

Many scholars have tried to explain the century of neglect that intervened between Darwin's recognition that our emotions were not frivolous actions of a mind gone bad and our own modern attention to his work. It was clear to Darwin that even the wildest and most irrational emotional outbursts were derivative of complex neuromuscular mechanisms that had conferred on the organism superior power in the process of natural selection. Yet his writing on emotion was marred by a Lamarckian concept of heredity and ignorance of the concept of child development to be introduced a generation or so later by Freud. These errors, based as they were on science accepted quite well in his era, ensured that the greater body of his work on emotion would be ignored until discovered anew by Tomkins and formulated in the language of information-processing.

It would be the shame of our era if Freud's contributions to the study of defense against emotion were to be ignored similarly by a generation of scholars quick and ready to pounce on those aspects of his work that cannot survive into this second century of psychoanalytic thinking. Error must be addressed, but what is true and important must be retained and celebrated. This chapter by Dr. Basch goes a long way toward impeding the tendency to scrap whatever has been shown to bear a flaw despite the validity of what remains. —DLN

IN SEVERAL PREVIOUS publications (Basch, 1983a, 1988, 1992a) I have traced the significance that recent studies pertaining to the development of reason and affect have for psychoanalytic theory and practice. Here I will try to correlate these findings in developmental psychology and neurobiology with the process of defense in psychoanalysis.

Freud's explanation for defense was based on his concept of the mental apparatus and its functioning. The mental apparatus was offered as a hypothetical model that Freud anticipated would someday have physical counterparts supplied by neurological discoveries. His speculations about how the mind/brain must work represent an amalgam of his knowledge of the biology and physics of his time and his investigation of language in neurological patients (Basch, 1975).

Freud (1895) hypothesized that the resting state was the optimal one for living organisms, and that their activity was in the interest of eliminating stimuli that interfered with that goal. At the same time, every organism is unavoidably put into disequilibrium by the demands of the self-preservative and the species-preserving instincts, and so is forced or driven into activity to satisfy these needs, thereby eliminating the unwanted stimulation. Although Freud thought of mental processes in terms of the flow of energy—a proposition now widely disputed—it is more important that he recognized that the basic function of the mental apparatus was the reception of signals and their transformation into dispositional messages, a concept still congenial today when the computer has replaced the steam engine as an analogue for mind.

As a matter of fact, the actual operation of the mental apparatus was not based on Freud's biological speculations, but on a hypothesis about the development of thought that he formulated when he studied the aphasias. These neurological deficits—the result of some insult to the brain—produce a separation between linguistic ability and sensory recognition. For example, a patient so affected may be able to indicate through proper usage that he correctly identified a piece of cutlery put in his hand, but then be unable to call it by name. Freud concluded that the separation of faculties reflected the manner in which the thought process originally developed, that is, in infancy and early childhood mental life consists of sensory images of objects which gradually become joined with their appropriate verbal designators. It is the joining of images and words that then makes possible the mental manipulation of experience that we call thought.

Though he never explicitly made the connection between his neurological theory of the development of thought and his psychological discoveries in the investigation of the neuroses, Freud always dealt with the neuroses as if they were functional aphasias. For example, a hysteric's symptoms reflected a failure to solve a conflict through thought, the explanation for that failure being that a forbidden wish had been separated from the words that could describe it in an effort to keep that wish from consciousness. The psychoanalytic cure consisted essentially of helping the patient to reunite, or connect for the first time, his forbidden wishes, experiences, and fantasies with appropriate words. Once talked about and thought about, the formerly unconscious wish no longer needed to be experienced symptomatically, but could be either dismissed or reasonably gratified in the manner of all conscious needs.

Freud gave the name "repression" to the process that kept word and image apart, repression being stimulated by the need to avoid the anxiety or unpleasure that forbidden wishes would have generated once they reached consciousness. As Freud said, " . . . to suppress the development of affect is the true aim of repression . . . " (1915a, p. 178). In those early days, Freud used "repression" as a synonym for defense (Freud, 1915b). Repression referred to the basic process that excluded forbidden ideas not just from consciousness but from thought (Freud, 1895). If it is successful, repression impoverishes mental life. If repression is in danger of failing, secondary mechanisms like isolation, projection, etc., are instituted to protect the psyche, and only then do neurotic symptoms appear.

This model of defense was satisfactory from the clinical point of view as long as the focus was on the psychoneuroses and the instinctual conflicts that precipitated them. However, Freud learned from the analyses of character and personality disorders that threats to the psyche came not only from within, in the form of instinctual overstimulation, but also from potentially traumatic perceptions. The psyche had to have some way of warding these off as well. Freud's clinical discovery of the defense of disavowal clarified this issue for him.

Disavowal, as Freud described it, is a process whereby the perceptual image is registered and acknowledged, while its affective meaning or significance for the individual is disregarded. So, to use an example from Freud's 1927 paper, a child who has lost a parent can be intellectually aware of the loss but remain unaware of the emotional impact that that loss might be expected to have, a situation clinically evidenced by the absence of mourning. It is important to notice that disavowal, like repression, depends for its efficacy on the separation of experience from affect, still bearing out Freud's (1915a) clinical insight that defense is always directed against affect.

Freud never dealt as systematically with disavowal as he did with repression—his references to this process are scattered throughout his writings, and there is a semantic and conceptual confusion between disavowal and denial in the literature. Elsewhere (Basch, 1981, 1983b, 1992b) I have dealt at length with these issues; here I will only summarize Freud's conclusions regarding disavowal. Freud described disavowal as a defense available when the need to preserve the reality-testing function comes into conflict with the perception of a significant environmental event that is potentially traumatic. The demands of reality-testing make it impossible simply to turn away from the offending perception, and a compromise is formed that attempts to serve both the pleasure and the reality principle. This is achieved by bringing about an ego split, one arm of which acknowledges the reality, while the other repudiates the meaning of the perception and substitutes a fantasy that protects the individual from the anxiety he would otherwise have to face.

Disavowal defends against anxiety-provoking external perceptions and is the counterpart of repression, the latter being directed toward similar demands from the inner world of the instincts. Disavowal is a ubiquitous process, whose presence is not in itself indicative of pathology, general or specific. With this discovery the concept of defense was expanded beyond the original concept of defense against instinct.

Freud did not try to deal with disavowal on the metapsychological level, contenting himself with its clinical explication. When we try to do so, we find that it cannot be done within the framework of the mental apparatus and its later variations described by Freud, a model whose structure and mode of functioning have also been called into question by analysts who see a contradiction between the brain/mind as an energy-processing apparatus and the more recent findings in biology, physics, and ethology that make that model obsolete. However, it is only now that developmental psychology and neurobiology have caught up, so to speak, with the clinical insights made possible by the psychoanalytic method, that we are able to account more adequately for both repression and disavowal.

The brain, we now know, is not an energy-processing but a signal-processing organ. What we call mind is the ordering function of the brain that selectively translates the welter of impulses that impinge on it through the sense organs and receptors into informative messages (Basch, 1976a). Human beings are not born with the totality of their message-processing capacity already in place. The manner in which messages can be organized goes through various stages as the organism matures; this is what we mean by cognitive development. Freud, like most psychologists then and now, equated cognition with reason, and cognitive development with the increasingly sophisticated use of language in describing our experience of ourselves and the world around us. He thought of affect as the conscious experience of drive tension and, in keeping with philosophical tradition since the time of Aristotle, as the antonym of cognition. However, the time-honored division between affect and cognition has been shown to be false and misleading. Affect, like reason, plays an important part in cognition, i.e., coming to know.

The more complex the animal, the more complicated is the decision-making process that guides behavior. Tropisms and reflexes orient and adapt the organisms lower on the evolutionary scale, choice of behavior is limited, and response follows a fixed pattern. In addition to inherited stimulus-response mechanisms common in lower animals, mammals also possess a more flexible way of adapting. The interposition of affective reactions between signal and response enables mammals to gauge their behavioral response, to learn from experience, and also to communicate what they have learned to others of their species. The variety and intensity of affect provide a way of categorizing experience and determining the response appropriate to it in a given instance. The degree of pleasure or unpleasure that attaches to a particular experience influences the meaning of an experience as well as the quality of the behavioral response it elicits. It also determines in part how similar or associated experiences will be interpreted and dealt with in the future. The pleasure-unpleasure principle familiar to us from Freud's writings also holds true for all animals that respond with affect to stimulation (Basch, 1976b).

The cognitive function of affect is twofold. That an observer comes to know the state of mind of another through affective signals is a matter of everyday experience. What is not so obvious is that affect can determine the state of mind, for affect may precede and determine how an event is judged rather than eventuating from that judgment. As a matter of fact, this holds true in the first case also. We often, perhaps usually, come to know the affective state of another person directly, basing our judgment of what he/she is feeling on the affective resonance set off within us by him or her. Probably the dichotomy between cognition and affect came into being because affect is experienced seemingly immediately and quite differently from the discursive process we call reasoning. The dependence on affect for determining behavior is more apparent in animals other than humans. We are no less dependent on affect; however, that fact has been overshadowed by the importance we give to language and the reasoning process made possible by it.

Darwin (1872) noted that the facial expression of emotion is similar in adult man, human infants, and animals, especially other primates. Furthermore, it is the same in all cultures, i.e., the picture of an angry caucasian baby is identified as being that by people of other cultures. Darwin suggested that these facial configurations were originally components of larger behavior patterns essential for survival that gradually came to have a reciprocal communicative function. They signal attitudes and test the reaction forthcoming from those exposed to the display before committing the animal to action, thereby making a truly adaptive response possible in most instances.

The idea that affective expressions were inborn, stereotyped, and universal was supported by the experiments of Darwin's contemporary, Duchenne, who, using electric stimulation, showed that triggering specific facial muscles automatically created emotional expressions independent of the subject's feeling state at the time. This is corroborated by neurological evidence now available indicating that affective expressions are under subcortical control. Psychologists did not do much with this work or its implications until Silvan Tomkins (1962, 1963) and his co-workers recognized its significance and carried it further. Tomkins suggests that initially the various affective responses are related to stimulus intensity and to intensity gradients and are probably transmitted by the autonomic nervous system. In other words, affective behavior patterns are, like the infant's perceptual capacity, inherited programs with which the infant meets the world. Each affect pattern has its mild and its extreme form and a range between the two, reflecting the subcortical brain's response to stimuli from within the body and from the sense organs in touch with the environment.

Although the affective response, being mediated by the autonomic nervous system, is a total bodily response involving body temperature, the skin, hair, glands, muscles, and viscera, in humans it is the face that has become the prime communicator of affective states. Let me just briefly list the main recordable and reproducible signs used by researchers (and by parents) to identify the nine ranges of affective responses in infants that form the basis for our emotional life. There is a continuum from surprise to startle, depending on the suddenness and intensity of stimulus onset, in which we see the infant's eyebrows go up and the eyes blink. The range from interest through excitement is shown on the face when the eyebrows go down, the eyes track the stimulus, and there is an attitude of looking and listening. The scale of mild enjoyment to joy is signaled by a smile, the lips widened and out, and slow deep breathing. On the negative side, there is the range from distress to anguish as indicated by crying, arched eyebrows, corners of the mouth turned down, tears, and rhythmic sobbing. Even more dramatic is the behavioral series beginning with anger and culminating in rage. Here the face is in a frown, the jaws are clenched, and the face is red. Disgust is shown by protruding the lower lip while angling the head forward, while dissmell is evidenced by raising the upper lip and pulling the head back. The range from fear through terror is manifested by a cold, sweaty face, with eyes frozen open, facial trembling, and hair erect. And shame through humiliation is demonstrated when both the head and eyes are cast down (Tomkins, 1962, p. 337; Nathanson, 1992).

Unpleasure and pleasure are not themselves affects, but the outcome of affective experience, and it is possible to establish what affect or combination of affects is responsible for the final result. What still needs to be explained is the affective experience itself. How is it generated and how is it communicated? If the postulation of a psychic energy is no longer a satisfactory explanation, how is the intensity as well as the quantity of affects that go into the experience of pleasure and unpleasure determined? How is it that the affective spectrum is essentially in place and operating effectively in human infants who cannot reason logically or reflect on their experience and evaluate it for its qualitative import?

Basically, affect responses are related only to stimulus density (the number and intensity of nerve impulses transmitted per unit time) and to the gradient of that stimulation (Tomkins, 1981). Surprise, interest, and fear, and their extensions are all the result of a continuous rise in stimulus intensity above a particular infant's nonreactive, resting level; which of these three reactions—surprise, interest, or fear—will be elicited is determined by the rate, height, and duration of the stimulus vector. Distress or anger reactions are manifested when stimulus intensity is maintained steadily at a higher than optimal level for a length of time. Joy and its variants result whenever there is a drop in the stimulus pattern, no matter what the nature of that stimulus may be; the degree of pleasure will be directly proportional to the rapidity with which the stimulus decreases. Shame is the result of an inadequate stimulus reduction. It occurs when the resolution of a stimulus gradient has begun but is not carried through to completion. The only exception to the quantitative determination of affect is the qualitatively triggered, protective withdrawal reaction of dissmell or disgust, two primary affects based on inherited avoidance responses triggered chemically by odors or tastes that register as noxious.

In the study of affect we find the biological foundation that explains the intensity of ideas without having to postulate a psychic energy. How body becomes mind, how tension becomes recognized as need, the "mysterious leap," as Freud termed it—all appear to be much less puzzling given the transformation of quantitative stimulus gradients into the experience that we associate with our affective/emotional life. It seems to involve the same sort of transformation that our brains are able to carry out when they take the purely quantitative stimulation of electrons in varying wavelengths that impinge on our sense organs and transform them into the imagery of sight, hearing, and so on.

We can now consider the question of what it is infants experience when they signal their affective state. Certainly no reflection is involved. It is the babies' way of adapting to stimuli in the only way they can, given their inability to move closer to what attracts them or to escape what hurts or frightens them. They can only engage the caretaker and induce her to do what babies cannot do for themselves. The highly developed facial musculature of the infant and the automatism of the affective reaction are ideally suited to setting up an error-correcting feedback system in the mother-child unit, in which the child provides the indicator by which the mother can judge whether her efforts on the child's behalf have been successful (Basch, 1982).

Here it should be noted that the adult has two ways of receiving and responding to affective transmission—cortical and subcortical. Obviously, the mother can make a judgment about the infant's appearance and then come to a conclusion regarding what the need is that her infant is signaling. But there is a more direct communication generated within the mother by her baby's sounds and/or appearance. Each mammalian species responds on the subcortical/autonomic level to the affective expression of its members, who, as one investigator said, "infect" each other with affect.* The infant's smile calls forth the smiling response in the mother due to an involuntary, subcortical response, and it is her own affective response that lets the mother interpret what her infant is experiencing. This three-step process—reception of affective transmission, involuntary subcortical response, and cortically mediated interpretation of one's own response—is the essence of what we call "empathy" (Basch, 1983c).

As the mere 26 letters in our alphabet can be combined to generate the wealth and nuance of our verbal language, so the even richer variations to be found in the respective ranges of each of the nine basic affects will, in time, blend and mix, using not only face and body but also the variations of the voice to communicate our feelings at any given time. Affect is a nonverbal language, sometimes complementing the spoken word, yet often, as Freud taught us, a counterpoint that (for those alert to it) reveals the consciously or unconsciously concealed truth behind the spoken words. Affect is the language of motivation and this is the reason that, as Freud noted, defense is always directed against affect.

Far from being opposed to or separated from cognition, affective response and affective communication are the basis for cognition and remain so throughout life. Even more important, affect is the gateway to behavior. Whether we react with attraction or avoidance, the intensity and persistence of our effort depend on the kind and degree of affect a particular idea can recruit or a particular experience can evoke. Although in adult life it is the combination and permutation of reason that attracts our attention, from the larger, developmental perspective reason is in the service of the affective system; it is an evolutionary and developmentally late refinement of the basic affective process. More primitive mammals, like infants, respond more or less stereotypically and in all-or-none fashion once affect has been mobilized. As human beings mature cortically, the possibility of organizing experience in increasingly refined fashion, the ability to anticipate, alter, and even generate experience through fantasy, and the capacity for reflection all influence the generation and mobilization of the affective response.

Reason not only permits human beings to refine and modulate the generation of affect, but it enhances both the range and the level of sophistication of human adaptation beyond that of any other animal. It is cortical activity itself, therefore, that is the protective barrier, the

---

*Since each of the nine innate affects is itself both a reaction to and an analogue of the gradient or density of stimulation that triggered it, each one of the infant's affects is a compact display of whatever triggered it. The displayed affect of one person can then act as the trigger for the affect of another.

Reizschutz (postulated by Freud, 1920) that modulates and modifies affective response so that we do not so easily become the victims of overreaction to the affective messages set off by external or internal stimuli. For example, we may hear a loud bang outside our window, but we do not startle and flee like an animal in the forest. Instead, we startle but then the voice of reason tells us that the noise may have been only a car backfiring and that we are in no immediate danger. If reason fails, of course, then the unmodified affect signal triggers commensurate behavior and we are, as the saying goes, carried away by the emotion of the moment.

It is now possible to supply the theoretical explanation for Freud's statements that repression (defense) is always directed against affect. Affect is the trigger for behavior. As long as forbidden wishes can be prevented from engaging affect, they will not be carried into action. Freud also suggests how the protective system operates, and here, too, recent work in developmental psychology and neurophysiology has given us further insight that corroborates Freud's ideas.

As was mentioned previously, practically speaking mind may be equated with the function of the brain, that is, the organization of stimuli into meaningful messages that lead to appropriate adaptation. Freud already wrote, in *Inhibitions, Symptoms and Anxiety* (1926), that anxiety signals that there is a threat to the integrity of the organism that must be dealt with. Modern affect theory refines this concept. Anxiety indicates that there is a nonoptimal gradient of stimulus acquisition that the cortical organizing function cannot arrange effectively. If neither escape from nor solution for the source of the disturbance is forthcoming, distortion of perceptions or of thought is instituted through defense mechanisms to make affect management and reintegration possible by at least eliminating the problem from active consideration.

The manipulations of perception and thought that we call defense mechanisms are nothing more than the usual cognitive mechanisms used in a pathological manner (R. Loewenstein, in Fine, Joseph, & Waldhorn 1969, p. 37). Under normal circumstances, the myriad signals that impinge on the brain must be sorted and classified according to their importance for the organism,* since one cannot pay attention to and effectively engage all of the millions of messages being generated at any given moment by the billions of cells in the nervous system. Only what is important at that particular time can be fully dealt with at all levels of mental organization. When this process is used in the interest of repres-

---

*That is, by the salience assigned to the signal by the nine patterns of stimulus contour.

sion or disavowal—i.e., used to conceal rather than reveal, hide rather than clarify—we call it defensive.

It is important to differentiate between defensive process and defensive mechanisms, the latter more properly called secondary defenses or secondary defense mechanisms. Primary repression, secondary repression, and disavowal are the first lines of defense. Mechanisms like displacement, isolation, denial, etc., are activated if the primary form of defense fails to hold. Defense mechanisms are a function of, and are made possible by, the fact that humans are not born with their behavior patterns in place; rather, they undergo a lengthy cognitive development. Defenses, by reversing or arresting that cognitive development, can selectively interfere with the synthesis of knowledge.

The work of Piaget (Piaget & Inhelder, 1969) is important here. Piaget's studies have shown that the development of reason proceeds in stepwise fashion. In infancy, problem-solving progresses in terms of sensorimotor activity without the benefit of evocative reasoning. Between the age of approximately 18 and 24 months, during what Piaget calls the preoperative period, the capacity for imaginative representation and evocative recall—i.e., recall independent of sensory stimulation— makes its appearance. A memory of past experience can now be generated and contemplated. Such a memory stands for or symbolizes what is no longer immediately present to the senses.

What Piaget did not deal with systematically was the affective component of infantile life. Given the work of Tomkins outlined previously, we may postulate that every sensorimotor experience is accompanied by affect and that the engram or memory of that experience records not only what affect is triggered, but also where it stands on the scale of pleasure/unpleasure. When evocative memory becomes a possibility, those experiences associated with significant distress or pain—the recall of which would mobilize dysphoria—will probably not undergo cognitive transformation but will continue to exist in their more primitive form. This defensive block to cognitive transformation in the interest of avoiding negative affect, along with the anxiety that would precipitate, corresponds to what Freud called primary repression—events that are blocked from conscious thought or reflection because they were never permitted to become preconscious, that is, never attained symbolic representation of the sort that words, for example, provide (Basch, 1977).

The act of imagination itself becomes the basis for the concept of self, the symbolic representation of the symbolizer's symbolic activity (Basch, 1979, 1988). The concept of self plays a major role in the third stage of the development of thought—the concrete operational phase of Piaget—beginning about the age of six or seven years. Only now do the constraints of logic come to govern preconscious and conscious thought. Prior to this development, contradictions could coexist between wish and the demands of environment, between impulse and adaptation. Now the demand for logical consistency as central for the ordering process of the brain creates a new potential for anxiety that must be dealt with (Basch, 1974, 1975, 1981). It is now that the reversal of affect, which Freud postulated as initiating secondary repression, is very much in evidence. What was once pleasurable is no longer so and what Freud called secondary repression is instituted. Infantile wishes (that is, dispositions toward behavior) that had attained imaginative representations are blocked from advancing to the level of concrete operations by being excluded from verbal manipulation. As Freud put it in the *Project* (1895), repression is not simply repression from consciousness but repression from thought. What cannot be talked about, to oneself or to others, is excluded from maturation and sublimation. This, as we know, is the fate of incestuous infantile wishes, and this secondary repression lays the groundwork for possible psychoneurotic and character neurotic pathology in later life (Basch, 1975, 1977, 1979).

But not only infantile instinctual wishes must be dealt with defensively—so must anxiety-provoking perceptions from the environment. Prior to the concrete operational period, anxiety-provoking perceptions could be dealt with through various forms of perceptual distortion (Basch, 1974). This becomes less acceptable once concrete operations and the need for logical synthesis dominate mental life. It is now that the defense Freud termed disavowal comes into prominence. The concept of self is a further refinement of the process that apportions affective investment and protects the organism from overreaction to stimulation. Here, two forms of memory identified by Tulving (1972)—semantic and episodic—are of significance. Episodic memories are those seen as relevant for the self-concept. Semantic memories are those that record general knowledge not germane for the self, at least not for the moment. Memories important for the self, one would expect, are much more likely to produce significant stimulation of affect. Perhaps more accurately, memories endowed with greater increments of affect become important for the self system (Basch, 1988).

Ordinarily, episodic and semantic memories are freely interchangeable. If, however, a particular perception or its memory is potentially disorganizing (that is, anxiety-provoking), interference with the transformation of information from the semantic to the episodic would accomplish the purpose of defending against affective stimulation without distorting perception and reality-testing as such. This is how the disavowal of memory is accomplished (Basch, 1983b, 1992b). The psychoanalytic interpretation, along with the working-through of such interpretations, promotes the cognitive transformation that once again unites affect with memory and experience (Basch, 1981). This is the essence of what is curative in Freud's technique.

REFERENCES

Basch, M. F. (1974). Interference with perceptual transformation in the service of defense. *The Annual of Psychoanalysis, 2*, 87–97. New York: International Universities Press.

Basch, M. F. (1975). Toward a theory that encompasses depression: A revision of existing causal hypotheses in psychoanalysis. In E. J. Anthony & T. Benedek (Eds.), *Depression and Human Existence.* Boston: Little, Brown.

Basch, M. F. (1976a). Psychoanalysis and communication science. *The Annual of Psychoanalysis, 4*, 385–421. New York: International Universities Press.

Basch, M. F. (1976b). The concept of affect: A re-examination. *Journal of the American Psychoanalytic Association, 24*, 759–777.

Basch, M. F. (1977). Developmental psychology and explanatory theory in psychoanalysis. *The Annual of Psychoanalysis, 5*, 229–263. New York: International Universities Press.

Basch, M. F. (1979). Mind, self, and dreamer. In R. J. Stoller (Ed.), *Sexual Excitement: Dynamics of Erotic Life*, Appendix A (pp. 224–231). New York: Pantheon Books.

Basch, M. F. (1981). Psychoanalytic interpretation and cognitive transformation. *International Journal of Psychoanalysis, 62*, 151–175.

Basch, M. F. (1982). The concept of "self": An operational definition. In B. Lee (Ed.), *Psychosocial theories of the self.* New York: Plenum Press.

Basch, M. F. (1983a). Affect and the analyst. *Psychoanalytic Inquiry, 3*, 691–703.

Basch, M. F. (1983b). The perception of reality and the disavowal of meaning. *The Annual of Psychoanalysis, 11*, 125–154. New York: International Universities Press.

Basch, M. F. (1983c). Empathic understanding: A review of the concept and some theoretical considerations. *Journal of the American Psychoanalytic Association, 31*, 101–126.

Basch, M. F. (1988). *Understanding psychotherapy: The science behind the art.* New York: Basic Books.

Basch, M. F. (1992a). The significance of a theory of affect for psychoanalytic technique. *Journal of the American Psychoanalytic Association, 39* (suppl.), 291–304.

Basch, M. F. (1992b). Repression and disavowal: A reappraisal. *Forum der Psychoanalyse, 8*, 173–186.

Darwin, C. (1872). *The expression of the emotions in man and animals.* Chicago: University of Chicago Press, 1965.

Fine, B. D., Joseph, E. D., & Waldhorn, H. F. (Eds.) (1969). *The mechanism of denial.* Monograph III, Kris Study Group of the New York Psychoanalytic Institute, pp. 3–57.

Freud, S. (1895). Project for a scientific psychology. In J. Strachey (Ed. & Trans.), *The standard edition of the complete psychological works of Sigmund Freud* (hereafter *SE*), Vol. 1. New York: Norton.

Freud, S. (1915a). The unconscious. *SE*, Vol. 14.

Freud, S. (1915b). Repression. *SE*, Vol. 14.

Freud, S. (1920). Beyond the pleasure principle. *SE*, Vol. 18.

Freud, S. (1926). Inhibitions, symptoms and anxiety. *SE*, Vol. 20.

Freud, S. (1927). Fetishism. *SE*, Vol. 21.

Nathanson, D. L. (1992). *Shame and pride: affect, sex, and the birth of the self.* New York: Norton.

Piaget, J., & Inhelder, B. (1969). *The psychology of the child.* New York: Basic Books.

Tomkins, S. S. (1962). *Affect, imagery, consciousness, Vol. I: The positive affects*. New York: Springer.

Tomkins, S. S. (1963). *Affect, imagery, consciousness, Vol. II: The negative affects*. New York: Springer.

Tomkins, S. S. (1981). The quest for primary motives: Biography and autobiography of an idea. *Journal Personality & Social Psychology, 41*, 306–329.

Tulving, E. (1972). Episodic and semantic memory. In E. Tulving & W. Donaldson (Eds.), *Organization of Memory* (pp. 378–403). New York: Academic Press.

12

The Archetypal Affects

Louis H. Stewart

A few years ago, a colleague asked, "Who would you prefer to operate on your acutely inflamed gall bladder: Ambroise Paré, Joseph Lister, or a third-year resident in surgery at any major teaching hospital?" Notwithstanding my awe for the contributions of the great 16th-century French battlefield surgeon responsible for our concept of emergency care and the 19th-century Scot who showed for the first time why operating rooms and delivery rooms had to be sterile, I would be far more comfortable with the young physician who knew so much more about the science of modern medicine. My friend continued, "And should you be troubled with some emotional difficulty, would you choose Freud, Jung, or a third-year resident at any major teaching hospital?" Perhaps my young colleague might know some aspect of modern neurobiology, or possess some expertise in a specific technique, but I really do appreciate the remark of an early supervisor that psychotherapy is "an old guy's game," an art rather than a science. Despite the many areas of disagreement we might have with either of those founders of our field, if our choices were limited as phrased, I think we'd do better with the old masters than with the talented beginner. Learning psychotherapy is more a matter of self development than learning surgery.

Long distinguished for his work as a Jungian analyst, Louis Stewart stands in the forefront of those who appreciate both the miracles of neurobiology and the accumulated wisdom and richness of human culture. Jung offered a poetic view of human development that encompassed myth and the history of whole peoples, as well as what happened between one specific infant and one set of parents. His psychology has become increasingly popular among those who seek more connection between religion and psychotherapy, also those who seek a cross-cultural appreciation of the personality.

It is the relation between affect and the soul that most occupies Stewart in this chapter. That he begins his offering with an epigrammatic quotation from Jung that might have been written by Tomkins is only the first surprise. Offhandedly, each of us tends to describe our friends in terms of the way they handle their emotions–some are angry, some shy, some (like the proverbial "type A personality") energetically avoidant of shame. Tomkins often said that personality involved the differential magnification of innate affect–from temperament, socialization by parents, other qualities of our milieu, and the specific experiences I have characterized as the software of life, each of us has learned to react to stimuli with a slightly different intensity of each of the nine affects. These highly idiosyncratic systems of affect management fall naturally into patterns. Stewart points out that each of the personality types described by Jung may be understood as a specific pattern of affect modulation. Throughout this contribution, Stewart shifts back and forth between the language of affect theory and the language of Jung, until by the end he has developed a highly personal way of understanding and expressing both.

Stewart and Tomkins corresponded about the material included in this chapter, the latter expressing his pleasure that Jungian psychology could be reformulated in terms of the innate affects. You may notice that some of Dr. Stewart's explanations differ significantly from those in the remainder of this book; his understanding of affect theory is based on the work published by Tomkins in the first two volumes of *Affect, Imagery, Consciousness,* and includes none of the changes in theory offered 30 years later when the final volumes were published. Despite the lack of congruence between this current chapter and the remainder of the book, I know of no better link between these two powerful ways of viewing the human condition than that offered here by Dr. Stewart.   –DLN

On the one hand, emotion is the alchemical fire whose warmth brings everything into existence and whose heat burns all superfluities to ashes. . . . But on the other hand, emotion is the moment when steel meets flint and a spark is struck forth, for emotion is the chief source of consciousness. There is no change from darkness to light or from inertia to movement without emotion.

—C. G. Jung, 1938, p. 96

THE AFFECTS ARE the life blood of the psyche. Without their ubiquitous presence in the psyche, life would be pale and drab, without value—in short, the underworld of death. But life is problematical, as the affects are quick to remind us. The heart-rending pangs of loss reduce us to lamentation and weeping; the icy grip of terror chills our blood as we quiver and quake. Yet the heart also leaps with joy and pounds with excitement. The emotions, in all their numinous power, plumb the heights and depths of the soul. Over the ages, philosophers have sought to reconcile the tranquil goals of reason with these titanic forces.

In analysis the affects can never be ignored. They are always present, whether openly expressed or felt beneath the surface; if seemingly absent, then they are much in the consciousness of the analyst. In Jung's theory of analytical psychology they are given appropriate attention as energy, value, source of imagery and new consciousness, and, of course, as troublesome, unruly, and capable of overwhelming consciousness. Perhaps most significant, the affects are the bridge between body and psyche, instinct and spirit. They reach back into the physiology of the body, to the chemical processes of the hormones, and neurologically to the areas of the "mammalian" brain. Phenomenologically they are a pervasive presence in the psyche, which fluctuates around a steady stream of subliminal awareness of mood, punctuated by intrusions of varying degrees of intensity of the more specific emotions. Developmentally, they appear in infancy as eruptions of primal energy of high intensity, normally of short duration, that interrupt a steady state of pleasurable interest and somnolent reverie. By adulthood they have been modulated in the crucible of family relationships and transformed into a complex and sensitive matrix of feelings and emotionally toned complexes. Yet the innate affects never lose their primal autonomy and original mode of expression, which can appear at any time under the proper circumstances. These primal affects, with their universal patterns of bodily innervation and expressive action, can be recognized in infancy and throughout life in humans everywhere. (See Table 12.1 for an over-view of the archetypal affects.)

THE NATURE OF EMOTION

The hypothesis I am presenting here as to the nature of the emotions has deep roots in my lifelong interest in the creative imagination, first in art, then in the archetypal development of the imagination itself and the transformative function of active imagination in analysis. Its more im-mediate origins lie in my analytic work with sandplay and other forms of active imagination. During recent years, while I was writing papers on sandplay and active imagination, I found my interest gravitating toward the affects. When I finally succumbed to this pull and looked carefully at the affects and their relation to play and the imagination, I found that they are intertwined in at least four significant areas: motivation, transformation, potentiation of imagination, and the forms of social games.*

The four ways in which the affects are enmeshed with play and the imagination exemplify two fundamental and reciprocal aspects of the psyche, namely *energy* and *transformation*. Children are motivated to play just for the "fun" of it; one might say that play is energized by the affect of joy. But play is "about" emotion in another way; children play out little dramas involving affects of a distinctly different flavor, such as distress, fear, anger, and shame. Careful observation of the day-to-day experiences of children reveals that they are forever playing out whatever it is in their life that arouses emotion. But in their play the effects of these emotions are transmuted through compensatory fantasies, liquidat-ing or cathartic experiences, and the like. Thus, one must conclude that during childhood, play and fantasy serve a transformative function in the equilibration of the personality. Later, in psychoanalysis, active imagination serves an identical transformative function in the "re-creation" of the wholeness of personality.

Imagination has a twin that finds its expression in the affect of interest and the dynamism of "curiosity." Play/imagination and curiosity/explo-

*I should like to acknowledge that during the early years of my interest in these subjects I was fortunate to have as collaborator my brother, Charles T. Stewart, pediatrician and child psychiatrist. It is now sometimes difficult to sort out his contributions from my own, but I take full responsibility for the form in which the ideas are presented here. (Stewart, C. T., 1981; Stewart, C. T. & Stewart, L. H., 1981; Stewart, L. H. & Stewart, C. T., 1981).

TABLE 12.1
The Archetypal Affects
From the Source (Primordial Self) toward the Goal (Realized Self)

THE REALIZED SELF

HIGHEST VALUES	THE SACRED	THE BEAUTIFUL	THE TRUE	THE GOOD	WHOLE-NESS	EROS	LOGOS
EVOLVED IMAGES	HOLY MOUNTAIN	ABUNDANCE AND BEAUTY OF NATURE	ORDERED COSMOS	UTOPIAN COMMUNITY	MANDALA	LUNA	SOL
EGO FUNCTIONS	INTUITION	SENSATION	THINKING	FEELING	EGO CONSCIOUS-NESS	FANTASY	EXPLORATION
APPERCEP-TION	Intangible	Tangible	Quantitative order	Qualitative order	Orientation	Being	Becoming
THE COMPLEX FAMILY EMOTIONS	The complex family emotions (Stewart, 1992) are mixtures, modulations, and transmutations of the innate affects. They develop in the family. The innate affects have clear, prototypical expressive patterns. By contrast, the expressive behavior of a complex emotion tends to be subtle, indistinct, idiosyncratic. The complex family emotions include jealousy, envy, greed, revenge, hatred, suspicion, deceit, slyness, guilt, and of course, love, affection, tenderness, devotion, deference, consideration, generosity, satisfaction, awe, trust, admiration, respect, reverence, compassion, mercy, and many others.						
SYMBOLIC CULTURAL ATTITUDES	RELIGIOUS	AESTHETIC	PHILOSOPHIC	SOCIAL	SELF-REFLECTIVE CONSCIOUS-NESS	IMAGINA-TION	MEMORY
EXPRESSIVE DYNAMISM	RITUAL	RHYTHM	REASON	RELATION-SHIP	REFLEC-TION	PLAY	CURIOSITY
RANGE OF INTENSITY FROM MILD TO EXTREME	Apprehension, anxiety, fear, terror, panic	Distress, sadness, grief, anguish	Irritation, annoyance, frustration, anger, rage	Disdain, dislike, contempt, disgust. (rejection toward other). **** Shyness, embarrassment, shame, humiliation. (rejection toward self).	Surprise, astonishment, startle	Enjoyment, joy, ecstasy	Interest, excitement
THE INNATE AFFECTS:	FEAR	DISTRESS	ANGER	CONTEMPT and SHAME develop out of the primal affective reflex DISGUST	STARTLE	JOY	INTEREST
EXISTEN-TIAL LIFE SITUATION	THE UNKNOWN	LOSS	RESTRIC-TION OF AUTONOMY	REJECTION	THE UNEX-PECTED	THE FAMILIAR	THE NOVEL
PRIMAL INNATE IMAGES OR IMPRINTS	THE ABYSS	THE VOID	CHAOS	ALIENATION	DARKNESS	DIFFUSE ILLUMINA-TION	FOCUSED ILLUMINATION

THE PRIMORDIAL SELF

ration are inseparably entwined in a dialectical process in which each potentiates the other. From this perspective, the affects joy and interest, with their parallel dynamisms of play and curiosity, appear as the proto-typical energic and dynamic expressions of the libido as what are known in Jungian psychology as lunar (eros/mythical) consciousness, and solar (logos/linguistic) consciousness.

My interest led me to two questions: Are other functions of the psyche similarly "energized" by specific affects? And what is the relation of the affects to Jung's concept of the *self*, the principle and archetype of orientation and meaning? This inquiry was spurred by recent studies of the emotions, which have demonstrated their universal modes of expression in all cultures. This idea was originally taken up by Darwin (1872) and has been supported by other studies of the evolution of the affects (Ekman, 1972, 1984; Izard, 1977; Nathanson, 1987). The subject was most thoroughly evaluated by Silvan Tomkins in the first two volumes of *Affect, Imagery, Consciousness.* Further support came from anthropological studies of play and games (Roberts & Sutton-Smith, 1970), which consistently demonstrate a fourfold categorization—games of *chance*, games of *physical skill*, games of *strategy*, and games around a *central person* (i.e., social games)—and from the field of literary criticism, in which the imagination is expressed in a tetravalent structure, as, for example, in Gaston Bachelard's (1938) four elements and their mythological personifications—the sylph, the gnome, the salamander and the ondine (Stewart, 1978). Everything seemed to suggest, then, that the structure of the primordial self could be represented in a fourfold affective system structured around a central affect.

Tomkins's studies pointed both to a twofold structure of affects that fit the analysis above of the libido and also to a specified number of "crisis" affects that seemed referable to the primordial self. Briefly stated, Tomkins identified a basic system of innate affects, which in his view have evolved in the mammalian species as a twofold structure of "positive" affects of life enhancement, namely joy and interest, and a structure of what he termed "negative" affects, namely distress, fear, anger, disgust, and shame, which have evolved as responses to the major existential crises of life. In addition, he identified startle as an affect of orientation, the "re-setting" affect. In his later years, Tomkins added a newly named affect, dismell, and he came to view contempt as a fusion of dissmell and anger, one that develops its own path through life.

An evaluation of Tomkins's work led to the following slight modifications of his views and a change in terminology. First, as I have said above, the affects of joy and interest can be understood as the archetypal affects of the libido. Second, in accord with Helen Lynd (1958), I understand contempt and shame as the two faces of a bipolar emotion. The stimulus to both contempt and shame is rejection. Whether one experiences contempt or shame is determined by the direction of rejection, i.e., whether it is turned toward the other or toward oneself. Consequently, I speak of the existential emotion contempt/shame. Finally, startle is the affect of orientation and the centering of consciousness. Thus, we arrive at a system of seven innate affects: the two life enhancing affects of the libido, joy and interest, and the four crisis affects of the primordial self, sadness, fear, anger, and contempt/shame, structured around the "resetting" affect of centering and orientation, startle.

Unfortunately, space limitations do not allow for a discussion of the mixtures and modulations of the seven innate affects described above. They are transformed in the family crucible; that is, they come into being simply and solely because there is a family (Stewart, 1992).

Thus, we may now say that:

1. The archetypal affective system is an inherited regulatory system of the psyche that functions as an unconscious energic, orienting, and apprehension-response system. It evolved to replace an earlier system of programmed instinct.

2. It consists of a dynamic system of seven archetypal affects, of which two, the affects of joy and interest, function as twin dynamisms of the life instinct (libido), making it certain that newborn mammals, and particularly humans, will enter the world with joie de vivre and divine curiosity. This assures an active engagement with the world through which the fundamentals for survival are acquired. In addition, there are four existential affects oriented to the basic crises of life in the world as it is. These are distress, fear, anger, and disgust. Disgust differentiates into in the bipolar emotion of contempt/shame. Each of these primal affects has evolved in relation to a specific domain of the world. Certain life experiences are the inherent stimuli around which the primal emotions constellate, namely *loss* (sadness), *the unknown* (fear), *restriction of freedom* (anger), and *rejection* (contempt/shame). The fifth existential emotion, startle, which has evolved in relation to the crisis of disorientation, has as its inherent stimulus *the unexpected*.

3. This archetypal affective system functions in roughly the following fashion. As I have said, each of the existential emotions is constellated by a particular life experience, the stimulus, which is a function of the characteristics of the world into which we are born. Thus the four crisis emotions, sadness, fear, anger and disgust (contempt/shame), comprise four basic modes of apprehension of the world and the self. In the

psychological functioning of the ego, these categories are experienced as Jung's (1921) ego functions of sensation, intuition, thinking, and feeling. The fifth existential emotion of the self, startle, appears as a category of orientation and as the function of ego-consciousness.

With what aspects of the world do joy and interest, the two archetypal affects of the libido, the instinct of life, correlate? Let us reflect on the two primary ways of experiencing life as expressed in the philosophical principles of being and becoming. Many efforts have been made to characterize these fundamental modes of life experience, for example, the *Tao* as the interplay of Yin and Yang, the alchemical images Luna and Sol, or the cosmogonic principles of antiquity, Eros and Logos. All of these concepts and images seek to represent the alternation of life experience between two modes which nevertheless seem to be united within a whole. Insofar as the archetypal affects of joy and interest may be considered prototypical forms of the expression of these life principles, they have presumably evolved in relation to these two modes of experiencing life. The inherent stimuli of these affects appear to be, respectively, *familiarity* and *novelty*. Play and curiosity are the prototypical, dynamic forms of expression of these affects in the psyche.

As we know, however, there is another realm in reference to which this system of archetypal affects has evolved, namely the subjective realm of the self. With respect to the self, then, these existential affects evoke the age-old categories of the beautiful, the holy, the true, and the good, Kant's ideas of reason. As psychological structures these categories are represented in Joseph Henderson's cultural attitudes: the aesthetic, the religious, the philosophic, and the social (1962, 1984).

4. It is not immediately evident just how the ego functions and the cultural attitudes have developed from the primal affective system of apprehension and response. While our knowledge of the evolutionary process is very limited, I suggest that the distinction between ego functions and cultural attitudes is related to two basic aspects of the archetypal experience, namely, the *impressive* and the *expressive*. It would appear that the ego functions have evolved from the impressive (apperceptive) aspect and the cultural attitudes from the expressive.

5. This brings us to the realization that there must be both a "stimulus," i.e., a life experience, and an unconscious "image/imprint," or the potential for such an "image/imprint," with which the stimulus connects; like a key in a lock, or better yet, as the half of a broken coin, which reconstitutes a totality, a symbol (Hillman, 1960, p. 286). Some ethologists, such as Niko Tinbergen (1951), speak of the "innate releasing mechanism"; others describe the "key tumbler" structures that release

patterns of instinctive behavior in animals and humans (Stevens, 1983, pp. 56–58). What might these unconscious "image/imprints" be? Inasmuch as they represent fundamental domains of life, they must be innate, primal, universal images. These are found in the universal images of pre-creation, the "void," the "abyss," "chaos," "alienation," and "darkness" (Campbell, 1959; Eliade, 1967; Schaya, 1971). Thus, in human experience the existential emotion of sadness is constellated by confrontation with "loss," of which the *void* is the primal innate image/imprint; fear is constellated by "the unknown," of which the primal innate image/imprint is the *abyss*; anger is constellated by "frustration," that is, restriction of autonomy, of which *chaos* is the primal innate image/imprint; and disgust is constellated by "rejection" of self or other, of which *alienation* is the primal innate image/imprint. Finally, the affect startle is constellated by the "unexpected," of which the primal innate image/imprint is *darkness*, the darkness of unconsciousness. The nature of the innate image/imprints of the affects of the libido, joy and interest, are not well understood as yet, although it would appear that they are two forms of *illumination*: blissful merger and focused insight.

6. The constellation of a primal affect occurs as follows. In response to a symbol (that is, a life experience that is "met," so to speak, by an unconscious, innate image/imprint, or the potential for such an image/imprint), there ensues a rush of feelings of a specific quality that we label as "the emotion." This is accompanied by a particular set of bodily innervations and a typical pattern of behavior. The consequence is a state of mind that both heightens and narrows the conscious field to focus primarily on the stimulus situation. This is a total reaction that for a varying period of time transforms the ego. It leads to heightened awareness within a narrowly focused consciousness, along with a rapid mobilization of energy that takes the form of a stereotyped behavior pattern accompanied by typical vocalizations, facial expressions, and bodily tensions.

7. It is important to specify now, as best I can, the prototypical behavior patterns of each of the archetypal affects. Let us begin with the twin dynamisms of the life enhancement affects, joy and interest. All the evidence suggests that the behavior patterns at the most basic level are, for play, leaping with joy, and, for curiosity, reaching for the moon. That is to say, the behavior patterns are expressions of the innate rhythms of the life instinct in forms that become in early childhood the function of play and curiosity, respectively.

It is somewhat more difficult to specify the behavior patterns of the affects of the primordial self (the crisis affects). Nevertheless, I am convinced that they have clear and immediate behavior patterns of a stereotyped and prototypical nature, which have evolved into highly differentiated functions of the psyche in the same way that play and curiosity have evolved from the primal expressions of the affects of joy and interest. My hypothesis is that the prototypical behavior patterns of distress, fear, anger, and contempt/shame may be characterized in their *expressive* aspects as "rhythm," "ritual," "reason," and "relationship." I suggest these terms as a kind of mnemonic device. As we shall see, distress is expressed and transformed through rhythm; fear is expressed and transformed through ritual; anger is expressed and transformed through reason; contempt/shame is expressed and transformed through relationship. It is apparent that rhythm, ritual, reason, and relationship are the irreducible elements, respectively, of art, religion, philosophy, and society. These are the innate categories of imagination; they appear as Joseph Henderson's (1984, 1985) cultural attitudes, the aesthetic, the religious, the philosophic, and the social. On the other hand, the prototypical behavior patterns of these same affects may be characterized in their *impressive* aspects, as an apperceptive focus on fundamental domains of the world: the tangible, the intangible, quantitative ordering, and qualitative valuing. These are the irreducible elements of our experience of the world as Kant's categories of understanding (intellect): objects in space; time and causality; quantitative, impersonal order; and qualitative, personal valuing. As psychological functions these are represented in Jung's ego functions: sensation, intuition, thinking, and feeling. (I want to mention that Jung's ego function of "feeling" is sometimes confused with "emotion" and emotionality in general. But emotion is not limited to a single ego function; rather, all of the higher functions appear to have evolved out of the primal affects.)

CHARACTERIZATIONS OF THE EXISTENTIAL EMOTIONS OF CRISIS

In the section that follows, I shall attempt to characterize briefly the affects distress, fear, anger, and disgust (contempt/shame), in descriptive and phenomenological terms, using material from various sources. This is a preliminary effort; I make no claims to completeness or finality. My purpose is to stir imagination and memory by bringing these affects to life. I shall relate them to the differentiated functions of the psyche that appear to have evolved from the affects.

Distress

At first hand, it may seem a long leap from the sad face, weepy eyes, sobbing and rocking behavior of the anguish of loss to the highly differentiated function of sensation and the cultural attitude of the aesthetic. Yet if we focus on the function of that behavior, it can be seen as an autonomous reaction of the psyche that assures a heart-rending experience of the significance of the loss that has occurred. It forces a total commitment of consciousness to the devastating feelings and sensations that are evoked by loss and to recognition of the barren *void* into which one is driven. The myth of Demeter and Persephone brings these images vividly to mind—the rupture of the primal relationship of mother and child, expressed at the cosmic level of the Great Mother in Her two aspects as Mother and Daughter, chthonic Goddesses of Nature and the cycle of death and rebirth. Demeter's barren world of despair is the primal *void* that is constellated by loss. In the myth, her experience is raised to the highest level of cosmic drama in which the constancy of her longing for Persephone and the limits to which she has to go to assure her return from the Underworld are emphasized.

It is not our purpose here to go into the intricacies of this myth, since I am seeking only to make evident the correlation of the basic images and theme of the myth with the "human" experience of loss. The expression of loss is a primal pattern that emphasizes the relation of the earth to the underworld in its aspect as the source of the fruits and beauty of the world. This, I suggest, is the channel of analogy at the primal level of the element earth through which ultimately evolved the ego function of sensation. As for the evolution of the aesthetic attitude, I would call attention to the fact that the transformation of the ego that takes place in anguish is one in which consciousness is narrowed to include only the longing for the lost loved one. The human experience of loss and its transformation shows that the rituals of mourning, e.g., the traditional rhythmic lamentations and the iconic focus, serve to keep the positive image of the beloved enshrined in the heart. The AIDS quilt shows this process so clearly—it is at once an expression of universal grief and a memorial of terrible beauty. From this, we begin to understand the artist's role in depicting the images of the world for all to enshrine in their hearts.

Fear

Let us look now at another existential affect for comparison. Our images of the expression of fear are distinctly different from those of sadness.

In fear, the eyes are wide and staring, the mouth is shaped into an audible or a silent shriek of horror, the hair stands on end, an uncanny feeling runs down the spine, and we quiver and quake. The primal behavior patterns are to run or fall in a shivering faint, i.e., to play dead. This pattern in its impressive (apperceptive) aspect is, I suggest, the prototypical form of the ego function of intuition, in that consciousness is directed to a desperate entanglement with the dreaded possibilities of the situation. At bottom, the phenomenology of fear can be understood only as a response to the "unknown," which in its spiritual aspect is Otto's "Wholly Other," and the "abyss" of Hellish terror. This is the channel of analogy which has led to the religious cultural attitude. In *The Idea of the Holy* (1923) Rudolph Otto has shown in a compelling tour de force how the most exalted of religious feelings have evolved from the primal experience of terror, "demonic dread." A living example of this is described in the Book of Job:

> In thoughts from the visions of the night, when deep sleep falleth on men, fear came upon me, and trembling, which made all my bones to shake. Then a spirit passed before my face; the hair of my flesh stood up. . . . It stood still, but I could not discern the form thereof: an image was before my eyes, there was silence, and I heard a voice saying, Shall mortal man be more just than God? Shall a man be more pure than his Maker? (Job iv. 13)

Anger

Anger presents another face of emotion, with eyes staring, brow contracted in a scowl, face flushed. Every muscle is tensed, the body is thrust forward ready to attack, and threatening growls or shouts may be heard. But perhaps the most distinguishing feature of anger is the fiercely focused attention to freeing oneself from the perceived threat to autonomy. The emotion drives one to strike out, to remove the intrusion that is creating chaos in one's world. There is perhaps no stronger engagement possible with the object than in anger. The primal behavior pattern is threat and attack. In its impressive (apperceptive) aspect, this pattern is the prototypical form of the ego function of thinking, in that consciousness is single-mindedly directed to a confrontation with a chaotic situation of extreme frustration. Is this not a first stage in thinking, that is, the identification and engagement with a problem? What follows then in subsequent reflection may be improved strategies for solving the problem. As we know from bitter experience, an angry outburst is often followed by a long period of "rehashing" the situation: I could have said that, or why didn't I do such and such, and so on. This is thinking, pragmatic attempts to set things aright, at least in one's own mind—still under the sway of the emotion, to be sure, but thinking nevertheless. There is still another way in which we may approach this difficult question. And here we may draw upon our understanding of the compensatory nature of the psyche—what cannot be achieved in the everyday world appears in unconscious fantasy. This is borne out by studies of children, who at an early age of three or four years will respond to parental restrictions on their behavior with compensatory fantasies, often involving an imaginary figure who is able to do what they would like to, and more. As children develop, these fantasies evolve into useful strategies for getting what they want.

It seems more difficult, at first, to see the potential development of the philosophic cultural attitude from the expressive aspects of the behavior pattern of anger. As we know, philosophy develops in relation to the value of the "true." The word itself derives from the two Greek words, philo and sophia, which together mean love of wisdom. The philosopher William James saw philosophy as an unusually stubborn attempt to think clearly, which captures a commonly held slant on the nature of a philosopher as one who thinks more deeply and obstinately than other people. The greatest frustration for a philosopher is not to understand something. Rodin's famous statue of the thinker shows a seated man with elbow on his knee, resting his head on his fist. His brow is furrowed as in anger, and he is obviously in a state of deep concentration. Is this not a link with the expressive qualities of the affect anger? That is to say, one sees the concentration of consciousness on gaining freedom from the restriction to autonomy, the fist and furrowed brow, expressive features related to such a response, whether it be the primitive one of a forceful physical attack or the concentrated thought of the philosopher.

A paradigm of the way in which reason must confront chaos and discover the cosmos within it is to be found in the mythical imagery of the "Babylonian Genesis." In this ancient Babylonian creation myth the hero Marduk must do battle with the Goddess Tiamat, whose domain is the Chaos of the abysmal waters. The state of Chaos that Tiamat creates, and represents, is vividly portrayed at the moment when she is confronted by Marduk, who challenges her to single combat: "She became like one in a frenzy (and) lost her *reason*" (my emphasis). But unswerving in the face of her fury, Marduk slays Tiamat, whose body he divides in two to form heaven and earth, a new cosmos (Heidel, 1942, pp. 40–43). The reciprocal relationship between anger and reason has been perceived by thinkers throughout the ages, as for example these comments from Seneca's treatise "On Anger":

Hesitation is the best cure for anger. . . . The first blows of anger
are heavy, but if it waits, it will think again. . . . Anger . . . is
the foe of reason . . . nevertheless [it is] born only where reason
dwells. (Seneca, II 29)

Disgust (Contempt/Shame)

What may we say about the innate basis of disgust? In the evolutionary
scheme of things it seems likely that it goes back to the primal affective
reflex whose function was the rejection of noxious, potentially poisonous
substances. This is accomplished either through a turning away from
such substances or, if they have been ingested, by vomiting up the con-
tents of the stomach before digestion has occurred. This behavior can be
observed throughout the mammalian species. In the dominance-
submission behaviors of the higher primates we can see that this affect/
reflex has evolved to a stage which is the precursor of the bipolar human
emotion I have called contempt/shame. Shame is perhaps the most painful of all the innate affects (Tomkins, 1963, p. 133, p. 185; Nathanson,
1987). The expressive features are bowing the head, turning away, covering one's face with the hands, and the like.

Contempt/shame is an acute evaluative function that finds others or
ourselves wanting. When we are contemptuous of others we turn up our
noses and then find ourselves alienated. When we experience someone
else's contempt, or our own, we hang our heads in shame and find
ourselves alienated. Nothing in the world has such a potential for inducing us to take stock of ourselves and our relationships with others. In the
twinkling of an eye, shame can shatter what but a moment before was a
comfortable sense of pride in our accomplishments, in our relationships,
in our very being. In this sense, shame is the mirror image of contempt.
Children are shamed by adults who point out to them the errors of their
ways, often in a manner which the child experiences as rejection. How
could you *do* that? You know better than that? For shame! Then may
follow banishment—go to your room until you can behave! The withdrawal of love, the most potent punishment available to parents, is the
ultimate meaning of rejection and the most powerful stimulus to shame.

Finally, in this dynamic of contempt/shame, we discover, surprisingly
enough, the basis for a further evolution that has occurred in humans,
namely the development of the ego function of feeling. As defined by
Jung, the feeling function is an evaluative function. It evaluates feelings;
that is to say, it evaluates the state of relationships. What do I really feel
about this person, this relationship? Is this right for me, or for the
family, and the like? As an evaluative function it may be compared with

the thinking function. The thinking function evaluates thoughts. The criterion against which the thinking function evaluates is the intrinsic ideal of *truth*, defined as logic, verification, and ultimately, wisdom. The feeling function evaluates feelings. The criterion against which the feeling function evaluates is the intrinsic ideal of the social domain, namely the *good*. This is the realm of human ethics and morality. Looked at from the broadest possible perspective, society and the social order depend upon a continuing, sustained effort to achieve the best possible synthesis of the desires of the individual and the needs of the group. This human ideal is sustained through the efforts of individuals of good will who struggle to create a social order in which the contending desires for power and love may find an equilibration that maximizes justice and cooperation.

In conclusion, then, I suggest that not only has the ego function of feeling evolved out of the contempt/shame dynamic, but that the highest values that make possible a viable social order are also to be found embedded in this toxic, painful, existential emotion. It seems evident that contempt/shame has evolved directly as a function of the social needs of the mammalian species.

SOME CLOSING THOUGHTS ON ACTIVE IMAGINATION

I have attempted to present a view of the self as it evolves out of the primordial depths of the unconscious toward the highest aspirations of the human spirit. In closing, I should like to discuss further the topic of active imagination. For Jung it was a technique that was applicable to any of the art forms — drawing, painting, music, poetry, dance, and so on, and, of course, sandplay (Stewart, 1981a, 1981b, 1982). It is also a technique of dialogue with autonomous personifications of the unconscious. The basic aim, according to Jung, is to give free reign to fantasy while retaining a conscious viewpoint. This broad spectrum of experiences, which can include phenomena of the transference as well, is what I recognize as active imagination.

The grounding place for me in this realm of bewildering manifestations is the syzygy (anima and animus), understood as the archetypal affects of the libido, joy and interest, and their dynamisms, play and curiosity. This means that there are differences in forms of the imagination at different developmental levels and on the different planes of the unconscious. In this sense, the symbolic play of childhood "pretend" is a form of active imagination. So is the experience in analysis when analysand and analyst are seeking congruence for an image constellated in the transference and countertransference medium (Davidson, 1966; Schwartz-Salant, 1982). While analysts have their individual styles and terminology, as well as preferences for particular media, it is helpful, or so I believe, to be cognizant of this process as an archetypal manifestation of the libido, which fits many media but which is forever preoccupied with the transformation of the archetypal affects of the self. These transformations appear in normal development and in re-creation in psychotherapy and analysis, no matter what the particular technique, in one or another of the four cultural attitudes of the realized self—the aesthetic, the religious, the philosophic, and the social—and in the fourfold structure of the mandala symbols or the twofold intertwining of the Tao, Yin and Yang, Luna and Sol, Eros and Logos.

REFERENCES

Bachelard, G. (1938). *The psychoanalysis of fire*. Boston: Beacon Press, 1968.

Campbell, J. (1959). *The masks of God: Primitive mythology*. New York: Viking.

Darwin, C. (1872). *The expression of the emotions in man and animals*. Chicago: University of Chicago Press, 1965.

Davidson, D. (1966). Transference as a form of active imagination. *Journal of Analytical Psychology, 11/2*, 135–146.

Ekman, P. (1972). *Emotion in the human face*, (2nd ed.). Cambridge: Cambridge University Press.

Ekman, P. (1984). Expression and the nature of emotion. In K. Scherer & P. Ekman (Eds.), *Approaches to emotion* (pp. 319–343). Hillsdale, NJ: Erlbaum.

Eliade, M. (1967). *From primitives to Zen: A thematic sourcebook of the history of religions*. New York: Harper & Row, 1977.

Heidel, A. (1942). *The Babylonian genesis*. Chicago: University of Chicago Press, 1956.

Henderson, J. L. (1962). The archetype of culture. *The archetype, proceedings of the 2nd international congress of Psychology, Zurich* (pp. 3–15). New York: S. Karger, 1964.

Henderson, J. L. (1984). *Cultural attitudes in psychological perspective*. Toronto: Inner City Books.

Henderson, J. L. (1985). The origins of a theory of cultural attitudes. *Psychological Perspectives, 16/2*, 210–220.

Hillman, J. (1960). *Emotion, A comprehensive phenomenology of theories and their meanings for therapy*. Evanston: Northwestern University Press, 1972.

Izard, C. E. (1977). *Human emotions*. New York: Plenum.

Jung, C. G. (1921). Psychological types. *Collected works 6*. Princeton, NJ: Princeton University Press, 1977.

Jung, C. G. (1938). Psychological aspects of the mother archetype. *Collected works 9*, part 1. Princeton, NJ: Princeton University Press, 2nd Ed., 1968.

Lynd, H. (1958). *On shame and the search for identity*. New York: Harcourt, Brace.

Nathanson, D. L. (Ed.) (1987). *The many faces of shame*. New York: Guilford.

Otto, R. (1923). *The idea of the holy*. New York: Oxford University Press, 1981.

Roberts, J., & Sutton-Smith, B. (1970). The cross-cultural and psychological study of games. In G. Luschen (Ed.), *The cross-cultural analysis of games* (pp. 100–108). Champaign, IL: Stipes.

Schaya, L. (1971). *The universal meaning of the Kaballah*. Baltimore: Penguin, 1973.

Schwartz-Salant, N. (1982). *Narcissism and character transformation*. Toronto: Inner City Books.

Stevens, A. (1983). *Archetypes: A natural history of the self*. New York: Quill.

Stewart, C. T. (1981). Developmental psychology of sandplay. In G. Hill (Ed.), *Sandplay studies: Origins, theory and practice* (pp. 39–92). San Francisco: C. G. Jung Institute of San Francisco.

Stewart, C. T., & Stewart, L. H. (1981, April). *Play, games and stages of development: A contribution toward a comprehensive theory of play*. Presented at the 7th annual conference of the Association for the Anthropological Study of Play (TAASP), Fort Worth.

Stewart, L. H. (1978). Gaston Bachelard and the poetics of reverie. In G. Hill et al. (Eds.), *The shaman from Elko*. San Francisco: C. G. Jung Institute of San Francisco.

Stewart, L. H. (1981a). Play and sandplay. In G. Hill (Ed.), *Sandplay studies: Origins, theory and practice* (pp. 21–37). San Francisco: C. G. Jung Institute of San Francisco.

Stewart, L. H. (1981b, April). *The play-dream continuum and the categories of the imagination*. Presented at the 7th annual conference of the Association for the Anthropological Study of Play (TAASP), Fort Worth.

Stewart, L. H. (1982). Sandplay and analysis. In M. Stein (Ed.), *Jungian analysis* (pp. 204–218). La Salle: Open Court, 2nd Ed., 1995.

Stewart, L. H. (1987). Affect and archetype in analysis. In N. Schwartz-Salant & M. Stein (Eds.), *Archetypal processes in psychotherapy* (pp. 131–162). Wilmette, IL: Chiron Publications.

Stewart, L. H. (1992). *Changemakers: A Jungian perspective on sibling position and the family atmosphere*. New York: Routledge.

Stewart, L. H., & Stewart, C. T. (1981). Play, games and affects: A contribution toward a comprehensive theory of play. In A. T. Cheska (Ed.), *Play as context. Proceedings of the Association for the Anthropological Study of Play* (TAASP) (pp. 42–52). Westpoint, NY: Leisure Press.

Tinbergen, N. (1951). *The study of instinct*. New York: Oxford University Press.

Tomkins, S. (1962). *Affect, imagery, consciousness, Vol. 1: The positive affects*. New York: Springer.

Tomkins, S. (1963). *Affect, imagery, consciousness, Vol. 2: The negative affects*. New York: Springer.

13

Trauma and Affect: Applying the Language of Affect Theory to the Phenomena of Traumatic Stress

Andrew M. Stone

Bad things happen to people, experiences that produce so much discomfort that they cannot be handled by mental mechanisms that allow the associated memories to remain in normal consciousness lest the affect triggered by such recall take over much of waking life. Recall that Tomkins suggested that the pain system is both localizing and motivating–when something hurts we are both drawn to the area of pain and motivated to reduce the pain message. Affect calls our attention not to some local condition, but to a much more general quality of our existence; it is, however, the primary source of psychological motivation.

Terms for the worst possible experiences include trauma, abuse, and torture, for which I have suggested the following criteria: (1) An experience can be called traumatic only when it produces dense and enduring negative affect. (2) Interpersonal action can be called abusive only when, by intention, it produces pain, dense affective experience, or massive sexual arousal in an individual who is helpless and otherwise unable to modulate it. (3) Torture involves the induction of pain or negative affect when these mechanisms are prevented from acting as motivations and are used only to convey information.

But how are we altered when forced to endure trauma, abuse, or torture, and for how long are we so changed? Dr. Stone focuses our attention on the military veterans he has studied and treated through the Post Traumatic Stress Disorder Clinic of the Philadelphia VA Hospital. He reviews what has been written about this group of illnesses, recasting it in the language of affect theory, and suggests how these scripted responses to maximal discomfort may be understood and altered with the use of these new insights. Central to his chapter is the understanding that the efficacy and efficiency of the treatments we can offer this cohort are improved significantly when we pay attention to the specific affects that underlie their complaints. —DLN

Nothing can be called trauma unless it triggers affect.
                                            — Donald L. Nathanson, 1993

DISTURBANCES OF AFFECT are central to all descriptions of traumatic stress and its sequelae. The experience of traumatization induces a profound transformation of affective and emotional life. So pervasive are the ensuing alterations that they cut across all the categories of symptoms noted in posttraumatic stress disorders. Reexamining what we know of trauma from the perspective of affect and affect theory can add to our ability to describe and understand the phenomena that comprise it. In an attempt to begin this task, this chapter briefly outlines a framework for considering the realm of affect. Using the proposed terminology, we will then review the affective dimensions of existing descriptions of traumatic stress and the symptoms of posttraumatic stress disorders. From the vantage point this provides, implications for assessment and treatment will be discussed.

What is the measure of trauma? How we define and determine this has been an issue throughout the evolution of psychotherapeutic understanding. Freud, Rank, and Janet (van der Kolk & van der Hart, 1989) all sought to link varying degrees of causality to different aspects of experience, ranging from birth to everyday life to incest and other more extreme circumstances, on the one hand, with diverse forms of psychopathology, on the other. For some, the result has been a reductio ad absurdum, in which determinism replaces responsibility. For others, the link between trauma and change remains one of the most inviting mysteries of the human mind.

How does trauma change people, in what ways, and by what mechanisms? The transformations accomplished by moments or hours of terror and helplessness can last a lifetime. How does this occur? And what can be done to alleviate the resulting suffering? These are questions that arise out of the clinical encounter with traumatized patients.

One such patient is a woman in her early forties whom we will call A. She comes to my office appearing somewhat angry and suspicious, although her behavior is polite and socially correct. She chooses the chair at the greater distance from mine and closest to the door. Nearly two years ago she was shot and critically wounded in an incident with an acquaintance that took place in her own home. After a long hospitalization and convalescence her physical recovery is complete, but her life is totally changed. She has moved to another area. She stays in her house. In a market, she scans the surroundings, expecting to be shot. Seeing a man with a hat like that of her assailant is enough to produce a marked physiological arousal response. She avoids contact with family and former friends. She has not been able to return to work. Her sleep is poor. She dreams of the shooting and its aftermath. After such dreams fear can leave her feeling weak for days. How can we best describe and understand what has happened to her? And what good can this formulation do her; how does what we say about her change what we can do?

Traumatic events are interactions of people and circumstances. As students we were asked whether the tree falling unattended in the forest made a sound; similarly, it is axiomatic that no event has been traumatic unless it affects a person. Neither the individual alone nor the event alone is sufficient to constitute a trauma. It is the conjunction of the event and the person that produces the trauma and the subsequent disorder. We must ask by what means, in what currency, is this interaction mediated? The natural candidate for this function is the affect system. It is the affective response to sensation and perception, modified through cognition and behavior, that determines the degree to which any event is to be considered traumatic. Indeed, the affective response is the variable that indicates and regulates the priority of any given stimulus in an organism's information-processing queue. The greater our understanding of the mechanisms of affect, the better will be our chances to comprehend the process of traumatization and its repercussions.

AFFECT THEORY

In order to speak of affect, we need, at least provisionally, to agree on a language for doing so. Based on the work of Silvan Tomkins (1962), we can speak of a finite number of innate affects, each of which is elicited by a particular contour of changing stimulus density or gradient. This feature enables us to discriminate beyond such simple distinctions as the level of pleasure versus unpleasure, and allows the designation of two positive, one neutral, and six negative affects. The precision made possible by this concept also allows a discussion of the interaction of different affects. It permits us to explore the dynamics of the relations between affect and action, affect and cognition, affect and experience. The innate affects, constellations of physiologic responses, are seen as underlying and forming the basis for the development of what is to become the unique emotional experience of a given individual. With the biologic substrate of affective response as a template, a person's memories, cognitions, and associations can accrete to become what we see as mature emotions. Awareness of these affects and emotions is referred to as a capacity for feelings. These clarified definitions of affect, feeling, and emotion, along with mood and disorder, as described more fully by Nathanson (1993, chapter 1 in this volume), complete the conceptual armamentarium to be used here.

PTSD DEFINED

With these concepts in mind, we can revisit and re-map the rocky terrain of traumatic stress and the disorders that may result from it. Beginning with the *DSM-III* in 1980, there was a widespread effort to operationalize definitions of psychiatric disorders in terms of observable behaviors. The criteria for posttraumatic stress disorder (PTSD) went beyond this, describing etiology as well as symptomatology. Other than the organic and substance use disorders, only PTSD among the categories of psychiatric illness includes the cause in the diagnostic criteria.

Our current diagnostic criteria fall into four groups. The previous nosology, *DSM-III-R* (American Psychiatric Association, 1987), required "an event that is outside the usual range of human experience and that would be markedly distressing to almost anyone." (There is nothing that prepares the average adult for the sight of a loved one being tortured or the experience of being buried alive.) In *DSM-IV* (American Psychiatric Association, 1994), this has been succeeded by a two-part stressor criterion. We are no longer asked to believe that such occurrences are indeed outside the usual range of human experience. There must be an event to which one is exposed, generally involving jeopardy to the physical person of oneself or another, and a specified response to that event, consisting of terror, hopelessness, or horror. The language of affect and emotion has arrived at the core of the disorder's definition. For the diagnosis of PTSD, it is not enough that such an event has been experienced—the event itself must also be *reexperienced* in some way that evokes the noxious quality of the original. "Reexperiencing symptoms" may include nightmares, intrusive recollections, "flashbacks" (dissociative reliving of the event), and intense discomfort triggered by reminders of the event.

The third diagnostic criterion calls attention to the normal human wish to avoid or escape noxious stimuli. PTSD patients describe a spectrum of such responses, ranging from amnesia for the signal event to blunting or numbing of all emotional experience. Despite these mechanisms, traumatic stress disorders continue to produce a fourth realm of problems— persistent symptoms of autonomic arousal, including difficulty initiating or maintaining sleep, increased irritability or outbursts of anger, decreased concentration, hypervigilance, and exaggerated startle responses. (These are examples for the purpose of illustration. The actual criteria require specified numbers of symptoms from each of the three clusters in order to make the diagnosis. The final requirement is that of duration.)

PTSD IN TERMS OF AFFECT THEORY

Each facet of our existing definitions of trauma and traumatic stress symptoms can be shown to refract differently with a more rigorous and specific set of definitions, moving from common or folk usage to a more narrow and technical sense of terminology. For example, affect theory both provides and requires a redefinition of our common experience of startle. In everyday language we tend to lump the innate affect surprise-startle (which lasts only a few hundredths of a second) with what follows

TABLE 13.1
Categories of *DSM-IV* Diagnostic Criteria
for Posttraumatic Stress Disorder

A. Experience of a sufficiently stressful traumatic event
B. Reexperiencing of memories of the event
C. Avoidance of trauma-associated stimuli and/or numbing of emotional response
D. Symptoms of increased arousal
E. Duration greater than one month

it. So it is that we describe what happens when a bomb goes off: First there is an unexpected explosion that triggers surprise-startle; attention is then removed from whatever had just then occupied us; now we turn our attention to the result of that detonation—more noise, smoke, fire, screaming, injuries of various severity. These new stimuli trigger such affects as fear-terror, disgust, dissmell, distress, and anger. Whoever is subjected to such a scene will recall the sudden explosion, the ensuing carnage, and the affects occurring in response to each and every minute part of this complex scene as one event rather than many. Any stimulus that recalls this scene will produce a new experience that is similarly condensed.

What startles us is by its nature very brief; in sharp contrast are stimuli that both last a long time and remain at terribly uncomfortable levels of intensity, thereby triggering the affect distress-anguish. "Distress" is not the only affect-linked language to be found in the definition of PTSD, for "intense fear, terror, and helplessness" are also mentioned. Thus, the genesis of the disorder is rooted in the experience of overwhelming negative affect.

Reexperiencing symptoms are not limited to imagery alone; what is reexperienced includes the affect occurring with the traumatic event. Surprise-startle, considered to be a neutral affect in response to a stimulus of sudden onset and offset, is also found prominently both as part of the initial stressor in many instances of PTSD and as part of the subsequent symptoms. The exaggerated startle response is one of the key arousal symptoms and has been studied as a psychophysiologic marker of the disorder (Butler et al., 1990). The irritability also described in the arousal cluster of symptoms may be seen as an increased likelihood of experiencing the affect anger, associated with a sustained increase in the overall level of stimulation.

Even the positive affects of interest-excitement and enjoyment-joy are involved in the manifestations of the syndrome, primarily through the change in the quality of living produced by their reduction. Decreased concentration reflects the deficit in interest, as do numbing and withdrawal. An incapacity for the expression of warm or tender feelings is also described. Alexithymia, literally the absence of words for mood or feeling, is another frequent finding in this group of patients, a clinical syndrome that has engendered its own line of investigation and thought. Thus, our most inclusive statement about PTSD would describe it as a disturbance in which the identification, regulation, and expression of affect are severely impaired. Both the source of the impairment—the traumatic stressor and the response to it—and the manifestations of the disorder can be most clearly described in terms of affect.

ALEXITHYMIA

Few groups of patients have proved as daunting for practitioners of verbal psychotherapies as those we now call alexithymic. Noted by Nemiah and Sifneos (1970), among others, to have little awareness of their affects, and indeed little perceptible external expression of them as well, these individuals are notable for their lack of progress in insight-oriented treatments. Their affective discomfort is often experienced and presented as a somatic discomfort that may lead to extensive and fruitless medical evaluation. Henry Krystal's work with concentration camp survivors led him to a view of trauma and affect that is delineated thoughtfully in his *Integration and Self-Healing: Affect, Trauma, and Alexithymia.* While working largely within the language and paradigms of psychoanalysis, he never allows the theoretical models to obscure his clinical observations. The richness and erudition of the text and of his examination of his own and his patients' experience in treatment make for rewarding, albeit demanding, reading. In defining the condition, Krystal sees the incapacity for reflective self-awareness as central. He describes the alexithymic patient as experiencing emotions as "vague and unspecific, as if they represented an undifferentiated form of affect precursors." They are also weak in "the cognitive aspect of emotion," which includes the sense of "meaning . . . and . . . the 'story behind it'" as well as the ability to identify and express feeling (p. 243). Krystal notes the common conjunction of alexithymia and anhedonia, describing poignantly the resulting constriction of emotional experience. Emerging from his exploration is the understanding that trauma alters profoundly the emotional and affective world of the survivor, and that any approach to treatment must take this into account. Dealing with cognition alone will not suffice.

DISSOCIATION AND AFFECT

Other lines of inquiry provide additional perspectives that we can use to look at affect and trauma. Some of the most illuminating material about trauma and affect comes to us through the efforts of those who work with dissociative disorders. In the BASK model, Braun (1988) proposes that the cleavage occurring in dissociation separates along the planes of *b*ehavior, *a*ffect, *s*ensation, and *k*nowledge or consciousness. One or more of these functions may be suspended when the level of stress is too great. Again, one must ask how a given level of stress or traumatic event becomes sufficient to require the use of such defenses. Here, too, affect can be seen as the key dimension.

One of the crucial determinants of dissociation is the level of affective intensity, both overall and in regard to specific negative affects. Clearly, these thresholds vary in people with different developmental experiences. Certain conditions, such as early abusive treatment, have been shown to predispose an individual to use the defense of dissociation. The work of Spiegel, Hunt, and Dondershine (1988) in looking at hypnotizability showed that this capacity, which normally is high in childhood and decreases with age, remained elevated in those with PTSD, further linking the dissociative mechanisms with that disorder. Affective ontogeny, the developmental history of the affective apparatus, may be greatly illuminated through studies of these variations in early experience as they relate to later disturbances. In those with the capacity to dissociate, what triggers the phenomenon? Various precipitants may be identified, but levels of intensity and degrees of distress are still components of the affective realm.

ASSESSMENT AND AFFECT THEORY

The experience of any given traumatic event can be described in terms of the succession of affects that comprise it. The major principle to apply here from Tomkins's work is consideration of the affect as analogous to the overall pattern of stimulation from which it is generated. A greater-than-optimal rate of increase in stimulation, for example, can produce the affect fear–terror, while a sustained excessive load may induce distress–anguish. His postulates regarding the role of changes in stimulus intensity in triggering affect can also be a guide in predicting the dynamics of how affects succeed one another in the course of an individual's response to events.

While affects occurring simultaneously with each other or with sense impressions, cognitions, and so forth, are said to be coassembled, another term is used when there is a succession of affects over time. Tomkins (1987) called these chains of affective variation "affect scripts." He saw them not only as occurring in response to given events, but also as being reproduced as repeated patterns in the life of the individual. Reconstruction of these sequences is a critical part of the therapeutic process, as it permits the reaction to the trauma to be, in effect, "unbundled" and traced to its diverse symptomatic ramifications. Each of the component affects of the memory will have its own set of associations, cognitions, sensations, and behaviors. The predominant affect of an individual's reaction to some situations may be a clue to the initial trauma response, or it may be a secondary layer of adaptation to reaction that has supervened in the course of the person's efforts to integrate and assimilate the experience. In either case, it is necessary to identify the affect, trace the association to the original trauma, and clarify the manifestation of the affect in the present symptom picture of the patient. Tomkins (1963) had earlier pointed out the relations among trauma, memory, and cognition. "An experience has to become traumatic by being transformed both in content and in retrievability by succeeding experience" (p. 386). This subsequent processing may be entirely internal and conceptual, or it may include other, external reinforcement. This is quite consistent with recent emphasis on early intervention as a way to reduce later trauma-related morbidity. It is not the event itself, but the way in which its associated affects and cognitions are assembled with it to make meaning, that constitutes psychological trauma.

CULTURAL FACTORS

Affect theory also provides a framework for understanding the differences in emotional life in general, and response to trauma in particular, that are found across cultural divisions. Since we accept that only the affects themselves are innate, we recognize that the experience and expression of the emotions arise from personal, family, and social learning through the life span. Traumatic events are a special case of such learning. It is only reasonable to expect that responses to trauma will also have both an underlying biological affective component and a conditioned expression that is mediated through the existing cognitive and emotional structures of the individual. The former is relatively consistent across populations, and the latter can take numerous forms. The work of Mollica et al. (1991), for example, demonstrates the manifestation of trauma in Cambodian refugee populations in ways that are both similar to and different from the constellation set forth in the American *DSM-III-R* and *DSM-IV* classifications. Both the work of this group and the efforts of institutions such as the World Health Organization to define the impact of trauma have tried to take into account the role of culture and language in order to determine the presentations of disorders of traumatic stress. Recognition of the factors involved in making the steps from affect to emotion can contribute to the development of this understanding.

NUMBING

This deliberate, almost plodding approach is made necessary by that part of PTSD which is a further layer of defense against affect: the numbing.

This symptom cluster alone may serve as sufficient evidence of the value of describing PTSD in terms of its affective phenomenology. What is "numbing" but a distancing or drastic reduction in intensity of all affective experience? While dissociative defenses may sever completely any connection between affect and cognition, the effects of the numbing response may range from that extreme to a more partial or selective reduction in both affect and awareness. This overlaps with but is not necessarily identical to the alexithymia discussed above. Patients report an absence of positive affect as well as a limitation of negative affect. While a patient's family may note great difficulty in expressing warmth or tenderness, the capacity for anger or fear may remain, despite attempts at reducing intensity. Many of the avoidance/withdrawal behaviors may be seen as efforts to limit the overall level of stimulation and to decrease opportunities for loss of control that may accompany affective overload.

The neurobiology of numbing is another intriguing window into the physiology of emotion. Work by Pitman, van der Kolk, Orr, and Greenberg (1990) has found evidence that stress-related analgesia is mediated by the endorphin system. Does this system override the interoception of affective cues or diminish the affective reaction in the first place? The soothing effects of exogenous opioids have been noted for millennia. The basis for their mechanism of operation is closer to being elucidated. While there are certainly other factors and systems involved in the numbing response — abnormal adrenergic function has also been demonstrated (Southwick et al., 1993) — the endogenous opioid system is a key contributor.

OVERLOAD

The opposite extreme of trauma-related symptomatology is that of overwhelming affect. The same traumatic events that we have defined as such by virtue of their affective intensity serve to destabilize the patient's hard-won but precarious equilibrium when they spring unbidden into awareness. They may have been stimulated by memory-specific external cues such as sights, sounds, or language. Or internal imaginal exposure may trigger a memory, with all its attendant affect. Affect itself, as it relates to a particular event or one's experience of it, can be a powerful reminder. Whichever of these pathways is followed, the images, sensations, affects, and cognitions of the trauma are revisited. Secondary affects arising in the present in reaction to this cascade may also be activated; one may become ashamed, dismayed, or enraged, to name but a few, merely at the experience of again being subjected to the overwhelming reexperiencing. Similarly, secondary reactions may occur to arousal symptoms with significant affective component, such as exaggerated startle or increased irritability and the loss of control of the expression of anger that may accompany it.

The excesses of affective manifestation in PTSD can take a variety of forms, as we have seen. It can be in the reexperiencing or in the arousal symptoms, as fear or anger, startle or distress. At times, the person may be relatively unaware of the nature or the extent of affect he is displaying: "My wife says I'm really off the wall." This man's expression of affect is not regulated by feedback from his own awareness of affect. When someone else informs him that his behavior is beyond acceptable limits, he may control himself, or withdraw, or become more enraged.

Affective and behavioral dyscontrol can enter a vicious cycle of positive feedback with substance abuse and dependence. While some patients may report using alcohol or other licit and illicit substances in an effort to regulate affect and mood, for most people this is not a viable long-term solution. Although alcohol and benzodiazepines can reduce anxiety transiently, they can also increase the risk of loss of control. While stimulants such as amphetamine and cocaine may brighten mood or enhance alertness temporarily, they may also increase the risk of fear, rage, and outbursts of violence. Use of nonprescribed substances has been found in a significant proportion of patients with PTSD (Keane, Gerardi, Lyons, & Wolfe, 1988), though it probably varies a good deal among various traumatized subpopulations. To the extent that it is an effort to self-medicate various symptoms, substance use can be a valuable indicator to the clinician as to which of the symptoms are most troubling to the patient. Any active substance use problem must be dealt with prior to or at least concurrently with any other treatment for traumatic stress syndromes.

A man we'll call B sits in my office this morning. He is in his early forties, and his face is deeply lined. He moves with the unconscious athletic sureness of someone who does physical labor for his daily work. In addition to being a Vietnam combat veteran with posttraumatic stress disorder, he is also a survivor of 18 years of intravenous opiate dependence; he has been drug- and alcohol-free for the past five or six years. Partly as a result of his uncontrollable anger, he is separated from his wife. Their 12-year-old son, who is developmentally disabled, lives with her. The man is telling me about his latest trip to "The Wall," the Vietnam Veterans Memorial in Washington, DC. In the past, he has gone there and come away in a rage. This time has been different. "I would stand there and the first tear would hit my cheek and I would want to kill. . . . All of a sudden I'd be all right, but I wasn't all right." On this visit, supported by two close friends, he decided to stay in his grief. He carried a poem written by another veteran that was an affirmation of mourning. He read it to himself as he stood there. He was able to remain focused in his sadness. He did not become angry. He cried for half an hour.

Many factors and much hard work on the part of this man and his family and their several therapists have led to his ability to make this step. The language of affect theory helps us to see what elements in his treatment have been most supportive of this change. He has had to overcome the numbing of the PTSD to recover the capacity for feeling, that is to say, for awareness of affects as they arise. In addition, he has had to overcome the habit of annihilating with chemicals any affect that did break into awareness. He has had to learn to recognize and identify the different negative and positive affects and his own patterns of dealing with them. Those patterns that were most maladaptive, such as the use of rage to avoid sadness, have been addressed both on a descriptive didactic level and in the experiential settings of therapy and daily living.

A second man, C, comes into my office a couple of hours later. Also in his forties, he's wearing the blue work clothes of his warehouse job. He's almost eight years sober, after years of PTSD, depression, alcohol dependence, and stimulant abuse. He's less educated and articulate than the previous visitor. He's called for this appointment to ask me about something he's noticed recently. It seems that one morning on the bus on his way to work, he was thinking of guys in his unit who had died, and as he remembered them, tears came to his eyes. Then, later, when he got to work, he felt good, "too good," and was very comfortable and confident—not out of line, just having a good time with people. Then, later that same day, passing a mirror, he saw his face, and wondered, "Where have all the years gone?" He wasn't upset by the thought, but pleased that now he was doing all right. He doesn't quite know what to make of all this variation in his state, and wonders if he is getting depressed again.

For him, the explanation is in terms of feelings. He, too, is gradually overcoming numbing, except that he is not sure how to manage the changes. From a relatively steady state achieved at great cost, he is mildly alarmed at noticing excursions in various directions, despite their not interfering with his functioning. The educational component here is about the return of feeling. The adaptive nature of numbing in the situation of protracted and repeated traumatization is compared with the maladaptive effect of prolonging the numbing into subsequent life. He is able to recognize that he is having feelings and that they can be differentiated from each other. Negative affects can be experienced, and their associations explored, without total decompensation if other defenses are adequate. We try to distinguish between sadness and depression. The capacity to feel enjoyment–joy is contingent on the capacity to feel. Accepting the passing experiences of awareness of affect is a life skill that he will need to practice in the world and bring back to the therapeutic situation for further evolution.

APPLICATIONS TO TREATMENT

Treatment is biopsychosocial and psychoeducational. As Friedman (1988) suggests, most pharmacologic intervention in PTSD is symptomatic. An understanding of the affective picture of the patient may help select agents that have efficacy in certain specific instances. The generalized adrenergic alerting that is reported as anxiety or "nerves" may respond to beta-blockers. Limiting this overall arousal may also reduce outbursts of anger and aggression, as Yudofsky, Stevens, Barsa, and Williams (1984) have shown in brain-injured patients. Continued outbursts of anger or rage may be seen as kindling phenomena that are reduced by use of carbamazepine or valproate. Antidepressant medications of several categories, including tricyclics, MAOIs and SSRIs, may all have application in certain cases. In each treatment, the profile of symptoms and likely side-effects will guide the selection of a medication. Behavioral methods (Solomon, Gerrity, & Muff, 1992), including relaxation, stress management, and biofeedback, may be concurrently or alternatively employed to reduce arousal and enhance control.

Psychosocial aspects of treatment will unfold according to the mode of therapy being employed. As Wolfe (1989) has pointed out, all psychotherapies for traumatic stress disorders involve some form of exposure, generally an imaginal exposure to the memory of the traumatic event. It is in the reaction to that exposure that the affect is elicited, and the task of treatment is that it be identified and regulated under conditions of safety for the patient. Here the educational component also plays a role, as the reintroduction of the patient to the innate affect repertoire will provide a cognitive framework within which to understand the healing process and its vicissitudes as they happen. Naturally, the affects elicited are not limited to those stimulated by imaginal exposure to traumatic memories. The therapeutic setting and relationship provide a real-time laboratory for the discovery and rediscovery of affective and emotional functioning that is deeply interwoven with the trauma-related changes.

How does all this bear on the evaluation and treatment of the patient called A? Just as the objective descriptive language of *DSM-III-R* is justified by its efficacy in guiding the clinician toward an appropriate treatment, a comprehensive affective inventory and formulation of this woman's presenting condition will help to frame her therapy. What are her strengths and weaknesses, and how do they connect with the circumstances of the trauma? The predominant affect of her dreams, memories, and symptoms is fear–terror. She can come to recognize it, to name it, to become more familiar with its effects on her. She will reassess its appropriateness in different circumstances. Her world has become a much more dangerous place than it used to be. While the fear is obvious to her, the depth of her anger is less so. Realizing that every day she still carries enough anger to want to kill the man who shot her is a necessary step toward determining how to lighten that load. What other vulnerabilities from prior events are restimulated by this one? What of the shame of being a victim? Naming this affect is also necessary in the course of coming to terms with a new reality and developing a worldview that permits one to function. Trust in her own judgment, trust in other people, the capacity to achieve enough safety to allow intimacy again are further goals that depend in large part on the resolution of the other obstacles that have been mentioned. Describing the affects gives us another map for healing. Such a map does not convey all the information of the territory it represents. Maps can be topographic, political, or otherwise descriptive of certain dimensions. The dimension of affect is crucial to our understanding of the workings of the mind. Having more specific language with which to describe it permits us to conceive and carry out assessment more precisely and treatment more thoroughly.

REFERENCES

American Psychiatric Association. (1987). *Diagnostic and statistical manual of mental disorders* (3rd Ed.). Washington, DC: Author.

American Psychiatric Association. (1994). *Diagnostic and statistical manual of mental disorders* (4th Ed.). Washington, DC: Author.

Braun, B. G. (1988). The BASK model of dissociation: Part I. *Dissociation, 1*, 4–23.

Butler, R. W., Braff, D. L., Rausch, J. L., Jenkins, M., Sprock, J., & Geyer, M. (1990). Physiologic evidence of exaggerated startle response in a subgroup of Vietnam veterans with PTSD. *American Journal of Psychiatry, 147*, 1308–1312.

Friedman, M. (1988). Toward rational pharmacotherapy for PTSD: An interim report. *American Journal of Psychiatry, 145*, 281–285.

Keane, T. M., Gerardi, R. J., Lyons, J. A., & Wolfe, J. (1988). The interrelationship of substance abuse and posttraumatic stress disorder: Epidemiological and clinical considerations. *Recent Dev. Alcohol, 6*, 27–48.

Krystal, H. (1988). *Integration and healing: Affect, trauma, and alexithymia.* Hillsdale, NJ: Analytic Press.

Mollica, R. F., Caspi-Yavin, Y., Bollini, P., Truong, T., Tor, S., & Lavelle, J. (1991). The Harvard trauma questionnaire: Validating a cross-cultural instrument for measuring torture, trauma, and post-traumatic stress disorder in Indochinese refugees. *Journal of Nervous and Mental Disease, 180,* 111–116.

Nathanson, D. L. (1993, October). *Toward a new psychotherapy.* Paper presented at the annual meeting of the Silvan S. Tomkins Institute, Philadelphia.

Nemiah, J. C., & Sifneos, P. E. (1970). Affect and fantasy in psychosomatic disorders. In O. W. Hill (Ed.), *Modern trends in psychosomatic medicine, Vol. 2* (pp. 26–34). Stoneham, MA: Butterworth.

Pitman, R. K., van der Kolk, B. A., Orr, S. P., & Greenberg, M. S. (1990). Naloxone-reversible analgesic response to combat-related stimuli in posttraumatic stress disorder: A pilot study. *Archives of General Psychiatry, 47,* 541–544.

Solomon, S. D., Gerrity, E. T., & Muff, A. M. (1992). Efficacy of treatments for posttraumatic stress disorder: An empirical review. *JAMA, 268,* 633–638.

Southwick, S. M., Krystal, J. H., Morgan, C. A., Johnson, D., Nagy, L. M., Nicolau, A., Heninger, G. R., & Charney, D. S. (1993). Abnormal adrenergic function in posttraumatic stress disorder. *Archives of General Psychiatry, 50,* 266–274.

Spiegel, D., Hunt, T., & Dondershine, H. E. (1988). Dissociation and hypnotizability in posttraumatic stress disorder. *American Journal of Psychiatry, 145,* 301–305.

Tomkins, S. S. (1962). *Affect, imagery, consciousness, Vol. 1: The positive affects.* New York: Springer.

Tomkins, S. S. (1963). *Affect, imagery, consciousness, Vol. 2: The negative affects.* New York: Springer.

Tomkins, S. S. (1987). Script theory. In J. Aronoff, A. I. Rabin, & R. A. Zucker (Eds.), *The emergence of personality.* New York: Springer.

van der Kolk, B. A., & van der Hart, O. (1989). Pierre Janet and the breakdown of adaptation in psychological trauma. *American Journal of Psychiatry, 146,* 1530–1540.

Wolfe, J. (1989, August). *Types of treatment and treatment selection in PTSD.* Paper presented at Department of Veterans Affairs Conference on Advanced Clinical Skills for PTSD, Baltimore.

Yudofsky, S. C., Stevens, L., Barsa, J., & Williams, D. (1984). Propranolol in the treatment of rage and violent behavior in patients with chronic brain syndromes. *American Journal of Psychiatry, 138,* 218–220.

14

Drama Therapy for the Treatment of Affective Expression in Posttraumatic Stress Disorder

Miller James

David Read Johnson

The language of the theater is often used as a metaphor: We speak of an operating theater, the theater of life, the staging of events, the drama of the moment. Many of the images we use in common language are drawn from what we have seen on stages and screens both great and small. If art is a representation of life, a way that the artist conveys new ideas about our shared world or encourages us to see it anew, then it makes sense to search the arts to see what they offer that can be used to assist the process of emotional renewal.

Those who have sustained emotional injuries while working in the theater of war may be assisted by therapeutic techniques based on a sound understanding of dramatic process. In this concise and deeply evocative description of their work with veterans whose response to emotional trauma includes dissociative defenses, James and Johnson explain how they have set up a theater of hope within which PTSD patients may experiment with the expression of feelings from which knowledge, control, or understanding has been shorn. Their use of theatrical method and metaphor throughout both this chapter and their clinical work may be seen as a way of approaching the inner life of the adult with dignity and safety, even though far removed from the system of treatment in which most of us have been trained.

Echoes of gestalt therapy, play therapy, and image-oriented psychotherapy abound. Viewed solely on the basis of the content of the material produced in such methods of healing, the differences are more salient than the similarities. The link, of course, is through the affect system; in this chapter you will learn new approaches to the release of feelings that otherwise threaten the equilibrium of your patients. Allowed affective freedom, these patients become able to process unconscious material long held out of awareness and to drop defenses that had made them unavailable for more cognitive methods of treatment. –DLN

Over the past thirty years increasing attention has been given to the nature and expression of the emotions (Nathanson, 1987, 1992; Tomkins, 1962, 1963). No longer viewing emotional expression as a mysterious or secondary function of the mind, investigators are studying the complex transformations of emotions that can lead either to a rich and mature emotional life or to feeling states that remain undifferentiated or superficial. Essential distinctions have been defined: *Affects* are primary, physiological expressions innate within the species; *feelings* are states of awareness of affects; and *emotions* are the fully integrated experience of feelings in the context of a person's life history and meaning structure (Basch, 1976; Tomkins, 1962, 1963).

As knowledge regarding the function of the emotions is revealed, interventions can be conceived that aim specifically to increase the capacity to express, regulate, and identify emotions. Nevertheless, most psychotherapists are unaware that theories of acting may contribute to their work; the methods used by actors to create representations of authentic emotion have much to offer therapists interested in developing treatments for impairments in emotional expression. In this chapter, we will describe our efforts to influence the emotional life of Vietnam combat veterans suffering from posttraumatic stress disorder through drama therapy based on acting theory.

We will first present the major theories of acting derived from the work of Konstantin Stanislavski. These methods will be linked to a system of treatment for the emotional impairment in posttraumatic stress disorder and then illustrated in three clinical examples showing the direct application of drama therapy to affective expression.

APPROACHES TO EMOTION IN THE THEATER

Theater has from its beginnings been a significant means by which civilizations symbolized and represented traumatic experience. Since the first moment when an actor stepped out of the chorus and spoke alone on the stage at Delphi, theater artists have been engaged in the exploration, understanding, and development of methodologies for the expression and regulation of emotion. For centuries, the theater profession has explored and practiced various ways of helping the actor become emotionally truthful and alive in a rich and full way. Theories of acting have ranged widely across a spectrum of orientation to emotion (Fink, 1990). Aristotle offered the first theory of drama in the *Poetics* (1968), proposing that the purpose of theater is to purge the audience of pity and terror through catharsis. While catharsis-oriented approaches to acting have emphasized the actor's capacity for intense emotional expression, the other extreme has involved more emotionally distant approaches that have emphasized the intellectual or educative function of the theater. The best example of this approach is that of Brecht, who believed that theater should enhance the audience's ability to reflect on the drama, through what he called the *alienation effect* (Willett, 1964). In his incisive book, *Catharsis in Healing, Ritual, and Drama* (1979), Scheff has reviewed the range of approaches to emotion and the issue of catharsis in the theater, and has pointed out their relevance and similarity to psychotherapeutic strategies. The conflict between direct and indirect approaches to emotion has occupied theater artists throughout the 20th century. Contrasting schools of thought have produced lively debate that parallels the contrasting approaches to the treatment of emotional conditions. Our search for a new way of approaching posttraumatic stress disorder will be rewarded by study of the major theories of acting, beginning with the modern master, Stanislavski.

STANISLAVSKI'S CONTRIBUTIONS TO THE STUDY OF EMOTION

Konstantin Stanislavski (1863–1938) was an actor, director, and writer who is without parallel in the modern world for his contribution to the art of acting and the understanding of theatrical emotion. In his mature years, Stanislavski provided perhaps his most rich contribution in the form of a comprehensive and systematic articulation of the actor's inner process (Moore, 1965). Stanislavski's experiments represent a process designed to achieve a "conscious means to the subconsciousness" (Moore, 1965, p. 13) and were carried out over a period of forty years. He explored and articulated much of what we now view as the foundation of modern practice in the theater. Over the course of his life, Stanislavski shifted from an approach that managed emotion directly to an indirect approach to emotional representation through physical action and somatic pathways (Mitter, 1992).

Early Model: Affective Memory

Stanislavski knew that actors must not wait for inspiration to hit like a bolt out of the blue but rather have to become fully emotional on cue. It was therefore of practical necessity that actors have at their disposal a method that could be applied consciously to evoke emotion. He therefore developed a technique called *affective memory*, in which the actors prepared themselves by calling up an emotionally upsetting event in their own personal life. Stanislavski was influenced in his thinking by the science of his day—particularly the Russian psychologist Ivan Petrovich Pavlov (1849–1936) and the French psychologist Theodule-Armand Ribot (1839–1916) (Simonov, 1962). Following these investigators, Stanislavski hoped that, by pairing an upsetting memory from the actor's real past with a situation in the text of the play, the appropriate emotion would be triggered when the actor came to that part of the play. The rehearsal process was therefore a process through which the text was associated with an emotional memory in order to produce a conditioned emotional response.

Stanislavski experimented by asking actors to recreate in their imaginations a specific memory from their own lives, directing his actors to focus first on the sensory material of the memory—the visual, auditory, kinesthetic, or olfactory experience of a specific past experience. Once done, and the emotion reexperienced by the actor, the next task was to transfer that emotion to the dramatic circumstances of the play.

This early approach to the portrayal of emotion was ultimately rejected by Stanislavski, whose actors felt constricted by the practice of emotional recall and prolonged analysis of the text. Indeed, it had the effect of diminishing the spontaneous expression of emotion, for his early rehearsal approaches interfered with the actor's abilities to act and improvise. Often it was difficult for the actor to call up the appropriate emotion on cue, despite several attempts at direct association through a number of methods.

Later Model: Physical Actions

Stanislavski hoped to provide the pathway to rich, truthful, human emotional expression through such conscious crafting of action. He came to understand that every important emotional experience leaves its trace on our central nervous system, producing a sensitivity that might react to such stimulation as a dramatic structure. "From many preserved traces of what was experienced, one great condensed, magnified, and deepened memory of emotions of the same nature is formed" (Moore, 1965, p. 51). Each actor contains a well of personal experience that he or she can explore through the given imaginary circumstances of the play. Each actor has an area of sensitivity (a pool of emotional experience) that can be recalled through the similar situations/actions of a particular play. If the stimulus is crafted consciously in the dramatic action, then organic human emotion will be expressed naturally through the actor's body without strain or hysterics.

> He must feel an emotion not only once or twice while he is studying his part, but to a greater or lesser degree every time he plays it, no matter whether it is the first or the thousandth time. Unfortunately this is not within our control. Our subconscious is inaccessible to our consciousness. We cannot enter into that realm. If for any reason we do penetrate into it, then the subconscious becomes conscious and dies.
>
> The result is a predicament; we are supposed to create under inspiration; only our subconscious gives us inspiration; yet we apparently can use this subconscious only through our consciousness, which kills it. Fortunately there is a way out. We find the solution in an *oblique* instead of a direct approach. In the soul of a human being there are certain elements which are subject to consciousness and will. These accessible parts are capable in turn of acting on psychic processes that are involuntary. (Stanislavski, 1961, p. 13)

The Magic If

Stanislavski provided the method to achieve the *oblique* approach to the subconscious. By a simple yet pivotal adjustment, he created a method through which actors are allowed through conscious means to stir the deepest emotions in themselves and allow those emotions to animate the fictitious character created in the presence of the audience. Stanislavski did not ask actors to believe that they *were* the characters in a given play, for that kind of practice both proved difficult and distorted the actors' sense of truth. Instead, as a stimulus to the creation of logical action and indirectly to the display of truthful emotion, he made a supposition: *If you (the actor) were the Prince of Denmark and the ghost of your father came back from the dead and told you that your uncle was a murderer, what would you (the actor) do?*

> Consequently, the secret of the effect of *if* lies first of all on the fact that it does not use fear or force, or make the artist do any-thing. On the contrary, it reassures him through its honesty, and encourages him to have confidence in a supposed situation. It arouses an inner and real activity, and does this by natural means. (Stanislavski, 1961, p. 44)

Physical Actions

In addition, Stanislavski did not ask actors what would they *feel*, but rather what they might *do* in the given imaginary circumstances if these were real. Stanislavski instructed actors to create a role out of the building blocks of physical and mental *activity*. He focused the actors' attention on the physical actions their characters required in order to perform their roles. He found that a detailed understanding and performance of these actions evoked in actors the relevant emotional state. Feeling followed bodily sensation and physiological arousal. Stanislavski was quite surprised by this discovery, which seemed counterintuitive: "the small truth of physical actions stirs the great truth of thoughts, emotions, experiences" (Moore, 1965, p. 23).

CONTRASTING INTERPRETATIONS: STRASBERG AND MEISNER

In the 1930s, the Group Theater under the direction of Harold Clurman, Lee Strasberg, and Cheryl Crawford (Clurman, 1975) took the lead in introducing the concepts and methods of Stanislavski to American audiences. The Group Theatre split into two basic systems that have influenced most contemporary American theater professionals, the first established by Lee Strasberg at his studio in New York City and known as the "method school" (Vineberg, 1991), and the other developed by Sanford Meisner at the Neighborhood Playhouse theater school in New York. For the past few decades these two schools have influenced the training of most actors, directors, teachers, and other theater artists who now practice in the United States. Each of these schools defines acting in specific terms and approaches practice in different ways. The concepts that most concern us here are the affective memory approaches of the method school and the imaginative/daydreaming process of the Meisner school.

The Method

The affective memory approach of the method school asks actors to recall their own emotional reactions to situations analogous to those appearing in the dramatic text and to apply their own personal emotions directly to the text. Strasberg focused almost exclusively on the early affective memory work outlined by Stanislavski, describing his approach succinctly in this passage:

> The best description of affective memory is in Proust's *Swann's Way*. That's how it works. You do not start to remember the emotion, you start to remember the place, the taste of something, the touch of something, the sight of something, the sound of something, and you remember that as simply and as clearly as you can. You touch the things, in your mind, but with the senses alive. (Vineberg, 1991, p. 107)

Strasberg expanded Stanislavski's conditioned response model to include free association as influenced by the psychoanalytic method of the time. Actors are encouraged to drift through their inner thoughts until something paralleling their theatrical role emerges, whereupon they focus on the image in more detail. This approach is often criticized because it directs the attention of the actor inward rather than toward the interpersonal interactions within the play. Elia Kazan wrote, "You see the worst misuse of emotional recall in actors who are really playing with something in themselves — not with the person in the scene. There is this glazed, unconnected look in their eyes and you know they're somewhere else" (Vineberg, 1991, p. 107).

Meisner Technique

The Meisner approach to theater is based on the assertion that "To act is to do and live truthfully under imaginary circumstances." This deceptively simple description of the art of acting can be broken down into two areas of study — *dramatic action* and *moment*.

The imaginative/daydreaming approach of the Meisner school assumes that the life experience of the actor provides an emotional history residing naturally in the body of the actor. It is not as important for the actor to remember actual life events as to be involved fully in the imaginative circumstances of the play. Following Stanislavski's later work, Meisner focused the actor on physical and psychological actions in the scene in order to evoke feeling states in the actor, who remains open to the potential meanings of these actions. Sanford Meisner writes:

> In other words, what I am saying is that what you're looking for is not necessarily confined to the reality of your life. It can be in your imagination. If you allow it freedom — with no inhibitions, no proprieties — your imagination is, in all likelihood, deeper and more persuasive than the real experience. So (emotional) preparation is a kind of daydreaming. It is daydreaming. It's daydreaming which causes a transformation in your inner life. (Meisner & Longwell, 1987, p. 79)

Thus, the actions of the play will draw on the "pools of emotion" that already exist in the actor. Thoughts, words, emotions, visual images, and affiliated sensory experiences will come to the actor's consciousness as a result of the physical embodiment of the imaginative actions. This done, and the attention of the actor placed on the other actors in the scene, the moment-to-moment interaction will be rich in emotion. In contrast to the method school, the Meisner approach to emotional expression is indirect, as described here by William Esper:

> Affective Memory means going back to a past experience, and it has a lot of problems. First of all, you have to teach the actor to do an Affective Memory. You don't have to teach anyone how to daydream. Next, you often run into a lot of resistance with an Affective Memory because the actor may not want to go back to it. You cannot keep going back to re-create your mother's funeral for thirty years. That's not healthy, it is not good for the actor. You don't need to do it either, because when your mother died it created an area of sensitivity to loss in you and that is what you need — that area of sensitivity. Then any daydream that plays on loss, losing something precious to you, is going to emotionalize you. When you get tired of one daydream, you can invent another. You know that there are just so many emotions that human beings are capable of: fear, anger, pain, joy, humiliation. It doesn't matter where it originates because once it's alive in the actor, it is easy to relate it to the circumstances of the scene. (in Mekler, 1987, p. 27)

The second concept is dramatic *moment*. Meisner was able to articulate and demonstrate that what actors feel on stage does not depend on them but rather on what is done to them emotionally by the other actor in the relationship. To attract the quicksilver of emotion the actor must achieve a state of concentration/attention that is totally involved with the other actor and away from self. Inspiration and emotional truth are not within the conscious control of the actor and should never be of self-conscious concern. Attention to the other actor intensifies participation in the imaginary circumstances and grounds the dramatic action, thus increasing the possibility of an authentic emotional response. If the actor is successful in the habitual performance of the appropriate action and can achieve full attention on the other actor in the scene, the result will be a rich and spontaneous emotional quality in the role.

Thus Meisner and Strasberg represent two divergent approaches to emotional preparation by the actor. Now let us examine the application of these principles to the treatment of posttraumatic stress disorder.

TRAUMA AND ALEXITHYMIA

It seems fairly well established that traumatic life experience interferes with the healthy development of the expression and regulation of emotion. Krystal (1988) has led the way in describing how psychological trauma can produce *alexithymia*, the inability to symbolize or represent emotional states in words. Krystal notes that alexithymic individuals often express their emotions in somatic forms, at the physiological level of affects, with minimal verbalization. Their emotions tend to be undifferentiated, vague and nonspecific; thus different emotional states such as sadness and fear are not readily distinguishable. Shame, in particular, seems to dominate (Stone, 1992). Lane and Schwartz (1987) have posited a developmental sequence of emotional awareness from which we may infer that alexithymic individuals operate emotionally at lower developmental levels. Their work is derived from the cognitive developmental theories of Piaget (1951) and Werner and Kaplan (1963), who have described the normative process through which bodily states are translated into images and then words (the microgenetic principle). It is not clear what biological or psychological mechanism is responsible for the fundamental impairment seen in alexithymia. It is possible that traumatic experience establishes a conditioned fear response to certain stimuli (both cognitive and emotional) that may serve as a powerful inhibitor of imagery. This inhibition must be overcome if the treatment of alexithymia is to succeed in helping patients access, identify, and express their emotions appropriately (Johnson, 1987).

Approaches to the treatment of posttraumatic stress disorder include both abreaction of emotion and insight, in proportions that vary in parallel with the theories of acting discussed above. Therapeutic strategies based on abreaction or catharsis attempt to access emotion directly as if to allow a release or purging of the mind. Dionysian in spirit, these approaches attempt to weaken the defenses against emotional expression in order to allow suppressed emotion to surface. Such catharsis was a significant element in early psychoanalytic therapy, the sodium amytal interview, and hypnotic age regression, all of which were used to treat posttraumatic stress disorder; it also operates with great effectiveness in Moreno's (1945) psychodrama.

In contrast, other approaches more Apollonian in spirit have argued that neither purging nor catharsis provides permanent relief, and that insight, cognitive integration, and learning are more powerful tools for healing. Freud turned away from catharsis and hypnosis when he declared that abreaction served more as an aid to memory than a true purge. Cognitive-behavioral treatments for PTSD have emphasized the establishment of cognitive control over traumatic material (Meichenbaum, 1977). These approaches view emotional constriction as a reaction to the fear of being overwhelmed by memory, and thus predict the return of normal emotional reactivity once safety is established.

DRAMA THERAPY METHODS IN RELATION TO EMOTIONAL EXPRESSION

Both of these approaches to emotion may be identified in the theories and methods of drama therapy that emerged in the 1940s—notably the system of role-playing within a therapeutic setting introduced by Moreno (1945). In this form, the Director (therapist) attempts to bring suppressed emotions to the fore by using role-play to remind the client of the problematic or traumatic situation with real people from the past. Psychodrama, like hypnosis or method acting, is a direct approach to emotion and catharsis.

In contrast, the developmental method of drama therapy (Johnson, 1982, 1986, 1992) emphasizes a more indirect method in which feeling-states of a more general nature are evoked in the client, and emotionally laden situations at some distance from the actual real-life ones are portrayed. This method is consistent with Scheff's (1979) proposal that the greatest potential for healing occurs at the point of *aesthetic distance*, which he defines as the midpoint between states of emotional immersion and cognitive distance. At aesthetic distance, one is simultaneously involved in the experience and able to keep it in perspective. Most trauma victims are unable to achieve aesthetic distance, instead fluctuating between states of flooding (i.e., under-distanced) and numbing (i.e., over-distanced). Treatment of their affective expression requires a technique that helps them achieve an intermediate level of emotional distance. In the developmental method, metaphoric and imaginative situations are used to diverge from the traumatic material, while offering analogues of the trauma. The skillful therapist maintains aesthetic distance by modulating the level of arousal and awareness within the session. As with Stanislavski's method of physical actions and Meisner's focus on the other actor, the developmental method utilizes physical movement, sound, and interpersonal interaction as the context to ground the expression of emotion. Once immersed in the immediate context of action and the presence of the other, the actor/patient will respond with appropriate emotion.

CLINICAL APPLICATIONS OF DRAMA THERAPY IN EMOTIONAL WORK

Our approach to trauma victims is consistent with the Meisner technique for emotional expression (James & Johnson, in press), based on therapeutic and aesthetic considerations of the clinical challenge they present. In this system of treatment, we help trauma victims work with their inner experiences and associated intense emotions (particularly shame) in a manner that protects them from becoming overwhelmed. Many of these patients fear that any symbolizing process may evoke a reexperiencing of the trauma, for the very act of replaying scenes reminiscent of their traumatic event may give rise to intense anxiety, an effect heightened by the physicality of dramatic role-playing. It is our belief that the Meisner approach to emotional expression allows the patient the greatest amount of control and safety.

Most of the Vietnam combat veterans who come to our center have told us that they avoid family events capable of triggering intense emotion, like birthday parties, weddings, and holidays. As a consequence, the trauma victim becomes cut off from the world of others. We use the theater as the medium through which patients may reconnect affect and experience in a safe and contained way, and then communicate that experience to their families and to the larger community so that they may gain acceptance. This task is consistent with the philosophy of the entire treatment program (Johnson, Feldman, Southwick, & Charney, 1994).

Our treatment takes place in a specialized inpatient program designed for Vietnam veterans who are suffering from posttraumatic stress disorder. These veterans participate in a variety of modalities of treatment, including individual, family, and group psychotherapy, psychoeducation, community service, as well as art, music, poetry, and drama therapies, over the course of four months. In the first phase of the program they review their traumatic experiences in depth and confront the negative consequences of their adaptation to the trauma. In the second phase of treatment they turn their attention to the future and prepare to make changes in their lifestyles in order to make room for new skills, attitudes, and relationships.

RELATIONSHIP LAB

During the treatment program at the National Center the drama therapist and patients meet two hours a week for the Relationship Lab. The drama therapist makes it clear that what the group members are expected to do is to provide their story: their feelings, thoughts, memories, dreams, and hopes for the future. The drama therapist asks the group what they want their wives, children, parents, and friends to know about the Vietnam combat veteran diagnosed with PTSD and their struggle to come home to the world. The drama therapist records their answers to these questions without judgment and encourages the group to express whatever occurs to them in that moment. Typically group members respond with answers like: "my inner pain of being forgotten; what it was like to come home and be spit on; what it is like to lose your innocence; how I feel like a stranger even in my family; that I feel betrayed; that I walk on a razor's edge; that I can't let go of the dead I carry inside; that I love my wife and children; that I am trying to make my life better but it is not easy; I am a human being not a monster; I hurt inside; and I am scared." After this articulation of purpose and focus of the work, we follow a four-stage process.

Stage 1. Identifying Relationships

Improvisational scene work is the format that is used in exploring the object relationships of the trauma group. The therapist asks the group to provide examples of *relationships*. The group responds by offering pairs of potential relationships to explore. Examples include doctor-patient, teacher-student, police-criminal, and more affect-laden family relationships like mother-son, father-son, and husband-wife. The therapist lists the relationships on a sheet of paper and then helps the group choose a specific relationship to examine.

The potential relationships that can be crafted with dramatic events, points of view, actions, and improvisation are limitless. The internal object relations that make up the Vietnam combat veteran's inner cast of characters come from his childhood past, adolescence, Vietnam experience, and more recent relationships: dead buddies, other soldiers in his past, boom-boom girls from good times on leave, generals, politicians from the past, the "new guy," the children that were killed, the Viet Cong, hippies, fathers, mothers, brothers, present wives, children, friends, therapists, bosses, the inner child that they once were, the teenager who was idealistic and patriotic, the beast inside that kills for pleasure, body parts, weapons, the jungle, the mosquitoes, water buffalo, monkeys, lizards, ants — all exist in the inner world of the war trauma victim. Each group member has a different story to tell about what it means to carry the burden of war trauma. Each group has a unique inner landscape.

What is striking in our experience is the very limited number of role possibilities that the trauma group members initially provide and how stereotypical their representations tend to be. This may reflect an inner world that is frozen, rigid, and constricted as a result of their traumatic experience. Encouraging the rediscovery of forgotten aspects of self in the internal world begins even in this early stage of role-playing. For instance, the group may be polled for different ways a father and son might talk other than destructively, or the therapist may ask, "How else could the husband behave in this scene?" The drama therapist encourages the exploration of the widest range of role, dramatic event, and feeling. The transitional space of daydream and imagination simultaneously contain representations from the traumatic past, relationships of the present, and potential relationships of the future.

Stage 2. Imagining the Action

Once the relational pair has been chosen, the next step is to create the *event* that connects these two characters in the given circumstances of the story. The event is the reason that these two characters are interacting. The therapist does not impose the given circumstances of the scene onto the group but rather allows the group to provide all of the material and then judge what material might be most beneficial to explore.

Preparation of the patients' emotional state involves an active process of imagery. We ask the trauma victims to *actively* imagine themselves in different situations. Rather than asking them to tell us what *did* happen to them, we ask them to imagine what *could* happen. Once trauma victims ask what could happen they can begin to daydream. It is our experience that this is very difficult for trauma victims at first. They tend to be obsessed with their own traumatic past and terrified of their own inner life/imagination. However, forcing their attention back to remember the death of a buddy is not only difficult, but unnecessary for our purpose. The real event of watching a buddy die in combat creates an area of sensitivity around loss in the mind of the trauma victim. By carefully crafting the imaginative relationships and dramatic events, a *dramatic container* is created that can attract the affect of loss already present in the trauma victim, hence the traumatic material is approached indirectly.

Thus the therapist moves group members away from the real autobiographical events of their lives and encourages them to imagine what *could* happen between, for instance, a father and son. The group is encouraged to make up the event, not be held hostage by their personal past but to enter into a transitional space by creating events that hold potential. The therapist writes down group members' responses on a sheet of paper, listening for the underlying themes, issues, and feelings that are provoked by this daydreaming process.

It is our experience that initially Vietnam combat veterans respond with events that reflect negative and abusive interactions and feelings. Examples of potential events in the father-son relationship have included that the son wrecked the car, the father has been drinking and beats his wife, the father missed his son's high school graduation, the father lost his job, or that the son got his girl friend pregnant. These spontaneously provided events reflect themes of abandonment, abuse, and violence. The feelings that are stimulated in the patient group are hopelessness, rage, fear, and remorse.

As the patient group sits, daydreams, and shares these imaginative events, strong emotions begin to brew in the group. The therapist can offer divergent directions for the group by pointing out that they are offering only the negative potential in the father-son relationship and can challenge them to create more positive potential events that could take place in this relational pair.

Long before anyone actually acts out a scene, the group slowly crafts the role-play with the facilitation of the drama therapist. This process warms up the players emotionally and provides information to the therapist about areas of emotional sensitivity in the group. From the list of potential events the therapist chooses one that seems most salient to the group. The event is best when it stimulates strong emotion in both characters of the scene. The task of the therapist is to observe the group and recognize areas of exploration that have meaning and emotional depth. In the Vietnam combat group it is not difficult to observe how emotion is held in the body: their rigid postures and muscle tension are obvious. The therapist observes the group to see when dramatic events bring them to life emotionally and when the group is filled with unexpressed feeling.

Stage 3. Establishing Point of View

The third step of dramatic crafting that takes place before the players actually act out a scene has to do with determining the *point of view* that each character has of the dramatic event and the given circumstances. If the scene is about a father and son and the son's decision to enter into the armed service, what views do each of the characters have about these circumstances? The therapist asks two veterans to take the stage. The therapist then asks the group, What is each character's attitude regarding the son going into the armed service? What might the father think about his son joining the army? Typical responses in this circumstance for the father's character might be: "The father will kill him before he allows his son to join the army," "he is terrified for his son's life," or "he does not want his son to make the same mistakes that he did." Next the group might articulate the son's point of view by saying: "I want to be like my father," "I am a man now capable of my own decisions," or "I want to seek my own adventure." Organic conflict is created in the scene when the points of view taken by each character are contradictory. The above examples are just a few of the possibilities in these circumstances. Many sessions could be devoted to exploring the father-son relationship alone, with all of the emotional possibilities that this relationship implies. It is important for the therapist to help the group articulate the various points of view as strongly as possible, to capture the point of view in strong language that has meaning for the character and actor.

Stage 4. Enactment

The fourth and final step in creating the improvisational scene now turns toward the living out of the dramatic circumstances in *action*. If the group has properly prepared the crafting of the dramatic events and point of view through the daydreaming process, the improvisations will be natural, real, and emotionally rich. The two veterans that have been asked to role play have been listening to the group articulate their various points of view and are already imagining actions that they might play. The characterizations are a combination of many group members' ideas and inclinations, and therefore do not exactly match the actors' own real experiences. This separation between the past reality and the current role will be the critical factor in evoking an authentic emotional reaction.

The given circumstances of the scene suggest actions that can be played by the characters. The therapist now articulates for the characters what they are supposed to do. Actions are the building blocks of theater, what the actor does on the stage in relationship to the other characters. Actions are articulated to the actors by the therapist. Actions may by physical or psychological. To pick up a cup or open a door is a simple physical action. Psychological actions may be to impress, to convince, to make amends, to take charge, to appease, or to warn. In the example of the father-son scene, if the father's point of view is that he will not tolerate his son's choice to enter the service, then his overall action might be to simply stop his son from joining the army. The father in the scene can achieve his overall objective by using a number of simple actions. The father may *reason* with his son, *plead* for his son's understanding, or *forbid* his son's choice. The father may utilize these three actions in any order and at any time in the scene.

The son in the scene may have for his overall action that he wants to become a man. Tools or actions that the son may play in the scene with his father might be to reason, plead, convince, explain, pacify, or demand. Once the therapist has articulated to the players appropriate actions for the given circumstances in the scene, then the improvisation can begin.

The two actors then act out the scene that the group has created. The therapist encourages them to perform their actions within these dramatic circumstances *as if* they were real. The therapist frames this role-play as an experiment to see if there is any truth in the scene. The actors are to focus their attention on the other actor in the scene and to respond truthfully, as they feel in the moment. If the preparation of the scene has been crafted organically and truthfully, then all the group members, not only the actors in the role-play, will have been free associating around the given circumstances and will be able to benefit from the role-play. As the actors act out the scene, the therapist may stop the role-play to allow others in the group to try out the characters or to ask the characters to switch roles. The therapist can introduce different group members into the role-play to allow them to explore their own feelings. The therapist may also stop the role-play to poll the group as to their thoughts/feelings on the scene. For example, the therapist may ask the group, What may be in the father's mind at this point in the scene, or what could the son do now to achieve his goal?

Paradoxically, it is not uncommon for trauma victims in this situation to spontaneously confess to the group specific and real traumatic memories from their lives. Many times, for instance, group members may describe specific incidents that have happened with their own fathers or incidents that have taken place with their own children. One veteran remarked after a father and son scene that his son was thinking about joining the army and that he was terrified that his son would make the same mistake that he had made in going to Vietnam. Our experience has shown that at this point the therapist may poll the group for similar experiences and will be rewarded with many spontaneous and emotional memories from the group.

DEVELOPING EMOTIONAL SKILLS: EXAMPLES

The following are three examples that illustrate the application of dramatic action, focus of attention on the other, and the sensitivity to the imaginative circumstances that allow for the development and expression of mature emotion in patients suffering from posttraumatic stress disorder.

Example One

One Relationship Lab consisting of eight veterans began with the drama therapist asking: What if you did not have all of these problems? What if you did not have PTSD? What if you did not have pain in your legs, or fear of crowds, or hopelessness, or lack of trust in authority or faith in others? What if your life had not gone in the direction it has; what might you be doing right now with your life? What would you rather be doing than getting treatment for memories of the war in Vietnam? The silence that fell on the group indicated they had been caught off guard by the supposition of the therapist. One veteran protested vehemently, "What is the point of thinking about what isn't real?" The drama therapist gently restated the question: "What if what I am asking you *could* be real, and we could reach in and remove the memories that you live with from the war, what would you be doing?"

The veterans seemed to have a visible physical response, as they began to daydream themselves out of the past and into a "what if" situation, a potential. There was a sense of playful participation as freely flowing associations were expressed and shared in the group. One veteran wrote on his paper that he would open a florist shop, another wrote that he would become an archeologist, one acknowledged an interest in divinity school, and one group member said sarcastically that he would run for president. Group members laughed, and a great deal of interest was evident in this seemingly ridiculous supposition. There was a burst of energy as the group debated whether or not a Vietnam veteran could ever

run for president. One-half of the group was vehement in their convic-
tion that this could never happen, that the public would never allow such
a thing, that it was so far-out, no one would ever vote for a Vietnam
veteran. An almost equal number in the group was willing to entertain
the idea that not only it could happen but it would be a good thing. The
drama therapist then asked the group to silently imagine themselves
giving a speech to a group of voters. This was done by guiding them
though real imaginative physical actions, i.e., see yourself leave the ho-
tel, get into a limousine, arrive at the auditorium, confer with aides,
discuss security with staff secret service, enter the auditorium and face
the crowd to give their speech to the audience. Each member of the
group was then asked to stand up in front of the other veterans (who
were now the voting public) and give a speech asserting their particular
agendas. The atmosphere in the room was playful, supportive, fun, and
the group enjoyed the improvisation. Associatively linked actions, images, improvised dialogue, and emotion came spontaneously and without strain within the dramatic context. Where the group had been depressed, fearful, hostile, the physio-affective expression was now
playful, light, spontaneous, and more tolerant of emotional complexity
and ambiguity. The group had a sense of intentionality of emotion,
energy, and creative collaboration.

The agendas that were asserted by the veteran/candidates were varied
but represented a consistent theme. The veteran candidates were concerned with poverty, lack of empowerment in the government structure,
homelessness, drug and alcohol abuse, poor health care for veterans and
their families, and the appropriate use of the American military power in
international conflict. A clear theme of the use of power and the relationship to authority was evident in the content of the improvisational forms,
reflecting core issues derivative of combat experiences: mistakes in combat
made by commanding officers based on lack of information, bad intelligence, or poor judgment that had resulted in needless loss of the lives.

At this point in the session, one veteran offered his own supposition.
He wondered if the Vietnam veteran candidate would ever be elected
after having been treated for PTSD. This clear reference to the theme of
stigma set off another burst of energy in the group, which signaled to the
drama therapist that this was a meaningful area of sensitivity for this
particular group. The drama therapist assumed that each of the group
members had had real experiences of being shamed and humiliated. The
drama therapist at this point did not ask the group to share their real
experiences with stigmatizing events, but rather, paradoxically, focused
the work of the group away from their personal experiences and onto
what could have happened to the imaginatively created character/candi-

date. The validation for this silently held hypothesis came from the group through the content of the scene work. Many references to the voting public being the "same people who welcomed us home from Vietnam" were spontaneously brought into the improvised dialogue between the candidate and his advisors as they decided how to handle a leak to the press regarding the candidate's psychiatric treatment for war-related memories. This scene evoked a moving group discussion as members spontaneously shared specific traumatic situations that they had suffered when they arrived home from Vietnam. The shame derived from their stigmatization by an American public that did not want to hear from the soldiers of Vietnam now came out in moving detail, with full affect. Many tears were shed, and support from the therapist and other veterans was evident.

This is an example of an aesthetic distance that allowed for the expression and containment of the intense emotions of sadness, loss, and abandonment. The physio-affective nature of dramatic improvisation offered an avenue for emergence of this previously fragmented, diffuse, murky area of emotional sensitivity in the veterans. In this moment, past, present, and future possibilities were integrated in a rich, potentially new representation of self and other against an emotional background of hope and forgiveness.

Example Two

This scene takes place between a Vietnam combat veteran and his son of 13 who are on a fishing trip. The son has become very curious about what his father did in the Vietnam war. During the scene the son describes seeing a "Rambo" film and asks his father: "Is that what war is like, Dad?" The scene required from the father/veteran a strong emotional response of fear that his own son might be seduced by the images of glory in war and try to follow in his father's ill-fated footsteps, and strong resolve to make his son understand that war is not what is portrayed in the movies or on television commercials. Though the group members found the theme very interesting, the first time it was portrayed the scene did not come to life, was without feeling, and both actors in the scene were frustrated. The drama therapist began by questioning the father/veteran in the scene.

THERAPIST Doug, you seem inhibited and shut down. When I first talked to you about the scene you had an emotional reaction, even just imagining the circumstances. Since we have started the scene you have been flat emotionally. Are you feeling stuck?

DOUG   Yes, I don't have any children and I wonder if that is why I can't get into this.

It appeared to the therapist that the action for the scene was not clear to the actors. He suspected that the scene needed a much stronger dramatic action to contain the depth of the emotion. The drama therapist asked the two players to perform the scene again.

THERAPIST   Doug, what are you doing in the scene?

DOUG   I am telling my son what it is like to be in war.

THERAPIST   I think I have made a mistake in not giving you a more specific and simple action to play in this scene. Let's try the scene again, and this time try to *confess* a difficult and shameful truth about yourself for a loved one. This is for the purpose of *redirecting* your son's thinking about the reality of this situation. Do you know how to confess something?

DOUG   I think so.

THERAPIST   Try to confess a painful truth about yourself.

The father and son try the scene again, and this time it appears to be more spontaneous, with more energy, and Doug seems to be more involved emotionally. There still remains something that is inhibiting the scene. The drama therapist notices that the focus of Doug's attention seems to be within himself and not on the other actor in the scene.

THERAPIST   Doug, try it again, with the same action, but this time put your focus of attention on your son, carefully look for the effect of your confession on your son's behavior.

DOUG   I'm not sure what you mean.

THERAPIST   What do you want your son to do with your confession?

DOUG   I want him to see my view, to be thoughtful and realize that war is not romantic.

THERAPIST   What would your son do that would let you know that you achieved your goal?

DOUG   He would be more afraid . . .

THERAPIST   What would you see in his behavior?

DOUG   He would be more thoughtful, serious, then I would know he was getting it.

THERAPIST   OK, Doug, then watch your son to see if you are successful in your objective. Try the scene again but don't look away from your son.

Doug tries the scene again, but has difficulty keeping his attention on his partner. The drama therapist notices that Doug is self-conscious and attending to his internal emotional state. The action seems to be specific and simple to do, but the focus of attention needs to be placed on the other actor in the scene to allow the self-consciousness to diminish. On the third try the drama therapist stands behind Doug and gently encourages him to place his attention on the other actor. Every time Doug breaks away from the interpersonal contact the drama therapist says in his ear, "look at him Doug." After a short pause, Doug's face flushes, as he begins to cry openly. He clearly comes to life emotionally as waves of grief, fear, and shame fill the dramatic action of the scene. Doug becomes momentarily afraid of the wave of emotion animating the dramatic action, and he again breaks the contact with the other actor.

DOUG   I . . . I . . .
THERAPIST   (*Still standing behind him, gently*) Let it come Doug, continue your action and look at your son.

Doug continues the dialogue of the scene and tells his son the story of seeing a young soldier die on the field and how he was not able to save the life of his comrade. This story is not a real experience from Doug's past. Both players are focused on each other, the veteran playing the son also becomes filled with emotion. The other group members are silent but completely attentive. Following the scene, Doug appeared drained but relieved, saying as he wiped his eyes, "Wow." In subsequent portrayals of this scene, Doug was able to become more proficient in playing this simple action, and his mastery reduced the fear of the emotion that the action called forth in the given circumstances of the play. Doug became more spontaneous, less self-conscious, and each time the scene was performed it was filled with rich, truthful emotion.

In this example, both the clarification of a dramatic action and the gentle insistence that the patient focus on the other actor produced the natural sensation of deeply felt emotion, which otherwise had been inhibited by the patient's avoidant defenses. Doug's relationship with his wife had been severely damaged by his inability, during emotional interactions with her, to stay focused on her and not withdraw. He reported that the work in drama therapy had been good practice for communicating emotionally with her.

Example Three

The topic of another scene in the Relationship Lab was an incident when a company of North Vietnamese soldiers overruns a marine unit, requiring hand to hand combat. What should have been a powerfully emotional event appeared flat, stale, and pretentious in the initial scene performed by three patients. One actor, Paul, who played the combat veteran in hand to hand combat, seemed particularly stilted, empty, and emotionless. The sense of heightened human power, the thrill of combat, was missing.

THERAPIST   Paul, can you tell me what you are doing in this scene?

PAUL   I'm acting out the combat.

THERAPIST   Paul, I think I have given you too general and vague an action to play. Let's see if we can craft together an imaginary situation that will suggest an action that you can play. Whom are you performing this movement for?

PAUL   (*After a pause*) I guess for the audience.

THERAPIST   Ah, here is a problem. What if we forget about the audience, and we think of someone else whom you could perform this kind of combat dance for. What if you imagined that you were before the God of War. Imagine that he is sitting on a throne and you approach him with your tribute of combat?

Paul becomes silent, his jaw sets, and there is an emotional response to this imaginative circumstance. At this point Paul responds to this imaginative supposition.

PAUL   I would bring my sword to him.

A yardstick is found that serves as a sword for Paul and the physical action of the scene is adjusted to begin with the presentation of the sword to the God of War for the blessing of the combat. This time as the scene begins Paul's movement is mesmerizing. He becomes filled with rage, and his movements become graceful and fluid. He appears cold and indifferent as he mimes the hand to hand killing of an enemy soldier. His eyes remind one of the sharks that you might see circling in the aquarium, cold and black. He now moves with freedom and emotional power that are contained and expressed by the action. All watching the scene held their breath as Paul performed his dance of killing.

Paul's emotional expression was produced by having him place his focus of attention on another character within the imaginative circumstance. The shifting of this object from actual memories of Vietnam to a metaphorical God of War provided the increased distance that moved Paul into the realm of aesthetic distance, allowing the emergence of the deeply held emotional state. Paul had been viewed as an automaton by his family; he had equated showing emotion with committing murder.

As a result of his work in the program, he made significant strides toward becoming emotionally alive, progress that was noted and appreciated by his family.

CONCLUSION

Our goal is to aid our patients in accessing, identifying, and regulating their emotional expression. Their condition of alexithymia has shut them down emotionally, and they are left with explosively aroused kinesthetic experience that is directed either outward in acts of aggression or inward in somatization and numbing. Pathways from kinesthetic arousal to imagery to authentic verbalization appear to be blocked. The imaginative container of the dramatic action may offer the veterans and other traumatized individuals a link to this inner symbolizing process and a safe and at times pleasurable method by which to express a more integrated picture of their inner experience. Our efforts are not restricted to the retelling of the story as it happened in reality, but to embracing the potential of unintegrated aspects of self, and through the group process to enhancing access to symbolic pathways of experience. Patients are invited to participate in a metaphorical space where they can begin to remember their own story and experience themselves as the locus of potential growth and transformation. This procedure opposes the maladaptive effects of posttraumatic stress disorder, which maps present experience onto past schemas of traumatic experience.

We have attempted to demonstrate that one way to access and transform diffuse, fragmented, and painful aspects of self and memory is through the method of physical dramatic actions. An approach to emotion that begins through the body may allow feelings to form and then be expressed safely through dramatic metaphor. It is assumed that the container of imaginative dramatic action organically attracts and expresses the person's inner areas of emotional sensitivity. Approaching emotion indirectly provides safety and allows the victim to reclaim and play with that emotion in all its potentiality.

In posttraumatic stress disorder, emotional work such as we have described can have a significant impact not only on individual patients' capacities to process and regulate their emotions, but on their relationships with family and friends. Intimacy is often severely impeded by the sequelae of posttraumatic stress disorder, since intimate relationships involve the emotions and their expression so fundamentally. The reenactment in a therapeutic laboratory setting of emotionally laden relationships, supported by the guidance of the drama therapist, offers patients an opportunity to explore and renew their commitment to be human, that is, to feel again.

REFERENCES

Aristotle. (1968). *Poetics*. (D. W. Lucas, Ed.). Oxford: Clarendon Press.

Basch, M. F. (1976). The concept of affect: A re-examination. *Journal of the American Psychoanalytic Association, 24*, 759–777.

Clurman, H. (1975). *The fervent years*. New York: Knopf.

Fink, S. (1990). Approaches to emotion in psychotherapy and theatre: Implications for drama therapy. *International Journal of Arts in Psychotherapy, 17*, 5–18.

James, M., & Johnson, D. (in press). Drama therapy in the treatment of PTSD. *Arts in Psychotherapy*.

Johnson, D. (1982). Developmental approaches in drama therapy. *International Journal of Arts in Psychotherapy, 9*, 183–190.

Johnson, D. (1986). The developmental method in drama therapy. *International Journal of Arts in Psychotherapy, 13*, 17–34.

Johnson, D. (1987). The role of the creative arts therapies in the diagnosis and treatment of psychological trauma. *International Journal of Arts in Psychotherapy, 14*, 7–14.

Johnson, D. (1992). The drama therapist in role. In S. Jennings (Ed.), *Drama therapy: Theory and practice, Vol. 2* (pp. 112–136). London: Routledge.

Johnson, D., Feldman, S., Southwick, S., & Charney, D. (1994). The concept of the second generation program in the treatment of posttraumatic stress disorder among Vietnam veterans. *Journal of Traumatic Stress, 7*, 217–236.

Krystal, H. (1988). *Integration and self-healing: Affect, trauma, alexithymia*. Hillsdale, NJ: Analytic Press.

Lane, R. D., & Schwartz, G. E. (1987). Levels of emotional awareness: A cognitive-developmental theory and its application to psychopathology. *American Journal of Psychiatry, 144*, 133–143.

Meichenbaum, D. (1977). *Cognitive behavioral modification*. New York: Plenum.

Meisner, S., & Longwell, D. (1987). *Sanford Meisner on acting*. New York: Random House.

Mekler, E. (1987). *The new generation of acting teachers*. London: Penguin.

Mitter, S. (1992). *Systems of rehearsal*. New York: Routledge.

Moore, S. (1965). *The Stanislavski System*. New York: Viking Press.

Moreno, J. (1945). *Psychodrama: Vols. I & II*. Beacon, NY: Beacon Press.

Nathanson, D. (1987). *The many faces of shame*. New York: Guilford Press.

Nathanson, D. (1992). *Shame and pride: Affect, sex, and the birth of the self*. New York: Norton.

Piaget, J. (1951). *Play, dreams, and imitation in childhood*. New York: Norton.

Simonov, P. V. (1962). *Method of K. S. Stanislavski and the physiology of emotions*. New York: Theatre Arts.

Stanislavski, K. S. (1961). *An actor prepares*. New York: Theater Arts.

Stone, A. (1992). The role of shame in posttraumatic stress disorder. *American Journal of Orthopsychiatry, 62*, 131–136.

Scheff, T. J. (1979). *Catharsis in healing, ritual, and drama*. Berkeley: University of California Press.

Tomkins, S. S. (1962). *Affect, imagery, consciousness, Vol. 1: The positive affects*. New York: Springer.

Tomkins, S. S. (1963). *Affect, imagery, and consciousness, Vol. 2: The negative affects*. New York: Springer.

Vineberg, S. (1991). *Method actors*. New York: MacMillan.

Werner, H., & Kaplan, S. (1963). *Symbol formation*. New York: Basic Books.

Willett, J. (1964). *Brecht on theatre*. New York: Hill & Wang.

15

Emotion and the Psychology of Performance: The Application of Affect Theory to Iconicity

Bruce G. Shapiro

My daughter is an accomplished actress, playwright, and director whose talents became obvious in early childhood. Everybody's children change in college, and we expected that she would leave the world of the theater and take up something reasonable, like psychology. After all, hadn't she been involved in my struggles to understand affect theory? Didn't she have her own private relationship with Silvan Tomkins (who always commented on the variety of her affective expression) and trade stories with him? Surely her interests would shift from the frivolous to the scientific.

In her junior year at Tufts University, she began to spout off about something called "iconicity," a theory of acting, or directing, or something theatrical taught by a new favorite among her professors. Suddenly we were not permitted to use the term "director" for the person who guided actors from their introduction to a script toward the eventual production; this function was now served by an iconicist. Words like "timbre" and "hyperpresence" invaded dinner conversation.

With all the sophistication of a professional therapist used to picking up new systems of thought and working within them in the effort to know a new person, I paid absolutely no attention to this language until my wife made one of her usual, calm statements of appraisal: "Isn't Julie just talking about some way of using affect theory in the theater? Everything she says seems to fit what you and Silvan write about."

Immediately I asked my daughter to explain iconicity much more slowly, at a pace suitable for the very young or the elderly. Bruce Shapiro, a Los Angeles-born actor and director, the author of *Divine Madness and the Absurd Paradox: Ibsen's Peer Gynt and the Philosophy of Kierkegaard*, innocent of formal training in academic psychology, had indeed entered the heart of affect theory even though he thought he was talking about the theater. Just as James and Johnson, in the previous chapter, recognized that the instructions given actors by the great coaches resembled the exhortations of expressive psychotherapists, Shapiro saw the essence of the drama as a matter of affective expression. Julie and I conspired to send him a copy of my book about affect theory, and we started the interchange that resulted in his presentation at the 1994 meeting of the Tomkins Institute, and ultimately, this chapter.

One of the most incisive points Shapiro makes here is the observation that actors experience and express real emotion about something that has not happened to them but to a character created by an author. What makes a character believable must have something to do with both the way that emotion is portrayed and the way it causes affective resonance with the audience. The iconicist responsible for the staging of the drama must ensure that the actors remain in synchrony with both the world created by the author and the effect on the audience of their portrayal of it. He points out that an actor who is uncomfortable expressing affect had better find another occupation, and that the search for authenticity is as important in the theater as it is in every other aspect of life. A narcissistic actor is more concerned with self-portrayal than the world of the character; a great actor must have the same affective flexibility we postulate for the healthy adult.

I have long maintained that the emotionally healthy adult is capable of experiencing the neutral state of no affect, free of the need to express or display affect from internal sources that are unrelated to the world of the moment. This hypothetical person would then be able to respond to any source with whichever of the nine innate affects this source would trigger solely on the basis of its stimulus characteristics. The affect so triggered would last only until noticed, and would lead to effective action in mode and degree suitable to that specific situation. From Shapiro's work we can see that the per-

fect actor is transparent to the playwright's purpose, displaying affect and affecting the audience exactly as scripted. It is the coloration brought by our own lives, complex and variegated as they are,
that makes us less than perfect as people and as actors, but so
fascinating to know and watch.

Because of my personal enjoyment of Shapiro's work, I regret
deeply that he and Tomkins never met. In college, the great psychologist thought his career would be as a playwright; it was from this
background that he developed the concepts of script theory.
Maybe that's why I made the error of thinking my daughter, with all
her knowledge and understanding of this work, would gravitate toward psychology. I guess there's more than one way to know feeling. –DLN

From the point of view of feeling, the actor's craft is the type.
—Oscar Wilde, 1966

The world we perceive is a dream we learn to have from a
script we have not written.
—Silvan S. Tomkins, 1962, p. 13

ACTING BRAINS

Neuroscience and technology have shown that human psychology, particularly patterns of awareness and cognition, is determined not
so much by sensory perception and intellect as by the brain's intrinsic
cadences and celerity. Neuroscientists have yet to ascertain the exact role
this timing plays in the activity of consciousness, but it is generally
acknowledged that these rhythmical characteristics may account for an
individual's dramatic performance tempo. This tempo is the speed at
which one acts upon the self-generated imagery of one's existence, imagery provided by the affect system.

Although there is no way of confirming whether or not humans have
neurological speed limits, the increasing presence of technology in our
intellectual environment may nevertheless be pushing those limits,
thereby causing a human psychological slowdown, a technology-induced
disorder of the affect system. The speed of technology may be surmount-
ing the image-generating capacity of the affect system that is so important to dramatic performance.

Dramatic performance is an innate human capability. It is an individual's capacity to endow one's total self with the form of one's mental creations. In other words, dramatic performance makes actual the perceptions of existence that are registered in the brain as images. Silvan Tomkins (1962) has pointed out the crucial role played by the affect system in the generation of these images. Thus, it is the affect system that provides human beings with the ability to use their natural capability for dramatic performance.

Human beings use dramatic performance to confirm their surroundings and thereby create a common environment for themselves in private and in society. The world in which we live and socially coexist is an agreed-upon world, and dramatic performance is the human venue wherein that agreement is established.

At a certain point in ancient history the idea of god, *theos*, entered the mass psychology of human society, and the human capability for dramatic performance, particularly with regard to action, was appropriated by religion in order to establish a common social environment. This event marked the beginning of *the*ater: a place where the creations or acts of god are viewed. Those individuals employed to portray these deitic acts were called actors, and they were trained to develop their natural capacity for dramatic performance. This theater then manipulated society for many centuries by dominating the human capacity for dramatic performance.

During the late 19th century, and concomitant with the rise of the science of psychology, religion peaked and began a slow decline. At that point, the director emerged like a high priest of the theater, which maintained its hold on human action and society by appropriating psychology as its new religion. The acting "system" of Constantine Stanislavski, the innovative Russian actor, director, and teacher, was preoccupied with psychological notions of character (Moore, 1965). This replacement of psychology for theism lasted for over half a century, peaking in the 1950s in America with the psychoanalytically influenced, system derivative process called "method acting."

In the present age, the theater, particularly with regard to imagery, has been appropriated by technology, which has emerged to reign over our private and common social environments. For some people this new world is an alienating source of anxiety, at least partly because its operating languages and hardware provide a continuously daunting source of stimuli. But, more urgently, technology has effectively displaced and disoriented the affect system by appropriating the image without allowing for any of the actual human interaction necessary to dramatic performance. Ironically, technology has disappropriated dramatic performance by the former's lack of interest in human action and psychology. Thus, the power of dramatic performance to pursue humanity has finally fallen back to the individual after centuries of domination by organized factions within society. However, in order to take full advantage of this power, we must also employ it to overcome the threat technology poses to the affect system.

Throughout history, actors have been those who made a profession of their human capacity for dramatic performance. In order to be effective artists in this new world of technology, those individuals who choose to become actors must concentrate on extending the tempo limitations that the brain, through lack of conditioning, tends to place upon dramatic performance. The new actor must train and exercise the image-generating capacity of the affect system, thereby overcoming in advance the potential damage of technology, while at the same time rehumanizing the art of dramatic performance in order to provide audiences with a similarly empowered capacity for affective imagery.

Actors, using their innate capability for dramatic performance, begin their work by consciously generating some idiosyncratic primary imagery. This primary imagery, rather than simply a response to the actual perceptions of existence, is prompted in the actor by a given set or source of stimuli, commonly a play. The distinction between existential perceptions and those produced by a given set of stimuli separates an individual's natural employment of dramatic performance and an actor's artistic employment of dramatic performance. In order to generate the primary imagery, when actors read and rehearse a play they transcend its dramatic form and learn to experience it instead as a source of stimuli. When cast into this source of stimulation, the actor's brain is prompted to create primary imagery; thus, the brain is really the primary locus of dramatic action. The actor's body and surrounding environment then serve as the stage for a created performance of this primary imagery.

An actor's dramatic performance is an iconic analogue, because its appearance represents some other corresponding, although not identical, object; that object is the idiosyncratic primary imagery generated in the actor's brain in response to the given set of stimuli. A play, or any other dramatic conception or material, may constitute the given set, or source, of stimuli. But the performance analogue that emerges is actually of the stimulated primary imagery and not of the source (or play). The process for developing such a performance is here defined as *iconicity* (Austin, 1971; Matejka & Titunik, 1984; Peirce, 1940).

ICONICITY

Iconicity means *the presence of imagery*. It is a process for the artistic creation of a dramatic performance. By rehearsing actors in the given stimuli of a source, iconicity evolves the performance analogue. This analogue is the virtual, rather than predetermined, outcome of the rehearsal process. Ideally, an audience viewing the performance analogue comes to recognize its initiating source.

Iconicity represents human life as a continuous cycle of stimulus integration. Thus the process is comprised of an integrated sequence of source stimulus conditions called *hyperpresences*. There are four of these hyperpresences (see Table 15.1), each consisting of three multidimensional, diversely related characteristics that integrate sequentially and hermeneutically. The integration is hermeneutic in the cyclical sense, because the actor recurrently encounters the characteristics of the hyperpresences during the intensive rehearsal process. This integration provides for the actor's natural generation of primary imagery and the concomitant creation of the performance analogue.

The four hyperpresences are *identity*, the *text*, the *stage*, and *consciousness*. Identity comprises the source material's overall semantic structure, the primary stimulus for logical thought. Text comprises the pragmatic distinctions of the source material's language, the primary stimulus for the verbal weave that forms and connects the lines of dialogue and patterns of cognition. The stage comprises the interpersonal actions of the source material's characters, the primary stimulus for the spatial and visual composition of the performance. The hyperpresence of consciousness comprises the source material's orchestration of affect, the primary stimulus for the dramatic performance tempos. In rehearsal, during the final hyperpresence of consciousness, the actor autogenously engages the affect system, stimulating emotion and authenticating the acting.

The culminating presence in the process of iconicity is the performance analogue. Thus, although iconicity is committed to its source material, it is always moving the actor away from that source toward the performance analogue and anticipated audience. During a performance, the affect system provides for the empathy that will draw the spectators into the analogue (Nathanson, 1986, 1992). Hence, the performance directs a transition away from the textual source material toward the actors as a source of stimulus for the spectator. Through affective resonance made possible by the spectators' willingness to drop what Nathanson (1986) calls the empathic wall, and the tide of associations to the affect triggered by the actors (Basch, 1983), the audience enters an empathic linkage with the actors. Ideally, this empathic link with the textual stimulus allows the spectator to experience an affect-inspired visual composition or image that constitutes a deep and powerful recognition of the source material. This recognition is the denouement of iconicity.

TABLE 15.1
The Hyperpresences of Iconicity

Each hyperpresence constitutes a set of stimulus conditions. In rehearsal, the actor is conditioned in and integrated through each hyperpresence.

Stimulus Conditions:

I IDENTITY Semantic structure	II TEXT Pragmatics of Dialogue	III STAGE Interpersonal Imagery	IV CONSCIOUSNESS Affect dynamics
Icon	Timbre	Locution	Sites of action
Index	Intensity	Perlocution	Feeling
Symbol	Intonation	Illocution	Emotion

I IDENTITY CHARACTERISTICS
Icon: a character or moment in a play that would be recognizable in any other situation or environment, such as a police officer or delivery boy, the action of shaking hands or kissing.
Index: the character in the play who points or guides the spectators through the action or plot; the character without whom the play would not occur as it does; there can be only one index.
Symbol: a character or an event in the play that discloses, reveals, or can be interpreted as information about the index that would otherwise remain hidden.

II TEXT
Timbre: the verbal quality of a line of dialogue that shows the character's physical or psychological disposition; for example, a character from Checkov's *Swan Song* who wakes up with a hangover and says, "My mouth feels like there's been a whole army camping through it."
Intensity: Intense dialogue focuses on moving the action; the tighter the focus, the more intense the line.
Intonation: Intoned lines are slogans or conventions of speech that comment on the given situation; they may be learned phrases, the ideas of playwright, simulated emotions, even jokes. Neil Simon writes cleverly intoned dialogue.

III STAGE
Locution: an utterance that momentarily isolates the actor in a physical or psychological disposition.
Perlocution: an utterance that accomplishes or hopes for an event or an action.
Illocution: an utterance that comments on or engages the situation.

IV CONSCIOUSNESS
Site of Action: the places in the body where the innate affect program causes bodily effects that can be recognized by both actor and spectator.
Feeling: indicates the actor's awareness that an affect has been triggered or set into action.
Emotion: an actor's understanding or interpretation of the affect based on the character's given set of previous experiences and information about that affect; emotion is actually the end-result of an affect script.

AFFECT THEORY AND THE PRESENCE
OF EMOTION

In the fourth hyperpresence of consciousness, the source material triggers the demeanor of humanness by providing affect to the developing performance analogue. Emotion draws the audience into the performance, where they begin their journey of recognition. A performance devoid of emotion will deaden the audience, leaving them emotionally and intellectually distant and alienated.

Our affects influence us deeply throughout life. They may oppress us, inspire us, interfere with our voice and speech, take our breath away, distort our faces, make us laugh or cry, and so forth. In any given situation, the forces of emotion motivate our actions and reactions. Throughout the 20th century, the interpretation and dramatic representation of the relation between emotion and human action have been dominated by a nostalgia for 19th century Romanticism and by pseudo-psychoanalytic thinking. However, the existential experiences we call emotions are actually the properties of an intricate neurological network called the *affect system*. Silvan S. Tomkins, who first presented this theory in the early 1960s, viewed "affect as the primary innate biological motivating mechanism" (1991, p. 5).*

Affects originate in and operate from their central location deep in the brain. From there, via the body's neural, biochemical, neuronal, and neurochemical infrastructure, the affect system has access to both the external stimuli of the world as they trigger our senses and also the internal brain circuitry of memory and cognition. The affect system also coordinates this external and internal information, enabling a person to achieve a conscious purpose or desired human condition. Tomkins referred to this purpose as the *image*, a blueprint innately created to confront the demands of existence. Finally, the experiences we call feelings and emotions are produced by and comprise the modus operandi of the affect system, enabling us to sustain the self-awareness we call consciousness.

The details of the affect system are extensive and complex, and this explanation of the salient features of the theory is predicated upon their relevance to the present subject. One comes to understand much that is

---

*Tomkins's four-volume study spans over three decades of research and requires careful reading and study. I owe much of my understanding about affect theory to Donald L. Nathanson, Executive Director of the Tomkins Institute in Philadelphia, Pennsylvania, both from his 1992 book *Shame and Pride: Affect, Sex, and the Birth of the Self*, which provides a lucid, comprehensive exploration of the affect system, and from our personal discussions of theory and practice.

essential about affect theory by studying its application to iconicity and dramatic performance.

Any practical application of affect theory is contingent on a basic understanding of the following essential features: (a) the nine affects and their stimulus characteristics, (b) the terminology and characteristics of affect theory, and (c) script theory (not to be confused with what the theater world describes in such terms as dramaturgy or play script analysis.)

Affect and Stimulus

There are nine innate, universal affects. Seven are designated pairs to reflect a heightening of the affect's intensity. The first two affects are positive: *interest-excitement*, and *enjoyment-joy*; a third affect, *surprise-startle*, is neutral and serves only to reset the system so that it may register an oncoming new stimulus; and the remaining six are negative affects: *fear-terror, distress-anguish, anger-rage, shame-humiliation, disgust*, and *dissmell*.

The production of affect is dependent upon some stimulus. That stimulus may come from the physical world outside the body, from the verbal or visual arts, from dreams, from memories, and so forth. The stimulus may originate from a source outside the self, or it may be entirely autogenous. The relation between the affect and its stimulus is not necessarily an equal one, for when a stimulus triggers an affect, that affect in turn amplifies the experience of the stimulus.

Whatever its source or origin, each stimulus occurs at a certain *density* and *gradient*, and it is these qualities of stimulation that determine the amount and type of affect produced. The production of affect depends also and equally on a time signature—the duration of the stimulus as well as how it grows in density. For example, a sudden, dense stimulus like a gun shot will trigger the affect surprise–startle. The sudden high density of stimulation and the equally sudden cessation of that stimulation are responsible for the way an audience feels startled by the unexpected firing of a gun during a play.

This fundamental aspect of affect theory—gradients and densities of stimulus—is of crucial importance to iconicity, particularly the hyperpresence of consciousness. The time/stimulus densities in the source material compose an orchestration of affect. This affect orchestration generates diverse cadence and celerity in the brain, providing a performance tempo for the acting while also serving as a metronome for the entire performance.

As I have explained, the source material is to be thought of by the actors as a given set of stimuli rather than a drama. In a drama, the affects are merely part of a verbal representation. But, as iconicity transcends the verbal dimension of drama, the affects represented there become stimuli for affect in the acting. Hence the actors do not imitate dramatized affects, they experience actual affects. Trained actors use the source stimuli to trigger actual affects in themselves and in one another, thereby providing a hyperpresence of consciousness for the performance.

The autogenous stimulation of affect is a complicated matter. Psychotherapists often see the phenomenon in their patients, who achieve it with varying levels of believability. Just as a patient's autogenous stimulation may often represent little more than a simulation, this is also a common problem with actors. On the other hand, whoever is successful at autogenous stimulation is usually committed to a belief in the set of circumstances, whether real or imagined, responsible for that affect stimulus.

Believability is not, however, the essence of successful autogenous affect stimulation. To believe in something really implies one's desire for that thing. For example, an individual may desire for there to be a God, hence that individual believes in God. A person may desire for a variety of reasons all sorts of different things, including the experience of any affect. Desire is defined by the concomitant need for its satisfaction; thus, when any of us desires the experience of some affect keenly enough, we may be able to stimulate it successfully autogenously by calling to mind any situation or experience characterized by the correct density or gradient of stimulation. An actor is not unlike the rest of us in this respect, because actors by nature genuinely and deeply desire affective experiences. They are not merely the impersonators of false characters. An actor who is not captivated by the affective experience should not be an actor. It is quite common for actors in training to discover their aversion to the affects, in which case they usually move on to another profession. Likewise, a patient who is successfully treated for an abnormal, disabling desire for some affective experience is also able to move on.

Affect Terminology and Characteristics

Strictly speaking, *affect* exists because something produced by the genetic code is capable of being *triggered* as a biological reaction to a stimulus. For example, the gun going off on stage at a moment when it is least expected triggers the affect surprise–startle, biologically causing a spectator to jolt upright in his seat.

Each affect produces a particular observable physical reaction that is its unique characteristic. This physical characteristic is manifested at a *site of action* on the body. The face is the most important of these sites, followed by the voice and by posture. In the extreme case of the gun going off, the affect of surprise–startle causes the spectator's whole body to show a reaction.

The various sites of action, most especially the face and voice, form one of the three multidimensional, diversely related characteristics that integrate the hyperpresence of consciousness with the three other hyperpresences. Sites of action not only express and display an affect, but, because the affect system is reciprocal, the very action occurring at the site also sends a message through the system back to the actor's brain where more affect is produced. In other words, what begins as an actor's imitated display of some affect is almost at once authentic because it triggers in the actor an innate biological mechanism that produces that affect. This is why, when discussing affect and acting, I refer to the actors rather than the characters they may be playing; characters are literary representations, while actors are people. The affects should become authentic in the acting rather than imitated, authenticity being key to the hyperpresence of consciousness.

When integrating with the first hyperpresence of identity, the site of action becomes an *icon of affect, a self-identifying image*, reflecting like a mask the actor's immediate condition of existence. But, unlike a mask, the sites of action are alive, especially the voice. Thus when integrated with the second hyperpresence of the text, the frozen stare on the face of fear becomes unmistakable as the *timbre* of terror. Finally, in the third hyperpresence of the stage, an actor may be so overwhelmed by an affect as to become an isolated figure, so consumed in the site of action that he or she must be *drawn out by the human interaction occurring on stage.*

Feeling, as defined by Basch (1976), involves our perception and awareness of an affect. It makes us aware of ourselves as well as our surroundings and situations. Unlike the sites of action that display affect, feelings are internalized experience signals that inform us an affect has been triggered. When the gun goes off on stage and the spectator jolts upright, startled, she is feeling what is happening to her body; she becomes aware of herself, of the amplified stimulus, and that she is watching a performance.

Feeling is a second multidimensional characteristic of the hyperpresence of consciousness. In the first hyperpresence, feelings *identify events* in the actor's mind, establishing and maintaining a conscious connection to the affect stimulus. Feelings direct the actor's sensibilities to all the happenings surrounding and involving the actor. Feelings connect the dramatic narrative to the actor's self-awareness. In the second hyperpresence, this self-awareness and sensibility of feeling *intensify the acting, inducing the actor to speak about the affect stimulus*, thereby expressing the actor's knowledge of what is happening. This language of feeling concentrates and focuses the acting, preventing general or indistinct behavior. Finally, in the third hyperpresence, because feelings orient the actor to the surrounding situation, they impel the actor to *commit or stage purposive acts* in an effort to manage the events that comprise the affect stimulus. Feelings educate the actor with information necessary to form a conscious response to the given situation.

Emotion (Basch, 1976) involves our interpretation of what we are feeling. This interpretation is based upon our memory of kindred, typified experiences and on our subjective experiential conditioning. Take the situation in which the stage gun goes off and the spectator experiences the typical sudden startling jolt, but this spectator also has conditioned herself not to be emotionally demonstrative at plays. She doesn't allow herself to cry or even to laugh at the appropriate times. Thus, when the gun goes off and she jolts in her seat at the surprise, it is as if she has momentarily forgotten that she is in the theater. In the next moment she remembers and is ashamed of herself for losing control. She sinks into her seat, hiding herself, reluctant to rejoin the performance.

Mood (Nathanson, 1992) may be defined as an extended state of emotion initiated by some current event or condition. For example, the spectator ashamed of losing control in the theater might well be unable to stop dwelling on her reaction, such that for the duration of the evening she may remain afraid that she may overreact every time she hears a loud noise. This complex, more-or-less constant experience of the combination of shame and fear may be considered a mood.

Emotions and moods together comprise a third extraordinarily important characteristic of the hyperpresence of consciousness. The emotions reflect an actor's thoughts about the affective experience. In the hyperpresence of identity, *emotions establish a symbolic relationship between the actor and the affect stimulus constituting a self-interpreted identity*. In the hyperpresence of the text, emotions *prompt the actor to explanations that are intonations about the affective condition*. These intonations often deploy *abstract stage gestures in order to manipulate* the affect stimulus to the actor's orientation. In the hyperpresence of the stage, the actor's emotions *allow for conscious ideas about the stage action* but they do not impel that action.

Moods, although they often prevail over the entire demeanor of the acting, must be thought of as a subpresence of emotion. They should be treated as a general mask of emotion over which the actor applies the other, more specific affects. Because a mood may be pervasive, an actor runs the risk of playing it too exclusively, veiling the other affects and defeating the specificity of life experiences the affects express. Moods also tend to be autogenously stimulated by constant dwelling on a past affective experience, the details of which may have already faded from the actor's memory; thus, mood is capable of diminishing the actor's sense of immediacy. In the plays of Anton Chekhov, many of the characters are said to be moody. But this moodiness should be considered an iconic feature in the hyperpresence of identity, not consciousness. My great-grandfather, even in old age, was a sour, moody man, but that did not prevent him from expressing enjoyment at seeing me when, as a child, I visited him.

An affect is *analogous* to its stimulus. Thus, when the spectator is startled by the gun, his body's reaction is explosive, like the gun. In this sense it is possible to know a stimulus without a direct experience of it. For example, after I have rehearsed and staged a play, my reactions to it have often grown cold. However, I can evaluate it as a source of stimuli by observing the spectators' faces during a performance. If no one is jolted when the gun goes off, I need a louder blank. If people look annoyed and hold their ears in pain, I need a softer blank. If people fall asleep during the play, the stimulus gradient may be too low; if people are jumpy and fidgety, it may be too high, and so forth. If the performance stimulus is effective, to some degree I will be able to see it duplicated analogously in the faces of the spectators.

In the same way that it is possible to know a stimulus by its affective analogue, it is also possible to feel an affect through *affective resonance* without actually experiencing its stimulus. This is extremely important in performance, because the dramatic stimulus of the narrative is not really happening to the spectator. The actor must employ a particular site of action in just the right way in order for the spectator to resonate with the displayed affect and thereby recognize what is happening in the action of the play.

For example, one might imagine a scene in a play where a man walks into a room occupied by a woman. The woman asks, "What are you doing here?" The spectator has no way of knowing what sort of stimulus the man's entrance constitutes unless the actor playing the woman employs a site of action in a manner reflective of a specific affect. This not only displays what she feels, but it also conveys the action, timbre, and direction of the dramatic narrative. It is through an empathic link with the actor's affective display that the spectator experiences this concomitant dramatic information.

Script Theory

It is not unusual for psychologists and sociologists to borrow terms and ideas from dramatic theory, and it is interesting to note that as a young man Tomkins contemplated a career as a playwright. But Tomkins's *script theory* is only remotely related to dramatic art, and it is not at all related to the techniques of script analysis commonly taught at drama academies.

Human life is filled with experiences that are distinguished one from another by sequences of affects. All such similar sequences of triggering source and resultant affect can be grouped together as a set of common experiences. The affect mechanism, operating in concert with the neocortical cognitive system, is responsible for this clustering of experiences; each cluster of experiences is stored in memory and recorded as a scene.

For example, all the incidents in a person's life that stimulated the affect anger–rage are grouped into a catalogue of angry events or anger scenes. This catalogue, which seems to be stored in memory as imagery, contains all the information from all the incidents that prompted the affect anger in that individual's life. Fairly early in our development, patterns of anger scenes are recognized and scripts evolve around them. These scripts form a nexus of anger scenes that become guidelines for dealing with whatever triggers anger throughout the rest of the person's life.

All the affects come to be involved in scripts and, because the affects are both innate and universal, all individuals share some common universal script guidelines. On the other hand, because no two people have identical affect life experiences, no two scripts are identical. Script theory is of particular importance to the actor for two reasons: First, it is through scripts that the logic or semantics of the source material (the first hyperpresence) is integrated with the patterns of consciousness generated by affect in the fourth hyperpresence. The source material, therefore, operates as an affect script rather than a play script; affect scripts are stimulus related, whereas play scripts are drama or literature related. The actor's work is dependent upon stimulus relationships.

Secondly, recall that the function of affect is to amplify the stimulus experience. Similarly, when a cluster of affect-related scenes occurs in the source material, the affect experience is increased by that nexus of scenes. In other words, even though a single stimulus might trigger the anger affect, the layering of five or six connected scenes of anger may lead to rage. It isn't that the single events themselves add up to rage, as if they became a new sort of summated stimulus, but that the clustering of scenes moves the subject from the mild to the extreme part of the affect's range (Tomkins, 1991). This is psychological script formation.

An actor playing King Lear must get angry in the first scene of the play and in many scenes thereafter; thus, the source material is a rage-producing anger script. However, an actor playing Lear without the benefit of an affect script will be confined to a series of anger imitations of only one dimension because the rage is actually based upon the agglutination of anger scenes and not so much on the events of the drama. Shakespeare understood the difference between multiple triggers for an affect and the layering of experience that pushes that affect toward its highest expression; it is the job of the actor to realize and reify Shakespeare's knowledge by making it happen to the audience.

Affect scripts, like each of the individual affects, also determine performance tempo; they are responsible for the forces of emotion that weave through the source. An orchestration of affect laces through the textual source, affects following one another or overlapping, integrating all the hyperpresences at the level of consciousness. But these affect scripts are based in part on the unique life experiences of each individual character, stimulus distinctions made in the first hyperpresence of identity. Thus, they incorporate the component of history or biography into the actor's emotional consciousness, influencing the actor's performance tempo. An actor playing Creon in *Antigone* would realize a very different anger script from what would emerge were he playing Lear, thereby distinguishing the actor's performance tempo from one performance analogue to the other.

Method acting sought to find ways to let the actor's own past emotional experiences serve as models for moments of affect in a performance. As a result, the method actor often projected or simulated psychological or emotional instability. Affect theory and script theory present a very different approach to the performance of emotion. With affect theory, the emotions are immediate, not recollected, and they are not based on the past life of the actor, but on the affect scripts found in the source material. It is possible for trained actors to abandon their own personal affect scripts and adopt those provided by a source if they are willing to learn to treat that source in part as a given set of affect stimuli made present by the process of iconicity.

For centuries the drama, particularly tragedy, has been subject to an Aristotelian set of dramaturgical or structural principles designed to produce and evaluate its effect. In *The Poetics*, Aristotle discounts the necessity of performance, suggesting that the spectator is emotionally involved in the events surrounding the drama's characters through what would today be described as the process of *identification* rather than anything to do with the actor's experience of affect. Aristotle therefore suggests that the telling of a tale is equivalent to the acting of it.* It is as if a psychotherapist could treat a patient by hearing about that patient or reading the patient's record! Thus Aristotle was wrong to discount the importance of performance in drama; it would be the same as eliminating a psychotherapist's face-to-face meeting with a patient. In fact, tragedy depends on actors for its effect because an audience does not empathize with the dramatic characters or events directly. Only the actors' experience of the given textual stimuli provides the affect that can move an audience. Even when we read a drama we are actually acting the play for ourselves, autogenously stimulating affects.

TO WHAT END

Iconicity did not begin as, nor was it ever meant to be, a theory. It is an aesthetic process, and what appears here as theory is meant to be part of an articulation of that process. Iconicity is not, however, open-ended, finding imagined false rewards in process alone. It has two specific goals, which are (1) the artistic creation of a dramatic performance, and (2) in the process and performance of that creation, definition of what a dramatic performance is. But, because the definition of a thing is linked to its use, iconicity is also troubled with purpose, with what an artistically created dramatic performance is meant to accomplish, its ethic.

I believe that in any age, all dramatic performance expresses the psychological pursuit of existence. For the present era, the art of dramatic performance is also meant to stimulate in the spectators a presence of imagery in order to ensure their continued presence in a technological world that is able to move intelligence faster than human beings are able to move it. The art of dramatic performance can condition us to keep up the skills necessary to manage our lives in the face of a technology that produces ever more intense affective experience.

Recently, I was shooting pool with an actor while we were talking about pauses. I told him that he paused too much on stage, that his acting was consumed with a tempo based on pauses, and that it was losing the intensity of specificity that iconicity is meant to promote. He felt the pauses were necessary to make transitions appear natural. To prove otherwise, I invented a game called three-second pool in which one must complete each shot before your opponent counts to three, or forfeit your turn. Within two or three games we were shooting just as well as or

---

*The reference may also be taken as saying that a plot should be based on actual events that apart from the drama would otherwise have been left unseen.

perhaps better than we had in regular pool. Then, by adding positive imagery to our cue strokes, we were soon able to shoot successfully on only a two-count. The same concept has long been applied in the world of chess.

That the brain keeps up, I think, has something to do with the affect system. The challenge of three-second pool triggered the affect interest-excitement, which sharpened all our other sensibilities. I have staged many plays, but only in the most recent, in which affect theory played a significant part of the process, was there that kind of sharpness in the performance. The affect system seems not only to provide feelings and emotions, but our understanding of it as a system also enables us to make intellectual advances. To an extent, the first three hyperpresences in iconicity are intellectual, making demands on the actors' thought processes. Together with actors, I had learned to advance from step to step through the process of iconicity to the third hyperpresence of the stage. But without the fourth hyperpresence of consciousness, the performance analogues were merely interesting, not involving. They weren't sufficiently integrated because they lacked the intellectual involution of the affect system.

In Australia and other countries around the world, there is a movement in education to displace the traditional art of dramatic performance along with actor skills training in favor of something called process drama. The prejudice on which this new agenda rests is the tacit awareness that in traditional dramatic performance the so-called talented students have been favored to the exclusion of the less gifted students, the result being that the educational benefits of drama were unfairly limited to those few talented individuals. By displacing artistic performance with process drama, and artistry with an aesthetic framework for the classroom, these educators have been able to (mis)appropriate the elements of drama, just as their religious counterparts did centuries ago. By using the dramatic elements uncritically to investigate social and psychological issues, these educators hope to include all students regardless of their innate or learned performance skills. However, because of their disdain for traditional performance and its associated artistic product, these educators have missed the point about what really is social, psychological, and even educational about the drama. Drama is an affect stimulus that (1) provides for common social and private environments, (2) develops an interplay of mental imagery, and (3) inspires learning, specifically through performance. The drama process movement has made creativity academic, overlooking affect in favor of pedagogy, discarding rehearsal—which surely is a form of study—in favor of curriculum, and dismissing the art in favor of the lesson. The more I learn about the psychology of emotion, and the centrality of the affect system for everything we know of as dramatic, the more certain I am that the health of a nation is integrally linked to the freedom of its theater.

Although the process drama movement does not exist in the United States, the drama here is under another form of attack. School boards in Boston and other major cities have recently extended the school day by one hour to boost the students' performance in traditional academic subjects. Naturally, this academic focus cuts further into already severely diminished extracurricular arts activities, such as drama. This decision is a mistake on the part of politicians and academic administrators, for without the *intellectual* stimulation supplied by the creative application of affect, students are denied experiences that might otherwise help them vault forward in their educational development. The social and educational role of theater and everything we know as the dramatic arts is neither frivolous nor unimportant to a culture in which introspection itself is under attack. The concepts of iconicity must lead one to a deeper appreciation of the importance of theater.

Iconicity provides for a very special kind of artistic freedom. Because it is not actor technique centered, but human centered, it frees the actors from distancing forms of analysis and interpretation. It allows the actor to respond like a normal human being to the given circumstances of the source stimulus environment. An authentic performer is one who freely engages a rich orchestration of affect with clarity and precision, while believably refining that orchestration into a performance tempo congruent with the source material. Furthermore, understanding acting and performance in this manner allows audiences a very different sort of recognition experience. The audience experiences a more authentic and less contrived stage event because what one sees is no longer an actor impersonating character, but a human being rehearsed in and committed to a composed set of stimuli made human by the affect system.

Psychotherapists in particular should find this type of artistic dramatic performance relevant to their own efforts, because they can use something like iconicity to initiate a new system of treatment that we might call stage therapy. Such therapy would be far more effective than any of the psychodrama techniques currently in vogue. The failings of psychodrama rest on its old-fashioned notions of dramaturgy and psychotherapy: The drama therapist assumes the role of a director and the therapy becomes a self-reflective performance given in an office where its consequences are both theoretical and to a certain degree manipulated by the therapist.

In stage therapy, the patient would be regarded within the parameters of a staged affect performance. This performance would be based on the patient's affect scripts and also be of the patient's own devising. Unlike a versatile actor, the ill patient has become stuck in some affective condition, prevented from responding authentically with whichever of the nine innate affects might be appropriate to any new stimulus. So the therapist's job is to study with the patient the patient's whole condition just as if it were a play, rehearsing in the office the source or sources of stimulus responsible for the condition in order to determine which are disrupting the patient's human interactions. The end result of stage therapy would be a reconditioning and reorienting of the patient toward the affect script(s) responsible for his or her discomfort, thereby restoring that individual's innate capacity for dramatic performance. Released from the therapist and the therapeutic situation, and from the formerly restricted self, the patient is freed to play affects in their freshly staged scripts, thereby performing a self-generated condition, or image, in a world of the patient's own perceptions.

REFERENCES

Aristotle. (1968). *The poetics.* (D. W. Lucas, Ed.). Oxford: Clardendon Press.

Austin, J. L. (1971). *How to do things with words.* (J. O. Urmsson & M. Sbisa, Eds.). New York: Oxford University Press.

Basch, M. F. (1976). The concept of affect: A re-examination. *Journal of the American Psychoanalytic Association, 24,* 759–77.

Basch, M. F. (1983). Empathic understanding: A review of the concept and some theoretical considerations. *Journal of the American Psychoanalytic Association, 31,* 101–26.

Matejka, L., & Titunik, I. R. (Eds.). (1984). *Semiotics of art: Prague school contributions.* Boston: MIT Press.

Moore, S. (1965). *The Stanislavski system.* New York: Viking.

Nathanson, D. L. (1986). The empathic wall and the ecology of affect. *Psychoanalytic Study of the Child, 41,* 171–87.

Nathanson, D. L. (1992). *Shame and pride: Affect, sex, and the birth of the self.* New York: Norton.

Peirce, C. S. (1940). *The philosophy of Peirce: Selected writings.* (B. Justus, Ed.). New York: Dover.

Tomkins, S. S. (1962). *Affect, imagery, consciousness, Vol. 1: The positive affects.* New York: Springer.

Tomkins, S. S. (1991). *Affect, imagery, consciousness, Vol. 2: The negative affects: Anger and fear.* New York: Springer.

Wilde, O. (1966). Preface to *The picture of Dorian Gray.* London: Collins.

16

Illegal Action–Official Reaction: Affect Theory, Criminology, and the Criminal Justice System

David B. Moore

Each cluster of humans has assorted for reasons that are difficult to discern, is maintained as such by forces that have been debated but poorly understood, and is threatened with dissolution by other forces that seem at once equally obvious but elusive. Social systems develop rules for behavior because individuals tend to operate, at least occasionally, in ways that decrease the efficiency of group function. There would be no such sets of rules unless what they opposed was powered by strong forces, and it is inevitable that where there are rules there will be those who break them—people who believe that their actions are proper under the circumstances or conditions at hand. Societal reaction to infractions of rules obeys the fashion of its locale and era, and varies over time as each group focuses on the success or failure of its techniques for the management of its laws.

Roughly speaking, these fall into two categories—systems that concentrate on the cognitive aspects of the rule violation under investigation, and systems that pay attention to the affective life of those who committed the crime and those whose lives have been changed by it. Working under the assumption that "revenge is a dish best served cold," the modern legal system is designed to protect the code of laws by providing an atmosphere as isolated from affect as possible. When the system works, it assures that the warring parties are represented by lawyers who will argue their cases before an impartial judge charged with the responsibility of ensuring that the jury of their peers is also held impartial and kept free from influence by emotion. In order for the process to work, the disputants must agree that they can be represented by others; they must accept the hypothesis that their own emotionality renders them unfit to speak with authority in the court of law.

Such a system offers obvious advantages. The strong cannot dominate the weak because both are equal the law; "normal" but potentially dangerous affective reactions triggered in the moment of discovery or apprehension are muted and modulated; the establishment of precedent avoids accusations of favoritism or prejudice. Yet there are disadvantages to a system that insists on such rigorous separation between rules and feelings. Moore's chapter addresses the growing sentiment that the current system for criminal justice used in the Western world has begun to fail. Evidence for this failure includes the all-too-common observation that the victims of crime feel little satisfaction at the close of the legal theater and that neither trial nor punishment seems to dissuade the perpetrators from committing further crimes.

Moore discusses the traditional dichotomy between authoritarian and permissive systems of control and offers as a new system the concept of authoritative management. The Wagga Wagga model of Family Group Conferencing is based loosely on work published by Australian criminologist John Braithwaite in his influential book, *Crime, Shame and Reintegration*. It is an approach to the current problems of our shared world that seems to make sense when viewed from the standpoint of affect and script theory.

Simply stated, Tomkins established that each individual human is born with the hardware and firmware for nine innate affect mechanisms that govern personality formation just as they control the ways we experience our world. We are "wired" to experience the two positive affects of interest–excitement and enjoyment–joy, the brief moment of surprise–startle that alerts us to what will happen next, and the six negative affects of fear–terror, distress–anguish, anger–rage, dissmell, disgust, and shame–humiliation. Each of us as adults seems to thrive best when we learn to maximize positive affect, minimize negative affect, and develop highly personal systems that foster the expression of all affect so these two actions may be performed. As Dr. Kelly suggested in Chapter 4, intimacy is a shared, private interpersonal relationship within which two people attempt to mutualize and increase the amount of positive affect available to them, and to mutualize and decrease the amount of negative affect occurring in their milieu; the system works best when they agree to express all affect so these two actions may be performed.

I suggest that a community is a shared, *public* interpersonal relationship within which a variable number of individuals attempts to mutualize and increase the amount of positive affect available, and to mutualize and decrease the amount of negative affect occurring in their shared world; the system works best when the community agrees to express all affect so these two actions may be performed. Positive affect is mutualized and increased by public celebrations such as entertainments and athletic competitions, while negative affect is handled through such mechanisms as public debate, absorption of material from news sources, and election campaigns. What we call mental health in the individual, and intimacy in the couple, is best understood as the sense of community when taken into the public world.

Crime, if limited in frequency, scope, and significance for a society, can be handled by methods that ignore these rules of affect modulation. It is only when the separation between the affective and cognitive systems for behavioral management fails to enhance community living that we must look beyond the traditional legal system for novel methods to assist the needs of the public at large. Moore's chapter introduces such a concept to the cohort of psychotherapists for whom this present text has been written and opens the door to a new kind of cooperation between the world of psychotherapy and the larger community it serves.   –DLN

T HE MODERN STATE has tended to seek greater control over the political environment, just as human society more generally has sought greater control over the physical environment. And just as human societies have employed technologies derived from a growing understanding of physics, chemistry, and biology to achieve greater control over the material and biological environment, political executives and the rational bureaucracies that answer to them have deployed new regulatory technologies in the quest for greater influence over society, politics, and the economy. Theories that inform these modern systems of social, political, and economic regulation all include a model of human nature. Methods of child-rearing, school education, workplace management, and punishment within the criminal justice system, for example, are all based on such models.

Some of these models are tacit, others explicit. They feature in debates concerning the best way to raise and educate children, run the factory or office, or deal with those who break criminal laws. Criminal law and the criminal justice system are currently of particular concern, not only because of the objective fact of the volume of crime – especially violent crime – being committed, but also because the extensive media attention given to crime evokes strong feelings, because criminal justice systems cost a great deal to maintain, and because organizations such as those supporting victims' rights are beginning to question the fundamental adequacy of current arrangements for responding to crime. While any criminal justice system will provide specific examples of problems that need redress, here I want to consider three questions concerning modern criminal justice in general.

First, how does the way in which modern criminal justice systems regulate behavior differ from practices in other regulatory systems? Criminal justice practice, like practice in all branches of politics, is ultimately justified in terms of theories about human nature, and this leads to the second question: How does the model of human nature and nurture on which criminological theories are based differ from the theories that inform other regulatory practices? Theoretical debate in criminology has revolved around differing conceptions of the relation between individuals and society. At the heart of the debate, in other words, has been a conflict between different schools of psychology. But a synthesis of these schools is now underway, and this leads to the third and final question: Does the integrated psychological model offered by affect theory suggest ways in which theory and practice in criminal justice might be altered?

CRIMINAL JUSTICE AND
OTHER REGULATORY SYSTEMS

Systems designed to regulate human behavior vary greatly. Families, schools, places of work and play, and prisons are all governed by complex rules of behavioral regulation and restraint. These rules differ from one institution to another, and from one culture to another. Beneath the diversity, however, are some common patterns in the methods of regulation and restraint. Families offer a good example. Psychologists now routinely assign parenting styles within families to one of three categories, which can be placed on a single spectrum. Permissive parenting styles are at one end and authoritarian parenting styles at the other. These two extremes share a tendency to shield children from the challenge of social and moral demands. Permissive parenting enforces too few rules, assuming a capacity for self-control in children. Authoritarian parenting enforces too many rules, relying on external control to restrain and remold behavior. Between permissive and authoritarian parenting is the golden mean of *authoritative* parenting, whereby a child's natural capacity for cooperation and empathy is fostered, legitimate commands are consistently enforced, and general norms of behavior are communicated (Damon, 1988, 1989). Authoritative parenting avoids authoritarian methods, whereby external control of behavior is imposed by punishment and threats of further punishment. In contrast to permissive parenting, however, authoritative parenting is clear and consistent about standards. It encourages self-regulation and self-control on the basis of a shared commitment to those standards. Its ultimate goal is self-regulation without the need for overt external reinforcement. Authoritative parenting fosters empathy, trust, and reciprocity, all of which are essential for lasting and harmonious social interaction in and outside of the family.

However broadly defined, the family is the first school of moral development and thus the most important system of social regulation (Okin, 1989). The family is unique in its mix of narrow responsibility to kin and broader responsibility to society in general. Nevertheless, the basic categories used to distinguish parenting styles within families can also be applied to other agencies of social regulation. The regulatory culture governing any place of education, work, or play can be placed on the same spectrum, ranging from authoritarian, through authoritative, to permissive. In spheres other than the family, however, different terminology is generally used to label these phenomena. An authoritarian culture in the political, legal, and social spheres is likely to be described as one that emphasizes social responsibilities but neglects or overrides individual rights. A permissive culture, in contrast, emphasizes individual rights but neglects social responsibilities. Again, the appropriate balance is achieved in an authoritative culture, where individual rights are protected but social responsibility is also valued and fostered. An authoritative culture is characterized by an interplay between individual freedom and collective order. The permissive approach promotes individual freedom from constraint. The authoritarian approach promotes collective order. The authoritative approach strikes a balance between these extremes.

The last line of defense for collective order in the modern state is the criminal justice system. But the institutions of criminal justice do not rely solely on authoritarian methods of priced and rationed tariffs for illegal behavior. Criminal justice agencies also aim to be "symbolic, ideological, hortatory" (Friedman, 1993, p. 10). They aim to teach as well as to threaten, to instill collective norms in the process of doling out individual punishments. The persuasiveness of the claim that the state is responsible for determining and disseminating moral norms tends, however, to wax and wane. In the late 20th century, many are not persuaded by the claim. This is another reason—added to burgeoning costs and the dissatisfaction of victims—why current procedures in the criminal justice system are being called into question. Nevertheless, the criminal justice system continues to promote collective norms. The nature of these norms changes over time, along with the punishments.

The changing nature of norms promoted by the criminal justice system can be attributed largely to more general changes in social norms and values. These changes in social values have, in turn, been hastened by the bureaucratic rationalization of social regulation that has occurred during the last century and a half. Responsibility for many aspects of social regulation has been transferred from civil society to the state, as public education, state-funded social welfare agencies, and public, uniformed police agencies have been established and expanded. These large public agencies have then been further rationalized; more specialized agencies have proliferated. Police agencies, for instance, were originally created with a very broad, tripartite mandate. They were established to "keep the peace," to provide miscellaneous and emergency services at any time, and to enforce the law (see Monkkonen, 1981). As the discretion of police departments was narrowed by political pressure and court decisions, police agencies came to focus on the narrowest and most readily measured police function, that of law enforcement. This general trend has been particularly pronounced in the United States, where the reality of a narrowly focused police role is reflected in the title "law enforcement officer." Under the law enforcement model, the police role is to act as gatekeepers, delivering up to the other agencies of the justice system those who have committed illegal acts.

The other agencies of this criminal justice system are also concerned with objective law enforcement rather than the more nebulous "peace-keeping." They emphasize retribution rather than the resolution of moral conflict. As the sense of any shared moral order has gradually declined, criminal justice has further emphasized the material rather than moral costs of wrongdoing. A modern theoretical justification for this approach has been provided by the "law and economics" movement, which applies to the analysis of law the rational choice theories that have dominated modern economics (Mansbridge, 1990). The methodology of law and economics is in the spirit of major trends in modern legal theory, which has become increasingly morally neutral, adversarial, and rights-oriented (Glendon, 1991, p. 3). Modern legal practice matches the theory, generally involving the search for victory through litigation rather than resolution through compromise. North American lawyers, somewhat more than their British Imperial or Continental counterparts, have "accepted the Hobbesian idea of law as command, together with the strict separation—postulated by Hobbes and elaborated by John Austin—between law and morality" (Glendon, 1991, p. 86). Law becomes an arena of combat rather than cooperation, of retribution rather than reconciliation. Understandably, this combative, retributive style is pronounced in the criminal law.

There is an apparent paradox here, however. Despite fostering combat, "law is now regarded by many Americans as the principal carrier of those few moral understandings that are widely shared by our diverse citizenry" (Glendon, 1991, p. 87). Nor is this faith in the cohesive power of law confined to the United States. As Jürgen Habermas and others have observed, law forms a link in all modern industrialized democracies between the economic, political, and social spheres (Habermas, 1988). It provides a measure of formal stability in an era of marital, geographical, political, and social mobility. Nevertheless, law can deplete politics. Tort law, for instance, is often seen as a simple—if costly—alternative to negotiation. Constitutional law has also become an important alternative arena of political decision-making; legislatures frequently cede to courts the responsibility to decide on tough moral decisions. Under these circumstances, "the skills of citizenship, not to mention those of statesmanship, have begun to atrophy" (Glendon, 1991, p. xiii). Similar claims can be made about the criminal law. It too can be seen to deplete politics. Certainly, the formal procedures of the justice system—in which criminal law is applied—provide important safeguards for rights. At the same time, however, these formal procedures deprive people of opportunities to practice skills of apology and forgiveness, of reconciliation, restitution, and reparation (Tavuchis, 1991). In assuming responsibility for social regulation when a citizen breaches a law and thereby challenges the moral order, the modern state appears to have deprived civil society of opportunities to learn important political and social skills. A comparison between informal and formal modes of discipline will emphasize this point.

Behind the complex formal disciplining processes of the modern criminal justice system are patterns similar to those observable in the social microcosm of the family. The same basic modes of response can be identified in the criminal justice system as in the family. At one end of the spectrum is the authoritarian response of command-and-control. The authoritarian response rightly condemns the victimization of one citizen by another, even as it then victimizes the individual offender in the name of the social collective. At the other end of the spectrum are the claims of a permissive culture that rightly values individual freedom. One act of victimization in civil society, it claims, does not justify an act of victimization by the state. Both the authoritarian and the permissive response are half-right. Few processes within criminal justice strike the right balance between the two. Few processes in contemporary criminal justice systems can truly be called authoritative. Like the authoritarian or the permissive parent, the state deprives members of civil society of the right to understand fully and deal with the consequences of a breach of the moral order.

Lawrence Friedmann's recent overview of crime and punishment in American history describes an interplay between the two extremes of authoritarianism and permissiveness. Perhaps, Friedmann concludes, "the siege of crime may be the price we pay for a brash, self-loving, relatively free and open society" (Friedmann, 1993, p. 464). (Allowing for some obvious differences in ownership of firearms, ethnic tension, wealth distribution, and prohibitionist policies, Friedmann's observations also apply to other societies settled during the second expansion of Europe. Nevertheless, the United States remains a sort of benchmark in the international criminological debate.) The United States can claim the world's most studied and most diverse criminal justice system — along with higher crime rates and a higher rate of incarceration than any other industrially developed nation. It also boasts the majority of the world's criminologists. Surprisingly, the U.S. criminal justice education industry shows only a modest commitment to educating its practitioners about the successes and errors of their forebears (Conley, 1993). The emphasis is on sociology and psychology rather than history and political economy. Yet historical accounts are essential to an understanding of the contemporary state of criminal justice.

An adequate criminological theory must account for the U-shaped plot of crime trends in modern industrialized democracies. Taking into account variations in the rates of different crimes, a long-term trend towards lower rates of crime in all of these countries has clearly been reversed since the end of the Second World War. Obvious material considerations — such as income inequality and the growth in the sheer number of possessions to be stolen — cannot alone account for the phenomenon of rising crime rates over the last half-century. Of the many explanations proposed, three have been subject to considerable discussion. James Q. Wilson's (1993; Wilson & Herrnstein, 1985) analysis accounts for the upsurge of crime in terms of a general loss of moral authority in all public institutions. Ted Gurr attributes the problem, more narrowly, to a loss of moral authority by the state. As Gurr (1989) sees it, however, the upsurge of the last half-century is merely an atypical blip in a long-term civilizing process. Roger Lane (1989) is less optimistic. He suggests that economic change has induced sociopsychological changes, the long-term consequences of which are less predictable and more disturbing.

The picture presented by Lane is the most complex of the three, and probably also the most persuasive. His suggestion is that change has occurred not just in the authority of institutions, but also in the psychology of the people who govern and are governed by those institutions. That argument is supported by evidence from other fields. Changes in social psychology appear to have been induced not simply by economic change, but also by the interplay of cultural and technological developments with economic factors. The cultural effects of theories counseling against "cultural repression" of any sort have, for instance, been considerable. Freudian theory's attack on shame as the basis of moral suasion and social deference is a good example of this. More importantly, the technology of the camera produced not only new ways of exposing people to observation and scrutiny but also vast industries of objectification (Broucek, 1991). One effect of these cultural and technological changes has been an alteration in the situations that now trigger shame and in the socially accepted responses to shame, the quintessential social emotion (Nathanson, 1992).

Such alteration in the mechanisms of social regulation represents major transformations in civil society. The sort of sociopsychological changes alluded to by Roger Lane include, for instance, the undermining of deference as an acceptable mode of social carriage, or of compromise as an honorable outcome, and the promotion of attack as a preferred response in impersonal encounters. These changes are reflective of more general changes in the socially acceptable responses to shame and anger (Nathanson, 1992), changes induced by developments in culture and technology. Where subtle methods of social regulation and control have been transformed or forgotten, the state is required to intervene with unsubtle methods of arrest and incarceration. Criminal justice systems may continue to promote collective norms, but the modern rational state ultimately lacks the emotional resources to maintain—let alone strengthen—the moral order. Under these circumstances, criminal justice will continue to be marked by an oscillation between permissiveness and authoritarianism.

There is, of course, a short-term advantage in all of this for elected officials. Any street poll with appropriately phrased questions will record a majority who feel that crime is on the increase and that tougher penalties are required for those who commit crime. The word "feel" rather than "think" is used advisedly here. Any mention of crime evokes understandable feelings of anger, prompting an urge to attack the source of that anger. But politicians – or, at least, their advisers – will know that the literature on deterrence is fairly clear about the effects of differential responses to crime. The most significant deterrent is the likelihood of apprehension, followed by speed of processing, followed, at a great distance, by the actual nature of the sentence. Potential offenders are deterred by the knowledge that they are likely to come to public attention and that their deeds will be exposed soon after the event, rather than by the nature of their subsequent sentence. Certainty and celerity are of far more significance than severity. The state, however, can guarantee neither certainty of apprehension nor, in the event of apprehension, celerity of processing.

What elected state officials can offer are angry words about crime and retribution for convicted criminals. They can offer severity. The temptation seems irresistible. A Republican presidential candidate offered to divert resources from the war in Vietnam to the war on crime at home. Twenty years later, a Democratic presidential candidate refuses a State Governor's clemency to a mentally incompetent prisoner on death row, then, having cleared that political hurdle, uses sporting metaphors – linking excitement with anger – to launch his own war on crime. Civil violence is met with state violence, a permissive culture with an authoritarian response.

Debate about youth curfews and boot camps, substance abuse and the war on pushers, gun control and violence, life imprisonment and the death penalty – all of these will continue to be fueled by fear and anger, disgust and distress. Politicians share these negative affects with potential voters. The simplicity of this emotional communion evokes the imagined solidarity of earlier times, when civil society was largely responsible for keeping the peace. Since these often romanticized earlier times, however, something very significant has occurred to the institutions of regulation and control. Responsibility for many of the activities that evoke negative affects has been ceded from civil society to the state. More specifically, responsibility for the negative aspects of social regulation has been passed to the criminal justice system and, in particular, to the police who act as gatekeepers of that system.

Other regulatory systems – schools, workplaces, commercial centers – have sought to retain any form of social regulation that involves the promise of excitement and enjoyment and to dispense with any form of regulation that does not. Schools call in police to discuss the unhappier sides of life – road trauma, substance abuse, teenage suicide. In the ab-

sence of effective methods to achieve compliance, schools understandably suspend or expel students whose behavior threatens the safety of the
school community. Police then deal with those same former students on
the streets. In the vast private-public spaces of shopping malls, people
are tempted with a tantalizing range of products. Police are then called
in to deal with those who help themselves. In schools, in shops, and on
the streets, police are left to deal with any behavior or event that evokes
fear, anger, disgust, or distress. Since the core of the police mandate has
been narrowed from peacekeeping to law enforcement, police have—
until very recently—not been enjoined to mobilize the resources of civil
society in response to these problems. Rather, they have been pressed
to remove offending elements and place them on the conveyor belt of
bureaucratized criminal justice. It is hardly surprising, under the circumstances, that police culture is marked by a solidarity in cynicism.

This bureaucratization of social regulation fits the pattern of increased
specialization common to all bureaucratic rationalization. It may, however, be producing unforeseen consequences. The development of a system that takes sole responsibility for authoritarian control and of a
department that takes sole responsibility for removing people from civil
society and feeding them into this system may be socially debilitating,
even criminogenic. It perpetuates the illusion that the state, rather than
civil society, is ultimately responsible for social order. The looming
promise of an authoritarian state response wherever and whenever required makes it easier for people to respond permissively to breaches of
social rules by children, friends, colleagues, and other citizens, where an
authoritative response would be more appropriate. The drug war provides one dramatic illustration of the consequences of this approach.
The focus of police on law enforcement rather than general peacekeeping
is one factor that has encouraged substance abuse to be treated as a
criminal matter rather than an issue of public health and long-term education. Current arrangements in criminal justice may also encourage a
tendency for both civil society and legislators to see individual liberty
conflicting with social responsibility, rather than complementing it.

What is the alternative to this destructive interplay between authoritarian and permissive approaches? The abstract answer is, of course, an
authoritative approach. But what practical form would such an approach take? Can greater responsibility for social regulation gradually
be ceded back to civil society? What mechanism would encourage greater
self-regulation? I argue that the answer may be found at the apparent
heart of the problem, at the point where civil law meets criminal law, and
where authoritarian policing meets its permissive critics. But to propose
changes in formal social regulation, one must first consider the com-

plexities of informal social regulation. One has to consider in greater detail what occurs when the moral order has been breached, invoking some response — informal or official. To account for breaches of the moral and legal order has been the traditional goal of criminology. Accordingly, the next section considers some of criminology's dominant themes.

CRIMINOLOGICAL THEORY: VARIATIONS ON UTILITARIAN THEMES

Crime evokes strong passions, ensuring that it remains among the most important political issues. Crime threatens personal liberty, defined in Montesquieu's broad republican sense as freedom from undue interference from above and from below, from the state and from the streets. Because it deprives people of liberty and dignity, crime evokes an apparently innate sense of justice and injustice (Gruter, 1991; Masters & Gruter, 1992). Indeed, media reports of crime produce the full gamut of affects — from surprise, anger, and fear, through distress and disgust, to interest, tempered by shame that one should feel anything positive in association with crime, and shame that one belongs to a community in which shameful violations occur. Crime also raises fundamental questions about the nature of altruism, empathy, and sympathy — and about the circumstances in which these social emotions fail to be evoked. Such questions are given particular prominence in debates about crime committed by young people, debates that are generally surrounded by an air of panic and crisis. The panic is understandable, since juvenile justice brings dramatically to the fore fundamental political-philosophical questions concerning the ways in which an individual should be nurtured into the moral community, and under what circumstances a person ought to be excluded from that moral community. Periodic crises in juvenile justice demand an answer to these questions (Moore, 1993).

At the heart of any answer to these questions is, as usual, a working model of the typical person. This working model then determines the nature of any practical response. Authoritarian responses to breaches of the law are premised on the belief that sociability is not innate, that it must be imprinted on a person through early punishment, and that it may require subsequent reinforcement. Permissive and authoritative responses, in contrast, hold with Aristotle that people are by nature sociable. Permissive responses are premised on a belief that this innate sociability will unfold of its own accord, with a minimum of interference. Authoritative responses are also premised on a belief that the capacity for empathy, altruism, and sympathy are innate, as is a basic sense of justice. Unlike advocates of a permissive response, however, advocates of an authoritative response believe that innate capacities will not develop fully without appropriate socialization. Sociable behavior must be fostered, rather than taken for granted.

As already noted above, modern criminological practice has tended to oscillate between two of these three responses. It has oscillated between authoritarian and permissive responses, between harsh and soft penalties administered by the state. This oscillation between harsh and soft penalties has taken place against the background of long-term trends toward less physically violent punishments and somewhat more respect—at least officially—for the individual rights of offenders. Authoritarian responses have been advocated by those who, following Locke, see the individual as a blank slate upon which all social norms are inscribed. The ideological impetus behind this philosophical position is clear enough. It is a view of individuals as being open to social engineering by philosopher-kings. It is a view that has been shared, in Robin Fox's heated words, by all "sanctimonious manipulators from Mill through Stalin" (Fox, 1989, p. 43). Criminologists of the classical school belong in this category. Closely associated with utilitarian political theory, classical criminology assumed that people were essentially rational. Accordingly, a person who broke the law had calculated that the pleasure arising from the transgression would exceed the pain of any subsequent punishment. Law-abiding citizens had reached the opposite conclusion. They were deterred from committing crime by the existing schedule of punishments, whereas law breakers were not deterred. If legislators and judges wished to reduce the rate of crime, therefore, they would need to raise the penalties for criminal behavior.

Most of the diverse criticisms of classical criminology have questioned this notion of the free-willed, rational actor. Such criticisms have been gathered under the broad and vague banner of "positivism" or, more recently, "determinism." They all hold that behavior is, to some degree, determined by factors beyond an individual's control. These factors may be biological, psychological, or sociological. Indeed, determinist theories have moved through this very fashion cycle, beginning with biological determinism in the late 19th and early 20th century. The fundamental scientific misunderstandings of the eugenicist movement, together with the link between "social Darwinism" and political reaction, subsequently brought theories of biological determinism into complete disrepute. The biological basis of human behavior consequently remained almost a taboo subject until the 1970s (Degler, 1991).

An alternative to biological determinism was provided by the psychological determinism of drive theories such as those of Freud and his followers. Drive theorists and proponents of other schools of psychology were subsequently challenged by behaviorism, which, with the usual ideological motivations, resurrected the Lockean idea of the blank slate infant. This sat well with the reformist impetus within the emerging disciplines of sociology and anthropology, many proponents of which, following Durkheim, have concerned themselves with "objective cultural facts" exterior to the individual (Fox, 1989). Psychological determinism was thus overshadowed—in academia and elsewhere—by social determinism. Mainstream criminological theory since the Second World War provides a good example of this development. Criminology has frequently urged legislators, law enforcers, and sentencers to be more understanding of law breakers, on the grounds that the latter are partly or wholly driven by their social circumstances.

All of these theories—those from a school of thought assuming the rational actor, and those from schools of thought assuming the actor whose rationality is bounded by biological, psychological, or social factors—seem at least partially plausible. Not surprisingly, the strongest empirical support has been found for theories that have managed to integrate aspects of both major schools of thought. To some degree, of course, theorists of the free-willed rational actor and those assuming determinism—whether biological, psychological, or social—are talking past one another. They are talking about different categories of law breaker. More significantly, both schools overlook the third, and probably largest, category.

So what are these three categories? We are concerned here with three sets of circumstances under which an individual fails to heed the moral imperatives underlying social rules and criminal law (Richards, 1987, pp. 625-626). The first set of circumstances is when a person fully understands the moral requirements of a situation and yet, despite this, acts immorally or illegally. We categorize such people as sinners. Lord, forgive them—though they know full well what they do!

The second set of circumstances is when a person is morally deficient—by birth or by socialization. Biology, psychology, and society have conspired to make such people incapable of distinguishing right from wrong. They may need to be physically constrained, but cannot be blamed. Lord, forgive them, for they know not what they do—nor are they ever likely to! They are more sinned against than sinners. Classical and neoclassical criminologists have been concerned with the first group. Most critics of classical criminology have been concerned with the second group.

But there is a third—and common—set of circumstances under which an individual may fail to heed moral imperatives. This is when a person misconstrues a situation. He is not aware of the full consequences of his actions. He fails to feel that his behavior is immoral — even though he may know that it is technically illegal. He knows not what he does — but may yet come to understand! Unlike the person who fully understands the situation but acts illegally anyway, the person who misconstrues a situation is not immoral. Nor is the person who misconstrues a situation amoral, in the manner of the person who cannot distinguish right from wrong. Rather than being immoral or amoral, the person who misconstrues a situation has failed to heed moral imperatives but is, nevertheless, potentially moral. This can be said of the majority of young offenders. It is also true of many older offenders who first entered the system as juveniles. Squaring off against the system that seeks to victimize them, they come to focus on themselves, rather than on the consequences of their behavior for the victims of that behavior. And yet, under circumstances that force them to understand those consequences, they will display a moral response.

This distinction between the immoral, the amoral, and the potentially moral is fine in theory. Legislators and other reformers have, however, found it difficult to put such distinctions into practice. Their efforts are constrained not only by the nature of existing institutions but also by contemporary modes of legal and political thought. The unidimensional "rights talk" that Mary Ann Glendon (1991) sees as having impoverished contemporary political discourse contains a clue to the problem. The language that evolved from the theories of Hobbes and Locke saw the political subject as a fully autonomous (property-owning, rights-bearing) individual. But individualism — an important safeguard of human rights — has been exaggerated in much modern legal and political discourse. The individual whose rights are protected from an overbearing state has also been construed as independent of social relations. A protective individualism has thereby been transformed into an alienating social atomism, with the subtle distinction between these two concepts rarely being made (Pettit, 1993, chapter 3). Anglo-American legal theory over the last century and a half has frequently not only emphasized individualism but also effectively promoted an atomistic view of the individual. "There is no such thing as society," often opines Baroness Thatcher, a modern philosopher of atomism.

Thatcher's intended target is collectivism, and her wrath is understandable. Modern social theory and rational bureaucratic practice, in their concern with social aggregates and state-induced reform, have frequently favored collectivist ways of thinking and acting. A confusion has arisen here between holism and collectivism. The holist thesis, an 18th-century reformulation of Aristotle, holds — correctly — that people are essentially social. Collectivist theories exaggerate this notion with the claim that individuals are "compromised by the operation of social forces and laws" (Pettit, 1993, p. 213).

Legal theory, then, has tended towards a view of the socially autonomous, atomistic individual. Social theory and political practice have tended towards a collectivism that focuses on social aggregates rather than individuals. The result is a legal-political culture that is tending towards an unstable "atomistic-collectivism." There are, of course, important social and political developments that run counter to this trend. But "top-down" reform from state and federal executives, legislatures, and judiciaries tends indeed to be marked by legal atomism and political collectivism. Attempts to reform criminal law "from above" certainly seem to operate within these boundaries.

Enduring reform — in criminal justice systems as in other spheres of politics — must come from below rather than above. As in any complex system, reform in criminal justice cannot be brought about simply by legislating for structural change. The framework of enabling legislation must come from above, but real reform must be brought about from below through an interplay of changing values and practices, an interplay that creates a sort of social feedback loop. A small change in practice leads to a slight alteration in values, which further alters practice, and so on. Over time, a slight change in the ground rules percolates up through the system, changing values and practices as it goes, and eventually changing large-scale structures (Lewin, 1993; Waldrop, 1993).

What form would such a change to the base of the criminal justice system take? Many current proposals for change continue to take one of two forms: the authoritarian response suggested by classical criminology's view of the rational but immoral actor, and the permissive response suggested by the view of the actor born amoral by dint of biology or rendered amoral by psychological and social forces. Atomist and collectivist views of individuals and society underlie these responses. The individual is an isolated, rational actor or, alternatively, a product of biological or social and psychological forces beyond individual control. The law breaker is thus construed as either immoral or amoral. Debate concerns the most appropriate level of retribution, and this is to be determined by the degree of criminal intent, the *mens rea*, the extent to which an individual offender is deemed immoral or amoral. The current bureaucratic solution to this dilemma takes the form of "intermediate sanctions," state-imposed penalties that cut prison costs, please administrators, and frequently bear the "community" label (Byrne, Lurigia, Petersilia, 1992). They are not quite tough and not quite lax.

A philosophy of individualist holism suggests a way out of the impasse of atomistic collectivism. It suggests an effective alternative to either a tough or a lax response, both of which are responses by the state, focusing on the perceived flaws of an individual offender, ignoring the immediate victim and the wider community of people affected by an offence. The offender passively accepts the official response, whether it be the tough response of legal officers, the lax response of welfare officers, or some intermediate compromise. A real alternative to these options would be a collective, participatory response that focuses not on the offender but on the offence. The alternative goal would not be to determine just deserts for the individual, but to heal the collective harm caused by the offence. The process would see the majority of offenders neither as people who fully understood the situation but acted immorally anyway nor as people incapable of distinguishing right from wrong. It would, instead, recognize that much offending occurs when a situation is misconstrued. The problem of misconstrual is more affective than cognitive. The problem is that certain social emotions, which discourage people from transgressing moral boundaries, have failed to register. It is a problem particularly common in juvenile justice, but also common among those adult offenders who have met the system when young and been provoked rather than deterred by it.

How does this explanation fit with that of classical criminology and its critics? In fact, it presents a profound challenge to both schools of thought. It turns their central concern on its head. Both classical criminology and its critics sought to answer one basic question: Why do some people commit crime? Their focus, in other words, was on social deviance. Durkheim well understood the reason for this focus; collectives define themselves by reference to what they are not, by reference to those who deviate from social norms (Garland, 1990). This method may promote social solidarity, but it doesn't produce sound social theory. Freud's flawed view of childhood development, for instance, developed in part as a back-projection from his adult patients. He would have done better to follow the empirical path taken by modern child psychology (Kagan, 1994). In a similar manner, criminology's proposals for preventing crime arose from hypotheses about and studies of those who committed crime. Here again, the approach should have been from the opposite direction. Rather than asking why some people commit crime some of the time, the more fruitful question would have been: Why do most people, most of the time, not commit crime?

Recently, a number of social theorists have indeed asked that question. Predictably, the nature of the answers they provide reflects their professional discipline, but their answers augment rather than contradict one another. Political scientist Tom Tyler (1990) finds that people have a commitment to the law when they perceive the processes of the justice system to be fair and where some participation in those processes is allowed or even encouraged. People's commitment to the justice system is determined by the justice of its processes as much as by its outcomes.

Psychologist Travis Hirschi provides a rather different answer (Gottfredson & Hirschi, 1990). He finds a crucial variable separating those who commit crime from those who do not. That variable is self-control. Legal sociologist John Braithwaite (1989) reaches a related conclusion. As he sees it, the crucial variable is the tendency to experience shame in relation to unacceptable behavior. Shame may be triggered both by the private contemplation of a socially unacceptable act and by public exposure in the wake of such an act. "Discretion shame" is experienced by contemplation of acts that are socially unacceptable. The experience of discretion shame is thus a safeguard against the more painful experience of "disgrace shame" (Schneider, 1977). Just as disgust protects the individual against biologically harmful substances, so shame protects the individual against socially harmful experiences (Tomkins, 1987). But in order to feel discretion shame, the individual must have a knowledge of the boundaries that separate the socially acceptable from the shameful. If social experience—or lack of it—has set those boundaries at the wrong point, shame will be triggered inappropriately. Individual and social damage can result if shame is triggered too readily, or not readily enough.

Learning what is and isn't considered shameful is an essential part of socialization. Families, as the first school of moral development, play an important role in this process—though they can also, of course, do a great deal of damage if they evoke shame inappropriately (Harper & Hoopes, 1990; Nathanson, 1987). The complexities of socialization require that the net of socialization be widened, that the efforts of families be supplemented by the efforts of other institutions, the most important of which are schools.

Broadening the net of socialization creates, as it were, a psychological system of checks and balances. But the net extends to the mass commercial media, and they, of course, have a different agenda from families and schools. The mass commercial media encourage neither self-control nor social responsibility, but, rather, promote an association between aggressive material consumption and the positive affects of excitement and enjoyment. In the process, they serve as the messenger in an "incongruous alliance between some of the most powerful corporations . . . and some of the . . . least articulate or important citizens" (Gilbert, 1986, p. 213). Parents and schools frequently complain of a tension between their efforts and those of the corporate media. They are given little support by contemporary law and politics, which "still have little room for the sorts of institutions where notions of, feelings about, the good are generated, regenerated, and transmitted" (Glendon, 1991, p. 143).

So families and schools tend to form some sort of loose alliance in an attempt to socialize appropriately the children in their care. And it is in the study of this socialization that Braithwaite's work in understanding moral, sociable behavior moves beyond that of his colleagues. Braithwaite recognizes patterns in the daily informal socialization techniques employed within families and schools. He then compares these patterns with common patterns in criminal justice. That comparison leads to some powerful conclusions about current practices. As he sees it, many of the means used by modern criminal justice systems work against their own stated goals. Most obviously, while the rehabilitation and social reintegration of the offender are generally (and cyclically) espoused as ultimate goals of criminal justice, the actual means employed by courts (i.e., incarceration) are as likely to achieve the opposite, to produce ritual humiliation and stigmatization (Garfinkel, 1956).

This conflict between aims and means in criminal justice arises from a failure to draw one simple but fundamental distinction. Modern Western theory and practice has generally failed to distinguish between shame put to destructive, negative ends, and shame put to positive, constructive ends. The obvious exception to this is authoritative child-rearing. Here a child may be castigated for unacceptable behavior, but is then ritually reaccepted a short time later with a hug and soothing words. In the process, a distinction is made at a deep, emotional level between the unacceptable act and the still acceptable actor. Authoritarian and permissive child-rearing both fail to draw this distinction. The authoritarian approach must punish the act and punishes the actor in the process. The permissive approach cannot punish the actor and so excuses, justifies, condones, or ignores the act. Proponents of tough or lax responses in criminal justice tend to repeat these errors. They engage in stigmatic shaming or do their best to avoid shame altogether. Braithwaite's model advocates the alternative of reintegrative shaming.

An adequate theory of the emotions is essential to explain this distinction, to explain how act can be distinguished from actor even as shame is experienced. A common argument distinguishes between shame, which involves a negative evaluation of the whole self, and guilt, which involves a negative evaluation only of the act in question. It is sometimes argued that shame is essentially affective, guilt essentially cognitive. One will hear proponents of a permissive approach in criminal justice argue that offenders who are "suffering from low self-esteem" should not have their problem exacerbated by further exposure to shame. They should be made to "acknowledge guilt" but not to "feel shame."

This account overlooks a far more important distinction. It overlooks the distinction between the basic physiological affect of shame and the more complex emotion of shame. The emotion of shame combines the present affect/feeling of shame with memories of previous experiences of the affect of shame (Nathanson, 1992). It combines these past and present feelings with knowledge of social rules governing the broad set of circumstances where shame is appropriate and the narrower set of circumstances where guilt — for intentional acts — is appropriate. The emotion of shame is thus both affective and cognitive. It is evoked by any action or event that has been socially recognized as bad. However, the raw affect of shame — evoked, in Tomkins's definition, by the sudden incomplete reduction of interest or enjoyment — this raw affect is neither good nor bad. It is a negative affect, yes; the organism seeks to avoid shame and responds when shame is registered. It alerts one to social danger. What follows, however, may be good or bad. What the actor does, and what is done to the actor, will have social consequences that can be judged according to collective standards concerning the bad and the good.

For complex reasons, modern criminal justice systems hold that it is good to evoke shame in order to stigmatize, in order to lower the recipient of punishment to a level considered more appropriate (Garland, 1990). The victim has been degraded, so must the offender be degraded by a shame that stigmatizes. Shame is employed to cast out the offending act together with the offending actor. This assumption that the cure must take a similar form to the disease is typical of magical thinking. An alternative approach need not make such assumptions. Shame could still be evoked by the process. But the shame would be followed by a strengthening rather than a severing of social bonds. The evocation of shame could promote reintegration into the community rather than stigmatization from it. Rather than punishing an isolated individual on behalf of the collective, it could encourage those connected by emotional bonds to victim and offender to heal the damage and minimize the harm caused by an offence. Individual rights could be protected but social bonds could be recognized and used constructively. This is individualist holism rather than atomistic collectivism.

As it happens, active attempts have been made since the early 1970s to introduce something close to this alternative philosophy into criminal justice systems in Western Europe and in North America. Programs operating under the title of "victim-offender reconciliation" have been established with the conscious long-term aim of collective restitution rather than individual retribution. Two decades of experience have shown that such programs may indeed have some long-term influence. The success of such programs is, however, strongly influenced by several factors. Counseling before meetings appears to be less than useful. An individualist approach has disadvantages. Most importantly, the position of these programs within, or in relation to, the criminal justice system is a crucial variable. The more deeply they are embedded in the system, the more likely they are to be corroded by the pervasive focus on the offender and by the exclusive concern with securing the appropriate level of individual retribution for that offender (Galaway & Hudson, 1990). This is corrosion by authoritarian philosophy. But victim-offender reconciliation schemes are also in danger of corrosion by permissive philosophy. The morally deluded are prone to confuse victim-offender reconciliation with mediation and conciliation schemes. Mediation and conciliation programs are important alternatives to court in cases involving parties of equal moral standing who are contesting some social good. Where victim meets offender, in contrast, the contest has already occurred — on the offender's terms. The parties are not of equal moral standing. Running victim-offender reconciliation on the format of mediation and conciliation schemes can foster the illusion that the parties are of equal moral standing.

Given the twin dangers of corrosion by authoritarian and by permissive philosophy, the logical point at which to position a scheme is at the front end of the criminal justice system. Small changes in practice based on large shifts in philosophy are possible within the existing institutional framework of criminal justice. They are possible at the one point where state officials currently and regularly exercise discretion in recruiting civil society to the task of social regulation. That point is the grey zone between legalism and welfarism known as juvenile justice. At this gateway to the system and to the start of the criminal justice conveyor belt, one "diversionary" or "intermediate" scheme after another has been tried, as fashion shifts from tough responses to lax responses and back again. Large bureaucracies engage in this tug-of-war between authoritarian and permissive philosophies. Police, caught in the middle, are subject to regular criticism by both. But by looking to civil society rather than the state for answers, police may be able to coordinate an authoritative alternative to authoritarian legalism or permissive welfarism.

The origins of the proposed model actually lie with the Maori of Aotearoa, though similar systems may be found among indigenous cultures in other parts of the world. The basic model involves the convening of a conference in the wake of an offence where offender and victim have been identified. The focus is on the offence, so multiple offenders and/or victims may be involved. Present are not only the victim(s) and offender(s), but relatives, friends, or colleagues of both. The conference convenor follows the introduction with a request for a version of events from the offender(s). This is followed by a version from the victim(s), followed by a version from the family members of victim(s) and offender(s), and a version of events from others present. In the process, the ripple effects of a single act of theft or violence are dramatically revealed to the offender(s). All present register fear, anger, disgust, distress, surprise, and shame. But there is a way out of this emotional miasma. Participants usually need little prompting from the coordinator to realize that cooperation is the shortest path from the negative to the positive. By reaching some collective solution to repair the material damage, the group begins to lay the basis for more important acts of symbolic reparation and the gradual restoration of trust (Moore, 1993).

This conference model has now been adopted in other parts of Australasia, with different agencies responsible for its administration in different jurisdictions. The prognosis seems best where the schemes are administered by police. For many members of the liberal intelligentsia, such a claim will seem counterintuitive. But it is not illogical. Consider the scheme's several aims: It aims to limit the numbers of people entering an authoritarian criminal justice system, while offering something better than the permissive alternative of doing nothing or the authoritarian-permissive hybrid of trying to govern the offender's soul with involuntary official-therapeutic treatments. Police are the first point of contact with offender and victim. Police coordination of the scheme minimizes contact with the criminal justice system. The scheme also aims to give equal weight to the needs of offenders and victims and of their respective communities of care. Victims appear readier to attend conferences convened by police, rather than by agencies which have traditionally focused exclusively on offenders. The underlying aim of the scheme is closer to the medical than the military model. It aims to minimize the harm caused by offending behavior. It does this while retaining appropriate safeguards of rights. So there are two nice paradoxes here. A focus on the offence actually produces a better outcome for victim and offender and those close to them. A focus on material reparation actually promotes symbolic reparation and restitution. Cooperation promotes reconciliation.

The most carefully designed version of the model currently deals only with offences committed by juveniles. It uses the longstanding police discretion to caution juveniles, but actually does something useful with that discretion rather than proceeding with the usual undignified farce of a bored or angry sergeant castigating a lone offender in the presence of a guardian. The traditional caution is now replaced by a conference, known variously as a Family Group Conference, a Community Account-ability conference, or some similar formula. A weekly panel considers cases for which the initial police investigation has been completed. If the offender(s) and victim(s) have been identified, and if the technical guilt of the offender is not in question, the panel may consider recommending that the case be dealt with by way of conference rather than court. The option is then put to potential participants. They may retain the court option, and they also have the right to leave a conference that has begun and have the case heard in court. There has been little evidence, however, of either option being exercised.

The panel deciding on cases consists either of police alone or of police, legal and welfare officials, and community representatives. The latter arrangement may be preferable, both because it brings other perspectives to the decision process and because it allays concerns about police ac-countability. If the conference process is proving effective, the propor-tion of cases dealt with by conference rather than court will increase. (Conferencing may also be used within the justice system as an option after court hearings, but it is appropriate only where victims willingly attend. The experience elsewhere with victim-offender reconciliation is that there is a tendency for the process to be seen as part of the punish-ment. Accordingly, a program of post-court conferences should be seen as supplementary to a program of conferences run as an alternative to court.)

The model discussed here uses police only as catalyst for a solution that is achieved by members of civil society. Police coordinate the initial arrangements. They provide a legal and in some cases physical safe-guard. In other respects, the scheme is run by civil society rather than the state. It is a reform from below, changing practices and values, rather than reform from above, changing structures. The scheme can thus be introduced as gradually as required. It can begin in relatively stable communities with small numbers of minor crimes committed by juve-niles. The panel considering cases may initially divert only a small num-ber of them to conferences. Experience suggests that, as the scheme proves effective, the panel will rapidly increase the number of victims and offenders who are offered the alternative process. Experience also suggests an important added advantage of the scheme, for conference participants carry the philosophy with them, ensuring that it is consid-ered for adoption in other areas. Schools have been quick to understand the implications of family conferencing — as have many families that had previously failed to develop authoritative rules of governance (see Alder

& Wundersitz, 1994). In this way, the philosophy underlying the scheme influences civil society. The maturity of the polity will determine the extent to which the philosophy and practice of authoritative, reinteg- rative shaming can be extended to less stable communities, more serious crimes, and older offenders.

For offenders who have misconstrued the circumstances, an authorita- tive response is preferable to the harsh measures of authoritarianism, which deprive people of basic rights to liberty and dignity. It is preferable to the lax response of permissive culture, which deprives offenders of the right to be made aware—to feel—the consequences of their behavior. For victims, who have been excluded from participation in modern jus- tice systems and who are currently used as passive exhibits in the state's search for retribution, this participatory authoritative model offers an even greater advance. The psychological model that best explains why the process works is affect theory. It accounts for the observation that basic common feelings seem to bind people together, evoke moral re- sponses, and encourage cooperation. Consideration of the conferencing model in the light of affect theory provides further justification for a shift from the extremes of atomism and collectivism to the synthesis that we are here calling individualist holism.

AFFECT AND SCRIPT THEORY: A BIOSOCIAL SYNTHESIS

I have argued that one can discern a pattern underlying the history of modern criminological theory and criminal justice practice. Theory and practice have been marked by the interplay of two views, the extremism of which has been exacerbated by an adversarial justice system. The view of the individual in criminological theory has oscillated between that of the free-willed rational actor, on one hand, and that of the actor deter- mined by biological, psychological, and social forces, on the other. Ac- cording to the first view, the social world is to be understood as a random collection of atomistic individuals. According to the second, the social world is to be understood as a collective, the individual constituents of which are determined by social facts outside themselves. These theoreti- cal positions suggest two responses in practice—authoritarianism and permissiveness. The authoritarian response is considered appropriate for the rational actor weighing the pleasure of crime against the pain of the official response. The authoritarian response is also considered appro- priate for the actor whose behavior is determined by innate drives, which must be broken by harsh measures (Miller, 1983). The permissive alternative is considered appropriate for the actor whose behavior is determined by social-psychological factors beyond individual control.

A stable synthesis of these views is not possible, for they are diametrically opposed. Free-willed rational agents do not belong in a world of puppets whose actions are determined by unconscious or external forces. A synthesis of two related positions is, however, possible. More persuasive than the collectivist model is an individualism that sees social structures as threatening but not overriding individual intentionality. More persuasive than the atomist model is a holism that sees individuals as essentially social agents "whose ability to think, or at least to think commonable thoughts, is a social property" (Pettit, 1993, p. 213). The unstable oscillation between the extremes of atomism and collectivism in theory and practice may be replaced by the stable synthesis of individualist holism. Here the subject of social theory and politicolegal practice is not the isolated rational actor or the socially determined emotive puppet. It is, instead, the individual enmeshed in a network of social relations, balancing personal and impersonal points of view, with emotions generally supplementing rather than undermining rationality (de Sousa, 1987; Frank, 1988; Nagel, 1986, 1991).

Atomism and collectivism can be dispensed with as useful models of self and society. They can be replaced with the mutually compatible models of holism and individualism. A single theoretical concept is still required to bridge the gap between large-scale social-structural accounts of human motivation and small-scale psychological accounts. The concept that bridges this gap between grand sociology and psychology is that of social capital (Coleman, 1990). Social capital is a measure of the number and strength of relations in a given community. It is less tangible than either financial capital or human capital—the accumulated skills and knowledge of a community. Nevertheless, social capital is a vital ingredient of stable, vibrant communities. Sophisticated comparative historical studies go so far as to suggest that "it is the key to making democracies work" (Putnam, 1993, p. 185). And it is social capital that is depleted when the criminal justice system, rather than promoting collective participation in the process of harm minimization, severs social bonds in search of retribution. It often does so in communities that can ill afford such depletion.

The concept of social capital has been something of a missing link in social theory. It links psychology with sociology, individuals with collectivities. The fundamental elements of social capital are interpersonal bonds governed by emotions, by affective resonance between individuals. Shared positive affect is the basic glue of society, whereas the ability of closely bonded individuals to mutualize negative affect in order to reduce it can be considered part of the healing mechanism of society. It is appropriate then that, just as the concept of social capital unites disparate concepts in social theory, a theory of affects and emotions has contributed to a similar synthesis within psychology. Apparently irreconcilable opposites have been synthesized.

Of course, the struggle within psychology has taken place between not two but three exaggerated positions. The subdisciplines of psychology have tended to focus on instincts and drives, on motor learning, or on cognition, all three reductionist approaches having proven inadequate to their self-allotted task. As in so many areas, the new synthesis revives many themes that were overlooked during the reductionism and academic bureaucratization of recent decades. Locke, it turns out, was half-correct when he claimed that there was nothing in the mind that was not first in the senses. His claim is patently not true for the individual, but it appears to be true for the species. Individual experience is not written onto a blank slate. It is interpreted via a network of innate, hardwired systems that have been selected for in human evolution (Gazzaniga, 1992). This is the story for the species, for the genotype.

The story for the phenotype is just as important. The software of experience—to use Nathanson's personal computing analogy—is not simply loaded into the hardware of the brain and body. The crucial breakthrough provided by Silvan Tomkins was to discern a level between the hardware and the software. Experience is "loaded"—interpreted, acted upon, and stored in memory—via this intermediate level, via the "firmware" of the affect system. Experiences of interest and enjoyment, surprise, anger, fear, distress, dissmell, disgust, and shame—all these basic physiological experiences shape character from birth. Developmental and evolutionary psychology continues to find empirical evidence for this profound insight.

The three main subdisciplines of psychology have traditionally managed to talk past one another because they have been concerned with different parts of the brain. The motor learning that fascinated behaviorists involves the core of the triune brain, as do the remnant instincts that behaviorism steadfastly denied (MacLean, 1990). The phenomena traditionally known as primary emotions, particularly fascinating to drive theorists, are registered largely within the hypothalamic-limbic axis. Cognition—psychology's most popular topic in recent decades—occurs in the thalamic-neocortical axis. The phenomena common to all three parts are the affects. Recognition of this intermediate system, this firmware between the hardware of the body and brain, and the software of experience, enables a synthesis of the competing schools in psychology. Certainly, sheer cognitive power makes humans special. We are distinguished from our mammalian relatives by "an abundance of random access type memory space in our neocortex" (Panksepp, 1990, p. 293). But it is the affect system that ties cognition in the neocortex to the rest of the brain and body. And this is why "human consciousness, at its core, is a feeling" (Gazzaniga, 1992, p. 203).

The modern rational-bureaucratic state, however, proceeds on the assumption that thinking rather than feeling, neocortical cognition rather than subcortical affect, is at the core of human consciousness. One of Darwin's many insights was to realize the folly of this position. He took the ethical theories of the Scottish Enlightenment and explained them in biological terms. Biologically based emotions are at the core of human social behavior, of which ethical behavior is a subset. Tomkins, building on Darwin's insights concerning human emotional expression, performed for psychology a task similar to that performed for ethics by Darwin. He stressed the biological basis of a consciousness located within a network of physiological systems. This model was proposed at a time when artificial intelligence was in the ascendancy within cognitive science, when consciousness was presumed by some to be analogous to complex binary information-processing within a single system (Gardner, 1985). But people do not become sociable, ethical, or moral on the basis of cool, rational reflection alone. As ethology has emphasized, we are a uniquely adaptable species of mammal but, like our closest relatives, we are born with certain innate capacities and tendencies. Sociability and certain basic ethical impulses seem to belong in this category (Alexander, 1987; Richards, 1987). In addition, the unique experience of each individual is filtered through the preexisting template of the affect system. Conscious design of political institutions must take both factors into account — the fixed capacities and tendencies, and the affect system that sets the boundaries of behavioral flexibility.

As Margaret Gruter (1991) has remarked in the specific case of criminal justice, "The effectiveness of law will be proportional to the degree to which the function of a particular law complements the function of the behavior that the law intends to regulate" (p. 21). The conferencing model described in this chapter seeks a better fit between law and nature. The law is invoked, as always, on the basis of a moral judgment made by earlier legislators and confirmed on the spot by a law enforcement officer. Instead of the further formal application of state law, however, the law is used as a safeguard around a more subtle, but more powerful process. In this process, the social capital of a small community affected by an illegal act is used to seek a better outcome for all concerned. Powerful affects are shared among the group. This affective resonance fosters empathy. Not only do offenders begin to grasp the victim's point of view, but the reverse occurs, making forgiveness easier, lightening the burden of the victim's anger.

The golden rule underlying the conference process is the golden rule of all human ethical systems – doing unto others as one would have done unto oneself. Under these conditions, crime is not the source of pride that it so readily becomes when the isolated offender wins in a game against the state. When the state is removed from the picture, crime becomes a source of shame. But that shame need not be debilitating. The pride that could counteract shame is also available in the collective conference setting. Pride is achieved through striving for and achieving goals. Interest registers in the striving; enjoyment in the achievement. Participants set goals to restore the damage through some sort of work on behalf of the victim or other work agreed to by the victim. The pride offered in a community accountability conference is doubly attractive. Agreeing to honor the collectively derived goals provides an opportunity for offenders to prove their worth, to restore lost trust and to rejoin the moral community.

The conference itself and the subsequent honoring of agreements reached in the conference provide important emotional lessons for offenders and victims. As Tomkins's script theory suggests, emotional lessons are important not for what is forgotten or suppressed but for what is remembered and transformed (Singer & Salovey, 1993). This is not a passive model, focusing only on affect, feeling, and memory. Like all lessons learned when affect and cognition produce emotion, these lessons are sufficiently powerful to influence future behavior. In the course of a conference, offenders who had previously reacted to shame by withdrawing and by attacking others are offered a lesson in the constructive avoidance of shame.

The conference process evokes basic affective responses, responses that may foster genuine individual and collective change. It does this within a network of relationships, not the dyadic relationships of punitive state officials and castigated offenders, but a state-coordinated network of relationships between offenders, victims, and their respective communities of care. The process is obviously not fail-safe. Where it fails, the traditional criminal justice system remains as a back-up support. But with a gradual rebuilding of social capital, with practice in the skills of apology, forgiveness, restitution, and reconciliation, real progress might be made.

As with all long-term reform, the justice system reform proposed here is designed to start from the ground up. It is a minor change in method, but one designed to foster a change in values by promoting the participation and collective education of all involved. It is educative for offenders, who are finally granted the right to understand the consequences of their actions. It is thus an authoritative alternative to the authoritarian cry for just deserts on behalf of the collective and to the permissive call for minimal state intervention on the grounds that not intervening at all is better than harmful intervention. The process is educative and liberating for victims. It is educative about the circumstances of the offender and the offence. It helps to liberate victims from the debilitating effects of chronic anger, shame, fear, dissmell, disgust, and distress. The process is educative for supporters of offenders and victims, who begin to contribute to the process of understanding the complex ramifications of a single offence. Finally, the process is educative for police, who have hitherto interpreted calls for community policing as meaning better policing *of* the community, rather than better coordination of self-regulation *by* communities. It is educative to witness a group of people, brought together to resolve an issue, pursuing cooperation rather than antagonism, seeking to minimize collective harm, rather than to maximize individual retribution. It is also educative for these state officials to see affects and emotions evoked in the pursuit of constructive rather than destructive ends. Affect theory accounts for these dynamics far more effectively than models which understand cooperation purely in terms of rational calculation (see Ostrom, 1990).

In the appropriate setting, a group will cooperate to transform contagious negative affects into contagious positive affects. Anger, fear, distress, dissmell, disgust, and shame are transformed into interest and enjoyment. This result cannot be achieved if people persist in responding to feelings of shame by attacking themselves, by attacking others, or by withdrawing (Nathanson, 1992). In a cooperative group, the only response that can transform negative affects to positive is the response of active avoidance. The most effective way to achieve this is to cooperate in goal-setting. The short-term goals are the very practical ones of negotiated agreement for reparation and restitution. The symbolic acts of apology and forgiveness invariably come to be considered at least as important as reparation of material damage and restitution for property loss. Longer-term goals include the restoration of trust and cooperation.

CONCLUSION

A colleague, who happens to be a police officer and an astute politician, recently made what seemed a throwaway remark about the conferencing scheme discussed in this paper. As he has been instrumental in piloting the scheme in Australia, the remark seemed worthy of reflection: "Get policing right, and everything else will flow from that." It sounded at the time like the opening gambit of a senior industrial officer at a difficult negotiating session. In retrospect, it bore the mark of the philosopher. The claim is less outlandish than it seems.

The institution of policing sits at the intersection of civil and criminal law. Modern police agencies were established first and foremost as departments of miscellaneous services and general peacekeeping. The modern community policing movement has arisen in part to reclaim the discretionary ground that was lost in the drive to a model of narrow law enforcement. Nevertheless, much of the damage appeared to have been done and appeared to be irreversible. Police had become, as Donald Nathanson exclaimed when he first learned of the scheme, "the embodiment of normative psychology!" Typically, there is also a deeper truth behind this exclamation.

Policing has become a symbol of the way in which the modern state has—inadvertently or otherwise—taken much of the responsibility for social regulation away from institutions of civil society. It has divided a single task of social regulation into multiple tasks of detecting, shaming, and reintegrating. It has apportioned those multiple tasks into separate departments, producing some unexpected results. One result is that detecting and shaming produce stigmatization, not reintegration, when performed by the impersonal state.

Civil society and the agents of the state are now realizing that a good deal of justice has been well hidden in the law and that, where possible and with all appropriate safeguards, it may be time to begin handing it back to the civil society from which it was taken. The most appropriate institution to initiate the change may well be the police. Balanced at the intersection of civil society and the criminal justice system of the state, police retain a certain discretion to decide, in many cases, how and where a problem should be handled. As police discretion has been reduced, however, more problems have been automatically hauled across the line separating civil society from the state. With the appropriate mechanisms of accountability, this widening net of state control might now be narrowed. The alternative is not the permissive absence of control, but the authoritative expansion of a net of community regulation within a civil society where individual rights remain safeguarded.

The scheme described here takes account of criminal justice practice, criminological theory, and the more fundamental, integrated psychology offered by affect theory. It offers a mechanism by which the juvenile justice system might stop treating young people as blank slates, as beasts to be tamed, or as purely rational, isolated individuals. If we must talk rights talk, then let us say that the process restores to young people the right to understand the consequences of their behavior. It offers equal time — and participation — to the victims of those young offenders. Their rights too should be enshrined. The process extends rights of participation to the community of care harmed by an offence in the process of minimizing that harm. That process powerfully evokes the full range of affects, which set the emotional boundaries of acceptable individual behavior and which strengthen the emotional ties that bind individuals together. This is an education for all participants. Its effects ripple through larger communities, perhaps hastening the day when the process can be extended to a wider range of offences and offenders. Greater responsibility for social regulation is thereby reclaimed from the modern state. In the process, civil society may be able to strengthen itself.

REFERENCES

Alder, C., & Wundersitz, J. (1994). *Family conferencing and juvenile justice: The way forward or misplaced optimism?* Canberra: AIC.

Alexander, R. D. (1987). *The biology of moral systems.* New York: A. de Gruyter.

Barkow, J. H., Cosmides, L., & Tooby, J (Eds.). (1992). *The adapted mind: evolutionary psychology and the generation of culture.* New York: Oxford University Press.

Braithwaite, J. (1989). *Crime, shame, and reintegration.* Cambridge: Cambridge University Press.

Broucek, F. J. (1991). *Shame and the self.* New York: Guilford.

Byrne, J. M., Lurigia, A. J., & Petersilia, J. (1992). *Smart sentencing: The emergence of intermediate sanctions.* Newbury Park: Sage.

Coleman, J. S. (1990). *Foundations of social theory.* Cambridge, MA: Harvard University Press.

Conley, J. A. (1993). Historical perspective and criminal justice. *Journal of Criminal Justice Education, 4,* 349–360.

Damon, W. (1988). *The moral child: Nurturing children's natural moral growth.* New York: Free Press.

Damon, W. (Ed.). (1989). *Child development: Today and tomorrow.* San Francisco: Jossey Bass.

Darwin, C. E. (1871/1981). *The descent of man and selection in relation to sex.* Princeton: Princeton University Press.

Darwin, C. E. (1872/1969). *The expression of the emotions in man and animals.* Chicago: Illionois University Press.

Degler, C. N. (1991). *In search of human nature: The decline and revival of Darwinism in American social thought.* New York: Oxford University Press.

de Sousa, R. (1987). *The rationality of emotion.* Cambridge, MA: MIT Press.

Donald, M. (1991). *Origins of the modern mind: Three stages in the evolution of culture and cognition.* Cambridge, MA: Harvard University Press.

Fox, R. (1989). *The search for society: Quest for a biosocial science and morality.* New Brunswick: Rutgers University Press.

Frank, R. (1988). *Passions within reason: The strategic role of the emotions.* New York: Norton.

Friedman, L. M. (1993). *Crime and punishment in American history.* New York: Basic Books.

Galaway, B., & Hudson, J. (1990). *Criminal justice, restitution, and reconciliation.* Monsey, NJ: Criminal Justice Press.

Gardner, H. (1985). *The mind's new science.* New York: Basic Books.

Gardner, H. (1993). *Multiple intelligences: The theory in practice.* New York: Basic Books.

Garfinkel, H. (1956). Conditions of successful degradation ceremonies. *American Journal of Sociology, 61,* 420–424.

Garland, D. (1990). *Punishment and modern society: A study in social theory.* Chicago: University of Chicago Press.

Gazzaniga, M. (1985). *The social brain.* New York: Basic Books.

Gazzaniga, M. (1992). *Nature's mind: The biological roots of thinking, emotions, sexuality, language, and intelligence.* New York: Basic Books.

Gilbert, J. (1986). *A cycle of outrage: America's reaction to the juvenile delinquent in the 1950s.* New York: Oxford University Press.

Glendon, M. A. (1991). *Rights talk: The impoverishment of political discourse.* New York: Free Press.

Gottfredson, M. R., & Hirschi, T. (1990). *A general theory of crime.* Stanford: Stanford University Press.

Gruter, M. (1991). *Law and the mind: Biological origins of human behavior.* Newbury Park, CA: Sage.

Gurr, T. R. (1989). Historical trends in violent crime: Europe and America. In T. R. Gurr (Ed.), *Violence in America, Vol. 1: The history of crime.* Newbury Park, CA: Sage.

Habermas, J. (1988). *The theory of communicative action.* London: Heinemann.

Harper, J. M., & Hoopes, M. H. (1990). *Uncovering shame: An approach integrating individual and family systems.* New York: Norton.

Kagan, J. (1994). *Galen's prophecy: Temperament in human nature.* New York: Basic Books.

Lane, R. (1989). On the social meaning of homicide trends in America. In T. R. Gurr (Ed.), *Violence in America, Vol. 1: The history of crime.* Newbury Park, CA: Sage.

Lewin, R. (1993). *Complexity: Life on the edge of chaos.* London: Phoenix.

Lewis, M. (1992). *Shame: The exposed self.* New York: Free Press.

McDonald, J. M., & Moore, D. B. (1995). Achieving the "good community": A local police initiative and its wider ramifications. In K. Hazlehurst (Ed.), *Perceptions of justice: issues of indigenous and community empowerment.* Aldershot: Avebury.

MacLean, P. D. (1990). *The triune brain.* New York: Plenum Press.

Mansbridge, J. (Ed.). (1990). *Beyond self-interest.* Chicago: University of Chicago Press.

Masters, R. D., & Gruter, M. (1992). *The sense of justice: Biological foundations of law.* Newbury Park, CA: Sage.

Miller, A. (1983). *For your own good: Hidden cruelty in child-rearing and the roots of violence.* London: Virago.

Monkkonen, E. (1981). *Police in urban America, 1860–1920.* Cambridge, UK: Cambridge University Press.

Moore, D.B. (1993). Shame, forgiveness, and juvenile justice. *Criminal Justice Ethics, 12,* 3–25.

Nagel, T. (1986). *The view from nowhere.* New York: Oxford University Press.

Nagel, T. (1991). *Equality and partiality.* New York: Oxford University Press.

Nathanson, D. L. (Ed.). (1987). *The many faces of shame.* New York: Guilford.

Nathanson, D. L. (1992). *Shame and pride: Affect, sex, and the birth of the self.* New York: Norton.

Okin, S. M. (1989). *Justice, gender, and the family.* New York: Basic Books.

Ostrom, E. (1990). *Governing the commons: The evolution of institutions for collective action.* Cambridge, UK: Cambridge University Press.

Panksepp, J. (1990). Gray zones at the emotion/cognition interface: A commentary. In J. A. Gray (Ed.), *Psychobiological aspects of relationships between emotion and cognition.* Hillsdale, NJ: Erlbaum.

Pettit, P. (1993). *The common mind: An essay in psychology, society, and politics*. New York: Oxford University Press.

Putnam, R. D. (1993). *Making democracy work: Civic traditions in modern italy*. Princeton: Princeton University Press.

Richards, R. J. (1987). *Darwin and the emergence of evolutionary theories of mind and behavior*. Chicago: University of Chicago Press.

Schneider, C. D. (1977). *Shame, exposure, and privacy*. Boston: Beacon. (Reprinted 1992, New York: Norton).

Singer, J. A., & Salovey, P. (1993). *The remembered self: Emotion and memory in personality*. New York: Free Press.

Tavuchis, N. (1991). *Mea culpa: A sociology of apology and reconciliation*. Stanford: Stanford University Press.

Taylor, G. (1985). *Pride, shame, and guilt: Emotions of self-assessment*. Oxford: Clarendon.

Tomkins, S. S. (1962). *Affect, imagery, consciousness, Vol. 1: The positive affects*. New York: Springer.

Tomkins, S. S. (1963). *Affect, imagery, consciousness, Vol. 2: The negative affects*. New York: Springer.

Tomkins, S. S. (1987). Shame. In D. L. Nathanson (Ed.), *The many faces of shame*. New York: Guilford.

Tomkins, S. S. (1991). *Affect, imagery, consciousness, Vol. 3: The negative affects: Anger and fear*. New York: Springer.

Tomkins, S. S. (1992). *Affect, imagery, consciousness, Vol. 4: Cognition*. New York: Springer.

Tyler, T. R. (1990). *Why people obey the law*. New Haven: Yale University Press.

Waldrop, M. M. (1993). *Complexity: The emerging science at the edge of order and chaos*. London: Viking.

Wilson, J. Q. (1993). *The moral sense*. New York: Free Press.

Wilson, J. Q., & Herrnstein, R. J. (1985). *Crime and human nature*. New York: Simon & Schuster.

Winson, J. (1985). *Brain and psyche: The biology of the unconscious*. New York: Anchor.

Wispé, L. (1991). *The psychology of sympathy*. New York: Plenum Press.

17

Some Closing Thoughts on Affect, Scripts, and Psychotherapy

Donald L. Nathanson

Something happens to you when the ideas of Tomkins permeate to the core of your being. Having seen a number of colleagues go through the process, I have begun to recognize a rhythm.

At first there is the excitement associated with the idea that all of our emotional experiences can be explained. We grew up feeling helpless in the throes of our emotions, just as we became helplessly aroused by a sexuality that always left us more than a bit confused and somewhat embarrassed no matter what had happened. The cognitive theorists offered to make things simple by organizing life in terms of cerain patterns of thought, but much as cognitive techniques serve to mute and modulate uncomfortable emotion, they do not provide a satisfying explanation of those experiences. The neurobiologists have shown a great many of the pathways over which emotion-related activity must travel, but as yet have not offered for these "primitive mechanisms" much of a role in healthy, adult life. Freud caught our attention for a long time when he linked the complex and swirling emotionality that surrounds sexuality to the general problem of emotion itself. But we knew instinctively that something about his theory didn't feel right. Little or none of our adult interest in, say, mathematics or sculpture really feels as if it had any

link to sexual arousal–you shouldn't have to explain all abiding interests as desexualized libido. And despite how different shame feels
from terror, Freudian theory said that both of these highly specific
emotions were forms of anxiety triggered by something that made
sexual energy travel along the wrong paths.

Tomkins offered us something different. A century earlier, Darwin
(1872/1979) had said that the emotions fell into clusters or families,
each of which was associated with highly specific displays on the
face and body. Where generations of later psychologists had as-
sured us that the "abc's" of mental function–affect, behavior, and
cognition–were separate and intrinsically different, from Darwin
alone we should have known that they were connected at some
deeper level. Every emotion is expressed by some bodily behavior
and is associated with a highly specific range of thoughts and style
of thinking. Afire with the same realizations that led some of his con-
temporaries to develop cybernetics, Tomkins added the what, when,
where, and why to how we had emotions. He developed a theory at
once so spare and beautiful and also so complex and daunting that
it requires a lifetime of study. It starts with the observations of Darwin
that we have evolved to react to certain stimuli with highly scripted
patterns of facial and bodily response that, instead of becoming
vague and vestigial as animal forms climb the evolutionary tree, become increasingly specific and discrete.

Nineteenth-century biology had contributed the idea that the major difference between living creatures and lifeless aggregates of
chemicals was that protoplasm was "irritable." Claude Bernard declared as the essence of biology the idea that in an experiment one
asked the cell a question by altering some aspect of its existence
and looking for the response of that cell. Life itself was thought to be
a matter of stimulus and response. Twentieth-century psychology
responded to the call of the biologists by studying mental life as
similar matters of stimulus and response. The search for stimulus-
response pairs has occupied most of academic psychology until
quite recently, when awareness of the importance of affect shifted
our attention toward these programmed physiological mechanisms
that influence or determine our eventual response. Human life is a
matter of stimulus-affect-response triads, not stimulus-response pairs.
Tomkins added that the evolving mind of the human being has allowed these clusters of affective behavior to be used in ever more
sophisticated ways. Ultimately, his was a theory of "minding," or what
he came to call "human being theory."

The theory occupied his entire professional life. Much like Darwin, who saw in every life form an opportunity to demonstrate his theory of evolution, Tomkins saw in every human action further demonstration of his theory of mind. Although he was an avid student of every scientific advance that might influence his work and drew heavily on evidence culled from the observations of psychotherapists, he did not offer any suggestions for the development of a new form of psychotherapy. Such responsibility falls on those of us who have come to understand and appreciate his work. In the five short essays that follow, each drawn from the pages of the *Bulletin of the Tomkins Institute*, I have tried to communicate some of the spirit of this work. –DLN

THE RANGE AND SCOPE OF OUR INTERESTS

IF PSYCHOTHERAPY IS the art through which people are enabled to optimize the use of their emotional, sexual, and cognitive functions, each system of therapy must involve some aspect of the affective and the cognitive systems of the brain, as well as some form of integration of both with sexuality. In an era of research that daily brings us new data about the machinery of life, it becomes increasingly important to offer some principle around which this information may all be organized. The affect and script theories of Silvan Tomkins provide just such an organizing principle, allowing maximal utilization of all research findings and maximization of therapeutic effectiveness no matter what one's preferred system of treatment.

Tomkins was the first to suggest that each of the nine innate affects has a specific function and that individual personality involves the gestalt of our life experience of those affects. He stated that each affect has its own address in the brain, not so much a grouping of neurons capable of approach by stereotactic instruments, but a complex program with subunits located throughout the limbic system and set into motion when signaled. Reasoning backwards from his analysis of the nature of the six basic affects (interest–excitement, enjoyment–joy, surprise–startle, fear–terror, distress–anguish, and anger–rage), Tomkins inferred that the affect system was based on one principle—programmed reaction to the combination of intensity and frequency of stimulation that he called stimulus density. Stimulus density, whether produced as the registration of external events through perception or by purely internal biological events, can only increase, decrease, or stay the same; the affects are therefore complex responses to simple physiological principles. Innate affect is the link between physiology and psychology. Only cognitive appraisal of the gestalt formed by the sequences of events we come to know as our affects can provide clues to whatever has triggered the innate mechanism. How we think about our affects and the scripts by which we react to them allow us to use neocortical cognition as a response to the conditions that triggered the affect.

Pattern-making is art, pattern-finding is science; great art and great science involve patterns of great significance. Tomkins knew that the innate affects were the heart of the problem studied by philosophers, novelists, and social scientists throughout the history of our species. What it means to be human depends on the expression and the management of these innate mechanisms. Yet it is from this simple statement that affect theory and script theory, its natural companion, veer off so dramatically from other systems for the explanation of human emotional function. Even though each innate affect involves brain mechanisms at every level from the molecular to the neuronal to the more complex yet subtle interplay of memorialized and current events, Tomkins insisted that the experience of affect requires one further body system. No matter what happened inside the brain, no matter how complex the activity sequence leading up to the moment when an affect was triggered, nothing could be called an affect unless and until it reached its programmed expression on the face. No matter what sets them in motion, the innate affects cause things to happen in the microcirculation of the face that makes privileged the highly patterned contraction and relaxation of the facial muscles. In order for normal emotion to take place, something must happen inside the brain to trigger one of the affect programs, after which the circuitry causes events outside the brain.

Only after the affect has been registered on the face and appraised as one or another of these innate patterns we come to experience from the earliest moments of life do we respond in the way we call emotional. Normal emotion (which includes everything we have ever considered as motivated behavior) cannot be said to have occurred until something happens inside the brain, goes outside the brain to the face, and then comes back into the brain for further analysis and processing.

The science of Tomkins's times was inadequate to offer more than a hint of whatever brain mechanisms might be involved. It was for this reason I suggested that affect might be studied by attention to its parts as long as no part is mistaken for the whole. A program may divided into its subroutines for purposes of evaluation and repair, but must be returned whole for proper use. Affect requires the services of certain structural effectors (neuronal paths along which affect-related messages travel) and chemical mediators that course through the blood as well as between cells of the brain. It is expressed at various sites of action, including but not limited to the face. Whatever happens at these sites of action is sensed by a system of receptors that transmit information to a central assembly where it is analyzed and/or used to trigger more affect. All this is set in motion by the organizing programs described by Tomkins.

Updating the computer analogy Tomkins first introduced in the 1962 conference he called "The Computer Simulation of Personality," I have asked that we consider all emotion a matter of hardware, firmware, and software (Nathanson, 1988). The software, of course, involves the way each of us has grown up in a family, a nation, and an era; it is the history of our affective life. Analogous to the firmware called ROM (Read Only Memory) chips that make possible the work of our personal computers, the firmware for emotion is the group of nine prewritten programs delineated by Tomkins. By the term hardware I imply both the sites of action for the firmware programs and the actual brain mechanisms triggered at all levels of emotional activity. Such an approach allows us a novel method of analysis for the work of scientists in gleaming laboratories filled with state-of-the-art machines capable of measuring minute quantities of substances hardly known to exist only a few years ago. Even a cursory examination of some recent, well-publicized "breakthrough" experiments suggests that the researchers might benefit from an introduction to affect theory.

A January 12, 1994 report in *The Philadelphia Inquirer* cited work from the Wisconsin Regional Primate Center attributing to endorphins the pleasurable feelings occurring in mother and child when they are reunited after a separation. "We think we have a handle on what may be the biochemical underpinning of mother-infant bonding," said Dr. Stephen Shelton. The newspaper article goes on to describe the researchers' theory that "this chemical reward for physical closeness evolved to keep mothers and offspring in a tight relationship. On a larger scale, they add, the phenomenon could be an evolutionary adaptation among social animals. 'They need to move together as a troop, and so [endorphin is] the glue.'"

Shelton and his colleagues separated young rhesus monkeys from their mothers, reuniting them after 20 minutes in a "strange environment"; the ensuing discomfort would normally have been relieved by "calming hugs" from the mothers. "However, the young monkeys were then given injections of morphine, which induced peaceful emotions independent of interaction with the mother. 'The young monkeys also moved around and explored the cage,' says Shelton, something they

wouldn't have normally done. 'We were filling up the endorphin receptors with morphine, so that (the) infant feels good without clinging to its
mother.' In a converse experiment, the researchers separated, then reunited the monkeys, but gave the young animals injections of naltrexone,
so that behavior that normally would turn on the endorphin system
would have no such effect. This time, the youngsters cried more and
sought to cling to their mothers more intensely than usual, indicating the
failure to trigger an endorphin calm was making them feel particularly
insecure."

How might this material be interpreted by a scientist familiar with
affect theory? Use of the Facial Affect Coding System (Ekman & Friesen, 1978) might allow us to determine which of the negative affects was
responsible for the discomfort seen in the baby monkeys, but we can
guess that they showed some blend of distress–anguish and fear–terror
that turned into enjoyment–joy when they were reunited with mother. I
have long maintained that enjoyment–joy is at least partially mediated
by endorphin release; Tomkins (1992, p. 50) sees it as an additional level
of amplification related to mood but not a primary part of the affect
mechanism. Innate affect is the most powerful and most specific of the
biological mechanisms that cause us to feel, but it is not the only one.
Endorphin and the reticular activating system are nonspecific amplifiers
that also make things happen around the body, mechanisms that I believe evolved much earlier than the highly scripted innate affect programs.

Infusion of any substance capable of activating the sites of action
normally associated with an affect can trigger enough of the pattern of
activation associated with that affect to be interpreted as the gestalt of
that affect. In other words, injection of morphine will bring about
enough of the pattern associated with enjoyment–joy to be experienced
as enjoyment–joy (contentment); morphine relieves distress–anguish and
makes unnecessary any further attempt to seek relief for whatever had
only a moment ago triggered distress.

Using this language, it seems clear that Kalin and Shelton have demonstrated (1) the ability of morphine to reduce distress–anguish (hardly
a novel conclusion), (2) the action of morphine in reducing thereby the
motivation provided by the innate affect distress–anguish (not surprising), and (3) the ability of naltrexone to alter the gestalt of events triggered by reduction of stimulus density and thus to confuse and distress
the infant monkeys who now found their response to maternal affective
resonance and affect modulation quite different from what they had
learned through experience. In no way have they shown that primates
form interpersonal associations or herds because they look forward to

the spurt of endorphin that "glues" them together. Rather, it still seems much more likely that social behavior is fostered by the entire affect system, which operates internally as a system of amplification bringing meaning, urgency, and importance to whatever function is assembled with it, and externally as a mode of communication allowing the viewing organism to understand the internal world of whoever is expressing affect.

Only a few months earlier, a series of articles in the *Wall Street Journal* claimed precise localization of the pathways for various types of fear, from mild anxiety through panic. The September 29, 1993 lead article quoted Joseph LeDoux, "a leading brain mapper at New York University" as saying, "When it comes to understanding what a feeling is, anyone's guess is as good as anyone else's. What we're trying to do is give a precision to emotion that hasn't existed before."

No matter what pathways are found for human emotion, no matter what chemicals are shown to be important in the travel of neural impulses along these pathways, it is essential to understand that nothing becomes an emotion until it travels outside of the brain to the musculature and microcirculation of the face, there to be assessed and interpreted as an affective response. Personality, which we understand as the differential magnification of innate affects that become altered and modulated and assembled into scripts throughout life, or thrown off balance by inborn or acquired variations in neural chemistry—this highly complex gestalt of factors can never be reduced to the simplistic form of precision that now occupies our leading brain researchers. Everywhere we see the antipathy toward complexity that leads some scientists to mistrust, eschew, and disavow the world of psychotherapy.

Our awareness of the affect system, of the enormously complex process of script formation, and the interplay of affect, experience, and biology, allows us to develop new methods of psychotherapy as well as to establish new connections to all fields of human study. In the world of emotion research the watchword is not simplicity but the ever-increasing sophistication of our analysis of complexity.

OLD CONCEPTS, NEW CONCEPTS

So much changes when you shift from the language of drive theory to that of affect theory. For years we have talked about patients with "impulse disorders," people who are said to be unable to limit the expression of drive forces and, therefore, behave in ways that upset other people. In the 4th edition of Hinsie and Campbell's *Psychiatric Dictionary*

(1970), an impulse is defined as "A stimulus that sets the mind in action . . . [A] basic impulse is an instinct, the source of which is a 'somatic process in an organ or part of the body' (Freud, S., *Collected Papers*, 1924)." The dictionary goes on to define as component impulses "sucking, biting, touching, defecating, urinating, looking (voyeurism), exhibiting, sadism, masochism, etc., all of which although they may be detectable in adulthood, will generally be expressed as forepleasure activities and will remain subservient to genital primacy." "Impulsive" children or adults are said to take "swift action without forethought or conscious judgement" because of "blind obedience to internal drives" against which they have not formed "an organized defense." Certain impulse disorders are attributed to failures of brain development. A generation later, Kaplan and Sadock's authoritative *Pocket Handbook of Clinical Psychiatry* (1990) lists for impulse control disorders the following definition: "The inability to resist acting on an impulse or drive that is dangerous to others or to oneself and that is characterized by a sense of pleasure when gratified" (p. 142).

One of the most important features of affect theory is the clear separation between drive and affect. The drives, which, like the affects, are part of the firmware of the brain, are built-in mechanisms that sense a need, indicate how that need may be satisfied, and initiate the activity required. Thus, the hunger drive responds to blood levels of glucose that fall below some critical set point and starts the sucking movements characteristic of the nursing baby. Stretch receptors in the bladder or distal colon transmit information about readiness to evacuate, after which the drive mechanism lets us know what we must do. The drives are absolutely specific about the location of the action to be taken. Affect, on the other hand, provides the sort of amplification that makes any information urgent and important, whether from drive, cognition, memory, perception, or any other source. Affect never provides localization, while no drive contains the kind of motivating information characteristic of the affects.

The drives inform us about a few, primitive activities needed for survival, activities so important that they must be performed even when the organism is too immature to understand why and to perform them intentionally. The affects can make anything urgent and important, even though they are by definition nonspecific amplifiers of anything with which they become associated. What does that tell us about patients who seem unable to stop performing certain actions or who seem "driven" to behave in ways that experience should lead them to control?

It is true, as in the case of trichotillomania, that certain repetitive behaviors may be linked to defects in brain mechanisms and controlled by medication; I think that the distress–anguish experienced by these patients is secondary to the push of the aberrant compulsive mechanism. When medical treatment is successful in relieving the symptom, the concurrent relief of the affective component is secondary to the cessation of the relentless stimulus that had triggered the affect. Incidentally, I suggest that such syndromes may be viewed technically as biological disorders of drives simply because the underlying mechanism is localizing, informs the organism what must be done, and initiates consummatory activity that is not necessary for survival.

But most of the patients who seem unable to curb some inappropriate and apparently impulsive behavior are not, as far as can be determined today, driven by an analogous repetitive source of information, but pressed toward action by some constellation of affects that has been magnified far out of proportion to the importance-to-life of the action they amplify. The hordes of people who seem transfixed by the slot machines at which they worship until depleted of coin, the man or woman who seems relentlessly available for sexual adventure despite the known and growing risks, the small child whose attention may be locked for hours to a Nintendo game that allows him to pummel or kill one "bad guy" after another, the partygoer who cannot imagine entering a room full of strangers unless "lubricated" by an amount of alcohol that will later render him helpless to resist the tendency to say and do things for which he will be embarrassed, the child who rushes out into the street even when mother has warned him again and again that this action places him at risk of death—all of these are instances of impulsive behavior due not to anything we can identify as an instinct-borne impulse but of affect incorporated in scripts we can learn to decode and alter.

The next time you see a patient whose behavior you might previously have passed off as "impulsive," look for the affect involved. Then try to determine whether this affect has become the source of psychopathology because of some hardware defect necessitating medication or some software problem we can "debug" with psychotherapy. Once you know the basic patterns of stimulus for each of the nine innate affects, it is relatively easy to figure out what might be responsible for the pathological amplification involved in a wide range of disorders previously quite difficult to treat. It is a lot easier to develop a treatment plan based on modulation of one affect than an entire psychoanalysis aimed toward complete revision of psychosexual development, especially when you understand that the behavior in question has nothing at all to do with the sexual drive!

THE CASE AGAINST DEPRESSION

The wife of a 42-year-old physician pushed him to call for an urgent appointment. He was described as suicidally depressed, had rejected all offers of help, but agreed to see me later that day. Within minutes of beginning our initial session he described anxiety that had increased steadily over a three-month period. A nearly fanatical platform tennis player, he had been sidelined by persistent, gnawing shoulder pain that his orthopedist claimed would remit were he to agree to the arthroscopic surgery he had been avoiding for six months. "I can handle pain easily, but this damn anxiety just won't quit. It eats away at me day and night and I've begun to think about killing myself. Do you think I have to be hospitalized for depression?" The chronic and worsening anxiety responded nicely to fairly low bedtime doses of the benzodiazepine clonazepan. Free of the crippling anxiety, he had no further thoughts of suicide, began to deal with his secret fear that he might succumb to the same rheumatoid arthritis that had constrained his mother to a wheelchair since his own childhood, and scheduled the relatively minor operation that eventually returned him to the level of competition he had enjoyed a year earlier. Through the course of our work he took a total of 11 tablets of medication.

The 82-year-old father of a friend began to withdraw from all social activity and sat slumped in a chair staring at the wall. "I can't remember things people tell me," he complained briskly with some asperity as his wife nodded in assent. "Things get into my ears and don't stay in my head. But I can remember things that happened 30 years ago as if it were yesterday. And I've lost my ability to read. And," in a voice so low it was almost inaudible, "I feel so unworthy. For so many years I've fooled people, but now I can't fool them anymore." All at once he began a sordid recital of infidelities committed years earlier, as if in hope that disclosure to his wife of these shameful secrets might reduce his pain. A full workup for dementia demonstrated far better cognitive and memorial function than one might have expected, while a battery of psychological tests suggested that he had a psychotic depression. Hospitalization, a wide range of psychotherapeutic interventions, and a wide variety of biological and somatic treatments were equally ineffective. A year later I still see this now-wizened old man in the neighborhood of my office, walking helplessly in the company of his vigorous wife, who can barely reconcile herself to the idea that some depressions resist all known treatment.

It is hard to avoid information about depression. *DSM-IV* lists more than a dozen forms of depressive illness and cites depressive complications of many other conditions, while nearly every day one of our journals presents an article about some new aspect of depression. Only the studiously avoidant remain unaware of the degree to which this cluster of discomforts is assigned biological causality; studies of blood flow and cerebral metabolism using brain imaging techniques of the greatest sophistication present more and more data about the neurobiology of depression even as more and more classes of medication are shown to relieve its symptoms. Intense debate swirls about the relative efficacy of therapeutic protocols based on psychopharmacology, cognitive theory, and psychoanalysis. There is even a journal called *Depression*.

And yet, with all this attention to what by now must be one of the best studied disease complexes in the history of psychiatry and psychology, I argue for the removal of the term from our nomenclature and its replacement by language more attentive to the affective experience actually involved. The system I propose would require a statement denoting the specific affects being experienced by the patient on a chronic basis. The first case presented might bear the label "Persistent Dysphoria; fear–terror with secondary distress–anguish; somatic precipitant," while the second might be "Persistent Dysphoria; inhibition of interest–excitement, cause unknown; possible biological shame syndrome." Diagnosis might be based on the affect pattern chart introduced at the 1993 meeting of the Tomkins Institute.*

If you listen carefully to the complaints offered by patients, it becomes clear that one may be mildly depressed or severely depressed for a few moments or for what seems like a lifetime or intermittently at varying degrees of severity. When depressed, one may shun contact with others or crave it incessantly. Some who suffer depression seek relief in hedonism, while others find pleasure nowhere and still others seem "driven" to suicide. Melanie Klein (1932), who more than any other psychoanalytic pioneer viewed the infant as a miniature adult, found evidence of a "depressive position" from birth. Where once there was a sharp distinction between symptom complexes characterized by the presence of depression or anxiety, now we see chronic anxiety being treated with antidepressants and chronic depression treated with antianxiety agents. Terms like "hysteroid dysphoria," "classical depression," and "atypical depression" are used to explain differences in symptom patterns as well as response to medication. Some schizophrenics seem to benefit from treatment with antidepressants, while nonschizophrenic patients with

---

*Reprinted as Figure 2.1 in this volume.

"delusional depression" fare better with antianxiety medication. In contrast, the cognitive-behavioral treatments for panic disorder and depression differ little.

The emergence of pharmacological agents capable of relieving the symptoms of some depressions but not others, or treating the depressive symptomatology of some patients but not the apparently identical complaints of others, should have suggested that more was wrong with our language than our medications. Of equal interest is the common observation that successful treatment with antidepressants relieves symptoms about which the patient had not complained, as well as symptoms rarely considered part of the depressive spectrum. Kramer (1992), whose *Listening to Prozac* opened this debate to a mass audience, adapted a paranoid style for hortatory purposes and suggested that the use of medication to improve the lives of people who did not have a recognized "disease" could be considered "cosmetic psychopharmacology" and was perhaps improper.

At issue here is the search for simplicity rather than the careful analysis of complexity. If, in the early days of psychoanalysis, all emotionality was to be explained on the basis of drive forces, then some simple, hydraulic mechanism had to account for depression. A depressed person had no "energy" to challenge life because the energy was being shunted somewhere else. Thus, anger thwarted or turned inward seemed an adequate schematic diagram for the energics of depression, and the search for ways of releasing that anger a reasonable therapeutic technique. By analogy, the medical approach to depressive illness has fostered a search for the ultimate antidepressant that will relieve all symptoms in all sufferers. The success of each new drug has led to its use in ever-widening segments of the population, followed first by steady decreases in the fraction of patients who achieve benefit (thus throwing that approach into disfavor) and then by renewal of the sturdy hope that the next drug will cure everybody. So thoroughly has psychoanalytic logic infused our culture that the concept of depression has remained unitary despite the mounting evidence that the term itself is a collective noun, a wastebasket into which are thrown a wide range of dysphorias.

The classification I have proposed would take note of the fact that six of the nine innate affects defined by Tomkins cause decidedly unpleasant experiences. By definition, all of the affects are brief, lasting a few hundredths of a second in the case of surprise–startle, and a couple of seconds in the case of distress–anguish and anger–rage. Our awareness that an affect has been triggered is called by Basch (1976) a feeling (this is the moment that the biology of affect turns into psychology), and the association of an affect with previous experiences of that affect is called an emotion (this is the interface between biology and biography). We use the term mood to speak of the internal loops through which affect and memory reinforce each other to produce the relatively continuous experience of any emotion. Through this mechanism, any negative affect may be experienced over a considerable period of time. If the relatively constant overload of work triggers distress–anguish that reminds me of what made me sob last year, and the rekindling of that remembered distress acts as an additional stimulus making me feel even more like crying, and the accumulated memories pile up to the extent that I begin to sob at television commercials simply because they trigger enough affect to make the protagonists matter to me, then I may be said to be in a mood characterized by fairly constant distress–anguish.

Persistent distress–anguish is often called sadness, persistent fear–terror is known as steady anxiety, persistent mild anger–rage is irritability or annoyance, persistent anger–rage at a higher density is thought of as being in a bad temper. Persistence of the affect shame–humiliation, when experienced as the withdrawal pole of the compass of shame, is a state of loneliness, hurt feelings, and bad thoughts about the self; when admixed with fear–terror it may be called guilt. (Since, when angry, parents often seek to adjust our behavior by producing guilt and shame in us, any psychosocial or biological disorder that produces enduring guilt or shame will be experienced as "anger against the self" even though these emotions have been produced by distinctly different mechanisms.) The bad moods associated with dissmell and disgust make us keep others at a distance and promote a wide range of interpersonal styles when paired with other negative affects.

There are, then, six families of bad mood, each of which when dense is likely to be described by its subject as depression. To those trained in affect theory, the persistent experience of shame is treated quite differently from the persistent experience of distress; for shame we investigate impediments to the positive affects of interest–excitement and enjoyment–joy, while for distress we try to reduce steady-state stimulus load. Both treatments are "antidepressant." Just as in a previous era we tended to use the term "psychosis" only when we were humiliated by our inability to get the patient to accept our arguments and renounce one or another group of scripts, we now think of a patient as "depressed" when conventional therapy does not remediate persistent negative affect. Despite the severity of the symptoms involved, the case presented in the opening paragraph of this section is an example of normal mood in that it really did involve an internal loop initiated by a discrete stimulus triggering normal affect that became involved with an internal script from which the subject could not extricate himself.

I do not mean to imply that treatment illuminated by affect and script theory is intrinsically easy. For example, every once in a while we see a patient whose chronic distress–anguish is a reaction to the steady experience of fear–terror; here it is the steadiness of the primary affect that then triggers a secondary affective reaction so that chronic anxiety is thus fused with distress. Despite the adequacy of their vocabulary for other matters, most people have few words with which to describe their feelings and lump such fusion products under the rubric of depression. (Often we are required to teach people the language with which they can become accessible to therapy.) In the example just cited, it seems only logical to expect that such a patient might experience relief from an antianxiety agent and feel much worse when given an antidepressant; the verbal psychotherapies might also work better were this situation recognized at its affective roots. I suspect that a cognitive therapist, by training less committed to the search for sources of affect stemming from infantile experience than her psychoanalytic colleagues, might trace distress backwards to anxiety and straightaway develop a systematic treatment for the underlying anxiety which therefore relieved the distress. This, naturally, would be considered successful therapeutic management of depression. If I am correct that the steady experience of any negative affect will be described as depression by anyone naive to the nomenclature of innate affect, then attention to the nature and source of any negative affect is antidepressant.

Sometimes, of course, the steady experience of negative affect is the result of aberrant neurochemistry; emotionality, no matter where placed on the yardstick of normality, must involve hardware as well as firmware and software. Tomkins suggested that the six basic innate affects evolved as amplifiers of simple qualities — increases and decreases in the levels or gradients of stimulation. Each affect amplifies a quite different stimulus condition, and amplifies it in a highly specific, discrete, and entirely memorable way. To the three basic negative affects (fear–terror, distress–anguish, and anger–rage) he added two discomforts that evolved as modulators of the drive hunger (the drive auxiliaries dissmell and disgust) and a final mechanism (the affect auxiliary shame–humiliation) that amplifies any impediment to the two positive affects of interest–excitement and enjoyment–joy. The firmware, of course, is the operating programs for each of these six negative affects, stored as subcortical action scripts dependent on intricate networks of neural pathways leading to activity at specific sites of action. All of these pathways comprise what I have defined as structural effectors and are dependent on chemical mediators that transmit messages along their course toward the actions we come to know as our affects. The system is so complex, its subunits so intertwined, its mechanisms involving so many layers, that there are lots of places for something to go wrong.

Here, I believe, is the reason there are so many different biological treatments for "depression," all of which work in some despite how inadequate they may be for other patients whose complaints and history seem identical. Even though we have come to understand the family of medications called antidepressants in terms of their effects on the neurotransmitters noradrenalin, serotonin, and dopamine, the action of some therapeutic agents seems unrelated to these compounds. I suspect that antidepressants work when they repair some part of the circuitry for the triggering, maintenance, and cessation of any affect. No one has as yet investigated the biology of any innate affect, for such is the mind-set of the contemporary neurobiologist that modern science searches for general solutions to the problem of disturbed emotionality rather than specific solutions to the problems caused by malfunctions in individual affect circuits. I have suggested that the serotonin reuptake inhibitors repair certain defects in shame biology, that the phenothiazines remediate some aspect of fear–terror, and that most tricyclic antidepressants are effective when symptomatology is canted in favor of the peculiar fusion of shame and fear known as guilt. Buspirone is highly specific for one form of the serotonin receptor; a much-advertised but largely ineffective remedy for anxiety when used in people who have never tasted a benzodiazepine, it is now touted for its ability to reduce "anxiety" in people whose "depression" is reduced by fluoxetine, sertraline, or paroxetine. If this therapeutic approach turns out to be valid, it suggests that certain aspects of the complex affective patterns presented by these patients may be traced to specific variations of the serotonin-related neurotransmitters. But there is no hope of explaining such effects in the absence of a clearly defined language for normal affect and a consequent redefinition of the broad and confused language for emotion based on the description of illness.

This is the problem presented by a language of science that confuses the effects of endorphin (endogenous morphine-like compounds) with the affect enjoyment–joy. The innate affect is triggered anytime stimulus density is reduced and is associated with highly specific facial displays. Gradual reduction in stimulus density is posited to trigger a smile, rapid reduction a laugh. Tomkins viewed endorphin as another, quite separate system of amplification also capable of creating the good feelings associated with enjoyment–joy but for different reasons under different circumstances. The amplification systems we know as our affects are formed in layers that have accreted through the long process of evolution. Some of these layers involve the innate affects described by Tomkins, and others do not. Disorders of mood can occur when there is something wrong in any layer, even though we humans are likely to describe any emotional experience as if it had been an affective response to a known and discernible trigger for ordinary innate affect simply because that is how we know our affects. The case sketched in the second paragraph of this section involved a disorder of mood in which the affect interest–excitement was shut down by biological mechanisms we still do not understand and for which we have no treatment. The symptom complexes presented by patients with dementia of the Alzheimer's type stem from primary lesions of memory storage and retrieval that make one poorly able to live in the world; yet these cognitive losses also involve the scripts for the modulation of affect, often making the patient "irrationally" emotional.

Only when we begin to investigate the psychopathology of emotion from the standpoint of normal affect mechanisms can we integrate the texts of neurobiology into the encyclopedia of psychotherapy. It is the affect and script theories of Silvan Tomkins that facilitate this new approach, and the best place to start would be with the replacement of the term "depression" by language both more precise and more useful.

STRESS AND TENSION

Until affect theory pointed the way to an integration of psychology and neurobiology, and script theory provided the links between normal and abnormal emotionality, it was reasonable for the psychotherapy establishment to use the term "stress" as a descriptor for the precipitant of a clinical syndrome. Long taken to represent a situation or event capable of inducing the cluster of responses that brings an individual into a therapeutic environment, it may perhaps be understood better as a relic of an earlier psychobiology.

The word "stress" appears everywhere in our field. While "depression" has become the nosologic wastebasket into which are thrown a medley of clinical syndromes characterized by the more-or-less steady experience of any negative affect or combination of negative affects, "stress" is the analogous container for a wide range of emotional discomforts that can be attributed to noxious experience. Take, for example, the following definition quoted from *DSM-IV* (1994):

> The essential feature of an Adjustment Disorder is the development of clinically significant emotional or behavioral symptoms in response to an identifiable psychosocial stressor or stressors. The

symptoms must develop within 3 months after the onset of the stressor(s). The clinical significance of the reaction is indicated either by marked distress that is in excess of what would be expected given the nature of the stressor, or by significant impairment in social or occupational (academic) functioning. . . . By definition, an adjustment disorder must terminate within 6 months of the termination of the stressor (or its consequences). However, the symptoms may persist for a prolonged period (i.e., longer than 6 months) if they occur in response to a chronic stressor (e.g., a chronic, disabling general medical condition) or to a stressor that has enduring consequences (e.g., the financial and emotional difficulties resulting from a divorce).

The stressor may be a single event (e.g., termination of a romantic relationship), or there may be multiple stressors (e.g., marked business difficulties and marital problems). Stressors may be recurrent (e.g., associated with seasonal business crises) or continuous (e.g., living in a crime-ridden neighborhood). Stressors may affect a single individual, an entire family, or a larger group or community (e.g., as in a natural disaster). Some stressors may accompany specific developmental events (e.g., going to school, leaving the parental home, getting married, becoming a parent, failing to attain occupational goals, retirement). (p. 623)

As you know, the syndromes of pathological adjustment to such stressors include what are described as prolonged anxiety, depression, conduct disorder, and various admixtures of these response patterns. Other syndromes, like the acute stress disorder and posttraumatic stress disorder, involve emotional responses to what our manual describes as an "extremely traumatic event" that has occurred in the immediate or more distant past.

This current use of the term derives from the confluence of two streams, one etymologic and the other scientific. The *Oxford English Dictionary* notes that "stress" first appeared in English as a shortened form of "distress." (Our language has always had a tendency to drop short, weak opening syllables, as in Cockney and American slang; this process is known as *aphesis*.) In Middle English (1150–1500), *distresse* and *stresse* often appear as variant readings in the same document, where they referred to "the action or fact of straining or pressing tightly . . . pressure applied to produce action, constraint, compulsion." Later meanings included "The overpowering pressure of some adverse force, as anger, hunger, bad weather," and "The sore pressure or strain of adversity, trouble, hunger, sickness, pain, or sorrow; anguish or affliction affecting the body, spirit, or community." A French word of similar but not identical meaning seems to have been absorbed into this shortened form of distress—*estrece* was an Old French term for narrowness, straitness, and oppression, adding another realm of imagery to the concept of stress.

So far, it would appear that the history of the word fits perfectly the sense to which Tomkins adapted it—a steady-state, higher-than-optimal level of stimulus density triggering a mechanism that produces an analogous but far more urgent biopsychosocial condition characterized by sobbing and other steady-state discomfort. What happened to shift this quite specific use of the word stress to indicate the far more general state of malaise referenced in *DSM-IV*? Tomkins (1991) comments that Freud was responsible for one part of the problem because he assumed that the birth cry was the prototype of *anxiety*:

> By confusing distress and anxiety, the latter term was given an initial connotation which made anxiety equivalent to psychic suffering of all kinds. By a further extension, everything which caused suffering or frustration of any kind became a cause of anxiety. Therefore, it was a brief step to the general postulate that any kind of "stress" or nonoptimal circumstance might produce "anxiety" in children and later, via generalization, in adulthood. . . . The common denominator of these meanings is some kind of "stress" which all animals will signal by some kind of "avoidance." (p. 494)

Even to the lay mind, there is a great deal of difference between distress and fear, between the steady, red-faced sobbing of the former and the frozen gaze, cold sweat, and pounding pulse of the latter. Freud, seeking a grand unifying theory, locked himself to the concept of libido as an energy source responsible for healthy sexual excitement when released properly but which, when blocked or frustrated, powered all forms of aberrant behavior and emotionality. Even though the classically trained psychoanalyst has by and large discarded libido theory as a serious explanation of emotionality, among psychoanalysts the general concept of "stress" or "anxiety" lingers to a greater degree than might be believed, simply because these are terms that unify rather than partition the negative affects. Freud blended the innate affects distress–anguish and fear–terror into a broader category of generalized negative affect, thereby conflating gradient and density triggers and thus obscuring the difference between them.

What Freud had joined together became more difficult to break asunder when Hans Selye began to study the effect on rats of relentless noxious stimulation. In a series of experiments beginning in the 1940s and described in powerfully written papers and books, Selye (1980) described stress as "the nonspecific response of the body to any demand." Nosologists are either lumpers or splitters, and Selye was a lumper par excellence when he asked us not only to place into one category everything that might affect the organism, but defined stress as whatever caused the "stress response." Right at the time when psychoanalytic language was being absorbed into the mainstream of North American culture, and Freud's sense of "anxiety" gaining acceptance as a descriptor of all emotional discomfort, Selye's demonstration of the endocrinologic effects of deadly stimulation now conflated into one word the entire range of mild and dense triggers. Suddenly there was a reason to fear anything that might produce stress and anxiety.

Reviewing his life work near the end of his career, Selye (1980) stated that all stimuli

> . . . have one thing in common: they increase the demand for readjustment, for performance of adaptive functions which reestablish normalcy. This rise in requirements is independent of the specific activity that caused the increase. In that sense, the response is *nonspecific*. The nonspecific adaptive response of the body to any agent or situation is always the same, regardless of the particular stimulus; what varies is the degree of response, which in turn depends only on the intensity of the demand for adjustment. Thus, it is immaterial whether the stress-producing factor or stressor, as it is properly called, is pleasant or unpleasant. A game of chess, a kiss, pneumonia, and a broken finger all produce the same systemic reaction, though their specific results may be quite different or even completely opposite. (pp. 127–129)

Selye spoke of a General Adaptation Syndrome (G.A.S.) with three stages:

1. An *alarm reaction* consisting of a *shock phase* in which "various signs of injury such as tachycardia, loss of muscle tone, decreased body temperature, and decreased blood pressure are typical symptoms." This shock phase may be followed by a *countershock phase*, a "rebound reaction . . . during which the adrenal cortex is enlarged and secretion of corticoid hormones is increased."
2. A *stage of resistance*, in which the organism adapts fully to the stressor, the symptoms improve or disappear, and the organism is left vulnerable to further insult.

3. A *stage of exhaustion*, in which the body's resources, having been depleted by the above reaction phases, prove unable to withstand further stress. "If stress continues unabated, death ensues."

Any student of the history of ideas will recognize the red thread running through these two conceptual frameworks, deriving as they do from quite different realms of observation. Both Freud and Selye believed that the organism is designed to remain at rest unless disturbed, at which time it must react in such a way that the disturbance is warded off or its effects minimized. In the post-industrial revolution system of thought from which both scientists emerged, the human is seen as a machine able to run smoothly unless stressed, at which time its energies must be diverted to defensive action. Despite the obvious and glaring flaws in Selye's argument (it is hard to imagine death as the expected result of stable and constant love), I suspect that his ideas were able to take hold easily in a world torn by global war ended recently by atomic weaponry that threatened the survival of all life forms. As far as I can tell from an examination of literally hundreds of articles and books on stress and stressors, the language of Freud and Selye remains dominant in our field.

In recent years the term "tension" has become a cognate for both stress and anxiety; patients are likely to attribute their symptoms to scripts such as "I've been under a lot of tension recently—really stressed out." The OED derives "tension" from the Latin verb *tendere*, "to stretch," as seen in such medical uses as bladder distension. Something is tensed when it is either stretched or strained, leading to the 18th-century sense of "a straining, or strained condition, of the mind, feeling, or nerves" associated with "straining of the mental powers or faculties; severe or strenuous intellectual effort; intense application," and the 19th-century sense of "nervous or emotional strain; intense suppressed excitement; a strained condition of feeling or mutual relations which is for the time outwardly calm, but is likely to result in a sudden collapse, or in an outburst of anger or violent action of some kind." Historically, a situation has always been described as "tense" when it involves steady-state, higher-than-optimal stimulation—a density rather than a gradient trigger for affect. Notice again how these older usages conform better to what we understand from affect theory than to the meanings toward which Freud and Selye wrenched them in order to fit their theoretical systems.

This difference between gradient and density triggers for affect is important. If you look at the derivation of the word "fear," you note roots that convey the sense of danger, ambush, or sudden calamity; "anxiety" derives from the root for choking. These are gradient triggers because something new is happening, and it is happening at a rate that is too much for the organism. Nothing new is involved in the steady stimulation that triggers distress or anger. Some "anxiety disorders" involve the biology and the psychology of the affect fear–terror (the sense of onrushing danger) while the sort of "constant anxiety" or "tension" physicians treat with benzodiazepines such as Xanax or low dose phenothiazines like Stelazine is more properly understood as distress–anguish. Syndromes involving fear require strategies for the assessment of danger, while syndromes involving distress demand search for and reduction of sources of chronic overload. Distinctions of this sort are essential to competent cognitive therapy, in which much precision is required in order to decrease the morbidity associated with whatever symptoms have brought someone into treatment.

This brings up an additional difference between the traditional language of our field and that of affect theory: It is unlikely that there would be any serious or life-threatening endocrinologic sequelae of affect that was permitted expression. A situation that triggers affect is not likely to become noxious as long as the affect can be expressed freely. It is only when conditions of nurturance preclude affective expression in the developing child, or sociopolitical forces suppress the cry of distress and the roar of rage, that the response to stress becomes deadly in the medical sense. Tomkins (1991) suggested that "much of what is called 'stress' is indeed backed-up affect and that many of the (reported) endocrine changes . . . are the consequence of backed-up affect as of affect per se. It seems at the very least that substantial psychosomatic disease might be one of the prices of such systematic suppression and transformation of the affective responses" (p. 14).

Go back to the paragraph above quoted from *DSM-IV* in order to verify these assertions. For each of the "stressors" indicated in our manual, try to imagine which of the six negative affects might be involved. Check out whether your clinical skills are improved when you look for fear–terror, distress–anguish, anger–rage, dissmell, disgust, and shame–humiliation alone or in their various combinations. See if your understanding of the specific psychosocial and biological triggers postulated for each of these affects can lead to the development of treatment strategies more sophisticated than the search for methods of "stress reduction." Watch your patients perk up when you teach them how to partition their emotional discomfort into easily recognizable categories that permit highly specific systems of solace. And smile with contentment as the work of psychotherapy is made just a little bit easier by this new approach.

SCRIPTS, THERAPY, AND THE MOVIES

Acceptance of affect theory requires certain shifts in our understanding of psychotherapy. If, indeed, each human must learn to live with and adjust to nine innate mechanisms that govern consciousness and are going to be triggered time and again from birth through death, and if personality itself may be defined as the biographically determined gestalt of those adjustments to innate affect, then psychotherapy must be defined in terms of both the individual affects and the patterns of affect management brought into treatment by each patient. People seek treatment when their scripted, habitual patterns of affect management prove inadequate and strand them in some noxious affective environment. The depth of therapy is roughly proportional to the centrality for each personality of the scripts that must be altered to achieve relief.

The pain of mourning, the unpleasant cascade of possible results of some anticipated action, the growing feeling of aversion for a once-loved partner, the idea that the presence of a more successful rival makes one unable to keep that cherished season ticket, or the partner whose testiness and irritability when immersed in a big case disturb the harmony of an otherwise successful marriage—the distress, fear, disgust, shame, and anger in each of these vignettes can be explained easily in terms of the gradients and densities of stimulation or interference with appetite responsible for each affect. Treatment is based on our clear understanding of affect dynamics, an understanding that we communicate with ease to the patient and that results in critical focus on causes and the development of strategies for remediation. Distress unassociated with some constant density stimulus, fear in the absence of some unfriendly gradient of information, disgust without some experience of betrayed expectation, shame where no impediment to positive affect can be determined, and anger in the absence of steady-state overload may be viewed as affects produced by errors of metabolism and treated with appropriate medication. Rarely does any of these situations require either long-term therapy or careful investigation of major operating scripts.

Two of the best known and most studied examples of treatment involving scripts are found in the world of psychoanalysis. Classical theory suggests that persistent personality dysfunction may be traced to compromised transit through the oedipal phase of development, while self psychology, the second generation of psychoanalytic theory and treatment, recognizes the importance of failures in parental attention during earlier phases of intrapsychic and interpersonal maturation. In each system of therapy, cure is achieved not by explanation of the "reasons" for the negative affects triggered so often and in such predictable situations, but through the establishment of a therapeutic relationship within which the patient experiences or lives through some approximation of an optimal nurturant sequence. The frequent success of such therapeutic approaches is undeniable. What must occupy our attention are the equally undeniable observations that some people are unable to achieve significant personality change even when treated by acknowledged masters of these crafts, and that others may become wholly different as the result of carefully designed therapeutic experiences that incorporate none of these techniques.

Fictive depictions of such transitions are among the most popular of our entertainments. Whether in the highly condensed form of poems, the more anecdotal genre of the short story, or the broad sweep of a novel, such demonstrations of personality change allow us to savor in privacy and under strict control our affective reactions to what is written. Plays, movies, and grand opera represent a gradient of affective expression operating at a far higher level of intensity. What happens during a play is by convention limited to the architecture of the theater, in which the proscenium arch defines the boundary between spectator and player, and the limitations of the unamplified spoken voice define the boundaries of affective communication. Opera is far more grand and grabs us more deeply because the music encourages an additional depth of affective involvement and because the singers are allowed to work with an intensity of affective expression rarely allowed elsewhere; that most great operas are performed in languages with which we are not fluent forces us to react more to the affective than the literary message. But it is in the contemporary film that most nontherapists are exposed to the emotional experience of another person at levels and intensities for which they have no parallel. Group efforts based on the cooperative work of writers, directors, actors, photographers, composers, musicians, artists, costume and set designers, and production staff, movies can provide peculiarly efficient affective experience.

Just as psychotherapy may involve attention to monoaffective dysfunction, some films may be viewed as monothematic discursions on violence, sexual success, humiliation, or that border between excitement and fear we call thrilling. Some, like "Remains of the Day" or "Dangerous Liaisons," based on major novels, allow us to grasp the complexity of a character at great depth and to understand why the individual in question is incapable of change. I wish to focus your attention on films in which character change is achieved, in which the protagonist enters as one kind of person and leaves as another. (Even the word "protagonist" is significant here—it derives simply from *proto*, for first and foremost, and *agon*, the arena within which the ancient Greek athletes competed.

Agony is the emotionality associated with intense effort, explaining in large measure our millennia of cultural addiction to sports as entertainment. The protagonist is the one who endures the most affective experience on the road to change.) Two recent productions, both considered trivial by most critics and moviegoers, bear contrast and comparison to one classic. "Switched" and "Groundhog Day" demonstrate one system for character change, while every one of the several versions of "A Christmas Carol" is based on another. Both systems have much to teach us about script theory.

In the simplest of terms, Ebenezer Scrooge enters our awareness as a man apparently allergic to positive affect. He presents a perfect example of what Tomkins describes as a scarcity script, in which it is taken for granted that the resources available on our planet are inadequate to take care of everybody, forcing one who intends to survive into a pattern of fearful and angry vigilance for the deadly possibility of loss. He undergoes a conversion experience when God removes him from the dimensionality of his ordinary experience to demonstrate the previously inapparent realities of his life, much as a denizen of Flatland might be removed above the plane of his existence to be shown the nature of line and polygon. Sudden immersion in scenes of Christmas past, present, and future triggers negative affect at a level far greater than that controlled by his scarcity script, inducing a shift to a polar opposite abundance script. Charles Dickens informs us that for the rest of his life, nobody kept Christmas better than Ebenezer Scrooge.

But what gave the rehabilitated Scrooge the idea to send food and presents to the Cratchit family? What made him able to accept love? I suggest that a fully articulated abundance script was always latent within his personality but kept from expression by fears overridden through the dramatic action of the short story. Sudden or miraculous conversion, whether religious or financial or political or romantic and whether from bad person to good person or good person to bad person, cannot occur unless the script for the "new" personality had been stored as a reasonably complete entity, awaiting activation by a suitably intense affective experience. The explosive awakening into sexuality seen in some adolescents and young adults, the sudden shift in behavior exhibited by those who have been released from poverty into wealth, and the wanderlust gratified by the gift of a first car are not conversions but an awakening into power that demands modulation through individual and interpersonal experience. Contemporary conversion analogues include the Transformer Robots that change from quite ordinary to extraordinarily powerful beings when deformed along predetermined joints, Billy Batson, the "crippled newsboy" of an earlier generation who was empowered to cry aloud the magic word "Shazam!" in order to turn into the omnipotent Captain Marvel, and weak but brilliant Dr. David Banner, who because of a "radiation accident" turns into the immensely powerful but quite infantile Incredible Hulk when angry. I recall a 1968 conversation with Jay Haley in which he commented that some people come to psychotherapists for ritual permission to become who they always wanted to be; this permission for conversion is certainly one of our roles.

Despite the attractiveness of such scenarios of conversion, and despite the reality that there may be much that is good in the worst of us and much that is bad in the best of us, most scripts for personal change are quite different. You and I did not achieve our current personalities because someone threw a switch and sent us on another track. Something like that did happen to a 24-year-old woman I met on a blind date 30 years ago in a city far from my home to which I had traveled to report some of my research in endocrinology. A slim, pleasant person apparently blessed with a bodily contour for which she was labeled beautiful, she came alive only at the end of our evening when she asked me to switch hats and answer a medical question. Until only a year earlier, she had developed no single secondary sexual characteristic—no axillary or pubic hair, no breast enlargement, never an adolescent skin blemish, no trace of a menstrual cycle—and no experience of sexual desire. Repeated examinations had demonstrated the presence of all the internal organs necessary for these phenomena, none of which components had yet been urged into action. At 23, a gynecologist had suggested she take birth control pills to "kick start" the system. Within a month she was the confused owner of a female body the match of any Hollywood starlet. "I feel like a boy with all of these things pasted on," she said. The normal transition of a prepubertal girl is more gradual and allows her to handle both the changes in self-concept and the reactions she triggers in male and female companions. This was a conversion for which she was less well prepared than she had guessed, and she was ready to opt for a life free from the sexual wishes of men. Writing in *The First Year of Life*, Spitz (1965) noted that most of the born-blind adolescents and adults whose congenital cataracts were removed by Von Senden in the 1930s regarded bright light and vivid color as an intrusion and wished for the return of their blindness.

It is true that a shame-bound adolescent or young adult may happen on alcohol as a shamolytic and feel competent when drunk and thus released into a desired constellation of attributes—this is a sham conversion with an ugly ending. Reread the short story "Flowers for Algernon" by Frances Parkinson Keyes or rent the videotape of the superb film "Charlie" made from it, in which Cliff Robertson plays a retarded baker's assistant who experiences a brief period of genius as the result of a brain graft that is later rejected. In sharp contrast is the enormous number of adults (and now children) whose innate or acquired defect in serotonin metabolism had caused a chronic shame disorder now kept in check by one of the SSRI medications, people who can now learn how to enjoy positive affect and new levels of competence without the relatively constant experience of impediment that can be handled only by actions mediated through the scripted patterns I have described as the compass of shame (Nathanson, 1992). Here, the careful use of medication has allowed a new, stable reality quite different from that offered on a transient basis by alcohol, which acts only to tantalize and seduce. When the SSRIs work in these cases, we can guess that normal learning had earlier been prevented by biological limitation. When proper medication permits normalization of affect physiology, emotional learning can occur with or without the aid of a psychotherapist, as a generation of us have learned since the introduction of effective antimanic agents.

Charlie wanted to become smarter, just as Billy Batson wanted to become stronger and more competent. Can you imagine Ebenezer Scrooge coming into therapy asking to become more kind and loving? I suspect that many people fear psychotherapy of any sort because they do not want to be the passive recipients or "victims" of change mediated by an outside force that turns them into something or someone they might not admire or know how to handle. Robert Louis Stevenson's "Dr. Jekyll and Mr. Hyde," the vampire genre, and "The Invasion of the Body Snatchers" are good examples of this culture-wide concern. Stories of sudden conversion are all the more intriguing because change is forced on one who least expected it.

Look next at the other group of stories of personal change as exemplified by the films "Switched" and "Groundhog Day." The protagonist in "Switched" is a callous seducer of women who is murdered equally callously by a trio of his targets and sent prematurely to Judgment where he is informed that he can avoid being sent to Hell if he can prove that any creature loved him. In order to fulfill this quest he is returned to life on earth, but as the kind of gorgeous blonde he used to seduce with gusto. Ellen Barkin gives a perfect performance as a man who awakens into female form, forced thereby to understand how a woman feels when she is valued for little more than her bodily contours and sexual availability. By the end of the movie, the protagonist has learned how to love both self and others—and, because of this new understanding of humanity, finds great difficulty choosing a final gender identity. The film suggests that only through the operation of a supernal force capable of fostering a new kind of evolution can so dramatic a personality transformation be mediated.

But it is to "Groundhog Day" that I wish to call your attention at greater length, for it offers much to anyone who is interested in the process of personal change. Bill Murray plays television weatherman Phil Connors, a nasty, heartless, cynical, misanthrope sent with his crew to record yet again the witless spectacle at Punxsutawney, Pennsylvania, a town made famous by its devotion to the legend that one can predict the length of winter from the behavior of a groundhog on a particular morning in February. The town itself seems more like a tape recording configured as an endless loop, for it is organized around the yearly repetition of this festival perpetuated by the broadcast media, and is as much slave to this flimsy set of scenes as the helpless groundhog, also named Phil. To the extent that Phil Connors is a godless man constrained to seduce, insult, and humiliate any man or woman in his path, his producer, Rita, as played by Andie MacDowell, is set up as an angelic force incapable of being fooled by evil. Just as the unwitting groundhog has been trapped into a yearly ritual in which he is surrounded by fools, Phil finds himself trapped in a time warp of a Groundhog Day that he is forced to relive without relief. No matter what he does, no matter whom he seduces, no matter what he steals or gives or tries, even if he engineers his own death, he is forced to awaken each morning to Groundhog Day in Punxsutawney, Pennsylvania. Nothing within the range of personal scripts that form his personality can release him from a Hell that has surely been devised by the same God who showed Ebenezer Scrooge the meaning of his life.

Slowly, carefully, Phil tries one strategy after another. Do you remember that wonderful scene in Eugen Herrigel's *Zen and the Art of Archery* (1953/89) in which the author tries to fool the Zen Master by releasing the arrow just as he used to squeeze the trigger of a rifle instead of learning what the Master was trying to teach? Phil begins to get the idea that Rita is the test of his salvation, and tries to achieve her love through the tricks he knows best. On occasion, she is taken in for a moment or even for a few hours, but always she rejects him for cause. The curse placed on him is also a blessing, for as each day dawns, only he will remember what happened before. To the extent that he is capable of change, he can grow in an environment that will be forgiving simply because it cannot assemble memories of his actions and share our disgust for his character.

He has entered a peculiar analogue of childhood, in which the optimal parent forgives our errors and encourages our attempts to learn. Day after day, Phil takes on one discipline after another, much in the way an adept is trained by a Zen Master in the ways of kendo, ikibana, archery, or any martial art while learning the spirit of Zen. Our heartless weatherman takes up jazz piano and ice sculpture, becoming a master of both.

We are left to wonder how many years, perhaps decades of immersion were required to achieve such facility and depth of character. Nothing that happens in Punxsutawney can occur without his knowledge. No child may fall from a tree, no street person die, no accident occur, no old lady become stuck in traffic by a flat tire but what he will know and thereby be forced to decide on some plan of action. Through his years of involvement in a single day he is like God for this island in time even though trapped as the most helpless of God's creatures. Phil as protagonist and we as viewers are released to the real world when he has evolved to the point where Rita sees him as he has become—a deeply loving and immensely talented man ready to take his place with a loving life partner. Nothing in the behavior of the character we met at the beginning of this film prepares us for this fully realized human. From the standpoint of script theory, Phil is the antithesis of Ebenezer Scrooge and forces us to recognize that some people know nothing about a potential that can only be made real through a lifetime of struggle.

Your own practice of psychotherapy will reveal many examples of each of these patterns of change. There are many times that you have acted to limit the affect that precipitated someone into patient status, just as there are situations in which you have given someone permission to make the transition to some much desired and well understood but deeply feared novel persona. Some who remain with us in long-term therapy may be blocked from change by what are in this era undiagnosable biological interferences with the normal plasticity of the affect system, while others find change difficult or impossible because of certain core scripts that have never been studied enough for us to devise adequate techniques for their alteration. But the struggle that makes up the real grunt work of day-to-day psychotherapy is the job of detecting the affect of the moment, determining the script within which it is being expressed, and designing systems for the alteration of those scripts that lock people within a character structure that prevents optimal growth through life.

REFERENCES

American Psychiatric Association. (1994). *Diagnostic and statistical manual of mental disorders* (4th Ed.). Washington, DC: Author.

Basch, M. F. (1976). The concept of affect: A re-examination. *Journal of the American Psychoanalytic Association, 24*, 759–777.

Darwin, C. (1872). *The expression of emotion in man and animals.* (Reprinted, 1979, New York: St. Martin's Press).

Ekman, P., & Friesen, W. V. (1978). *Manual for the facial affect coding system.* Palo Alto, CA: Consulting Psychologists Press.

Herrigel, E. (1953). *Zen and the art of archery*. New York: Pantheon. (Reprinted, 1989 New York: Vintage).

Hinsie, L. E., & Campbell, R. J. (1970). *Psychiatric dictionary* (4th Ed.). New York: Oxford University Press.

Kaplan, H. I., & Sadock, B. J. (1990). *Pocket handbook of clinical psychiatry*. Baltimore: Williams & Wilkins.

Klein, M. (1932). *The psycho-analysis of children*. London: Hogarth.

Kramer, P. (1993). *Listening to prozac*. New York: Viking.

Nathanson, D. L. (1988). Affect, affective resonance, and a new theory for hypnosis. *Psychopathology, 21*, 126–137.

Nathanson, D. L. (1992). *Shame and pride: Affect, sex, and the birth of the self*. New York: Norton.

Oxford English dictionary (1933) *on compact disc*. New York: Oxford University Press. (CDROM version published 1987) Ft. Washington, PA: TriStar Publishing, International Computaprint Corporation.

Selye, H. (1980). The stress concept today. In I. L. Kutash, L. B. Schlesinger, & Associates (Eds.), *Handbook on stress and anxiety: Contemporary knowledge, theory, and treatment* (pp. 127–143). San Francisco: Jossey Bass.

Spitz, R. (1965). *The first year of life*. New York: International Universities Press.

Tomkins, S. S. (1963). Simulation of personality: The interrelations between affect, memory, thinking, perception, and action. In S. Tomkins & S. Messick (Eds.), *Computer simulation of personality: Frontier of psychological theory* (pp. 3–57). New York: Wiley.

Tomkins, S. S. (1991). *Affect, imagery, consciousness, Vol. 3: The negative affects: Anger and fear*. New York: Springer.

Tomkins, S. S. (1992). *Affect, imagery, consciousness, Vol. 4: Cognition*. New York: Springer.

Index